THE OPEN EMPIRE
A HISTORY OF CHINA
TO 1600

Also by Valerie Hansen

Changing Gods in Medieval China 1127–1276

Negotiating Daily Life in Traditional China:
How Ordinary People Used Contracts, 600–1400

THE
OPEN
EMPIRE

A HISTORY OF CHINA
TO 1600

VALERIE HANSEN

W. W. Norton & Company
New York • London

The text of this book is composed in Granjon
with the display set in Trajan
Composition by Matrix Publishing Services, Inc.
Maps by Carto-Graphics
Manufacturing by Quebecor
Cover illustration: *Qingming shanghe tu* (Peace reigns on the river) by Zhang Zeduan.
Courtesy of The Palace Museum, Beijing, China.

Further acknowledgments and credits appear on pp. 437–40, which constitute a continuation of the copyright page.

Library of Congress Cataloging-in-Publication Data
Hansen, Valerie, 1958–
    The open empire : a history of China to 1600 / Valerie Hansen.
        p.   cm.
    Includes bibliographical references and index.
    ISBN 0-393-97374-3 (pbk.)
    I. China—History.   I. Title   II. Title: History of China to
    1600.
    DS735.H25   2000
951′.01—dc21   99-41325

ISBN 0-393-97374-3 (pbk.)

W. W. Norton & Company, Inc., 500 Fifth Avenue, New York, N.Y. 10110
                    www.wwnorton.com

W. W. Norton & Company Ltd., 10 Coptic Street, London WC1A 1PU

    6 7 8 9 0

CONTENTS

MAPS

ACKNOWLEDGMENTS

My greatest debt—to the scholars writing about Chinese history in English—is documented in the endnotes and suggestions for further readings. In addition, several colleagues carefully reviewed draft chapters and generously offered many suggestions for revision: Cynthia Brokaw, Bruce Brooks, Eric Henry, Jean Johnson, David Keightley, Victor Mair, Jonathan Karam Skaff, Anne Underhill, and Lothar von Falkenhausen. The students and teaching assistants in History 315 at Yale have heard these lectures and read through much of the material: Susan Comins, Noah Friedman, Pat Giersch, Felix Giron, Guo Haini, Shih-shan Susan Huang, Simon Kim, Lee McIsaac, Larissa Schwartz, Charles Wheeler, and Yi-Li Wu, in particular, shaped my understanding of the sources. The distant memory of Nathan Sivin's review of Mark Elvin's *The Pattern of the Chinese Past* prompted me to check the original Chinese-language texts for all the passages quoted in translation, many of which Liu Heping and Katherine Peipu Lee helped to locate. Many colleagues, including Thomas F. Arnold, James Boyden, Ann-ping Chin, Deng Xiaonan, Robert B. Gordon, Thomas R. H. Havens, Stanley Insler, Kegasawa Yasunori, John Major, John Merriman, Peter Perdue, Rong Xinjiang, Paul J. Smith, Jonathan Spence, and Zhang Guangda helped to answer queries in the course of writing.

Special thanks go to those who reviewed the entire manuscript. James Hargett and R. Bin Wong both offered many useful suggestions about how to make this a better textbook, and my editor Steve Forman taught me to abandon the conventions of monograph writing so that I could pro-

duce something more enjoyable to read. Pei-yi Wu checked the manuscript in record time and alerted me to many errors, as did Elizabeth
Owen, who scrutinized the copyedited manuscript with her characteristic professionalism. Sam Subity and Robert Stilling tirelessly and cheer-
fully tracked down permissions, and Alice B. Thiede did the maps.

This is the third book-length manuscript Barend ter Haar has read for
me, this time in the midst of taking care of two very young children. (One
page has the outline of a child's hand on it with the explanation "Sorry,
Merijn puts his fingers on whatever I write.") His careful comments on
nearly every page of the manuscript, requesting clarifications, pointing
out contradictions, suggesting further readings, and challenging my
interpretations, made this a much better book than it was before he read
it. When my original draft expressed surprise that Guan Daosheng was
able to continue painting even after giving birth to four children, Barend
wrote, "Some people write books while bearing children! (and have nice
husbands)."

Barend was right about that, too. How can one thank one's spouse
without sounding sappy? Suffice it to say that my husband Jim
Stepanek's profound skepticism about academic writing goaded me to
write a book that would appeal to all readers.

I drafted much of this book during the year 1995–1996 that we spent
in Beijing, courtesy of Yale University, who granted me paid leave of
absence, and Echlin Inc., who hired Jim to open their China office for
them. Within weeks of our arrival, our family adjusted to my working at
home. Claire, not yet two, summarized our new routine: "Lydia take bus,
Daddy take car, Mommy take work." When I wondered how we could
politely refuse a neighbor's invitation for a play date, Lydia, just five,
forthrightly explained, "My mommy is writing a book so we aren't free
until after four." We made many long trips in the Echlin company car to
the sites mentioned in this book. Since our return from China in the fall
of 1996, our family has continued to grow, with the birth of our son Bret
on May 17, 1997. Our baby-sitter in Beijing, Wang Shufeng, our baby-
sitter in Branford, Marty Hull, and the Children's Discovery Center in
Branford provided childcare that made it possible for me to write.

I am finishing this manuscript with great relief—and equally strong
awareness that Pei-yi Wu was right when he compared books to military
fortifications. Like walled cities, monographs rest on a secure foundation
of thorough research. In contrast, this manuscript, he sagely pointed out,
depended heavily on the research of others and so resembled open countryside that could be attacked from any vantage point. One justification

for writing a history that covers nearly 3,000 years is that it is worth recording the state of our knowledge at a particular time—in full anticipation that much of what is said here may be challenged and revised in this rapidly developing field.

June 23, 1998
New Haven, Connecticut

THE USE OF PINYIN

The pinyin system for romanizing Chinese has its origins in a system of romanization developed in Soviet east Asia in the early 1930s and employed later that decade in parts of China. With some modifications, pinyin itself was introduced by the Chinese in the 1950s. It is now the official romanization system in the People's Republic of China, has been adopted by the United Nations and other world agencies, and has become the system most commonly used in scholarship and journalism, largely supplanting the older Wade-Giles system. The pinyin system is pronounced as it looks, in most cases, the most important exceptions being the pinyin "c," pronounced like "ts," the "q," which is pronounced like "ch," the "x," which is pronounced like "sh," and the "zh," which is pronounced like "j."

The great woman poet Li Qingzhao, whom we will meet in chapter 7, has the family name Li. Chinese family names always precede given names; most, like Li, are only one syllable. "Qing" is pronounced "ching," while "zhao" sounds "jow" in English. The great teacher Zhu Xi, also in chapter 7, is pronounced with "Zhu" like "jew" in English and "Xi" close to the pronoun "she." Cao Cao, a powerful general in chapter 3, is pronounced "tsow tsow."

To avoid confusion, places are given in their modern-day equivalents. Two provinces in China have very similar names: Shanxi and Shaanxi, which have identical pronunciations, "Shan-she" (Mandarin speakers pronounce the first "shan," in the first tone, and the second "shaan," in the third tone). Changan, now the modern city of Xian, was often the capital of China before 1600. It is in Shaanxi province.

There follows a table of conversions between pinyin and Wade-Giles romanizations. The index to this book includes the Wade-Giles equivalents for all personal names entered there.

Pinyin	Wade-Giles	Pinyin	Wade-Giles	Pinyin	Wade-Giles	Pinyin	Wade-Giles
a	a	cong	ts'ung	gong	kung	kei	k'ei
ai	ai	cou	ts'ou	gou	kou	ken	k'en
an	an	cu	ts'u	gu	ku	keng	k'eng
ang	ang	cuan	ts'uan	gua	kua	kong	k'ung
ao	ao	cui	ts'ui	guai	kuai	kou	k'ou
		cun	ts'un	guan	kuan	ku	k'u
ba	pa	cuo	ts'o	guang	kuang	kua	k'ua
bai	pai			gui	kuei	kuai	k'uai
ban	pan	da	ta	gun	kun	kuan	k'uan
bang	pang	dai	tai	guo	kuo	kuang	k'uang
bao	pao	dan	tan			kui	k'uei
bei	pei	dang	tang	ha	ha	kun	k'un
ben	pen	dao	tao	hai	hai	kuo	k'uo
beng	peng	de	te	han	han		
bi	pi	deng	teng	hang	hang		
bian	pien	di	ti	hao	hao	la	la
biao	piao	dian	tien	he	ho	lai	lai
bie	pieh	diao	tiao	hei	hei	lan	lan
bin	pin	die	tieh	hen	hen	lang	lang
bing	ping	ding	ting	heng	heng	lao	lao
bo	po	diu	tiu	hong	hung	le	le
bou	pou	dong	tung	hou	hou	lei	lei
bu	pu	dou	tou	hu	hu	leng	leng
		du	tu	hua	hua	li	li
ca	ts'a	duan	tuan	huai	huai	lia	lia
cai	ts'ai	dui	tui	huan	huan	lian	lien
can	ts'an	dun	tun	huang	huang	liang	liang
cang	ts'ang	duo	to	hui	hui	liao	liao
cao	ts'ao			hun	hun	lie	lieh
ce	ts'e	e	o	huo	huo	lin	lin
cen	ts'en	en	en			ling	ling
ceng	ts'eng	er	erh	ji	chi	liu	liu
cha	ch'a			jia	chia	long	lung
chai	ch'ai	fa	fa	jian	chien	lou	lou
chan	ch'an	fan	fan	jiang	chiang	lu	lu
chang	ch'ang	fang	fang	jiao	chiao	lü	lü
chao	ch'ao	fei	fei	jie	chieh	luan	luan
che	ch'e	fen	fen	jin	chin	lüan	lüan
chen	ch'en	feng	feng	jing	ching	lüe	lüeh
cheng	ch'eng	fo	fo	jiong	chiung	lun	lun
chi	ch'ih	fou	fou	jiu	chiu	luo	lo
chong	ch'ung	fu	fu	ju	chü		
chou	ch'ou			juan	chüan	ma	ma
chu	ch'u	ga	ka	jue	chüeh	mai	mai
chua	ch'ua	gai	kai	jun	chün	man	man
chuai	ch'uai	gan	kan			mang	mang
chuan	ch'uan	gang	kang	ka	k'a	mao	mao
chuang	ch'uang	gao	kao	kai	k'ai	mei	mei
chui	ch'ui	ge	ko	kan	k'an	men	men
chun	ch'un	gei	kei	kang	k'ang	meng	meng
chuo	ch'o	gen	ken	kao	k'ao	mi	mi
ci	tz'u	geng	keng	ke	k'o	mian	mien

*From *People's Republic of China: Administrative Atlas* (Washington, D.C.: Central Intelligence Agency, 1975), pp. 46–47.

Pinyin	Wade-Giles	Pinyin	Wade-Giles	Pinyin	Wade-Giles	Pinyin	Wade-Giles
miao	miao	qi	ch'i	shuo	shuo	ya	ya
mie	mieh	qia	ch'ia	si	ssu	yai	yai
min	min	qian	ch'ien	song	sung	yan	yen
ming	ming	qiang	ch'iang	sou	sou	yang	yang
miu	miu	qiao	ch'iao	su	su	yao	yao
mo	mo	qie	ch'ieh	suan	suan	ye	yeh
mou	mou	qin	ch'in	sui	sui	yi	i
mu	mu	qing	ch'ing	sun	sun	yin	yin
		qiong	ch'iung	suo	so	ying	ying
		qiu	ch'iu			yong	yung
na	na	qu	ch'ü			you	yu
nai	nai	quan	ch'üan	ta	t'a	yu	yü
nan	nan	que	ch'üeh	tai	t'ai	yuan	yüan
nang	nang	qun	ch'ün	tan	t'an	yue	yüeh
nao	nao			tang	t'ang	yun	yün
nei	nei	ran	jan	tao	t'ao		
nen	nen	rang	jang	te	t'e		
neng	neng	rao	jao	teng	t'eng		
ni	ni	re	je	ti	t'i		
nian	nien	ren	jen	tian	t'ien	za	tsa
niang	niang	reng	jeng	tiao	t'iao	zai	tsai
niao	niao	ri	jih	tie	t'ieh	zan	tsan
nie	nieh	rong	jung	ting	t'ing	zang	tsang
nin	nin	rou	jou	tong	t'ung	zao	tsao
ning	ning	ru	ju	tou	t'ou	ze	tse
niu	niu	ruan	juan	tu	t'u	zei	tsei
nong	nung	rui	jui	tuan	t'uan	zen	tsen
nou	nou	run	jun	tui	t'ui	zeng	tseng
nu	nu	ruo	jo	tun	t'un	zha	cha
nü	nü			tuo	t'o	zhai	chai
nuan	nuan	sa	sa			zhan	chan
nüe	nüeh	sai	sai	wa	wa	zhang	chang
nuo	no	san	san	wai	wai	zhao	chao
		sang	sang	wan	wan	zhe	che
		sao	sao	wang	wang	zhen	chen
ou	ou	se	se	wei	wei	zheng	cheng
		sen	sen	wen	wen	zhi	chih
		seng	seng	weng	weng	zhong	chung
pa	p'a	sha	sha	wo	wo	zhou	chou
pai	p'ai	shai	shai	wu	wu	zhu	chu
pan	p'an	shan	shan			zhua	chua
pang	p'ang	shang	shang	xi	hsi	zhuai	chuai
pao	p'ao	shao	shao	xia	hsia	zhuan	chuan
pei	p'ei	she	she	xian	hsien	zhuang	chuang
pen	p'en	shen	shen	xiang	hsiang	zhui	chui
peng	p'eng	sheng	sheng	xiao	hsiao	zhun	chun
pi	p'i	shi	shih	xie	hsieh	zhuo	cho
pian	p'ien	shou	shou	xin	hsin	zi	tzu
piao	p'iao	shu	shu	xing	hsing	zong	tsung
pie	p'ieh	shua	shua	xiong	hsiung	zou	tsou
pin	p'in	shuai	shuai	xiu	hsiu	zu	tsu
ping	p'ing	shuan	shuan	xu	hsü	zuan	tsuan
po	p'o	shuang	shuang	xuan	hsüan	zui	tsui
pou	p'ou	shui	shui	xue	hsüeh	zun	tsun
pu	p'u	shun	shun	xun	hsün	zuo	tso

THE OPEN EMPIRE
A HISTORY OF CHINA
TO 1600

INTRODUCTION

The Chinese have been writing history books almost from the beginning of Chinese civilization itself. We know more about China's past than about the history of any other civilization on earth. It may seem surprising, then, that this book can add anything to such a long, well-documented history. Yet, each year produces stunning archeological finds that are adding to what we know. The new information is illuminating areas neglected by traditional historians of China writing before 1600. Court historians, who were hired to write top-down chronicles about emperors, ministers, and generals, almost totally ignored ordinary men and women, non-Chinese minorities, and economic and social changes that defied the compartmentalization of Chinese history into dynastic periods.

New evidence forces historians to reexamine the way Chinese history is conceived and organized. Was the Middle Kingdom perpetually hostile to non-Chinese foreigners, for example? While formidable geographic boundaries, including high mountains and extensive deserts to the west ensured that few outsiders traveled to China and that few Chinese traveled abroad, those who made the hazard-filled journey brought back information and technology from foreign lands. The spectacular success of Buddhism, originally an Indian system of belief that became one of China's most established religions, is an example of how receptive the Chinese could be to foreign beliefs in the premodern period.

THE GOALS OF THIS BOOK

This book breaks from the traditional model of Chinese history, now called the dynastic cycle, that exaggerates the importance of the emperor and minimizes the contribution of other social groups to the historic record. The traditional dynastic history is still employed but on a parallel track, without obscuring other trends in Chinese history that had a far greater impact on daily life, such as the introduction of Buddhism, the exchange of ideas and technology along the Silk Road, the evolving role of women, changing views of the afterlife among ordinary people, and the Mongol conquest. This book explains why recent spectacular archeological finds have caused historians to rethink received wisdom about the past. At the same time it highlights writings—both fictional and non-fictional—about women and family life. And it draws on visual evidence whenever possible to give the reader a more vivid sense of the dramatic changes taking place during the long time-span covered by the book.

This new approach results in a view of China before 1600 that differs from what readers might expect. These sources depict an empire that incorporated different regions and different peoples as it was taking shape and that remained open to outside influence throughout its long history—not a central kingdom closed to foreign influences. We shall encounter a few women who won fame for their own accomplishments and many more who managed their family's estates—even, paradoxically, when their feet were bound. An exclusive focus on religious treatises led many earlier Western analysts to think that each layperson subscribed to the teachings of only one tradition, be it Daoism, Confucianism, or Buddhism. Yet new archeological and textual evidence shows that individuals could simultaneously believe in elements of all three traditions as well as have other beliefs about the afterlife that are not even mentioned in canonical religious sources.

Buddhism entered China during the period of division between the third and sixth centuries, and continued to grow during the succeeding Sui (589–618) and Tang (618–907) dynasties. This process does not fit easily into the dynastic cycle model, which assumes that all important changes occurred within one dynasty. The official history of the Han dynasty (207 B.C.–A.D. 220) quotes an edict written by the emperor that provides some of the earliest evidence of the new religion. But if one relied only on these traditional histories, one could miss the introduction of Buddhism, which had a far greater impact on ordinary life than the shift of a dynasty.

The introduction of Buddhism is only one of the many changes in Chinese history that the official record slights. Chinese bureaucrats wrote histories for other bureaucrats and with their ruler in mind. Based on records composed by court officials, the official Chinese histories give the most coverage to the groups the bureaucrats thought most important: the emperor first, high officials, and then lower officials. The resulting sources reveal much about the concerns of the Chinese state, including the well-being of the emperor and all the problems of his empire. These annals contain debates among learned officials who tried to devise taxation policies, to build a strong army, to feed the people, and to govern well. They also document the abuse of power by emperors, regents, evil ministers, and eunuchs.

THE MODEL OF THE DYNASTIC CYCLE

Those viewing Chinese history through the model of the dynastic cycle saw the following patterns: all founding emperors were strong. Able to command sufficient support to reform the tax system, the founding emperors raised enough monies to fund a powerful military force that conquered vast stretches of territory. Because they inevitably lacked the founders' charisma, the successor emperors gradually ceded power to eunuchs, ministers, generals, and the families of the emperor's many consorts. By the end of the dynasty the ruling emperors deserved to be overthrown. According to the dynastic cycle, last emperors were often evil and always weak. Bad last emperors presided over the loss of the dynasty to the powerful founders of the next dynasty, who would immediately charge their officials with writing the history of their unscrupulous predecessors. This starkly simple model had a certain appeal, not least that it always justified rule by the reigning dynasty.

The model of the dynastic cycle has many weaknesses, the greatest of which is its blind acceptance of a dynasty's self-definition, a point made by the instructor of a survey class in an apocryphal tale told by one of my colleagues. Near the end of the semester, my colleague relates, a student asked the prominent historian teaching the class, "What is a dynasty?" The rest of the class roared, thinking the student had not learned even the most basic facts of the course. Yet the professor courteously asked whether the student wanted the long or the short answer. The short answer, of course, was that dynasty referred to a family who retained the emperorship for generations.

The long answer, though, requires more complex analysis. A dynasty is a convenient fiction that allows different people, often not members of the imperial family, to assume power, all the while maintaining the pretense that a given family continues to rule. The first long dynasty in China, the Han (207 B.C.–A.D. 220), illustrates the problems with the concept. At the beginning of the dynasty, a man named Liu Bang (reigned 206–195 B.C.) defeated the preceding Qin emperor to found a new dynasty. But after Liu's death, his wife, herself from a different family, took power while propping up two sons (one of whom she is rumored to have murdered) on the throne. When she died, two loyal ministers succeeded in restoring the throne to the Liu family, who ruled for about a century until another regent took over. By the second century A.D. a pattern was established in which consort families and eunuchs fought for power, leaving the emperor powerless; yet the myth persisted that the same family ran the country.

This four-hundred-year period retains the name of the Han dynasty, even though Liu Bang's descendants served as mere figureheads much of the time. Chinese historians use the names of dynasties because they are useful organizing concepts. The ease of terminology should not blind us to the fictions implied in the use of dynastic names.

By focusing too much on events at court, the model of the dynastic cycle assumes that nothing much happened *between* dynasties. Traditional court historians tended to describe these interludes as periods of chaos and disunity that ended only when the country was reunified by force of arms. If we were to look at the twentieth century through the lens of a traditional court historian, we would characterize the period from the 1911 fall of the last dynasty to the end of the twentieth century as a period of chaos and disunity because China and Taiwan are separate political entities.

But, as was so often the case in the past, chaos and disunity have brought forth vitality and innovation. In the course of the twentieth century, China, Hong Kong, and Taiwan, though not united, have experienced stunning economic growth, remarkable industrialization, and the widespread modernization of agriculture—not to mention dramatic changes in how people live and think.

The idea that Chinese civilization attained its greatest heights only during times of unity should therefore be regarded with skepticism until more consideration is given to the forgotten, yet vigorous, interludes between dynasties. This book reexamines prevailing assumptions about the benefits of unity, if only to light a candle in the darkness. It will take years of painstaking research and archeological work to flesh out our understanding of the periods between powerful dynasties.

ARCHEOLOGICAL SOURCES

Since the beginning of this century, Chinese archeologists have made a series of important discoveries, of which the terra-cotta warriors guarding the first emperor's tomb outside the modern city of Xian is only one.

Chapter 1, about the society of the people who produced the first writing, could not have been written before the discovery in 1899 of the earliest oracle bones. Oracle bones record the outcomes of divination sessions conducted by the ancient kings. Scratched on ox scapulas or tortoise shells, the oracle bones cover all matters of state—ranging from battles against enemy peoples to the king's own health. Traditional historians list the kings in order as if the first Chinese kingdom, the Shang (ca. 1766–1045 B.C.), was a dynasty like its successors. Yet careful examination of these first written records shows the area they ruled to have been quite small—perhaps only 200 kilometers (125 miles) across (see map, p. 18).

The transition from the Qin to the Han dynasty provides the clearest example of how archeological discoveries have prompted historians to rethink the version of the events given in the official histories. Traditional historians depict the first Qin ruler as a tyrant who was overthrown because of his brutal rule. But archeological excavations have uncovered a legal manual from the Qin dynasty in the grave of a low-ranking clerk who heard legal disputes. Contrary to the traditional view, the Qin dynasty implemented a rigorous legal code that distinguished between murder and manslaughter, between the legal killing of a handicapped infant and the illegal murder of a healthy infant. This archeological discovery suggests that the founder of the Han dynasty was able to lead a successful peasant rebellion against the Qin not because the first emperor was so unpopular—as earlier historians have maintained—but because people objected to the Qin founder's selection of his incompetent second son to succeed him (see chapter 3).

Archeological evidence has also illuminated how the Chinese people understood the hereafter. Scholars have always been able to study Buddhist and Daoist writings and literati views about the afterlife, but newly excavated tombs make it possible to see what goods people placed in their tombs. By the time of the Qin dynasty, clay models, such as the terra-cotta warriors, replaced the sacrificial victims of earlier times. The tomb of a noblewoman from the Mawangdui site in Hunan province, located in central China, dates to the second century B.C. It contains her home furnishings in her sitting room and three rooms packed with the forty-eight bamboo suitcases of goods she planned to take on her journey to the next world. Even more significant, her tomb contains a T-shaped banner depicting her as an elderly woman walking with the aid of a cane. This, the first portrait in China to show a historical personage, provides a glimpse of beliefs about the afterlife in the centuries before Buddhism entered China—beliefs that are not described in the written sources.

Literary Sources: The Use of Fiction

In addition to drawing on official histories and archeological materials, this book turns to unofficial writings of various kinds to find out about the lives led by the vast majority of Chinese in the course of history. Some of these materials, especially those from fiction, have long been known to historians who have shied away from them because they are not conventional sources.

As early as 1000 B.C., Chinese peasants sang songs about work, love, betrayal, and their religious lives. These were later edited to become the anthology *The Book of Songs*. Writers, both male and female, produced memoirs in which they advised their children how to run their households, described their own marriages, mocked contemporary superstitions, and even raised veiled criticisms of the state. In the tenth century A.D. the number and variety of these sources increased dramatically after the spread of woodblock printing, which heightened the number of books in circulation. These works have always been available to those few who could read Chinese, but a spate of translations in recent years has made them newly accessible to Western readers. Because of their vivid nature, this book frequently cites translations of long passages from primary sources.[1]

Several prominent women—including China's first woman historian, first woman poet, and first woman artist—left a written legacy. The vast majority of women left no permanent record. Unless a particular woman held the reins of state, as dowager empresses often did, or led a rebellion, as one woman did in the years before the Mongol conquest (see chapter 9), the dynastic histories record little about women. Pressed to explain how one woman, Empress Wu, who reigned from 684 to 705, managed to be crowned emperor in her own right, traditional historians can only accuse her of aberrant sexual practices. We know now that she was able to take advantage of the prolonged illness of her husband the emperor to place her kinsmen in high court positions from which they supported her rise to power.

Often this book uses fictional sources unconfirmed by other materials to explore the lives of women. The dramas written in the twelfth and thirteenth centuries under the conquest dynasties, when peoples of the steppe and the forest ruled China, depict male–female relations at a time when no other sources do so. Some experts in the field of literature—and some historians as well—are bound to object to this use of fiction to illuminate the past. These critics argue, as a matter of faith, that each piece of writing is a literary creation, and that one cannot take literary writing as a factual description of life at the time. They have a point. Several centuries hence, should a naive extraterrestrial historian depend exclusively on situation comedy or soap opera scripts, it would develop a distorted view of postwar American life. Yet even purists must grant that television scripts contain information not readily available in *The Congressional Record*. Similarly, Chinese fiction from the premodern period contains information about women not available in histories written by bureaucrats.

One fictional protagonist in particular, a young woman named Yingying, or Oriole, appears in several chapters here. Many analysts believe she was based on a real person, a jilted lover of the writer Yuan Zhen (779–831), who wrote a memorable short story about her (see chapter 6). In the original story Oriole chooses to sleep with her lover even though they are not married; after he rejects her, she is able to marry another. Once created, she proved so appealing that dramatists in subsequent centuries rewrote her story to conform to prevailing views about women in their own times. By the twelfth century, Oriole had bound her feet, and by the fifteenth, dramatists wrote skits maligning her for her willingness to engage in premarital sex. The world in which women lived had constricted considerably since Oriole's first appearance in the ninth century. When other women from fictional sources appear in the following pages, it is because their creators take pains to describe them in real-life situations. The details about their clothing, housing, and general concerns had to ring true before readers would believe in the fictional protagonists.

Artistic Sources: What Paintings Reveal

This book draws on artistic sources for the same reason: to supplement the historical record. Many of China's most famous paintings, like those of birds and flowers, depict imaginary landscapes or nature. Because such paintings shed little light on the human world, this book focuses on the few surviving real-world scenes, starting with Chinese bronzes in the first millennium B.C. Although the lack of accompanying documentation makes analysis difficult, these bronzes do suggest contemporary views of minority peoples, daily life, and ritual. Paintings from later periods depict even more varied subjects. One of the most lifelike, a 5-meter- (16-foot) long scroll depicting a city and its surroundings, turns out to be anything but realistic. The twelfth-century Qingming scroll portrays a city devoid of hunger, pain, poverty, and, curiously, even women.

This book runs the risk of interpreting visual sources at face value, but it is a risk worth running, because art reveals the visual world of the premodern Chinese as their artists conceived it, if not as it actually looked.

Structure of the Book

This book presents the history of China from the first writing in 1200 B.C. to the arrival of the Jesuits in 1600. To make better sense of the past, it divides premodern Chinese history into three periods: Inventing China (1200 B.C.–A.D 200), Facing West (A.D. 200–1000), and Facing North (1000–1600).

Part I: Inventing China

Although traditional Chinese historians dignify the Shang, and their successors the Zhou (1045–256 B.C.), with the label dynasty and credit them with uniting China, we must view such claims with skepticism, for surviving sources document the point of view of only those who used Chinese characters. Chinese-speakers were not the only people to inhabit the landmass now occupied by the People's Republic of China. Non-Chinese peoples made a significant if not always thoroughly documented contribution to China's history. Rather than seeing a fairly homogenous society like China today, historians and archeologists now depict an ancient China populated by many different groups, including some who did not speak Chinese and some nomadic and forest-dwelling peoples whose way of life differed from that of the sedentary Chinese.

We must not forget the other peoples also residing in China at the time. Archeological finds have so far produced indecipherable scripts in both Jiangxi and Sichuan provinces; our picture of ancient China will undoubtedly change dramatically should these written materials ever be understood. The imposing and yet puzzling Sanxingdui site in Sichuan (discussed in chapter 1) shows that equally sophisticated if undocumented peoples coexisted with the early Chinese-writing kingdoms, but as the centuries passed, the Chinese conquered larger and larger stretches of territory, leaving little trace of the original inhabitants.

Even at this early date, and with such a fragmentary and unusual source base, one can detect the considerable contributions of non-Chinese peoples to ancient Chinese civilization. In retrospect it may seem natural to their descendants that those who wrote Chinese should have conquered their rivals, but in fact, nothing was foreordained about the millennium of fighting that preceded the creation of the Chinese empire in 221 B.C.

The Shang kept their records in a language ancestral to modern Chinese, and they minimized the role of the non-Shang peoples—whether they spoke the same language as the Shang or not—whom they absorbed and conquered, region by region. Identifying the role of the non-Chinese peoples marks one of the most interesting new areas in ancient Chinese history, and analysts have had to use all the new tools of archeology, linguistics, and DNA (deoxyribonucleic acid) analysis to do so.

This period comes to a dramatic close with the unification of the Chinese landmass for the first time in 221 B.C. under the leadership of the Qin dynasty. Although the Qin ruled the empire for a brief fourteen years, this short-lived dynasty imposed standardization throughout its territory. The succeeding Han dynasty built on the legacy of the Qin to lead a unified empire for more than four centuries. By the end of the Han dynasty, Chinese-speakers had conquered much of the territory of the Chinese empire, and they drove many of the non-Chinese-speaking groups to remote mountain areas on the fringes of the empire. Although the Han dynasty collapsed in the early third century, the landmass of China had been filled by a Chinese-speaking population who dominated the historical record from then on. Even the archeological record conveys much less sense of regional diversity than had existed at the beginning of this period.

Part II: Facing West

In the second century A.D. the arrival of the first sizable group of Buddhist missionaries from India and Central Asia marked the beginning of the era in which China faced west toward the Central Asian oases and India. The arrival of these missionaries coincided with the rise of organized Daoism, an indigenous religion that attracted adherents in different times and places throughout Chinese history. This was the one time in China's long history before the nineteenth century when some Chinese, especially those drawn to Buddhism, acknowledged the cultural superiority of another civilization. India was both the birthplace of the Buddha and the heartland of his church. Chinese monks traveled over land and by sea to India to obtain original texts, and they stayed long years to master the difficult Sanskrit of the Buddhist texts. Many important Buddhist texts were translated into Chinese during this period, and Sanskrit loanwords that entered the language then are still in use today.

In the early fifth century, when Faxian (active 350–414), the first monk to keep a travel diary of his trip, arrived in India, his hosts in north India welcomed him, saying, "Wonderful! to think that men from the frontiers of the earth should come so far as this." From their point of view, China was indeed a distant frontier. Fourteen years later, when the pilgrim decided to return to China, one of his companions announced his resolve to stay behind in the land of the Buddha, where the level of learning was high and monastic discipline rigorously observed. Swept away by India, the monk vowed, "From the present time for ever till I obtain the condition of Buddha, may I never again be born in a frontier country."[2] Few Chinese, before or since, have referred to their homeland as a frontier country.

Lay Chinese also adopted Indian ways, whether in fashion, music, or art, which can still be seen in China's extraordinarily beautiful Buddhist cave complexes. The Buddhist establishment required large infusions of cash, and it looked to the merchant community to provide it. Religion and trade came hand in hand as proselytizing monks traveled in the company of merchants along the different silk routes around the Taklamakan Desert. The Chinese sold the Indians silk, and Chinese merchants bought gems and Buddhist relics in exchange.

Indian influence continued undiluted during the glorious years of the Tang dynasty (618–907). The many Buddhist monasteries in the capital conducted regular services for the dead, celebrated Buddhist festivals, and ran pawnshops, hostels, baths, hospitals, and pharmacies. The massive Buddhist cave site of Dunhuang, in the far northwest province of Gansu, contains a wall painting showing how extensive the holdings of a single central Chinese monastery were. A tenth-century manuscript from Dunhuang shows Buddhist missionaries still trying to persuade the Chinese to give up traditional ancestor worship for the Buddhist promise of redemption. The protagonist of this popular narrative, Mulian, a monk with the childhood nickname of Turnip, travels through hell to search for his dead mother. The traditional Chinese underworld, envisioned as a series of underground prisons, has expanded to include special sections for those committing crimes against the Buddhist church, such as trespassing on monastic land.

While many Chinese admired Indian civilization, most could not disguise their horror of the unlettered steppe peoples who began to raid Chinese territory with greater and greater success in the ninth and tenth centuries.

Part III: Facing North

Starting in the tenth century, China's orientation shifted north. Much of the time, China, or large sections of it, came under the rule of the northern peoples, of whom the Mongols are the best known. The rest of the time China was fighting those peoples, trying to keep them out of its territory. Although their armies traveled swiftly on horseback and used violence to great effect, the nomads had to develop methods of governing the sedentary, literate empire to the south. Most Chinese looked down on these steppe peoples who lived close to the animals on whom they depended and who had no written culture.

These peoples nevertheless had their own reasons for emulating the Chinese, and they were selective about which elements from China to adopt and which to reject. The people who under one ruler followed so many Chinese customs that they seemed to become totally Chinese could, under the next ruler, return to their own language, dress, and marriage practices. Cultural borrowing could go two ways, even though traditional prejudices only saw foreigners becoming more Chinese, not less.

Three different northern peoples conquered large areas of Chinese territory during this period. The Khitan Liao, who controlled much of the steppe north of China, continued to govern a small section of northern China, including the region around the modern city of Beijing, even after the founding of the Song dynasty and the unification of north and south in 960. In 1125 a forest people from Manchuria, the Jurchen, conquered first the Khitans and then all of north China, which they ruled under the dynastic name Jin. The Song were forced to retreat to the area south of the Huai River, where they ruled for a century and a half as the Southern Song dynasty. Because China was divided, and north China was ruled by non-Chinese tribal peoples while south China remained under a Chinese dynasty, chapter 7 treats the Song dynasty and chapter 8 the conquest dynasties of the Liao and Jin, which are often neglected by conventional accounts.

In 1234 the Mongols took north China, and in 1276 they defeated the Southern Song to take south China. For the first time, a non-Chinese people had conquered both north and south China. Although some officials remained loyal to the fallen Song dynasty, others served in the Mongol administration.

In 1368, the founder of the Ming dynasty defeated the Mongols and forced them to retreat north to Mongolia. There the Mongols did not disband but maintained their claim to rule China. The threat of the Mongol attacks cast a long shadow over the Ming dynasty for the course of its history, and on different occasions, the Mongols made successful forays into Chinese territory that only confirmed Chinese suspicions of non-Chinese.

No wonder the ruling dynasty sought to erect a barrier around China's borders. To the north it rebuilt the Great Wall—actually a series of stone and earthen ramparts, not one continuous wall. Because the dynasty could not construct a similar barrier to the east along its coast, it banned private ownership of boats and all private trading. In addition, it passed a series of regulations designed to make all contact with foreigners difficult. The dynasty could try to dictate the conduct of its officials, but it could not patrol China's entire coastline. Powerless against smuggling and piracy, it could not prevent foreign goods—whether Japanese silver or New World cash crops like tobacco—from entering the empire.

When the Jesuit missionaries from Italy arrived in China in the sixteenth century, they found an empire with closely guarded borders. One of the first to arrive, the Catholic teacher Francis Xavier (1506–1552), was never allowed to disembark in China, and he died on an island off the coast at Canton (now the city of Guangzhou). The Jesuit missionary Matteo Ricci (1552–1610) managed to enter the empire in 1583. Forced to stay in the south, near Guangzhou, only in 1601 did he reach Beijing, where he continued to be observed by a host of suspicious officials. Naturally, the Italians described China as a closed kingdom.

The early European missionaries had no way of knowing how recently these obstacles to foreign contact had been erected. Like many visitors to China since, they fell into the trap of assuming that what they encountered had always been there, and they were encouraged to do so by a historical tradition that had consistently minimized the contributions of foreign peoples.

This book aims to show just how different—and just how open— China was in the centuries before Ricci and his fellow Europeans arrived.

INVENTING CHINA

(CA. 1200 B.C.–A.D. 200)

CHRONOLOGY

ca. 1766–1045 B.C.	SHANG KINGS
1300–1100 B.C.	*Sanxingdui culture, Sichuan*
1200–1180 B.C.	*Reign of King Wu Ding*
ca. 1200 B.C.	*Lifetime of Lady Hao*
ca. 1200 B.C.	*First characters written on oracle bones*
1050–1045 B.C.	*Zhou conquest of Shang*
1045–256 B.C.	ZHOU DYNASTY
1045–771 B.C.	WESTERN ZHOU
1000–600 B.C.	*Songs in* The Book of Songs *composed*
900–800 B.C.	The Book of Changes (Yijing, *or* The I-Ching) *written down*

THE BEGINNINGS OF THE WRITTEN RECORD

(ca. 1200 B.C.–771 B.C.)

> Crack-making on xinyou (day 58), Que divined: "This season, the king should follow Wang Cheng to attack the Xia Wei, for if he does, we will receive assistance in this case."
> "Praying to lead away this sick tooth (?), the *ding* sacrifice will be favorable."
> "*You* sacrifice a dog to Fu Geng and *mao* sacrifice a sheep."
> "Sick tooth will be favorable."[1]

With thousands of such texts, the Chinese written record begins. These sentences, written in graphs clearly related to later Chinese characters, all appear on one turtle shell bottom, or plastron, dating to the reign of King Wu Ding, who reigned between 1200 and 1180 B.C., during the Shang dynasty, ca. 1766–1045 B.C.

Each time the king solicited the advice of his ancestors or other nature deities, he recorded the topic of the inquiry and the possible outcomes. First the diviners of the Shang-dynasty kings dried the shells and bones. They then dug hollows to make the bones thinner so they would crack more easily when heated. The king named the topic of his concern. The priests then applied heat, usually from a hot poker, to the bones. The bones tended to crack wherever hollows had been dug, and the priests numbered the cracks. The cracks were then interpreted. The origins of this practice may lie in animal sacrifice. Ancient peoples, it is speculated, examined the burnt bones of their offerings to see whether the gods had accepted their sacrifice. Only after the cracks had been analyzed did the engravers record what had transpired, marking this on the original bone they had placed in the fire. (We know the cracking preceded the writ-

ing because very few characters have cracks running through them. They must have been written after the bones and plastrons cracked.) These consultations were elaborate rituals, accompanied by music, dancing, and sacrifices, sometimes animal or human.

This particular text concerns the king's plans for battle, his toothache, identifying which ancestor caused it (could it have been Fu Geng?), and the most appropriate sacrifice for relieving the pain. The king checked with the divine powers thought to control the world on matters small, as here with the toothache, or momentous, like battles involving his entire kingdom. The quantities of texts are enormous: fully thirteen hundred texts concerning rainfall date to King Wu Ding's reign.[2]

This plastron constitutes only one selection from over two hundred thousand fragments of either plastrons or scapulas that have been discovered and deciphered since 1900. Before the discovery of these records, usually called oracle bones, scholars could consult a history compiled during the first century B.C. to learn about the Shang rulers (ca. 1766–1045 B.C.). This history provided a series of brief vignettes about the rulers of ancient China, which it listed in order, but revealed little about their subjects or Shang society. The careful deciphering of the oracle bones, coupled with painstaking analysis of Shang archeological sites, especially the royal burial grounds in Anyang (500 kilometers or 300 miles east of present-day Xian), constitute one of the most exciting intellectual breakthroughs in twentieth-century history.

Subsequent generations refined the characters they used to write, but to this day, when someone transcribes oracle bone writing into modern script, readers can still make sense of it. Because the Shang people used Chinese characters to write, we can infer they spoke Chinese. By the time of the Zhou conquest in 1045 B.C., the Zhou people had also adopted the Chinese writing system and spoke Chinese. Although we view the Shang through the dark, scratched lens of the oracle bones, we know slightly more about their successors, the Zhou dynasty (1045–256 B.C.), because the earliest classics, including *The Book of Songs* and *The Book of Changes*, date to their rule. They used the concept of the Mandate of Heaven to justify their conquest of the Shang, setting an example for all succeeding dynasties, who would claim they had defeated the previous dynasty not because of superior strength but because their supreme deity, Heaven, had willed them to do so.

Because they wrote and spoke Chinese, the peoples of Anyang—the Shang and Zhou—are the ancestors of today's Chinese. Determining their ethnic origins is a knotty problem. We do know, though, that as the Shang and Zhou peoples conquered more and more territory, they absorbed many different non-Chinese peoples.

China is the only civilization in the world to use the same writing system for over three millennia, and the Chinese are justifiably proud of this long historical tradition. But this tradition can mislead us into thinking that the people at Anyang were the only people resident in China. Neither the Shang nor the Zhou created a polity large enough to govern all of China. Large pockets of territory were occupied by peoples who did not speak Chinese, and about whom, accordingly, we know very little.

The discovery of the earliest Chinese writing has become one of the lasting myths of Chinese history—something on a par with the story of Isaac Newton's discovery of gravity while watching apples fall from a tree. It is a great story, and like all great stories, the identities of the major players vary according to which version is being told.

Dragon Bone Soup and Early Chinese Writing

The most widely accepted version begins with a malaria epidemic that struck Beijing in 1899. The city's residents, like many modern urbanites, showed great susceptibility to new medical fads. One of the most popular cures for malaria was to grind dragon bones into a powder and then to drink a soup made from them. With no dragons available, Chinese pharmacies marketed the scapulas of cattle and the undersides of turtle shells as dragon bones, and they did a brisk business selling them to ailing customers.

One of the customers for the dragon bones was related to a scholar who specialized in the study of ancient Chinese writing, or paleography. Earlier generations had studied the different forms of characters used before 221 B.C., when a reform had standardized the script, and the field of ancient writing experienced a revival during the eighteenth and nineteenth centuries. The scholar's curiosity extended to all things, whether ancient writing or medicine. When he examined the latest remedy prescribed for his relative, he was stunned to see scratches on the dragon bones that resembled ancient Chinese writing on bronze vessels. He immediately went to the druggist to buy out his entire supply.

The source of the dragon bones proved to be a town called Anyang in the central Chinese province of Henan. There, enterprising peasants had dug up large quantities of bones and shells in the ground. They noticed the scratches on them, but they did not realize the scratches were actually ancient writing, since they looked so different from modern characters. Because the peasants thought scratches would lower the value of the bones and shells, they rubbed them off before they sold them to druggists. The shell that led to the discovery of the oracle bones proved to be an exception. Since it contained characters the peasants had not managed to efface, it provided the first clue to the earliest Chinese writing.

Like all major discoveries, the recognition of the early writing seems obvious in retrospect. But few men had the imagination to think that scratches on dragon bones could be related to the elaborate characters on bronzes.

Once the identification of the scratches had been made, Chinese and foreign scholars began to take rubbings of scapulas and turtle shells, and their collections quickly reached into the thousands. Some had the foresight to publish ink rubbings of the bones, which allowed other scholars to work simultaneously identifying characters. Each character had to be matched with its modern equivalent, a laborious process that continues even now. Within ten years scholars had identified over five hundred characters, or about half the characters appearing on the bones available to them. Many of those they could not read were proper names, of people or places. Since then, scholars have identified some three thousand graphs, half of whose meanings they know.

The Oracle Bones

As early as 4000 B.C. Chinese diviners had heated scapulas to solicit the opinions of the spirits, but only some three thousand years later, at Anyang, did they write down the questions they posed and their interpretations of the cracks. As we've seen, the people used two types of writing material: the undersides of turtle shells and scapulas of cattle or water buffalo. The oracle bones show a limited number of calligraphic styles, which do not correspond one-on-one with the names of the priests, suggesting that scribes, and not the diviners, carved their analysis on the bones. Once the carving was completed, the scribes rubbed some kind of pigment, perhaps ash or cinnabar, into the cracks to make the writing stand out more clearly.

They used a complex language, with a clear grammatical structure, suggesting that these ancient peoples had first developed a script several hundred years before they wrote on the oracle bones. The telegraphic language of the oracle bones includes few of the elaborate formulas one would expect to see when addressing the gods. The difficulty of scratching characters encouraged concision in writing. Scribes abbreviated the questions asked verbally so they could fit more easily into the allotted space.

The need to use as few Chinese characters as possible on oracle bones meant there was a division between terse literary language and the more prolix vernacular. This difference between the written and spoken languages persists today. As China enters the twenty-first century, when so many use cellular phones, operators transmit messages to beepers in a concise language with none of the repetitive patterns so characteristic of modern spoken Chinese. We can glimpse the basic structure the Chinese use today in the ancient oracle bones.

How Chinese Characters Work

Most people using the alphabetic language have an exaggerated sense of the difficulties of the Chinese language, fueled by the daunting number of characters claimed necessary for literacy. American university students, who learn between six hundred and seven hundred characters in first-year Chinese, approach the three thousand they need to read a newspaper in third-year Chinese. A newspaper font holds seven thousand characters, while a new dictionary lists over eighty thousand. This astounding number looks more intimidating than it is, for many of the entries record variants of the same character, while other entries list rare characters whose pronunciation and meaning are unknown. Children take ten years to learn to read and write Chinese characters, only slightly longer than it takes students to master written English.

In fact, identifying individual characters differs little from the recognition of individual words or phrases, which is how most people read alphabetic languages. The most well-known examples of Chinese characters are those that resemble the word they depict, but one still has to study the characters before one can recognize them. Human 人 and wood 木 are examples. Many of these basic characters appear on the oracle bones. Sometimes the Chinese combined two elements to make one character: a pig 豕 under a roof 宀, say, meaning "family" or "home" 家.

The vast majority of characters, though, were not formed in this way, but of two elements: a radical, which indicated the general topic of the word, and a phonetic element, which indicated the sound. In the most ancient writing system, many characters had the same sound but different meanings. The character *xiang* 象 could mean elephant or image; if one adds the radical for person, then *xiang* 像 means image, not elephant. It seems likely that the ancient Chinese added radicals to make it easier to distinguish among different words with the same pronunciation.

Admittedly, an alphabetic language makes it easier to look words up in a dictionary, but these two elements (the radical and the phonetic marker) permitted an educated guess at the meaning and pronunciation of an individual character. Chinese is famous for its many words with the same pronunciation but different tones, or pitches. The character for "place or direction," *fang* 方, is pronounced in a high, flat tone in Mandarin, the dialect most widely spoken in north China that is the official language of both China and Taiwan. When the flower radical is added 芳,

it takes on the meaning of "fragrance," with the same pronunciation and tone. When one adds the speech radical 訪 , it means "visit," and is pronounced in a low tone. When a native speaker encounters an unfamiliar word, he or she can guess at the pronunciation and then try to think of a word with that sound and a meaning related to the radical, much as we might ascertain a word's meaning by analyzing its roots.

Today we judge writing systems by how efficient or cumbersome they are, and most English speakers tend to think of characters as an impediment to literacy. Indeed, China's literacy rate remains low, as one would expect of a large developing nation. But Hong Kong, Singapore, and Taiwan all use Chinese characters, and they have attained a higher literacy rate than the United States. Personal computers also facilitate teaching children large numbers of characters.

Ever since Westerners began to study Chinese, they have used different romanization systems to transcribe the unfamiliar sounds of Chinese into the alphabet. Students of China moan that seven or eight different systems exist, although two are used more often than the others. One was developed in the nineteenth century by Western missionaries, the Wade-Giles system, and the other, pinyin, was developed by Chinese scholars after 1949. This book uses the pinyin system, and a list of pinyin-Wade Giles equivalents appears in the front of the book. (The index gives both pinyin and Wade-Giles spellings for figures and places mentioned in the text.) Several of the letters in pinyin, like x, q, z, and c, are unpronounceable to English-speakers, which can be frustrating. These letters, in fact, depict sounds that do not exist in English.

The Advantages of the Chinese Script

The early Chinese writing system offered the people of Shang certain benefits. Only a few scribes had to be able to read and write, and they could afford the time to learn the existing set of characters. Whenever the Shang conquered a new people who spoke Chinese or a related language, little adjustment was required. But if the subject people spoke a different language, they could continue to speak their native tongue, while their priests could assign Chinese characters to preexisting words in the conquered people's language.

Because characters resembled modern numbers, and could be *read* by anyone regardless of native dialect, a people could adopt characters even if they did not *speak* a related language. Speakers of all languages, whether Americans, French, or Chinese, pronounce numerals differently, but everyone knows the meaning of 1, 2, and 3. The same held true for Chinese characters. Because the subjugated people did not have to learn the Shang dialect, China remained home to many dialects even as the use of Chinese script spread. We do not know what languages the subject peoples spoke, but we do know that in more recent times, the Chinese expanded into new territory by conquering speakers of non-Chinese languages in southwest and south China. Linguistic analysis of loanwords into ancient Chinese suggests that some of the peoples subdued by the Shang spoke languages in the Austro-Asiatic family, which includes modern Khmer and Vietnamese. Even so, Chinese characters proved so useful they could even be borrowed by speakers of languages in other language groups, like the Japanese, whose word order differs completely from that of Chinese—which is why Japanese can be so difficult to learn! Although writing clearly had many uses, and the Shang may have written characters on wood or cloth, the only materials to survive over three thousand years of burial are the oracle bones and bronzes with inscriptions on them.

The Content of the Oracle Bones

A 1936 find of 17,088 turtle shells and eight pieces of scapula confirmed what archeologists had suspected since the first bones and shells from Anyang had surfaced: the local diggers were marketing records that had been intentionally placed in the ground by the people of the Shang.

In one sense, the oracle bones can be classed as religious documents because they recorded communications with ancestral spirits and nature gods that some scholars see as similar to the communications of a shaman with spirits of the other world. Many of the oracle bones touch on questions relating to sacrifice: Would a certain ritual succeed? What animals or humans should be sacrificed? In what quantities? To which ancestors? Some divinations, like those asked by people in other ancient societies, sought to ensure that the coming day or night, or the coming ten-day unit, would occur unmarred by disaster.

In another sense, equally important, these oracles constituted political documents because they recorded matters of state in a theocracy with the Shang king at its apex. Would the highest Shang deity Di support the king if he sent his troops to a certain kingdom? Should the king launch new settlements? Sometimes the king asked about his own expeditions or hunting trips, and sometimes he asked about the weather in his kingdom and its effect on agriculture. Matters of state also included the personal concerns of the king, like his health, his toothaches, his dreams, even his consort's childbearing.

One side of a plastron, or turtle shell bottom, read:[3]

KINGS AS SHAMANS

This intriguing bronze statue of a man with his head in the jaws of a beast is still the focus of a debate in Shang-dynasty studies. Is he a king communicating with the spirit world through the body of the beast? If so, then the early Shang kings were themselves shamans. Others argue that this bronze, found in Hunan, sheds light on belief in an unrelated kingdom farther south, not the Shang kingdom.

[Preface] Crackmaking on *jiashen* (day twenty-one), Que divined:

[Charge] "Lady Hao's childbearing will be good."

[Prognostication] The king read the cracks and said: "If it be on a *ding* day that she give birth, it will be good. If it be on a *geng* day that she give birth, there will be prolonged luck."

[Verification] After thirty-one days, on *jiayin* (day fifty-one), she gave birth. It was not good. It was a girl.

The terms in brackets have been added to clarify the different sections of the text. The bone begins with the preface, which explains which priest presided over the shell cracking on which day. The charge states the topic, the prognostication gives the interpretation of the cracks, and the verification gives the actual outcome.

In the case of this text, one version, on the right side of the plastron,

A TYPICAL ORACLE BONE: BOY OR GIRL?

This illustration shows an oracle bone (actually a turtle shell bottom) used to ask about Lady Hao's childbirth. The charge is phrased positively on the right side of the turtle shell bottom ("Lady Hao will give birth in a good way") and negatively on the left side ("Lady Hao will give birth and it may not be good"). The verification on the right reads: "It really was not good. It was a girl." This inscription shows that, even as early as 1200 B.C., sons were preferred to daughters.

phrases the topic positively: Lady Hao will give birth in a good way. (Lady Hao, a wife of King Wu Ding, is called Fu Hao in many texts; Fu means "lady" while Hao is the name of her natal kin group.) The king read the cracks, and concluded that his wife's birth would go well, as long as she gave birth on one of two days in a ten-day cycle, the *ding* or *geng* days. Inscriptions frequently state that the king did the prognostication. Although he may still have relied on his priests to interpret the cracks, only he was thought to have the power to communicate directly with his ancestors.

The verification on the Lady Hao oracle bone explains that she did not give birth on either day, but on the *jiayin* day, and that she gave birth to a daughter rather than the hoped-for son. The other version of the divination, which appears on the left side of the plastron, abbreviates the right side, dropping the prognostication section, and phrases the charge negatively:

> [Preface] Crackmaking on *jiashen* (day twenty-one), Que divined:
> [Charge] "Lady Hao will give birth and it may not be good."
> [Verification] After thirty-one days, on *jiayin* (day fifty-one), she gave birth. It really was not good. It was a girl.

The two sides of this text, one phrased positively, the other negatively, allowed diviners to test different sides of the proposition, much as someone today might say, she loves me, she loves me not.

The Lady Hao text provides poignant documentation of the Shang preference for sons. It also suggests that the oracle bones may not have been edited as much as some analysts feared. The largely positive nature of the oracle bone texts, which usually record good weather or victories, suggests that even the oracle bones may have been censored, with the result that only those recording positive outcomes were kept. But this important text shows that the Shang recorded failed prognostications in addition to their successes.

The path to the source of the dragon bones was not easy to uncover. Those who had marketed the dragon bones as medicine did not wish to disclose their original location, and the peasants who had rubbed the writing off had to be persuaded that the relics had greater value if unharmed. Once they realized the potential value of the bones, they began to manufacture forged dragon bones. Opponents of the discoveries seized on these forgeries as proof that the oracle bones had all been fabricated, with the sole purpose of discrediting ancient Chinese civilization. One scholar of ancient writing remained convinced that the bones could not be genuine. Earlier historians would have mentioned them in their accounts, he thought, and it would have been equally impossible for bones to remain in the ground for such a long time without decaying. Archeological finds eventually proved him wrong. By the time archeologists began to dig at Anyang, nearly thirty years had passed since the discovery of the dragon bones.

The Discoveries at Anyang

The digs at Anyang provided a physical setting for the society that had produced the oracle bones. Plundered as they were, the massive royal tombs still bore evidence of their original magnitude. Deep ramps, sometimes over forty feet long, led down to the tombs. At the bottom of the pits stood the remains of large wooden chambers, as much as nine feet high, which the deceased were thought to occupy after their deaths.

Easily the most stunning find at Anyang came when archeologists opened the tomb of Lady Hao, the woman who gave birth to a daughter rather than a son. One of sixty-four consorts of the Shang king Wu

Preparing the King's Grave at Anyang

The depth of the pit indicates that a large labor force must have dug the deep hole long before the king's death. When he died, the laborers built a wooden chamber for his body, and filled in the grave with soil and other materials.

The Highest Quality Bronzes

Some of the bronzes in Lady Hao's tomb, like this bird-shaped wine vessel, illustrate the apogee of bronze-making technology in the twelfth century B.C. This vessel, 45.9 centimeters (18 inches) high and weighing over 16 kilograms (35.2 pounds), shows exquisite craftsmanship. Note especially the dragon and the small bird perched on the head of the vessel. Because it was the only royal tomb at Anyang that was never disturbed by grave robbers, Lady Hao's tomb contained over three hundred bronzes when it was excavated.

Ding, Lady Hao lived sometime around 1200 B.C. Other inscriptions record that she led her own armies into enemy states, took captives from other tribes, had her own lands outside the capital, and conducted certain sacrifices including those of captives. This formidable woman is the first person mentioned in the oracle bones whose remains have been positively identified. Lady Hao's tomb contained, among other items, 3 ivory carvings, close to 500 bone hairpins, over 500 jade objects, and nearly 7,000 cowry shells, which were used as money. Sixteen corpses, including those of men, women, and children, were buried in different places in her grave. The spectacular bronzes included 5 large and 18 small bronze bells, over 200 bronze ritual vessels, and over 130 bronze weapons, some of which Lady Hao may herself have used in battle. As magnificent as this find was, it remains the tomb of a consort and can only hint at the potential magnitude of the royal tombs across the river, none of which has been found undisturbed.

How to Cast a Bronze Vessel

The staff of the Shanghai Museum made this model to illustrate the process of casting a bronze. The first step was to make a prototype out of clay, fire it, and then use soft clay to make a mold around it. Then craftsmen cut that mold into pieces, leaving a hole into which to pour molten bronze. After the mold was fired, molten bronze was poured into the mold, allowed to cool, and then removed from the mold.

The Art of Making Bronzes

As beautiful as they are technically advanced, the bronzes made by the Shang stand in museums all over the world and regularly command hundreds of thousands of dollars at auction. Their familiar green patina masks their original highly polished, shiny golden yellow. Some are truly massive, with the heaviest bronze cast by the Shang weighing 875 kilograms (1,925 pounds, or nearly a ton). People living in China began to make bronze vessels just before 2000 B.C., with bronze-casting techniques reaching full maturity at Anyang.

Only a society with significant resources could produce bronzes in such large quantities. First it had to mine the necessary ores. The average composition of Shang bronzes was 80 percent copper, 13 percent tin, and 7 percent lead. An addition of tin makes pure copper harder. Lead contributes to the fluidity of the molten metal but leaves the final product softer. Because the casters understood the properties of these different metals, they varied their proportions depending on the item to be produced. Mirrors had to be shined to a high gloss, so they contained up to one-quarter tin, while weapons used little lead, which would have made them too soft. The 468 bronzes from Lady Hao's tomb weighed over 1,625 kilograms (3,500 pounds) and would have required nearly 10 metric tons (11 tons) of ore.[4]

The next and most time-consuming stage in the process of bronze casting was to make a mold. The first step was to produce a model of the desired bronze vessel out of clay. Another layer of clay was applied to the surface of the model in order to make a mold. Once the hollow clay mold had dried, it could be cut into different sections. A layer of clay—of the desired thickness for the bronze vessel—was removed from the original clay model, which became the core. With the core at the center, the sections of the mold were reassembled, and the casters then poured the molten metal between the mold and the core. The casters then waited for it to cool, which could occur within seconds. They then opened the mold and removed the vessel. After the vessel had been cast, workers polished it with a series of abrasives progressing from rough to fine.

The artists covered the surface of the bronzes with dense interwoven motifs that remain curiously abstract. One can make out individual animals the artists depicted, often dragons and birds, and complex animal masks, but the artists' choice of patterns remains unexplained.

The Antecedents of Modern Chinese Cuisine at Anyang

The people at Anyang produced many different types of bronze vessels. They used vessels of a certain shape to cook meat, to hold cooked grain, to pour wine, and to drink from, at elaborate rituals they performed for their ancestors. They, like Chinese today, distinguished between the staple starches and the accompanying cooked meat dishes. This division between cooked dishes and starches goes very far back in Chinese history but it cannot predate the agricultural revolution, which occurred sometime around 10,000 B.C. in China. At Anyang, the main starch consisted of steamed grain, usually millet. All the starches were cultivated crops, while many of the ingredients in accompanying cooked dishes were gathered wild plants or hunted animals. Although the now omnipresent technique of stir-frying had not yet been developed, most cooked dishes were meat stew.

Like their descendants, the residents of Anyang believed that their ancestors retained their desire for food, even when dead. Modern Chinese in Taiwan and Hong Kong frequently offer food to their deceased kin; only when the dead have partaken of the offerings do the living partake.

The oracle bones say nothing of what the ancestors ate, but a later poem, dating to the third century B.C., provides an elaborate description of the food offered to them.

The kin of the deceased addressed this poem to the newly dead in the hope of persuading them to partake of the joys of life, which included food:

> O soul come back! Why should you go far away?
> All your household have come to do you honor; all kinds of good food are
>   ready:
> Rice, broom-corn, early wheat, mixed all with yellow millet;
> Bitter, salt, sour, hot and sweet: there are dishes of all flavors.
> Ribs of the fatted ox cooked tender and succulent;
> Sour and bitter blended in the soup of Wu;
> Stewed turtle and roast kid, served up with yam sauce;
> Geese cooked in sour sauce, casseroled duck, dried flesh of the great crane;
> Braised chicken, seethed tortoise, high-seasoned, but not to spoil the taste;
> Fried honey-cakes of rice flour and malt-sugar sweetmeats;
> Jadelike wine, honey-flavored, fills the winged cups;
> Ice-cooled liquor, strained of impurities, clear wine, cool and refreshing;
> Here are laid out the patterned ladles, and here is sparkling wine.[5]

What spirit could resist such an invitation?

Although the individual dishes mentioned in this poem were eaten in the south, the poem's anonymous author divides food into the two categories used by those casting the Anyang bronzes. He starts with a brief mention of the starches—rice, broom-corn, wheat, and millet—but quickly proceeds to the heart of the meal, the dishes. Even today all Chinese food consists of two components: starches, often rice, and cooked dishes of mixed meat and vegetables. The people of the Shang offered food and wine to a host of deities whom they thought of in a hierarchy, with some ranking above others and some taking orders only from those above them.

The Pyramid of Shang Society

The oracle bones allude to a divine hierarchy headed by the supreme deity Di, who controlled the outcome of battles. Other important gods controlled the Yellow River and mountains. Underneath Di and the nature gods stood the ancestors of the royal family. The long-dead outranked the more recently dead, who in turn outranked the Shang king. Because the Shang believed one could communicate more easily with those in nearby tiers, the king could not approach Di directly, but he could communicate with his recently dead kin in a reciprocal relationship. The king needed their help to rule, but they needed his offerings, sometimes numbering several hundred cattle, to stay powerful. The king made offerings to his ancestors in a specific ceremony. Because the junior and senior ancestral spirits also had a similar relationship, the newly dead ancestors were then thought to perform the same ceremony for their more senior kin. Only the senior kin could pass on the king's request to Di. This divine hierarchy possessed certain bureaucratic characteristics. The ancestors were expected to perform a certain task for a fixed sacrificial fee. While no one living could address Di directly, many approached his subordinates, the ancestral spirits.

According to the oracle bones, the Shang king ranked first in human society. As the head of the royal lineage, he conducted sacrifices to the ancestors from which he, and other members of the lineage, claimed descent. Although modern Chinese are justly famous for their strong sense of family, one looks in vain for information about family structure under the Shang. The little evidence that survives pertains to the royal house, and historians of the period use the term *lineage* to denote a group of people claiming descent from a common ancestor. It is quite possible that different family structures coexisted in different regions and even within the Shang kingdom, but the surviving texts, like Lady Hao's oracle bone, concur that because they carry on the family line, sons are better than daughters.

The Harvard archeologist K. C. Chang's careful analysis of oracle bone records suggests that the royal lineage was further divided into ten smaller groups, or branches, and that succession alternated between different branches of the royal lineage; his explanation is not accepted by all.[6] Other members of his lineage, and the women from families who could marry with them, constituted the aristocracy of the Shang. Also privileged, though less so, were the court officials and landed lords, who organized into lineages with branches as well. Additionally, the oracle bones refer to "the multitude," who cleared and cultivated the land. In an analysis of 939 excavated tombs at Anyang, archeologists found that the only graves containing weapons were those of men. These tombs were also arranged along family lines, with members of the same lineage buried together.[7]

Scholars could only guess at the extent of the king's power before Anyang was excavated, when they uncovered the number of corpses buried with the Shang kings. Hierarchy defined the relationships even among corpses. Noble-born accompaniers-in-death, who were probably killed at the time of the king's death,[8] ranked first. With their bodies, which were buried intact near their ruler, they had their own coffins and grave goods. The bodies of the tomb guards, also intact, lay near their weapons. At the base of the Shang hierarchy came the prisoners of war, whose heads and limbs were cut off and then buried. Like many ancient peoples, the Shang believed the dead king would occupy his tomb after his death, and because he needed the services of all those who worked for him while alive, they had to perish when he died. The prisoners of war, sentenced to perish in the greatest numbers, outnumbered the accompaniers-in-death by more than twenty to one.

Many of these prisoners came from the Qiang people, who lived to the west of the Shang and may have been speakers of a different language belonging to the Tibeto-Burman family. The captives constituted a large workforce the king could call on to clear land or from which he could cull his sacrificial victims. One chilling oracle bone inscription mentions a ritual in which different numbers—ten, twenty, or thirty—of Qiang victims can be sacrificed.[9] The total number of Qiang proposed as victims in all the oracle bones reaches over seven thousand. Lady Hao's husband, the Shang king Wu Ding, conducted a sacrifice at which five hundred Qiang were killed at one time.

ANCIENT P.O.W.s

These clay figures depict male and female prisoners of war from the Qiang people who were captured by the Shang and served as laborers and even sacrificial victims. A wooden shackle around their waists connects their necks and wrists.

The Nature of the Shang Polity

The Qiang was one of over thirty non-Shang states mentioned in the oracle bone inscriptions. Scholars have struggled to determine the nature of Shang relations with these alien states and to draw the borders of the Shang polity—both knotty problems. Anyang, many argue, was the site of the royal tombs, not the Shang capital, which some scholars tentatively place near Shangqiu, Henan, some 160 kilometers (100 miles) away, although no excavations have yet produced any archeological evidence in support of this view. According to the great Chinese historian Sima Qian (145–ca. 90 B.C.) in his important book, *Records of the Grand Historian*, completed during the first century B.C., the Shang constituted a dynasty that preceded the Zhou, who preceded the Qin and the Han, his own dynasty. The historian Sima had access to some books now lost to us, but because he did not have any archeological evidence available to him, he exaggerated the sense in which the Shang resembled the powerful dynasties of his own time.

Records of the Grand Historian states that the Shang capital shifted many times, probably to various sites north of the Yellow River. Frequently on the move, the Shang king met with his subordinates, hunted, and led military campaigns—all means of asserting his power. Scholars have attempted to map the movements of the Shang kings by linking place names appearing on the oracle bones with known historical place names. Although individual identifications may remain suspect, one can still get a rough sense of the king's routes. The Shang king traveled frequently within a circle 400 kilometers (250 miles) in diameter; he took some longer trips, 650 kilometers (400 miles) to the northwest and the southeast. His men rounded up livestock from the residents of the places the royal entourage visited, but his officials did not collect taxes on a regular basis from a set territory. The king's camp served as a shifting base of operations rather than as a fixed capital with all the trimmings of a state. A recent reassessment of the evidence concerning Shang geography concludes that the area under its direct control stretched from Anyang to a point only 200 kilometers (125 miles) west.[10]

In what sense, then, did the Shang constitute a state? The Shang kings could mobilize thousands of people to carry out large-scale projects, like clearing land and building tombs, and they could order the mass killings of Qiang slaves. Some people who belonged to the king's personal entourage worked for the king as full-time metallurgists, diviners, or scribes. If the Shang formed a state, it was a soft state, whose stability hinged on the king's frequent visits to his subordinates and their domains, and whose bureaucracy remained divine rather than human.

Shang Relations with Other States

One of many peoples vying for power in China at the time, the Shang commanded forces numbering in the thousands—as many as thirteen thousand in one campaign, according to some sources—and they took prisoners in even larger numbers, one oracle bone claiming thirty thousand.[11] The seemingly innocent queries about clearing land in the oracle bones may actually refer to Shang conquest of nomadic peoples whose land had to be cleared. The oracle bones further record that other peoples submitted tribute to the Shang king in the form of horses, dogs, and cattle. Indeed, many of the scapulas and turtle shells the Shang used for prognostication came from outside Shang territory. Even a whale scapula has been found at Anyang, a hint that the people who originally found it lived beyond the landlocked Shang territory. Other rare animals found at Anyang include elephants, monkeys, and rhinoceri, evidence that the climate in ancient times was both warmer and wetter than today. Their presence reminds us that the people of the Shang lived along the Yangzi River in a small but fertile band of wetlands near green forests inhabited by these tropical animals. It is possible that the climate of north China was slightly warmer and wetter than it is today, further facilitating the cultivation of agricultural crops.

The Illiterate Contemporaries of the Shang in Sichuan

The discovery of the Sanxingdui site in Sichuan (on the outskirts of Chengdu, some 640 kilometers, or 400 miles, southwest of present-day Xian) dramatically illustrates the cultural variety of Bronze Age China during the age of the Shang. The residents of this ancient city pounded dirt between wooden forms to make giant earthworks. At its base their city wall was 47 meters (150 feet) wide, and one side ran one kilometer (three-fifths of a mile) long. The residents of Sanxingdui could not read or write, but they mobilized labor to make large public works.

Although the presence of certain artifacts in specific layers of soil dates the site to the same period as the Shang, 1300 to 1100 B.C., some of its artifacts differ dramatically from anything at Anyang. Two sacrificial pits found in 1986 contain many splendid items, including jades, rare blades, and bronzes. The bottom layer of pit number 2 contained over fifty enormous bronze masks, some stretching 120 centimeters (4 feet) wide. Completely unlike the few bronze masks found at Anyang, these masks have sharply angled features with large protruding eyes. No one knows how the masks were used, but evidently they were made locally, since the clay cores inside matched the clay in the burial pit itself. Investigators specu-

MYSTERIOUS MASKS FROM SICHUAN

The finds from the Sanxingdui site in Sichuan have no counterparts elsewhere in China. This mask is 65 centimeters (25 inches) high and fully 1.38 meters (54 inches) across. This perplexing, enormous bronze head has eyes that stick out 16 centimeters (6 inches). The square hole in the forehead, and two similar holes on the side suggest the mask may have been attached to an inner core—perhaps a tree trunk.

late that the masks were cast on the site of the pit, in preparation for the ceremony to be held there. Interestingly, the placement of jades, bronzes, and other objects reveals that they were first broken and burned before being placed in the pit, suggesting that some type of ritual took place before the pits were filled.

The most striking artifact from the pit is a bronze statue 182 centimeters (6 feet) tall, on a base 80 centimeters (2.5 feet) high. The figure wears clothing of several layers consisting of an underskirt of different lengths front and back, undershirt, and outer tunic gathered at one side. Two eyes appear on the skirt below waist level. It is unlikely that people wore such outfits on a daily basis. The bare feet and intricate silken clothing suggest a man of high birth who presides over a ritual of some type: later Chinese often thought shoes unclean and even dangerous to wear on ceremonial occasions. The head of the figure resembles the masks from the tomb, and his fingers form a circle as if he originally held something—perhaps an elephant tusk, or perhaps a torch of some type,

THE TALL PRIEST FROM SICHUAN

This 182-centimeter- (6-foot-) tall bronze statue (left) is unlike any other excavated in the territory of modern China. From a site contemporary with the Shang kingdom that contains no written material, the identity of this magnificent Sanxingdui figure continues to perplex scholars, who debate the meaning of the elaborate designs that are clearly visible in the drawings of the figure (right).

which would make sense in a ritual context. This extraordinary statue resembles much smaller human figures from a site 500 kilometers (300 miles) to the northeast, Baoji, Shaanxi, dating to the tenth century B.C., whose fingers also form circles. The stylistic similarity suggests that trade routes may have connected the two sites. Metallic analysis also indicates trade with settlements downriver.

The lack of documentation from the Sanxingdui site prevents reconstruction of its ritual context, but the stunning bronze faces are evidence that a civilization distinct from Anyang existed there. Our vision of ancient China must expand to include these peoples who could make bronzes and jades as technically sophisticated as those at Anyang.

The Caucasoid Corpses of Xinjiang

The unusual climatic conditions of the northwest Chinese desert have preserved over a hundred corpses of another people present in the modern region of Xinjiang between 2000 and 500 B.C. The dessicated corpses look surprisingly like Europeans. The corpses have the facial characteristics (round eyes and large noses) combined with the coloring (light hair and fair skin) we expect of Europeans, not Chinese. Some of them were over 1.8 meters (6 feet) tall, an unusual height for the ancient Chinese. The surviving individual graves do not reveal whether these peoples controlled any territory, but they contain plaid textiles resembling those of Europe, suggesting these peoples used looms different from those in use in the Shang heartland. Some scholars have speculated that these Caucasoid peoples traveled to the modern borders of China in horse-drawn wagons, which would have made it possible for them to travel long distances overland. Others suspect these peoples even introduced chariots, although no archeological evidence supports this point of view.

A few early oracle bones suggest that chariots were indeed a new technology brought in by outsiders during the reign of King Wu Ding, Lady Hao's husband. The oracle bone character for chariot shows much variation, suggesting the scribes struggled to depict a new and foreign piece of technology for which they had no preexisting word. Before the introduction of the chariot, the people of the Shang did not use wheeled carts, and they had not yet domesticated the horse—the two crucial preconditions for the development of the chariot. One early oracle bone describes such a hunting expedition saying: "On *jiawu* (day 31) the king went out

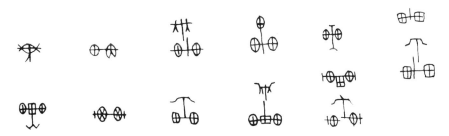

THE APPEARANCE OF THE CHARIOT AS SEEN IN
CHINESE CHARACTERS

The eleven signs for chariot illustrate the development from a simple two-wheeled cart to a vehicle with three or four wheels. The great variety of forms suggests the introduction of a new, foreign technology, which different scribes drew in individual ways before one graph became standardized.

in chase of rhinoceros. The Minor Vassal harmed the chariot and horse, overturning the king's chariot; Prince Yang fell out."[12] This description of the accident is perhaps the earliest mention of the chariot, a two-wheeled vehicle pulled by a horse.

We cannot be sure which non-Chinese people introduced the chariot to the people of the Shang. Whatever the specific technological contributions of the Caucasoid peoples, their presence reminds us that many different peoples came to China during the years of the Shang kingdom, and we know little about them.

The oracle bones mention many groups living at the same time as the Shang. Of the eight groups whose names appear with some frequency on the oracle bones, the Zhou, in alliance with the Qiang (the sacrificial victims mentioned in the oracle bones), conquered the Shang. Oddly, the early oracle bones frequently mention the Zhou people, but those of the last period do not—even though that period came to an end with the Zhou conquest. The Zhou conquerors justified their act by claiming that the Shang had lost the Mandate of Heaven.[13] This claim became the rationale for all those who sought to overthrow the ruling dynasties in succeeding years.

The Mandate of Heaven

Some one thousand years after the end of the Shang, the historian Sima Qian used a series of exaggerated stereotypes to depict the extreme excesses of the last Shang king in his *Records of the Grand Historian*. Most modern analysts see Sima Qian's account as a legend and not an accurate historical account. According to Sima Qian, the last Shang king liked the company of women, drank too much, enjoyed "depraved songs" with erotic lyrics, and hosted orgies. At the same time he raised taxes while generally neglecting matters of state. When some of his subjects objected, he invented a new way of punishing them, by roasting them on a rack. He turned some of his critics into mincemeat, others into dried meat strips. He appointed evil officials, and his good officials drifted away from his palace to serve the Zhou.

When the Zhou king's advisors urged him to invade the Shang, he refused, saying, "You don't know the Mandate of Heaven yet." Then the last Shang king killed an official who dared to criticize him by cutting his chest open while he was alive, so that the king could examine his still beating heart for signs of virtue. When he heard this, the Zhou king launched his invasion and defeated the Shang troops, and the last Shang king plunged to his death in a fire. The Zhou king then impaled the head of the dead tyrant on a pole for all his vanquished subjects to see.[14]

One of the great prose masters of classical Chinese, Sima Qian described the event in such powerful language that his account shaped later conventions about how one dynasty ended and another began. The Zhou king first refuses to invade because he does not have the Mandate of Heaven. For the Zhou people, Heaven, and not the Shang god Di, represented the supreme divine force. Unlike the Western Christian conception, the Zhou concept of Heaven did not refer to the home of the virtuous dead. For the Zhou, Heaven was a more generalized force, similar to the Western sense of the cosmos, whose support was essential for a given king to reign. The Zhou king later changes his mind about attacking the Shang, the historian implies, because Heaven had come to support his claim to be king.

Later thinkers interpreted the Mandate of Heaven as a check on evil rulers. If an emperor could not govern, they believed, Heaven would show that it had withdrawn support for the dynasty by sending natural disasters in the form of earthquakes, unusual celestial events, excessive rain, or drought, and/or man-made disasters in the form of peasant rebellions. Some philosophers argued that the people had the right to rebel against a bad king. Prudent rulers, then, were obliged to monitor the skies and their subjects for any early signs of Heaven's disapproval.

This view implies that China's masses could revolt if they did not support a given ruler. In the student protests of May 1989 leading up to the Tiananmen Square massacre, countless commentators remarked that the Communist party had lost the Mandate of Heaven. It is less often remarked that new dynasties used the Mandate of Heaven to justify their overthrow of another dynasty only after the fact. One dynasty could lose the Mandate only if another took it by establishing a new government. If widespread opposition to a dynasty arose, yet the ruler managed to suppress it before he was overthrown, then he could retain the Mandate. The Mandate of Heaven proved to have lasting influence because it justified all successful overthrows just as it justified all dynasties that clung to power.

The concept of the Mandate of Heaven emerged at the time of the Zhou conquest, but it fit neatly into the later scheme of the dynastic cycle, which was developing as Sima wrote his *Records of the Grand Historian* in the first century B.C. It made historical events seem the outcome of divine will—even though divine will could be discerned only after the fact.

The Zhou Conquest of the Shang

In spite of the vivid description in *Records of the Grand Historian*, the Zhou conquest remains shrouded in obscurity. Although the Shang troops grossly outnumbered the Zhou troops at the decisive battle (Sima Qian gives the Shang troops as seven hundred thousand versus forty-eight thousand Zhou troops),[15] the Zhou defeated the Shang.

Until very recently historians debated the actual date of the Zhou conquest. The Grand Historian Sima Qian mentions the calendar year only for events occurring after 841 B.C., when he was confident of his chronology. For earlier events, including the Zhou conquest, he specifies the order of events without giving any dates. Analysts tried to reconcile Sima Qian's relative chronology and other historical sources with known astronomical data, and they proposed over twenty possible dates for the conquest between 1127 and 1018 B.C. In the past decade historians have reached a consensus, based on astronomical data, that the conquest occurred between 1050 and 1045 B.C.

Once the Zhou had defeated the Shang, they established their capital along the Wei River, where it remained until 771 B.C., the year when the Zhou transferred their capital east from the Wei River valley (near the modern city of Xian in Shaanxi province) to the city of Luo. Historians have traditionally called the first half of the dynasty the Western Zhou, and the period after 770 B.C. the Eastern Zhou, but these designations grossly overstate the stability of the polity. Like the Shang, the Zhou was but one kingdom among many, even if it was the only one whose existence is documented. Although the Zhou dynasty did not come to an official end until 256 B.C., its power was so circumscribed after 770 B.C. that historians call it the Eastern Zhou, which they usually divide into two halves: the Spring and Autumn Period (770–481 B.C.) and the Warring States (481–221 B.C.) (see next chapter).

Divination in the Zhou: The Book of Changes

Like the Shang, the Zhou kings divined with the help of bones and shells, and they also used a leafy herb with white flowers called yarrow. Diviners manipulated the stalks of the yarrow in groups of six and then decided which hexagram, or configuration of six lines, the stalks indicated. The possible configurations ranged from six solid lines to six broken lines to form sixty-four possible permutations, or hexagrams, as they are usually called. *The Book of Changes* (*Yijing*, sometimes written in English as the *I-Ching*), first written down in the ninth century B.C., consists of the diviners' notes to these sixty-four hexagrams. Some of the hexagrams describe an event in the natural world and then cite a similar pattern among humans. An example is the second-line statement in hexagram #61, "Centered Sincerity":

A calling crane in the shade,
Its young harmonizes with it.
We have a good chalice;
I will down it with you.[16]

A conclusion concerning the outcome of divination follows many such images; such statements include words like "auspicious," "inauspicious," "danger," and "distress."

Including rhymes and puns, the unannotated text of *The Book of Changes* poses many interpretive difficulties. Because the original text contains so much abstruse language, we must look to archeological and other textual sources to learn about life during the Zhou.

The Sources of Zhou History

An extraordinary source, the classic *The Book of Songs* (also translated as *The Book of Poetry* or *The Book of Odes*), contains the first songs from ancient China. The songs vividly depict the lives of commoners in addition to those of the lords they served. The earliest songs date to 1000 B.C., the time of the Zhou conquest, while the later ones come several centuries later. An oral tradition holds that the famous teacher Confucius (ca. 551–479 B.C.) culled the collection's 306 songs from more than 3,000 songs; yet, in fact, only some 300 songs survived in his own time. Although most scholars today doubt that Confucius edited the book, *The Book of Songs* enjoyed the treatment accorded to all the writings of the great sage. Reprinted many times, it was studied by generations of students, who cherished the beauty of the songs.[17]

The earliest songs consisted of unrhymed four-character lines, many of which describe temple ceremonies or sacrifices. These songs probably began as ritual chants to accompany ceremonial music and dancing. As centuries passed, poets began to use rhyme, to divide their songs into stanzas, and to treat more varied topics including battles and eventually love.

The Book of Songs

A late song, and one of the most informative, details the many economic exchanges between the lord of an estate and his dependents—male and female—who work the land. As the song progresses through the year, it punctuates its account of human activities with the names of the birds, bugs, animals, flowers, and foods present in that particular month. The people described live close to nature, intensely aware of the changes in the landscape around them.

Several different people speak in the course of the long song, although they are not named. The song begins with the lord of the estate speaking in the seventh month of the year, during the summer when Scorpio (the "Fire") dips under the horizon at dusk:

> In the seventh month the Fire ebbs;
> In the ninth month I hand out the coats.
> In the days of the First, sharp frosts;
> In the days of the Second, keen winds.
> Without coats, without serge,
> How should they finish the year?

The lord's obligations to those on the estate, both high and low born, include providing them with clothing. When the song shifts to women, they are busy feeding leaves to silkworms in the spring:

> But when the spring days grow warm
> And the oriole sings
> The girls take their deep baskets
> And follow the path under the wall
> To gather the soft mulberry-leaves:
> "The spring days are drawing out;
> They gather the white aster in crowds.
> A girl's heart is sick and sad
> Till with her lord she can go home."

The women sing as they work. The song does not reveal the source of the girl's sadness, although it seems she has parted with her lover, but it suggests her grief will ease on marriage to another man. The women's work continues:

> In the seventh month the shrike cries;
> In the eighth month they twist thread,
> The black thread and the yellow:
> "With my red dye so bright
> I make a robe for my lord."

We learn that the women on the estate spin thread and sew the clothing the lord gives out before the arrival of winter. Their husbands also provide him with animal skins:

> In the days of the First we hunt the racoon,
> And take those foxes and wild-cats
> To make furs for our Lord.
> In the days of the Second is the great Meet;
> Practice for deeds of war.
> The one-year-old [boar] we keep;
> The three-year-old we offer to our Lord.

Living on recently cleared land, the residents have their pick of the abundant wildlife around them. Like the dependents on a medieval European manor, they divide the kill with their lord, who gets the larger, older animals.

One of the men tells his wife what to do in winter:

> In the tenth month the cricket goes under my bed.
> I stop up every hole to smoke out the rats,
> Plugging the windows, burying the doors:
> "Come, wife and children,
> The change of the year is at hand.
> Come and live in this house."

The song ends with the harvest festival in the house of the lord:

> In the tenth month they clear the stack-grounds.
> With twin pitchers they hold the village feast,
> Killing for it a young lamb.
> Up they go into their lord's hall,
> Raise the drinking-cup of buffalo-horn:
> "Hurray for our lord; may he live for ever and ever!"

This song, quite possibly a work song, gives a clear sense of life on the estate, which was the main economic unit during the Western Zhou. The people on this estate provided their lord with a share of their crop, the hunt, and the textiles they made, and he, in turn, gave them clothing and invited them to feasts. Although they worked throughout the year, the people in this song always seem happy and even wish their lord a long life, but, in fact, life must have been very difficult and food shortages frequent.

While everyone prospers in this work song, other songs express the dissatisfaction of the common people, although in veiled terms. One song addresses a "big rat," a term that may refer to the lord of the estate:

Big rat, big rat,
Do not gobble our millet!
Three years we have slaved for you,
Yet you take no notice of us.
At last we are going to leave you
And go to that happy land;
Happy land, happy land,
Where we shall have our place.

The workers on this estate threaten to leave their lord unless he lowers his exactions. To them, the frontier offers freedom from the burden of supporting their lord.

The Concerns of Women

Some of the songs in *The Book of Songs* give full voice to the emotions of women, who often remain silent in other sources. As the work song obliquely suggests in its description of the young girl's sadness, women could enter into sexual relationships before marriage. One hard-to-interpret song juxtaposes a seduction with a deer, whose corpse is wrapped with white grass:

In the wilds there is a dead doe;
With white rushes we cover her.
There was a lady longing for the spring;
A fair knight seduced her. . . .

"Heigh, not so hasty, not so rough;
Heigh, do not touch my handkerchief
[which was worn at the waist].
Take care, or the dog will bark."

Although the girl does not want to be discovered, she willingly participates in the tryst. The poet begins by mentioning the dead deer and the proper way to bury it, one scholar explains, so as to suggest that the man who seduced the girl failed to marry her—the proper way to fulfill his obligations to her.

As some of these songs hint at the first sexual experience of women, others disclose the disappointment of failed relationships. One moving song, narrated by a woman, describes a marriage gone sour. It starts on a light note:

> It takes a very stupid dolt
>> to bring cloth to trade for silk.
> He didn't come to trade for silk,
>> he came to bargain for me!

The man pays for the bride, and once he has consulted two kinds of oracles (both shells and yarrow stalks), her parents provide her with a dowry. The narrator then warns of the dangers of premarital sex by comparing a virgin to the untouched mulberry:

> Before the mulberry has shed,
>> its leaves are so glossy!
> Beware, oh dove!
>> eat not the fruits of the mulberry!
> Beware, oh girl!
>> dally not with a knight!
> A knight's dalliances are overlooked,
>> but a girl's are never forgiven.

Girls may engage in premarital sex, but at their own risk, for a double standard exists. After marriage, her husband proves to be unfaithful:

> The girl didn't change,
>> though the knight was deceiving.
> The knight was inconstant,
>> his favors cast this way and that.

The marriage lasted for only three years before her husband left her. The song ends with the abandoned woman's lament:

> My brothers ignore me,
>> if they knew, they'd jeer at me.
> When I calmly ponder it,
>> I see I have hurt myself.
>
> We were to grow old together as one
>> but growing old has made me an object of scorn.
> The Qi has its banks,
>> the marsh has its sides.
> During the gay times of hair tied in girlish horns,
>> the chatter and laughter were so pleasant.

The promises and oaths were so earnest,
    I never thought it'd change.
That it would change was unthinkable to me
    and now all is ended.

The Book of Songs evokes human feelings with great sensitivity. Because inscribed bronzes, another important source for this period, provide a different perspective from *The Book of Songs*, they make it possible to outline the government and economy of the Zhou.

The Bronzes of the Western Zhou

Inscriptions on bronzes reveal that the Zhou kings, like the Shang kings before them, worshiped their ancestors. They all conducted elaborate rituals in their family temples, where they made offerings to their ancestors. The nobility recorded honors they had received from the Zhou king on bronzes they commissioned. They cast the texts in hard-to-read places, like the bottoms or inside walls of vessels, which would usually have been obscured by the food offerings, or on the backs of bells, which could only have been read from behind the bell-rack. The texts were written for the benefit of the ancestors; the living hoped the messages would be conveyed to the dead when the bells were struck. One bell inscription read:

> I, Cai of the junior branch of the House of Xing, made my Accomplished Ancestor Mu Gong's great bells.
> May they be used to make the Accomplished Divine Men [the ancestors] rejoice and be happy; may they be used to pray for good fortune, long life in a position of high emolument, and unmitigated happiness.
> May sons and grandsons forever daily strike and rejoice in
> these bells; may they forever treasure and use them.[18]

These bronze inscriptions follow a fixed format progressing through the past to the present and then on to the future. They begin with the accomplishments of the person who paid for the bronze and his ancestors. If the Zhou king has awarded the bell donor any honors, this section mentions them. The middle section explains to whom the bronze is dedicated, here the Accomplished Divine Men, and may include the names of specific ancestors. The final section expresses the desires of the donor, who seeks fortune, official positions, success, and the well-being of his future sons and grandsons. Most of the texts on bronzes, like this one, largely concern the hopes of the donors, but a few touch on historic events leading up to the grant, especially in the first section.

A Battle in the Zhou

One text describes a chariot battle that occurred after the Xianyun people, based in a place called Xun, had raided a Zhou garrison. The bronze,
dating to the ninth century B.C., recounts the events leading up to the re-
ceipt of honors by a Zhou warrior named Duo You. When the Zhou king
ordered the Duke of Wu to respond to the attack, the Duke dispatched
Duo You to strike the alien people:

> On the morning of *jiashen* (day twenty-one), striking at Mai, Duo You cut off
> heads and manacled prisoners to be interrogated; in all, using the duke's chari-
> otry to cut off the heads of two hundred and . . . five men, manacling twenty-
> three prisoners to be interrogated, capturing one hundred and seventeen of the
> belligerents' chariots, and taking back the captives from among the people of
> Xun.[19]

The text then describes the awards given out:

> Duo You then presented the captives, heads and prisoners to be interrogated to
> the duke. Duke Wu then presented them to the king, who addressed Duke
> Wu, saying: "You have pacified the Jing Garrison; I enrich you, awarding you
> lands and fields."

This passage conveys the basic elements of the Zhou political system. At
the pinnacle of human society, the king had the ability to award lands to
his subordinates. Unstated here, the lands were occupied by people, whose
obligations included supplying their lord with crops and the goods described in the idealizing work song from *The Book of Songs*. In exchange
for the land grants, the lords were also to provide the king with troops.
They in turn could make grants to their subordinates, as the Duke of
Wu does in this inscription for Duo You:

> On *dingyou* (day thirty-four), Duke Wu was at the Presentation Hall and com-
> manded Xiangfu to summon Duo You, who then entered into the Presenta-
> tion Hall. The duke personally addressed Duo You, saying: "I began by giving
> you sanctuary; you have not transgressed but have succeeded in affairs and
> made a great catch. You have pacified the Jing Garrison; I award you one
> tessera [four-cornered tablet], one set of golden bells, and one hundred catties
> of *haoyou*-bronze."

These gifts reinforce the system of privilege that allowed a king to commission the highest number of bells, with his subordinates allotted fixed
numbers of bells depending on their rank. The last sentence expresses
Duo You's hopes for the future: "May my sons and grandsons eternally
treasure and use it."

Texts appearing on bronzes hardly constitute objective records of the past. Because Duo You is recounting his exploits to his ancestors, we cannot accept this one-sided casualty list—in which he took all the captives and beheaded all the victims—as a reliable account of his battles with the enemy. If we discount his bias, we still learn much about chariot warfare, which required long years of training to master. Duo You's decision to commission such a text reveals much about Zhou ancestor worship. By informing his ancestors of his honor and the gifts the duke gave him, he hoped to gain their approval.

Ancestor Worship

The Book of Songs makes it possible to reconstruct the ritual context of the Western Zhou bronzes. The songs describe family gatherings in ancestral temples where ancestors are invited to join in elaborately staged feasts.

In one song, a young boy in the clan is designated the impersonator, whom the spirit of the ancestor, often his grandfather, is thought to enter during the ceremony. The boy remains still throughout the ceremony. The chief of the lineage takes the role of pious descendant who conducts the ritual, and a third figure, the officiating invoker, serves as the go-between connecting the impersonator and the pious descendant. The song begins with a description of the lavish food prepared for the ancestors:

> We manage the furnaces with attentive movements;
> The foodstands are very grand;
> Some contain roasted meat, some broiled meat.
> The noble wives are reverently quiet.
> The meat platters are very numerous.
> The visitors and guests
> Offer toasts and pledges to each other.
> The ceremonies are entirely according to rule;
> The laughter and talk are entirely to the point.
> "The divine protectors have arrived.
> May they bestow on us increased felicity,
> May we be rewarded with longevity of ten thousand years."[20]

This song, like the work song above, presents different speakers, but where that song shifted from lord to cultivator, and man to woman, this song alternates between the living and the dead. First the living family members request good fortune and long life from the dead. The officiating invoker then consults an oracle, though the song does not specify which type, and interprets its response, which purports to be the reply of the ancestors:

> "Fragrant is the pious sacrifice,
> The spirits enjoy the wine and food,
> The oracle predicts for you a hundred blessings.
> According to the proper quantities, according to the proper rules,
> You have brought sacrificial grain, you have brought millet;
> You have brought baskets, you have arranged them;
> We will forever give you the utmost blessings,
> Ten-thousandfold, myriadfold."

The spirits begin by admitting they like the food and wine served and by praising their descendants for following the exact sacrificial procedure. They then promise their descendants exactly what they have asked for: blessings in large quantities. Now that the conversation between the living and the dead has ended, the ritual comes to its conclusion:

> The ceremonies are now completed,
> The bells and drums have given their signal;
> The pious descendant goes to his place,
> The officiating invoker makes his announcement:
> "The spirits are all drunk."
> The august impersonator then rises,
> The drums and bells escort away the impersonator.
> The divine protectors then leave the temple.

The officiating invoker closes off the part of the ritual involving the dead by explaining that the spirits have had their fill and have become drunk. When the boy impersonator leaves, the ancestral spirits, or the "divine protectors," leave with him. This is the signal the servants and the women have been waiting for, and they remove the ritual dishes, while the menfolk go to another place for their feast. After the men listen to music and eat and drink their fill, they summarize the ritual exchange that has occurred.

> "The spirits have enjoyed the wine and food
> They will cause the lord to have a long life. . . .
> By son's sons and grandson's grandsons
> Shall his line for ever be continued."

This last line calls to mind several last lines of texts cited above. The work song ended with the field workers toasting their lord: "May you live forever and without end!" The bell inscription concluded: "May sons and grandsons forever daily strike and rejoice in these bells; may they forever treasure and use them," and Duo You's bronze closed with his wishes for his descendants, "May my sons and grandsons eternally treasure and use it [the bronze]."

Indeed *The Book of Songs* and the bronze inscriptions show many rhetorical similarities. Both types of documents contain much parallel language, many formulaic expressions, and much internal rhyme. Many of the lines from the earliest songs in *The Book of Songs* are only four characters long. So too are many lines on the bronzes, especially in the final sections.

The linguistic similarity occurs because both *The Book of Songs* and the closing sections of the bronze inscriptions contain the prayers of the living. These messages, we have seen, echoed the messages of the spirits to their descendants. This remarkable linguistic coincidence reminds us that both the inscriptions on bronzes and the earliest songs in *The Book of Songs*—even *The Book of Changes* for that matter—contain ritual language and little of the spontaneous exchanges of daily life. The phrasing follows fixed patterns established centuries earlier and preserved by careful observance of ritual.

The Continuity of Shang and Western Zhou Society

The Shang oracle bones reveal much about the king and little about his officials or the people who worked the land, while the gradually expanding source base for the Zhou, biased as it is toward ritual language, still provides information about a greater variety of people. Even so, our overriding impression must be of the continuities between the Shang and the Zhou. Both peoples used oracles constantly. The Shang king consulted oracle bones for momentous matters of state, like the launchings of military campaigns, and for personal matters, like his toothaches. The Zhou kings continued to use oracle bones at the same time they consulted the hexagrams indicated by the yarrow stalks, and their subjects used oracles to determine whether they should marry or what the ancestors were saying during their ceremonies.

Both the Shang and the Zhou peoples employed their literacy to record their campaigns against their voiceless neighbors, whom they pushed farther away from the heartland of the Yellow River valley. The Shang and Zhou were both soft states with incipient forms of taxation and uncertain borders. Gifts from subject to ruler provided the major source of royal income, while in exchange the kings granted their subjects land, ritual privileges, and the right to use certain utensils. The kings could call on their subordinates to provide them with troops, while the subordinates could easily defect to the side of a ruler they thought more powerful.

The Book of Songs describes the obligations of farm laborers to their lord, whom they gave agricultural produce, hunted animals, and cloth. A sharp division of labor characterized the estate, on which men could farm and hunt, while women gathered mulberry leaves, spun thread, dyed textiles, and made clothing. *The Book of Songs* even affords a glimpse of the eagerness of the virgin and the sadness of the jilted. In the twelfth century B.C., women like Lady Hao could lead their own troops in battle, but even they felt pressure to bear sons, not daughters. A few centuries later, the inscriptions on Zhou bells chime the prayers of the living for their sons and grandsons—not for their daughters and granddaughters. The precedence of sons over daughters is visible in the early oracle bones, and it extends even to today's China, in which many families hope their one permitted child will be a son, not a daughter.

For all the magnificent breakthroughs of the last century, from the deciphering of the oracle bone script through to the careful analysis of Shang and Zhou artifacts, much remains unknown. We have no idea how many people either polity governed. No exact chronology exists for either dynasty, and no one can say with any certainty where the borders of either state ended or where their enemies' territory began. The greatest gap in our knowledge concerns the illiterate contemporaries of the Shang and the Zhou, like the residents of the Sanxingdui site in Sichuan, who occasionally left behind startlingly beautiful yet startlingly different artifacts. What did these people make of their literate, bronze-casting, chariot-borne, ancestor-worshiping, oracle-dependent, and above all, predatory neighbors? We shall never know, for in China as elsewhere, history is written by the literate, and by them alone.

CHRONOLOGY

1045–256 B.C.	ZHOU DYNASTY
770–256 B.C.	EASTERN ZHOU
770–481 B.C.	SPRING AND AUTUMN PERIOD
636–628 B.C.	*Reign of Double Ears (Chonger)*
551–479 B.C.	*Lifetime of Confucius*
ca. 500 B.C.	*First money circulates*
481–221 B.C.	WARRING STATES PERIOD
ca. 480–ca. 400 B.C.	*Lifetime of Mozi*
400–300 B.C.	The Commentary of Mr. Zuo *written down*
ca. 372–289 B.C.	*Lifetime of Mencius*
ca. 310–ca. 210 B.C.	*Lifetime of Xunzi*
300–200 B.C.	The Way and Integrity Classic, *an amalgam of different teachings, assumes its current shape*

THE AGE OF THE WARRIOR AND THE THINKER: DOUBLE EARS AND CONFUCIUS

(770 B.C.–221 B.C.)

The earliest historical records in China chronicle an age of ceaseless warfare. For centuries following their conquest of the Shang polity in 1045 B.C., the Zhou rulers maintained control over the subordinates to whom they had awarded land, titles, and honor, but in 770 B.C., two dependent states made an alliance with some tribal peoples to overthrow the Zhou king. The defeated Zhou then shifted their capital east, near the modern city of Luoyang on the Yellow River, where a new king ruled as a symbolic head over competing regional leaders, who commanded armies far superior to his. From time to time the Zhou king recognized one ruler as more powerful than the others, but no polity ever succeeded in conquering all its neighbors. Some of the more than one hundred contending polities contained as much territory as a modern European nation, while others consisted of only a walled town or two. State borders were often ill defined. Eventually some seven states came to predominate. The "central states" (*zhongguo*), as they were called at the time, were all located in the region of north China, around the Yellow River. (The singular form of the same term, the "central state," is the name for China in modern Chinese.) Because the Yangzi River marked the southern frontier of the Chinese cultural area, historical sources provide little information about the indigenous peoples living south of the river.

As these early Chinese speakers conquered the river valleys of north China, the original residents retreated farther into the border regions or into less accessible mountain areas. The written record expanded to reflect the standpoint of more than one kingdom—it was no longer limited to oracle bones and bronzes written from the ruling king's point of view—but it still lacked the perspective of the non-Chinese, who did not keep their own records and whom the Chinese continued to regard as

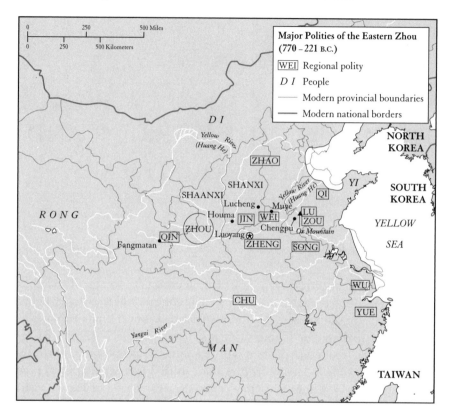

less civilized. The people of the Zhou classified their non-Chinese neighbors into four groups: the Rong and Di tribes to the west and north, the Yi to the east, and the Man to the south. Many of these groups also lived in less-populated mountain pockets within the central states. As we see in this chapter, many Chinese had regular contact with the non-Chinese, especially the Rong and the Di. For all the mixing that occurred, the Chinese reluctantly acknowledged their debt to the alien peoples, from whom they learned to fight with cavalry rather than with chariots. As certain polities conquered more territory, the general awareness of the cultural differences between the Chinese and the non-Chinese intensified.

Historians divide the six centuries of warfare (from 770 to 221 B.C.) comprising the Eastern Zhou period into two halves. The first half they call the Spring and Autumn period (770–481 B.C.), after the book entitled *The Spring and Autumn Annals*.[1] Much of what is known about the Spring and Autumn period comes from a book entitled *The Commentary of Mr. Zuo*, which purports to explain the different events in *The Spring and Autumn Annals* and which was written down only in the fourth century B.C. The second

half of the Eastern Zhou is called the Warring States period (481–221 B.C.).[2]
By the fifth century B.C., the Zhou had become so weak that it was forced
to share power with the ruler of the Jin polity, but the official end of the
Zhou dynasty came only in 256 B.C., with the death of the last Zhou ruler.

THE COMMENTARY OF MR. ZUO AND THE SOCIETY IT DESCRIBES

The rulers of the different Chinese states, which numbered more than
one hundred at the beginning of *The Commentary of Mr. Zuo*, regularly
vowed friendship with each other by making blood covenants before the
gods. Just as regularly they violated these pledges so they could fight to
erase a perceived slight, to vanquish a threat to their homeland, or to resolve a succession dispute. And battle they did. *The Commentary of Mr.
Zuo* describes over 500 battles among polities and over 100 civil wars
within polities—all in the 259 years between 722 and 463 B.C.

At the beginning of the period, a hierarchy divided society into different social strata, with birth determining to which lineage a man belonged.
The lineages of rulers related to the Zhou kings ranked at the top. Under them were the lineages providing ministers for those kings and then
the lineages of high officers. At the bottom of the aristocracy were the
knights, or "men of service." Below them were the laboring peoples.

Several rulers rose to prominence during these difficult times. Duke
Huan of Qi (reigned 685–643 B.C.) was the first man whom the Zhou
king recognized as lord protector. (The Chinese term *ba* is often translated as "hegemon," though "overlord" or "alliance chief" better conveys
the meaning.) Although he did not write it, the duke's prime minister
Guan Zhong (?–645 B.C.) has given his name to one of the earliest, and
longest, works of political philosophy in Chinese, *Guanzi*, which is a mis-
cellany of later writings. *Guanzi* sketches a well-developed system of rewards and punishments that, although never implemented, influenced
later theories of government. The book also describes how rulers can
manage the economy by manipulating the money supply. Because *The
Commentary of Mr. Zuo* says little about either Duke Huan of Qi or Guan
Zhong, we are left wondering what either man was like.

The Commentary of Mr. Zuo says much more about the second man to
gain the title of lord protector, the ruler Duke Wen of the Jin polity, who
was often called by his nickname Double Ears (Chonger). Although the
text never explains this unusual nickname, it may have referred to an extra flap of skin, resembling a second ear, that hung on each side of his

THE TRIUMPHAL RETURN OF DOUBLE EARS

This picture of Double Ears's triumphant reentry into his capital, Houma, was painted almost two thousand years after the fact. Because no portraits of Double Ears done during his lifetime survive, we do not know whether his ears had an extra flap. This artist has painted him with normal ears.

head; this was probably a physiognomic sign that he was destined to be a great ruler. It is also possible that he used the characters for "double" and "ears" to write down the pronunciation of his name in a different language and that his ears were perfectly normal. As we examine the life of Double Ears as recounted in *The Commentary of Mr. Zuo*, we must keep in mind that our source was written at least two centuries after the events it describes; therefore, it is not as reliable as a contemporaneous source would be. *The Commentary of Mr. Zuo* attributes many innovations to the great leader Double Ears, whereas, in fact, other unnamed figures may have been responsible for these changes.

Born to a non-Chinese mother, Double Ears fought with his half-brothers to gain control of their deceased father's realm, which he won after nineteen years in exile and then ruled for only eight, from 636 to 628 B.C. He was such a successful leader and skillful military strategist that the Zhou king recognized him as the lord protector of all the other polities, and after his death awarded him the title Duke Wen.

The Struggle of Double Ears to Win His Realm

When Double Ears was born, his father, Duke Xian, ruled the Jin realm, an ancient polity that had originally been the territory of the younger brother of an ancient Zhou king. Overlapping with much of the modern province of Shanxi (which lies directly east of the province of Shaanxi), the Jin polity lay to the north of the Zhou capital. Its capital was located in Houma. Comprising fertile river valleys among mountain chains running north to south, the area commanded an unusual resource: extensive salt marshes that still produce salt today. The mountains remained home to non-Chinese peoples like the Rong, while the Chinese speakers tended to settle in the lowland river valleys.

THE MASS PRODUCTION OF EXQUISITE ART

Hundreds of bronzes have been found at Double Ears's capital, Houma, in today's Shanxi province, which was a major bronze production center in the Jin kingdom. Only recently have scholars discovered how China's exquisite bronzes were made and realized that craftsmen used mass-production techniques. This buffalo-shaped vessel was excavated from Houma and dates to the fifth century B.C. Its design was created by a single stamp pressed twenty-three times on different parts of the mold of the buffalo's body. The pattern shows the face of a mythical *taotie* animal to the left, with two smaller dragons above its face, and ribbons on the right.

Double Ears's father took four wives: one from a Chinese state, who produced no sons, and three from different segments of the neighboring non-Chinese people, the Rong. He also took concubines, one of whom had been his father's. The Rong wife who bore Double Ears never became a favorite. The two other Rong wives also bore the king one son each. One of these Rong women, Lady Li, brought her sister with her to the Jin capital when she married. Because rulers saw marriages as a means of building alliances, and because they could not be sure that one daughter would bear a son, they often sent other female relatives with the bride. When the bride could not produce a son, if a secondary wife produced an heir, the baby boy could cement relations between the two states. These marriage practices testify to the low status of women, even among the ruling stratum. At the same time, many stories reveal that even the most powerful of men remained terrified of their mothers.

Both Lady Li and her sister, the secondary wife, bore Duke Xian sons. Lady Li succeeded in winning the king's favor, although the king did not name her son to be his designated heir because he preferred the son of the Chinese concubine of his deceased father. Even though he never married this woman—it would have shocked his courtiers to ratify such an incestuous match—Duke Xian chose her son to be his primary heir. Each mother angled for the success of her son, but Lady Li and her sister succeeded in having three of the duke's sons, including Double Ears, exiled to distant cities within the Jin polity. As was the practice of the time, the duke made grants of territory to these sons, who were expected to rule them in exchange for providing their father with troops when he needed them. Once a son had been awarded an outlying territory, he was not expected to compete to succeed his father (although sons often did).

At this point, Double Ears's chances of ascending the throne seemed slim. Lady Li then succeeded in creating the impression that the designated heir sought to poison his father. The heir, who realized he could not accuse Lady Li without offending his father, killed himself, and Double Ears and his half-brother fled to the territory of the Di people, one of the so-called Four Barbarian nations. There they awaited news from their realm, and in 651 B.C., they heard that their father had died. In all her plotting, Lady Li assumed that because birth determined succession, only the duke's sons could succeed him. Accordingly, she had not anticipated that the duke's ministers could kill her son and the other claimants to the throne. Yet that is exactly what they did, even though they did not belong to the ruling lineage. In fact, all over the central states, ministers were seizing power from high-born families, showing the very tenuous hold the ruling lineages had on power during the Spring and Autumn period.

Himself the child of a non-Chinese mother, Double Ears stayed twelve years in the territory of the alien Di people. There he took a mistress who bore him two sons, who were thus only one-quarter Chinese. But since their grandfather and father were both Chinese, they too were considered Chinese. When the time came for Double Ears to leave the Di territory, he urged his lover to marry if he did not return within twenty-five years. She pointedly responded: "I am already twenty-five years old! If I wait twenty-five more years then marry, I will have one foot in the casket. I beg to wait for you."³ Her spirited reply indicates the active role of women in the Spring and Autumn period. Women may have been judged primarily on the basis of their ability to bear sons, and they may have been only one of several wives, but they could still voice their own preferences. Like Lady Li, they often intervened in the affairs at court, which only complicated the infighting of their male kinfolk.

Double Ears apparently had other unusual physical features that marked him as a future ruler. In addition to his ears, "the prince's ribs were all grown together," which the text takes as a sign of great strength. When Double Ears left Di territory to begin his years of wandering from state to state, several loyal ministers accompanied him, showing that, even though they had inherited their positions, their personal loyalties to Double Ears outweighed their family obligations.

Throughout his travels Double Ears demonstrated the qualities expected of a great ruler, as shown in his visit to the large kingdom of Chu, south of the Yangzi. Its ruler invited Double Ears to a banquet, at which he asked Double Ears what he would do to repay his host if he regained the territory of Jin, which had been his father's realm. Double Ears replied:

> If, due to your kind assistance, I am able to return to Jin, and if Jin and Chu should take up arms and meet on the plain of battle, then for your sake I will withdraw my forces for a distance of three days' march. If, having done that, you fail to command your troops to withdraw . . . I will go round and round with you!⁴

Of course, this promise returned to haunt Double Ears, but his willingness to make it shows him to be a true leader. He was careful to make a promise that he could actually keep, thus enabling him to establish his credibility. When an advisor of the Chu ruler requested permission to kill Double Ears, the Chu ruler rejected his offer, saying Double Ears was destined to rule.

After the death of his half-brother, Double Ears took over the Jin polity with the help of his brother-in-law. His first measures included enlarging his army to three times its former size. In 632 B.C. he faced his first real test when his forces went into battle at Chengpu against those of Chu. The Chu troops were commanded by a renegade general who disobeyed his ruler's order to retreat. After persuading two of the small polities allied with Chu to join forces with him, Double Ears honored his earlier promise by ordering his forces to withdraw—to the dismay of his own officers. Yet, after the agreed-upon three days had passed, the tenacious Chu general still wanted to fight the Jin troops.

Double Ears and his opponent were continuing a military tradition dating back to the Shang and the Zhou. Their forebears treated war as a kind of sacrifice, gathering at the ancestral temple before they launched an expedition and returning to offer the victims—whether their corpses, their heads, or only their left ears—to the spirits. Their society had two classes: birth into low-born families meant military service running alongside chariots, whereas birth into high-born families qualified one to ride in chariots. In this world, only a privileged family could afford to provide its sons with the long training necessary to learn how to balance a flimsy vehicle pulled by four charging horses.

Although the battle occurred on schedule the next day at Chengpu, the Jin troops staged a retreat, which tricked the Chu forces into attacking. They suffered a stunning loss. Even though Double Ears had shown himself to be the most powerful ruler within the central states, he still adhered to the ancient ritual forms by presenting the Zhou king with four hundred horses and a thousand men taken from the Chu forces. The Zhou king in turn recognized Double Ears's position by naming him lord protector and awarding him various insignia appropriate to his new rank. When later historians list the five great hegemons of the Spring and Autumn period, they always include Double Ears and Duke Huan of Qi, while the identities of the three others vary, depending on the source.

After Double Ears's victory, the rulers of several small polities also acknowledged the dominant position of Jin by taking an oath before the gods:

> All of us will support the ruling house of Jin and will inflict no injury upon one another. If anyone should deviate from this alliance, may the bright spirits strike him dead and cause him to lose his army; may he enjoy no good fortune in his state, and may this extend to his grandsons and great-grandsons, whether young or old.

The phrasing of this oath, especially its final clause, evokes the formulaic language of the Western Zhou bells (see previous chapter), and indeed the form harks back to the ancient rituals of the Shang and Zhou.

Such oaths, called blood covenants, bound the participating states to adhere to the agreement. Should they violate the terms of the agreements, they agreed to be struck down by the gods. The ceremonies concluded with the sacrifice of an animal, whose blood was smeared on the lips of the participants as a symbol of their vow. *The Commentary of Mr. Zuo* records several hundred alliances, evidence that the participants frequently violated them to go to war and then to form other alliances anew. Soon after the alliance was concluded, Double Ears died. At his funeral, his coffin emitted a noise like an ox's lowing, an ominous hint that his heirs would encounter difficulties, which indeed they did as they plunged into repeated war with their father's former ally, the Qin polity.

Changes in the Art of War after the Death of Double Ears

The reign of Double Ears (636–628 B.C.) marked the end of an era. When he defeated the Chu army at Chengpu, the Chu side presented only seven hundred chariots. Estimates vary concerning how many men accompanied each side. Classical texts prescribe 70 foot soldiers for each chariot, but casualty figures from other battles suggest a much lower number, somewhere between 10 and 30. In addition to the foot soldiers, each chariot carried three skilled warriors. While the driver struggled to maintain control of the vehicle, the commander of the vehicle stood to the left and aimed his bow and arrow at the enemy, while the man to his right shielded him. Chariots cost much money to produce, and they frequently overturned or got bogged down in the mud. The largest chariot armies at this time numbered 10,000 soldiers, most of whom lived in the cities belonging to their rulers.

A dramatic change in warfare occurred in the sixth century in both ancient Greece and ancient China. In both societies, chariot warfare led by aristocrats gave way to infantry battles, in which common farmers fought. This change in warfare reflected a political shift. Because ordinary farmers could rise to lead infantry armies, they challenged the hold of the traditional chariot-based aristocrats.

In 540 B.C. the ruler of the Jin polity fought the Di people, who had sheltered Double Ears a century earlier. Because the Di and the Rong, both members of the so-called Four Barbarian nations, had never fought with chariots, their infantry made them a formidable opponent, especially on their own terrain. Chariots could intimidate opponents fighting on a flat plain, but when they ran into the ravines of mountainous areas, they became hopelessly mired targets. Quick to recognize the disadvantages of chariots, the Jin commander ordered his men to give them up and reorganized the fighters into an infantry consisting of five-man units. When those nobles who had manned the chariots objected to the loss of their privileged position, he ordered them executed—and so began the process of erasing the sharp social distinction that divided those on the chariots from those who ran alongside them. Over time, as the sons of aristocratic families lost their exclusive claim to the chariots, they also lost their lock on all leadership positions. In warfare with infantry, anyone could rise up the ranks to become a general, and the ensuing social flux occasioned much comment—and much consternation—among observers at the time.

When their chariot armies proved unable to defeat the cavalry of enemy peoples, rulers opted for a more efficient and more ruthless means of fighting, although they continued to maintain chariot corps in addition to infantry forces. They staffed their armies with infantry who took vows to respond to their general's commands with unquestioning speed. In order to field larger armies, sometimes with over several hundred thousand men, they had to develop new ways of deriving income from their territories. They found that the traditional means of awarding estates to subordinates, who in turn granted land to their own subordinates, did not produce the necessary revenue because the subordinates did not provide enough troops or supplies for larger armies.

Instead, officials dealt directly with cultivators, who paid taxes in grain or money and who served in the army. In 548 B.C., the ruler of Chu, the powerful rival of Jin, surveyed all the land in his kingdom so that he could tax it. Between 543 and 539 B.C. the ruler of the neighboring Zheng state created a grid of irrigation channels and grouped his residents into clusters of five households that were required to provide him troops. This survey facilitated the reclamation of land throughout the Zheng realm.

A rise in agricultural productivity and in tax revenues made it possible for the central states to expand their armies. The men in these armies came in unprecedented numbers, and they carried iron weapons, better swords, and thicker armor.

The people of the central states were using iron now for both weapons and agricultural implements. Iron came into the central states from the northwest, where archeological sites with iron implements and skeletons of Europoid stock have been dated between the tenth and seventh centuries B.C.[5] Cultivators had been using largely wooden implements to farm their fields, but starting sometime in the sixth and fifth centuries B.C. they began to tip their tools with iron. The first plows were pulled by human force, but the introduction of metal required the greater strength of draft animals. The use of a plow with an iron blade made it possible both to irrigate more fields and to cultivate lands that had previously been too difficult to till.

The shift from chariot warfare to infantry, with the accompanying increases in army size, created a demand for a new type of general. Rulers could not allow men to lead their troops simply because their fathers had been commanders before them. Instead, they sought expert generals who knew how to fight. They believed that the art of war could be taught, and the first treatises on warfare began to circulate in this period. The most well known, *The Art of War* appeared between 453 and 403 B.C. and is attributed to Sun Wu, a general who, if he really existed, lived in the late sixth century B.C. Sunzi, as the text refers to him, stressed that the entire army had to be trained to follow the orders of its general unquestioningly.

Many of Sunzi's teachings ran directly counter to the practices of armies during the Spring and Autumn periods. He attacked heroism as a useless virtue that often brought death. His most radical teaching held that the most successful generals avoided war when possible:

> To bring the enemy's army to submit without combat is the highest skill.
> Therefore the best is to attack his stratagems and deliberations, the next best is
> to attack his system of alliances, the next best is to attack his army, and the
> worst is to attack his cities. . . . Therefore he who is skilled in the use of
> armies brings the enemy's army to submit and does not engage in combat.[6]

The art of war—in a quasi-mystical way—promised to teach students to identify weaknesses in their enemy and to understand the right moment to attack.

Because *The Art of War* fails to mention a major change in warfare, the introduction of cavalry, we can conclude that cavalry was not yet used in the second half of the fifth century B.C. As difficult as it is for us to envision, all the battles that occurred before the fourth century B.C. involved only chariots and infantry—not soldiers on horseback. Although the horse had been domesticated long before the time of the Shang kings, and although horses pulled their chariots, the people of the central states did not ride horses.

Surviving sources do not permit exact dating for the adoption of cavalry, but one text, *Intrigues of the Warring States*, includes a tale showing the reservations the Chinese harbored about using mounted troops as their northern neighbors did. One exchange between a king of the northern border state of Zhao and his advisor concerns his decision to order his troops to form a cavalry in 307 B.C. The Zhao king explains, "I propose to adopt the horseman's clothing of the non-Chinese nomads and will teach my people their mounted archery—and how the world will talk!"[7] He then explains that to ease the transition, he too will wear the new clothing required to ride on horseback: trousers and a shirt, rather than the preferred long gowns of those who did not work the fields. This fictional tale assigns the date of 307 B.C. for the adoption of cavalry by the central states, and indeed archeological evidence confirms that horseback riding spread into central China sometime during the fourth century B.C. while fighting on horseback came at the end of the same century.

As the king of Zhao discussed his decision with an appointed advisor, so too did other rulers of the central states avail themselves of professional advice. Rulers during the Warring States period hired advisors on the basis of their skills, not their lineage.

The Demand for Experts

A first-century B.C. collection of anecdotes about the rulers of the Warring States, *Intrigues of the Warring States*, documents this belief in expertise. In one story, a man named Feng Xuan, who seeks a job as an advisor to a ruler, sends an intermediary to approach Lord Mengchang:

> "What is the gentleman partial to?" asked Lord Mengchang.
> "He has no partiality," was the reply.
> "What is he especially capable of?"
> "Nothing."
> Lord Mengchang laughed. "So be it," he said, and admitted him.

Initially Feng Xuan lives up to his employer's low expectations as he seems bent on improving the terms of his employment. Yet, every time he seeks a raise, whether in the form of better food, a carriage, or support for his mother, he sings aloud to his sword, which he calls "Longsword." And every time Lord Mengchang grants his request.

When Lord Mengchang asks which of his retainers can collect debts for him in his own territory, a small area called Xue, Feng Xuan volunteers to go. He matches his lord's tallies with those of all the people owing debts, and then gives out an order—in his lord's name—to forgive all the debts. This may be the earliest tale to document the practice of lending money with interest, although the interest is forgiven in the tale. He hurries back to Lord Mengchang, who asks what Feng Xuan has bought with the returned money, because he does not yet realize that Feng Xuan did not bring him any money.

> "My lord, you asked me to see if there was anything your house lacked," answered Feng Xuan. "It was my humble opinion that your castle was filled

with precious objects, that your stables and kennels abounded in steeds and coursers, and the lower palaces with beauties. It seemed that one thing only was lacking, and that was fealty. This I bought, my lord."

When Feng Xuan recounts what he has done, Lord Mengchang disapproves, but he does not dismiss him.

The following year Lord Mengchang loses his position with the ruler of Qi and is forced to return to his own Xue territory, where the people enthusiastically welcome him some distance from the city. He acknowledges his debt to Feng Xuan, who modestly replies:

> The wiliest rabbit must have three burrows before he can even preserve his life. At the moment you can scarcely rest secure with only one. I beg my lord allow me to dig him two more.

He then arranges for his lord to regain his former position, and he secures him a new ally as well.

Feng Xuan's intermediary described him accurately at the beginning of the tale when he said he had no special talents. He offered Lord Mengchang a far more important skill: acumen. Throughout the period of the Warring States rulers hungered for that skill, and tutors strived to impart it to their students. Some teachers, like Sunzi, taught the acuity of the battlefield. Others, like Confucius, despised warfare and sought to teach a different type of skill—one that could be used to reform the world of men. Although Confucius was born at the end of the Spring and Autumn Period, in 551 B.C., he died at the beginning of the Warring States period, in 479 B.C., and his teachings very much reflect the emphasis on acumen of his contemporaries.

The World of Confucius

Historical sources contain surprisingly little information about the man who would become China's most renowned thinker. The man whom today we call Confucius was born to the Kong family in Qufu, Shandong, and given the name Qiu ("hill"). During his lifetime he was called Kongzi, or Master Kong. Confucius is the translation of the little-used title, Kong Fuzi ("Master Kong"), adopted by the Jesuits in the sixteenth century.

Confucius was born to a man who had the rank of knight, or "man of service," which was the lowest-ranking group of the nobility. As a young man, he held several low-ranking positions managing accounts and watching over livestock. Then he began a career as a tutor to ambitious young men who wanted to learn the art of ruling. Throughout his

life he claimed to seek employment as an advisor to a ruler, but surviving sources disagree about whether he gained office. If he did, it was only
briefly and in a low position within his native state of Lu, where he returned after traveling to several other polities and where he taught until his death in 479 B.C.

Confucius has been called China's first private thinker (in contrast to
earlier political thinkers who served as ministers or generals), and his survival hinged on his ability to attract students, whom he welcomed as long
as they brought a token payment. Coming from a variety of backgrounds,
ranging from moderately well-off to aristocratic, his students all had the
leisure to study with him. None worked the land.

Our only source for understanding the teachings of Confucius, *The
Analects* (meaning "discussions and conversations" or "arranged discourses"), presents Confucius as his disciples, or their disciples, remembered him. Because Confucius lived at a time before written books
circulated, his conversations were first orally transmitted and then written down later. Just as the gospels present different impressions of Jesus,
so too does *The Analects* give us different impressions of Confucius, all
in the same book. No longer than several chapters of the Bible, the book
may have assumed its current shape as late as the first century B.C., when
the first reference to a book entitled *The Analects* appears. As biblical
scholars have in recent years shown that each of the gospels is composed
of different layers of text, quite possibly by different authors, so too have
Confucian scholars begun to question the textual integrity of *The
Analects*.[8] Throughout history, though, most Chinese believed *The
Analects* contained Confucius's original teachings and read it as one unit.

The Teachings of Confucius

The most-quoted passage from *The Analects* appears in the book's opening: To have friends coming from afar: is this not a delight?" (1.1).[9] Confucius's reputation as a serious thinker often overshadows his gregarious
nature: Confucius liked talking to people, and he spent much of his life
in conversation. Although the staccato format of *The Analects* makes it
difficult to reconstruct his teachings, the writings capture the stimulating yet perplexing experience of speaking with the master.

Confucius sought to end the warfare of his time by restoring the Zhou
dynasty in Lu, where he lived. Confucius claimed all along that he did
not introduce any new ideas, maintaining that he was seeking simply to
return the disordered realm to an earlier time. "I transmit, I invent nothing. I trust and love the past" (7.1). We cannot accept this claim at face
value, for Confucius did innovate. Like Sunzi and his art of war, Con-

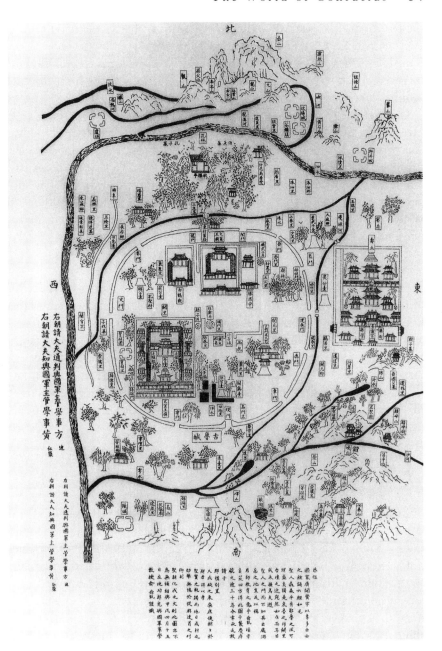

THE HOMETOWN OF CONFUCIUS

This map, carved on a stone tablet between 1037 and 1121, shows the hometown of Confucius, Qufu, in modern Shandong province. Although Qufu has added broader thoroughfares and tourist hotels, the many temples of Confucius and his followers are still intact, making Qufu one of China's leading tourist attractions today.

fucius taught skills that the well-born of antiquity had never had to study. Confucius believed that he could teach his students how to behave virtuously and how to govern, claims that no one in the ancient society he so revered had ever made because they assumed sons of high-ranking families were born to this knowledge.

In his concept of ritual (*li*), Confucius also introduced something new. His contemporaries used the term to refer to specific rituals, but Confucius recognized an abstract quality common to them that applied to the forms of all social interactions. If men could learn to employ this quality, he taught, society could be reformed. The word *ritual* may today suggest the rigid following of fixed forms that deny the individual an opportunity for self-expression. But to Confucius, ritual offered the individual the best opportunity to develop his own humaneness (*ren*), an essential quality also translated as "benevolence," "goodness," "exemplary humanity," and "manhood-at-its-best."

One analyst has suggested the example of a handshake as a rough illustration of Confucius's concept of ritual in modern life. Although one has to learn under what circumstances to shake hands and when to extend one's hand, one can use handshaking to express delight, reluctance, or even repugnance on meeting another. The rituals Confucius discussed, many of them deriving from the ancestral worship of the Zhou, had many more steps than a simple handshake; but if they were learned correctly, they too could express one's innermost humanity. Confucius emphasized that the rites had to be performed with feeling:

> The Master said: "Authority without generosity, ceremony without reverence, mourning without grief—these, I cannot bear to contemplate." (3.26)

Ritual, then, should not be an empty form.

Ritual allowed people to express emotion, but one had to understand the rituals in order to understand what sentiment was being displayed. Like a handshake, these rituals could be confusing, sometimes impenetrable, to people outside one's own culture. *The Analects* depicts Confucius teaching within a closed world of rulers, advisors, and advisors-to-be, whom he often addressed as "you several gentlemen," and who understood the ritual vocabulary he employed. When he made pronouncements about historical figures, he expected his listeners to know who he was talking about, yet he bemoaned the failure of so many beyond his immediate circle to understand him.

Outside this narrow world of the gentlemen remained the common people, who could respond to a good ruler but who could not master more subtle teachings: "You can make the people follow the way, you cannot make them understand it" (8.9). The Way was Confucius's term for his own teachings. By extension, it also referred to the means of governance used by the ancient sage kings, which Confucius hoped to restore through his teachings.

Confucius looked down as well on the non-Chinese peoples in the border regions: "The Di and Yi who have rulers are inferior to the various nations of China who are without" (3.5). Yet, they too, like the common people, could respond to a gentleman's presence. At one point Confucius pondered moving east to live among a group resident in the Shandong Peninsula, and was asked, "It is wild in those parts. How would you cope?" The Master said: "How could it be wild, once a gentleman has settled there?" (9.14). Also outside Confucius's world stand women. *The Analects* mentions neither Confucius's mother nor his wife.

Although he said little about his own family, Confucius advocated implementing his teachings first within individual families. Strikingly, he described a small family unit, in which sons lived together with their wives and their parents. The main bond in the family, Confucius stressed repeatedly, is that between parent and child. Children should obey and honor their parents, even when they disagree with them. Because one's parents raised one from birth, one owes them an enormous obligation that can never be repaid. During their parents' lifetimes, children should obey their wishes, as after their deaths, children should continue for three years to conduct family affairs just as their parents had.

Although Confucius used the gender-blind classical Chinese terms "child" and "parent," his disciples were all male, and Confucius clearly was more concerned with the obligations of sons to their parents than with those of daughters to theirs. *The Analects* describes how Confucius chose suitable husbands for his daughter and his niece (5.1; 5.2), revealing, as do other sources, that when women married, they left their natal families and were able to return only for occasional visits.

No records describe the reaction of ancient Chinese women to Confucius's teachings, but an anthropologist who has worked in modern China and Taiwan, Margery Wolf, has argued persuasively that Chinese women's conception of the family was different from that of men. Men generally considered the interests of a larger family unit stretching back to their ancestors and forward to their descendants. Because only men could worship their ancestors, only sons could carry on the family line. In contrast, women tended to focus on a uterine family consisting of themselves and their own children, whether daughters or sons.[10] When the interests of the uterine family conflicted with those of their husband's extended family, women worked on behalf of the uterine family, even

when such maneuvering ran counter to Confucius's emphasis on obeying one's parents—and for women, one's parents-in-law. These findings,
though from a modern setting, caution us that Confucius described ideal,
not actual, families, and that men and women could conceive of the family in different ways, although the historical record rarely presents
women's views.

Confucius advocated 3 years (in practice 25 or 27 months) of mourning for one's parents. Even though his contemporaries thought this
period unusually long, Confucius insisted on it. Although Confucius advocated a long mourning period, he did not explain what happened to
one's parents after they died.

In one of his most famous conversations, a disciple raised the issue of
the supernatural with Confucius:

> Zilu asked how to serve the spirits and gods. The Master said: "You are not
> yet able to serve men, how could you serve the spirits?" (11.12)

The next topic elicited much the same response:

> Zilu said: "May I ask you about death?"
> The Master said: "You do not yet know life, how could you know death?"
> (11.12)

Confucius's refusal to discuss either topic has often prompted students of
religion to say that since Confucianism has no teachings about the spirits or death, it cannot be a religion. Still, Confucius did not deny the existence of spirits, and he strongly advocated the performance of rites.

Confucius stressed the obligations of the individual because he believed
that, provided each person could tap into his own humanity while ad-
hering to the dictates of ritual within his family, the realm as a whole
would be reformed and the Way restored. One need not serve a ruler in
order to bring about reform. When someone asked Confucius why he
did not hold a government post, he cited one of the classics, *The Book of
Documents*:

> "Only cultivate filial piety and be kind to your brothers, and you will be con-
> tributing to the body politic." This is also a form of political action; one need
> not necessarily join the government. (2.21)

This idea runs through much of Confucius's teaching. One can influence
the world simply by behaving as a gentleman at home—even when the
world around one is engulfed in chaos.

If rulers developed benevolence, Confucius hoped they would then be
able to check all the chaotic forces ravaging society, but he never delin-

eated the precise mechanism by which this political transformation would occur. Throughout he remained adamant that good rulers would never resort to coercion to govern. As he explained,

> Lead them by political maneuvers, restrain them with punishments: the people will become cunning and shameless. Lead them by virtue, restrain them with ritual: they will develop a sense of shame and a sense of participation.

Succeeding generations wrestled with this prohibition on the use of force, which many found unworkable, but Confucius offered no support for punishments because he felt the ruler who stooped to coercion could never command the people's respect. Confucius acknowledged the difficulty of rule by equating governing with the movements of the cosmos: "He who rules by virtue is like the polestar, which remains unmoving in its mansion while all the other stars revolve respectfully around it" (2.1). Like the North Star, a good ruler could indicate the direction for all of his subjects to follow.

Intensely idealistic, Confucius sought to end warfare with his teachings that emphasized ritual and man's innate capacity for benevolence. As influential as Confucius's teachings became, and he is certainly the best-known Chinese thinker in China and in the West, he never succeeded in ending the violence around him. Confucius's teachings continued to be preserved and expanded in the centuries after his death in the small polity of Lu, and the Han-dynasty *Records of the Grand Historian* provides a poignant description of the Confucians' powerlessness when an opposing force attacked their city:

> From within came the ceaseless sounds of strings and songs, for in that place the Ru [Confucians] still recited and chanted, practicing ceremony and music.[11]

In 479 B.C., Confucius died an obscure teacher with few students. Confucianism was not yet a school, and many of his extant sayings were still to be invented. No one could have predicted that his ideas would have become the most influential in all of China, and indeed, a complex series of events had to occur before his thought, with many modifications, was installed as state orthodoxy in the second century B.C.

Ritual in the Time of Confucius

Although Confucius and his disciples often discuss particular aspects of a given ritual, *The Analects* contains no overall description of rituals similar to those cited earlier from *The Book of Songs*. Chapter 10 of *The Analects* contains a host of individual prescriptions, some so detailed that

many think the chapter may have been lifted from a ritual manual and
added later to the text:

> A gentleman does not wear purple or mauve lapels; red and violet should not
> be used for daily wear at home. . . .
>   With a black robe, he wears lambskin; with a white robe, deerskin, with a
> yellow robe, fox fur. (10.6)

Chapter 10 provides no context for such regulations. Elsewhere in *The
Analects*, Confucius mentions that archery and drinking have ritual significance:

> A gentleman avoids competition. Still, if he must compete let it be at archery.
> There, as he bows and exchanges civilities both before the contest and over
> drinks afterward, he remains a gentleman, even in competition. (3.7)

The reader cannot help wondering what the purpose of such rituals
was—or what they looked like.

Fortunately, many vessels depicting ritual occasions survive from Confucius's time. Their style breaks with all earlier Chinese art. Instead of
the raised, abstract animal designs on the ancient bronzes, the anonymous
artists of the Warring States inlaid smooth metal scenes of lifelike human figures engaged in a host of activities. These bronzes bear no accompanying texts, and as one analyst has noted, the figures they show
are resolutely anonymous. One can identify people by their tasks, but the
lack of individualized features make it impossible to recognize specific
historic figures. Some of the earliest bronzes showing human activities
and clay molds used to make the inlay have been found in Houma,
Shanxi, in the Jin realm. The rulers of the Jin, who were responsible for
so many of the innovations in fighting during these tumultuous times,
may also have patronized the first artists to depict human activities on
bronze vessels.

Ritual Activity as Shown on the Vessels of the Warring States

In earlier times, the Shang and Zhou kings had retained a monopoly on
bronze production and awarded their subordinates vessels, or the right
to make them. By the time of Confucius, lower-ranking lords had taken
over the production of such vessels, which they cast to record their own
victories, whether on the battlefield or in a ritual competition. A recurring theme on the vessels, as in *The Analects*, is ritual activity, showing
that, while many of his anonymous contemporaries shared Confucius's
concern with ritual, their views of it differed dramatically.

Confucius expressed his distress each time one of the newly risen feudal lords violated a ritual prescription. In his own homeland of Lu, the Three Houses of Huan, who were three noble clans descended from the same seventh-century lord, regularly infringed on the prerogatives of the increasingly decrepit Zhou king and the equally powerless lord of the Lu state. They worshiped the wrong mountain, performed an inappropriate ceremony, and hired too many dancing girls (3.26; 3.2; 3.1). Confucius's belief in a system in which rulers enjoyed the privileges due to their rank was undiminished, even though the system was unraveling before his own eyes.

Insubordination to one is opportunity to another. The violations of ritual regulation that so distressed Confucius allowed the newly ascendant rulers to demonstrate that they were the social equals of the rulers they hoped to depose. They rejoiced that they could hold ceremonies emulating those of the Zhou court, and they commemorated those ceremonies on the new bronze vessels. The bronzes they commissioned provide a valuable glimpse of ritual at the time of Confucius.

One of the earliest known representations of a battle during the Eastern Zhou appears on a wine vessel dating to 500 B.C. It was found in Lucheng, Shanxi (400 kilometers or 250 miles east of modern-day Xian). Although fragmentary, the ewer contains a few clear scenes. On its neck stand three fish, symbolizing prosperity. Immediately below them is pictured a structure with three figures: one is seated and drinks from a horn, as does the figure on the far left. The middle figure appears to be dancing or playing an instrument. Several birds fly overhead. Below them is an elaborate and macabre battle scene between two groups of people wearing different clothing. One group wears sleeveless chain-linked tunics with leggings; the others have on leotard-type clothing close to the skin. The tunic-wearers bear an array of weapons including spears, bows, and arrows. The figure standing in the center, perhaps a commander, wears a more elaborate hat than his fellow hunters and holds his spear horizontally. A flag hangs downward from the spear's point, while a severed head dangles close to his body. Other victims are shown. To the left, one cross-hatched, leotarded body lies with an arrow piercing its heart. On the right, another figure in a tunic prepares to behead his victim. Above him stands another person, perhaps a woman, in a leotard, with her hands in fetters. She appears to be the prisoner of the figure in a tunic carrying a pole.

This vessel provides unusual documentation of the differences in clothing between the victorious Chinese-speaking lords (in tunics) of the central states and their defeated enemies (in leotards). The vessel juxtaposes ritual observances and brutal fighting. The Shang and Zhou had offered

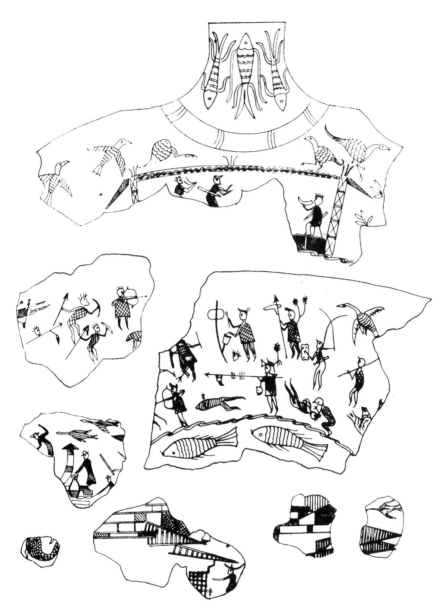

BATTLES AND RITUALS AT THE TIME OF CONFUCIUS

A wine vessel (ca. 500 B.C.) from Lucheng, Shanxi province, depicts a battle during the Eastern Zhou. *The Analects* gives detailed instructions for rituals but does not explain their link to warfare. Here the king is seen presiding over a ritual, while below him his troops defeat an alien people, who may not speak Chinese.

their battle victims to the gods, and this vessel testifies to the continuing link between the drinking ritual in the top register and the battle shown below it, but its fragmentary nature precludes further analysis.

A much-better preserved vessel, also from Confucius's time, shows a

NEWS DIGEST IN BRONZE

This drawing of a stunning, detailed bronze from 500 B.C. shows a hunt and a host of other activities. Reading in a clockwise direction, the quadrants show two men playing a drinking game with tallies and an orchestra (upper right), a battle in which an attacking army scales earthen ramparts (lower right), a water battle with men both rowing and swimming (lower left), and a hunt in which archers use arrows with silk cords attached to shoot ducks (upper left).

hunt and a battle. The long robes and elaborate headgear of those on the vessel suggest that they may have been participating in an official ritual event. The top band shows mulberry-leaf picking. The next band depicts a hunt, as does the left-hand side of the third band. The long-robed hunters use bow and arrow with a silk cord attached to shoot ducks. On the right, two men play a drinking game with tallies. The winner's cup contains three horizontal lines, which denote tallies, while the loser has none—so he will have to drink the wine being prepared behind him.

Underneath the two figures is a full orchestra of the Warring States period, with bells suspended from a rack (left), chiming stones (middle), and stringed instruments (right).

The fourth band shows a battle. The sharp diagonal lines (right) represent the earthen ramparts the attacking army scales as it assaults a walled city, while the men inside shoot arrows at them. In the water battle shown on the left, the figures standing on the two boats look unrealistically stable, while crouching men paddle below, and fish and soldiers swim underneath. Here, too, the attackers and defenders have different hairstyles. The victors in the battle wear three-cornered hats, while the victims have plaited hair. At the point where the two boats touch, a figure in a tricorner hat grasps the braid of his victim as he drives his blade into the victim's head.

The chronological relationship between the different bands is not explicit, but it seems likely that the battle shown on the bottom half of the vessel preceded the elaborate ritual shown above it. Only after the battle had ended and the people in the tricorner hats had slaughtered their braided enemies could they celebrate by staging an elaborate ritual with drinking games and archery competitions.

These vessels cast the rituals of the Warring States in a completely different light than does *The Analects*. Confucius had much to say about how rituals should be performed, but he did not remark on the occasions on which rituals occurred. For Confucius, ritual provided a forum for the individual's benevolence to develop. The inlaid bronze vessels of his time may exaggerate the violence of the battlefield because they were cast to commemorate a given ruler's victory. Still, they depict many of the same activities Confucius discusses—archery, music, dance, and hunting—in addition to grisly battles he did not mention. Battles may not have preceded all rituals, but the inlaid bronzes document that the Chinese, whether they wore tunics and leggings or three-corner hats, were taking territory at the expense of the non-Chinese speaking peoples around them. The bronzes also attest that violence often accompanied ritual, a link shown even more vividly by the finds at Houma, Shanxi.

Ritual and Blood Feud

A group of unusual oaths, recorded on stone and jade, was found in some four hundred pits located outside the capital city Houma of the Jin polity that Double Ears had once ruled. Dating to sometime between 499 and

489 B.C., the 656 documents found at the site varied in length and format, but each document recorded an oath to kill the members of an enemy clan, led by Zhao Ni. Some of the oaths were taken by individuals, others by groups of up to one hundred men who all vowed to support their ruler, who was named Zhao Yang. The way these oaths were buried indicated that the men followed the same ritual procedure for blood covenants as had the allies of Double Ears when they commemorated his victory. One such oath at Houma read:

> If I, Hu, dare to fail to strip bare my heart and vitals in serving my lord, or dare to fail to adhere thoroughly to Your covenant and the mandate granted in Dinggong [an ancestral temple of the Zhou] and Pingsi [a town near the Zhou capital]; or dare, in any respect, to initiate breaking of the faith or dispersion of the alliance, causing an interruption in the guardianship of the two temples; or dare to harbor the intention of restoring Zhao Ni and his descendants to the territory of the state of Jin or join in a faction to summon others to convenant with them; may our former rulers, far-seeing, instantly detect me and may ruin befall my lineage.[12]

Like the allies of Double Ears, they smeared their lips with the blood of the sacrificed animal as they took their vows before the spirits of their former rulers. They then buried the written text of their oath along with the sacrificed animal in a pit. The oaths at Houma, though, differ from those recorded in *The Commentary of Mr. Zuo* in an important respect. In the time of Double Ears, rulers entered into blood covenants on behalf of their realms and they called on spirits of rivers, mountains, the sun, and the moon to enforce the oaths. By Houma, a little more than a century later, they entered into covenants as individuals, showing how weak kin groups—and how strong individual households—had become during Confucius's lifetime. Interestingly, they looked to the deceased ancestors of the Jin rulers to enforce the oaths. The finds at Houma document a mass vendetta between two kin groups. Similar feuds probably occurred in other regions at the time. No wonder Confucius so longed for the rulers of his time to behave as gentlemen.

A WORLD BREAKING APART: THE DIFFERENCES AMONG CONFUCIUS'S DISCIPLES

The bronzes of the Warring States provide graphic testimony that Confucius's contemporaries did not share his optimistic vision of ritual. Similarly, *The Analects* documents divisions among even his disciples, some of which surfaced during his lifetime, others only after his death in 479

B.C. The textual history of *The Analects*, as given in a third-century A.D. catalogue, helps to explain why the book so clearly documents these incipient conflicts:

> The *Lunyu* [*Analects*] contains the teachings that Confucius spoke in responding to disciples and contemporaries, and the lessons learned from their Master that the disciples spoke to one another. Each disciple of the time made his own record. After their Master's death, his followers collectively edited and collated these; hence they are called the "collated teachings" [*lunyu*].[13]

Because individual students contributed separate sections to *The Analects*, the book retains each disciple's personal sense of his teacher in a way that no composite text written by committee could. If one reorders *The Analects* so that one reads all of Confucius's conversations with one disciple before proceeding to those with the next, one can see the sharp differences that caused the Confucians to break up into eight rival schools by the middle of the third century B.C.

Like Confucius, who led his own study group, his disciples developed their own followings in the years after his death. A late chapter in *The Analects* foreshadows the divisions among Confucius's students. One student belittles another's understanding of friendship (19.3). A third criticizes the way the first trains his students, while the first responds that his critic does not understand the "doctrine of the gentleman" (19.12). The critic accuses another of not attaining benevolence, and a fourth concurs that the other can indeed be difficult (19.15, 19.16). These students disagree about fundamental issues in Confucian thought—the nature of friendship, the behavior of the gentleman, and the attainment of benevolence—and they appear actively to dislike each other as well.

Mozi's Criticisms

Born just as Confucius was dying, the iconoclastic Mozi (480?–400?) formulated his teachings directly in response to Confucius. As in the case of *The Analects*, the text of *Mozi* we read today was written down several centuries later, after his disciples had divided into different, conflicting groups.[14] Mozi's name has puzzled commentators for generations. Because the word *mo* means 'ink' or 'tattoo,' some have speculated that the thinker was branded as punishment for a crime. Tattooing was a particularly humiliating punishment because it permanently scarred the body, a gift from one's parents. Others speculate that he bore the unusual surname because he was non-Chinese, and, indeed, his teachings convey a sympathy for non-Chinese peoples. In one anecdote, Mozi demonstrates a deep understanding of how to make a wheel from wood, suggesting that he may have been a carpenter. It is significant that Mozi borrows many terms from Confucius but not the distinction between the gentleman and the common people.

As the fighting of the Warring States continued in the fifth century B.C., the number of contestants dwindled to four major contenders—Qi, Jin, Chu, and Yue—which Mozi named, though other, smaller states survived as well. When these states' defenders argued that their survival demonstrated their righteousness, Mozi responded with his characteristically acerbic wit:

> In ancient times the Son of Heaven enfeoffed over ten thousand feudal lords. And yet now, because of the annexation of one state by another, these ten thousand domains have all disappeared and only the four remain. But it is rather like the case of a doctor who administers medicine to over ten thousand patients but succeeds in curing only four. He cannot be said to be a very skilled physician.[15]

Mozi accepted certain basic Confucian prescriptions, like the superiority of the ancient sage kings who had attained righteousness, yet he felt that Confucius overemphasized bonds with acquaintances and relatives. To illustrate his point, he gave his famous example of thieves who "steal from other families in order to benefit their own." They fulfilled their obligations to their immediate family members, as Confucius had instructed, but at everyone else's expense.[16] Mozi proposed an alternative to Confucius's hierarchy of obligations centered on the family. Mozi argued that each individual had an obligation toward all the other people in human society, and he advocated "impartial caring" (*jian ai*, often misleadingly translated as "universal love") as a solution to society's ills. Strictly defined, the term Mozi used, *ai*, means "love," but he did not mean that everyone had to love everyone else without qualification. Individuals simply had to consider how their actions would affect everyone in society, not just the people they knew personally.

Mozi's emphasis on equity also caused him to challenge Confucius's teachings about long mourning periods because they cost society too much. Mozi ridiculed Confucians for advocating elaborate funerals and a lengthy mourning period yet refusing to discuss spirits and the afterlife, saying: "To maintain that there are no spirits and to study the sacrificial rites is like studying the ceremonies for treating guests without having any guests." Mozi's criticisms of funerals hinged on several points.

The Confucians, he felt, depended too much on the income they earned from presiding over funerals: "When there is a death in a rich family, they [the Confucians] are overwhelmed with joy, saying, 'This is our chance for food and clothing!'" He also objected to the Confucian requirement that one mourn one's eldest son, one's spouse, one's mother, and one's father for the same three-year period because he felt it was obvious that a parent deserved more mourning than a spouse or a child.

Mozi produced a unique analysis of the problem of lavish funerals. He first described the reputed funeral practices of three non-Chinese peoples who had lived beyond the borders of Chinese states in the distant past. People in the south beyond the Yue territory had the following customs:

> When their first son was born, they cut him up and ate him, saying this would be beneficial to the next son. When their fathers died, they loaded their mothers on their backs, carried them off and abandoned them, saying, "One can't live in the same house with the wife of a ghost!"

His second example came from people who lived south of the Chu kingdom: when their parents died, they scraped the flesh off the dead person's bones and threw it away. A people who lived to the west, beyond the state of Qin, cremated their dead. Because Mozi chose these examples for their shock value, it is possible he exaggerated or even made them up.

Each of these practices horrified his Chinese readers, who buried the bodies of their parents whole and refrained from doing any damage to the body. Mozi understood how repellent his examples were, yet he explained why he introduced them: "If we examine the practices of these three lands, we find them too casual and heartless, while if we examine those of the gentlemen of China, we find them too elaborate." He proposes specific measures for controlling the costs of funerals—for instance, limiting the thickness of coffins, the number of clothes for the dead to wear, and the size of the grave pit. Although marred by repetition and a poor prose style, Mozi's ideas followed a logical progression. In later generations, his followers, the Mohists, would further refine his rhetorical techniques to produce China's most sophisticated logic. In the centuries following Mozi's death, his followers battled with the Confucians over the contentious issues of music, funerals, and spirits, but they all agreed that the gentleman had to remain engaged in society if he was going to reform it. The followers of another new school of thought dating to this time argued instead that the best method of reforming society was to withdraw from society.

Withdrawing from Society: An Alternative Way

Several passages in *The Analects*, possibly added later, suggest that the prescription of dropping out of society appealed even to some of Confucius's own disciples. In a late chapter, Confucius's disciple Zilu encounters a farmer who asks him, as he continues to plow the land:

> Instead of following a gentleman who keeps running from one patron to the next, would it not be better to follow a gentleman who has forsaken the world?

Zilu asks Confucius his view, and Confucius responds:

> One cannot associate with birds and beasts. With whom should I keep company, if not with my own kind? If the world were following the Way, I would not have to reform it. (18.6)

Confucius's response here emphasized the need to remain active in this world, but elsewhere in *The Analects*, he leaned toward the alternative proposed by the enigmatic farmer. Although he often said he sought office, and urged his students to accept it, he rejected three employment offers in the course of *The Analects*.[17] As he explained his reasoning, "Shine in a world that follows the Way; hide when the world loses the Way" (8.13). If one concluded that the Way did not prevail, then Confucius's advice overlaps with that of the early text, *The Way and Integrity Classic*, an amalgam of different teachings that assumed its current shape sometime in the third century B.C.

The Way and Integrity Classic

The Daodejing, or *The Way and Integrity Classic*, is known today as a Daoist text, but this label is misleading. At the time the text took shape (in the third century B.C.) there was no clearly identifiable group who could be called Daoists. Instead, there were only individual teachers who were not necessarily thought of as Daoist. Only in the first century B.C. was the label "Daoist" attached to *The Way and Integrity Classic*. At that time, "Daoist" referred to any teacher who practiced breathing techniques, meditation, or austere eating regimes in the hopes of extending his life span or even of gaining immortality. These individual teachers did not belong to an organized religious community.

Such teachers may have been among the multiple authors of the book, which has been traditionally attributed to one man named Laozi, or Old Master. The styles of different authors are visible in different sections of the text.

Translated countless times into English, sometimes even by those who could not read classical Chinese, its teachings appear more tangible in translation than in the original. The text consists of some five thousand characters, partially in rhymed couplets, testifying to its origins as an orally transmitted text. Some of these teachings are addressed to the ruler of a state.

The book opens by stating the ineffability of the Way:

> The ways that can be walked are not the eternal Way;
> The names that can be named are not the eternal name. . . .
>
> Mystery of mysteries,
> The gate of all wonders![18]

Different passages in this text emphasize the quality of *wuwei*, sometimes incorrectly translated as nonaction. The skilled translator Victor Mair defines *wuwei*, saying: "It indicates spontaneity and noninterference; that is, letting things follow their own natural course."[19] As one verse explains:

> Nothing under heaven is softer or weaker than water,
>   and yet nothing is better
>   for attacking what is hard and strong,
>   because of its immutability.

Water embodies the quality of *wuwei*, but so too do women and infants, who manage to get their desires even though they are weak.

The Way and Integrity Classic advocates that rulers emulate the female:

> In the congress of all under heaven,
>   the female always conquers the male through her stillness.
> Because she is still,
>   it is fitting for her to lie low.

He who governs, "the sage" in the phrasing of *The Way and Integrity Classic*, should adopt the principle of allowing things to follow their natural course because "Ruling a big kingdom is like cooking a small fish." If one pays too much attention to the state, or the small fish, it will be spoiled.

Like *The Analects*, *The Way and Integrity Classic* looks to the past for its model states:

> Let there be a small state with few people,
>   where military devices find no use. . . .
> Let the people go back to tying knots

to keep records.
Let their food be savory,
   their clothes beautiful,
   their customs pleasurable,
   their dwellings secure.

This vision of an ancient state undisturbed by war evokes the idealism of Confucius, but *The Way and Integrity Classic* takes pains to distinguish its teachings from those of Confucius:

Abolish sagehood and abandon cunning,
   the people will benefit a hundredfold;
Abolish humaneness (*ren*) and abandon righteousness,
   the people will once again be filial and kind;
Abolish cleverness and abandon profit,
   bandits and thieves will be no more.

The text targets Confucius's values of sagehood, humaneness, and right-eousness, and Mozi's emphasis on profit. It then reevokes the purity of those things that have not been touched by human hands: undyed silk and unhewn logs. And should the listener still lean toward Confucian values, the text counsels, "Abolish learning and you will be without worries." Another early text also attacks the teachings of Confucius, but the approach of *Zhuangzi* is far more direct than the oblique phrasing of *The Way and Integrity Classic*. *Zhuangzi* was also classed as a Daoist text in the first century B.C., but we must remember that no organized Daoist religious movement existed during the fourth and third centuries B.C., when the text was composed. Instead, individual teachers taught disciples about a variety of subjects, like those mentioned in *The Way and Integrity Classic*.

Zhuangzi: *The Use of Paradox and Humor*

Where *The Way and Integrity Classic* often addresses the ruler of a state, *Zhuangzi* focuses on the individual and presents a series of anecdotes featuring Zhuangzi, a persona possibly linked to a historical figure who lived from 355? to 275 B.C. Zhuangzi taught in a way like no other early thinker. He delighted in paradox and challenged the reader to abandon preconceived notions, often by making the reader laugh. In contrast, *The Way and Integrity Classic* never uses humor. Like all the other early classical Chinese texts, *Zhuangzi* contains many interpolations, but scholars concur that one person wrote the first seven chapters.

Zhuangzi refuted many of Confucius's teachings, often by having a character named Confucius denounce ritual and benevolence in favor of emptiness. In one anecdote, a fictive Confucius discusses studying with his favorite disciple, Yan Hui. One day Yan Hui announces, "I've forgotten humaneness (*ren*) and righteousness!" Confucius, here a mouthpiece for Zhuangzi, says, "That's good. But you still haven't got it." On another occasion, Yan Hui says, "I've forgotten rites and music!" Confucius replies, "That's good. But you still haven't got it." More time passes, and then Yan Hui and Confucius have the following exchange:

> "I'm improving!"
> "What do you mean by that?"
> "I can sit down and forget everything!"
> Confucius looked very startled and said, "What do you mean,
> sit down and forget everything?"
> Yan Hui said, "I smash up my limbs and body, drive out
> perception and intellect, cast off form, do away with
> understanding, and make myself identical with the Great
> Thoroughfare."[20]

Confucius then asks permission to become Yan Hui's student. Yan Hui's answer reveals a belief hinted at in *Zhuangzi* and more fully developed in later Daoism. Through self-cultivation, men can become invincible and avoid death.

Zhuangzi's choice of Yan Hui betrays his close familiarity with *The Analects*, for Yan Hui is the one disciple whom Confucius credits with having attained benevolence. *The Analects* records his attempt to understand his master's teachings about benevolence in unusual terms:

> The more I contemplate it, the higher it is; the deeper I dig into it, the more it
> resists; I saw it in front of me, and then suddenly it was behind me. Step by
> step, our Master really knows how to entrap people. He stimulates me with lit-
> erature, he restrains me with ritual. Even if I wanted to stop, I could not. Just
> as all my resources are exhausted, the goal is towering right above me; I long
> to embrace it, but cannot find the way. (9.11)

This imbues Confucius's teachings with a mystical component, and on several occasions Confucius responds to the queries of other disciples in equally elusive ways. Yan Hui is talking about an ideal Way, or *dao*, and he cannot explain how to achieve it.

But where Confucius maintained a serious tone in his conversations recorded in *The Analects*, Zhuangzi indulged in a paradoxical humor for which he became well known. Zhuangzi set out to convince his listeners and his readers that they could not be certain of what they knew:

> Once Zhuang Zhou [Zhuangzi] dreamt he was a butterfly, a butterfly flitting and fluttering around, happy with himself and doing as he pleased. He didn't know he was Zhuang Zhou. Suddenly he woke up and there he was, solid and unmistakable Zhuang Zhou. But he didn't know if he was Zhuang Zhou who had dreamt he was a butterfly, or a butterfly dreaming he was Zhuang Zhou.

This theme runs through much of *Zhuangzi*, which seeks to persuade its readers that they cannot take any belief for granted.

Zhuangzi achieved his greatest eloquence when he tried to persuade his listeners that death should not be mourned. Here, of course, he was challenging contemporary Confucians who advocated elaborate funerals. Zhuangzi compared death to the marriage of Lady Li, the Rong woman who married Double Ears's father, Duke Xian of the Jin state. Before her marriage, which Zhuangzi says occurred after she was taken against her will, Lady Li was terrified of leaving her home to join the duke:

> Lady Li was the daughter of the border guard of Ai. When she was first taken captive [by Duke Xian] and brought to the state of Jin, she wept until her tears drenched the collar of her robe. But later, when she went to live in the palace of the ruler, shared his couch with him, and ate the delicious meats of his table, she wondered why she had ever wept. How do I know that the dead do not wonder why they ever longed for life?

Zhuangzi's comparison is instructive. Lady Li, the daughter of non-Chinese parents, feared living in a Chinese palace. As the border woman ignorantly feared Chinese civilization, so too do the living fear death.

A later chapter of the *Zhuangzi*, and one that may have been added to the core text, presents a dream dialogue between a skull and Zhuangzi about the realm of the dead, in which the skull extols the joys of being dead. When Zhuangzi incredulously asks the skull if he would refuse a chance to return to life, the skull replies, "Why would I throw away more happiness than that of a king on a throne and take on the troubles of a human being again?"

Scholars have always assumed this was yet another example of Zhuangzi's playful rhetoric, but a tomb in northwest China, at Fangmatan, Gansu, has produced an extraordinary bamboo manuscript suggesting that Zhuangzi's contemporaries may indeed have believed in the resurrection of the dead. The record, drawn up by a low official for the court, describes what happened to a man with the surname of Dan:

Dan injured a man by stabbing him in Yuanyong village; and because of it he killed himself with his sword. They exposed him in the market. Three days later they buried him outside the south gate of Yuanyong. Three years later Dan was able to be restored to life.

The report then goes on to explain that an official of the underworld, who determined each person's individual life span, realized that an error had been made and that Dan had died prematurely, so Dan was allowed to return to the living, but with a scar on his neck where he had killed himself.[21] This unique document sheds light on the often unrecorded beliefs of ordinary people about a netherworld populated by officials who could change their minds about the fate of the living.

The most frequently recurring paradox in *Zhuangzi* concerns the advantages of the disadvantaged. Crippled men have difficulty walking but they are able to live long lives since they are exempt from labor obligations and military service. Certain trees also manage to avoid being cut down. Daoists are often said to love nature, perhaps because of the passages in *The Way and Integrity Classic* emphasizing letting things run their natural course. But Zhuangzi described the ongoing deforestation he saw taking place around him without ever condemning it.

Witnesses to the Degradation of the Environment: Zhuangzi and Mencius

Zhuangzi set one tale in the polity of Qi, where a carpenter and his apprentice see a giant serrate oak "broad enough to shelter several thousand oxen." When the apprentice asks why he does not cut it down, the carpenter replies:

> It's a worthless tree! Make boats out of it and they'd sink; make coffins and they'd rot in no time. Use it for doors and it would sweat sap like pine; use it for posts and the worms would eat them up. It's not a timber tree—there's nothing it can be used for. That's how it got to be that old!

Then, in a plot twist only Zhuangzi could imagine, the tree appears in the carpenter's dream to protest being called worthless and describes the plight of trees in third-century B.C. China:

> What are you comparing me with? Are you comparing me with those useful trees? The cherry apple, the pear, the orange, the citron, the rest of those fructiferous trees and shrubs—as soon as their fruit is ripe, they are torn apart and subjected to abuse. Their big limbs are broken off, their little limbs are yanked around. Their utility makes life miserable for them. . . .

> As for me, I've been trying a long time to be of no use, and now that I'm about to die, I've finally got it. This is of great use to me.

The tree's survival illustrates the use of the useless, one of Zhuangzi's favorite themes, but it also documents the extensive cutting down of trees taking place during his lifetime.

A contemporary of Zhuangzi's, Mencius (372?–289 B.C.) was born in the town of Zou, very near to Confucius's hometown, in the polity of Lu, where he studied Confucian teachings as a young man. He described the destruction of the countryside to make a very different point:

> Bull Mountain was once beautifully wooded. But, because it was close to a large city, its trees all fell to the axe. What of its beauty then? However, as the days passed things grew, and with the rains and the dews it was not without greenery. Then came the cattle and goats to graze. That is why, today, it has that scoured-like appearance. On seeing it now, people imagine that nothing ever grew there. But this is surely not the true nature of a mountain?

Bull Mountain began as a deeply forested hill but was transformed by its human neighbors.

Mencius then explained why he has introduced this example:

> And so, too, with human beings. Can it be that any man's mind naturally lacks humaneness (ren) and righteousness? If he loses his sense of the good, then he loses it as the mountain has lost its trees. It has been hacked away at—day after day—what of its beauty then?[22]

A central question for Mencius was whether men were endowed with good or bad natures at birth. As the environment had altered the nature of Bull Mountain, so too could it transform people. Mencius believed that men were born good, and he cited as proof the common human impulse to jump into a well to save a drowning child. In explaining his views of human nature, Mencius needed a clear example of something that had lost the qualities with which it had been originally endowed. Tellingly, he chose the natural environment around him, which, he felt, bore no resemblance to its pristine state.

Mencius and Xunzi: The Continuing Confucian Debate

The views of Mencius and Xunzi are often contrasted, because Xunzi (ca. 310–ca. 210 B.C.) thought only assiduous education could counteract the original weaknesses of human nature. When they looked at adults, the two men saw different entities. Mencius saw an originally good person who, like Bull Mountain, had been corrupted by his environment while Xunzi saw an originally evil person who had been improved by careful study and continuous education.

Like Confucius, the two thinkers focused on the question of how to govern, but they lived in a different age from his. In the two centuries between Confucius and his successors, the Zhou dynasty had become so weak that neither Mencius nor Xunzi could seriously advocate their return to rule. They both advocated unification under a competent ruler, whom they no longer expected to be descended from the Zhou. As the fighting among the various regional states persisted, both men developed new solutions to the political crisis engulfing the realm. Mencius, because of his positive view of human nature, felt the people could be trusted to select a new ruler, and he reinterpreted the ancient concept of the Mandate of Heaven to mean that a ruler could rule only with the support of his subjects. Mencius did not grant the people the right to voice their opinions, though. That was reserved only for the king's ministers. Because rulers should serve their subjects, Mencius thought, those who did so would come to win the support of all the people and be able to unify the realm. Mencius spent much time defending the different and irregular successions of the past, but he always claimed to see the workings of Heaven in them, even when the new emperor killed his predecessor, as the founder of the Zhou did the last Shang ruler. Any ruler could learn the correct principles and become a sage, and once he did, he could unite the realm. Mencius saw his own role as the teacher of such a king.

By Xunzi's time, after the turn of the third century B.C., the political situation of China had shifted again. Three major states vied for power: Qi to the east, Chu to the south, and Qin to the northwest. The few smaller states that had survived the fighting, including Xunzi's home of Zhao, maneuvered among these three. Little is known of Xunzi's family background, but he may have been descended from a noble family living in the state of Zhao. At the age of fifteen, just after the turn of the third century B.C., Xunzi traveled to the state of Qi to study at the Jixia Academy, then a center of political thinkers. The Zhou, on its last legs, finally collapsed in 256 B.C. when the powerful state of Qin, organized along lines deeply distasteful to Xunzi, finally defeated it.

Xunzi visited the Qin court just before its conquest of the Zhou. He described the Legalist policies of the Qin rulers accurately, saying, "They employ them [the people] harshly, terrorize them with authority, embitter them with hardship, coax them with rewards, and cow them with punishments."[23] This was a far cry from the polestar government advocated by Confucius, and Xunzi predicted the Qin could not last: "Qin has been victorious for four generations, yet it has lived in constant terror and apprehension lest the rest of the world should someday unite and trample it down." The ideal ruler for Xunzi, the ruler he called the true king, would govern with the support of the people. Under his rule, "no man of virtue shall be left unhonored; no man of ability shall be left unemployed; no man of merit shall be left unrewarded; no man of guilt shall be left unpunished." A meritocracy would replace the system of privilege that had prevailed in the past. Many of these ideals resemble those of Mencius, but Xunzi's vision of the state left more room for laws and punishments than did the vision of Mencius.

The Economic Thought of Mencius and Xunzi

Mencius and Xunzi both advocated specific policies that addressed the pressing political and economic concerns of the day. As the regional rulers continued to cast about for an efficient means of taxing individual households, Mencius suggested they look to the well-field system of the ancient Zhou kings, which superimposed on the land a tic-tac-toe grid (which looks like the Chinese character for well 井). Eight families worked the individual plots around the central square, which they cultivated together. They took the output of their own plots, while the ruler received the proceeds of the central, communally worked square. Although this system was never implemented, that did not lessen its appeal for Mencius, because it guaranteed the ruler an income while protecting the people from excessive taxation, a problem that Mencius and Xunzi both mention.

Mencius's example of the well-field system suggests a completely undeveloped market economy. Yet, when Mencius debated a rival who thought everyone should till the land so that all could be self-sufficient, Mencius replied that even peasants exchange grain to buy cloth, cooking vessels, and tools. Mencius's warning that impoverished peasants had to borrow from moneylenders testified to the growth of the economy. He also mentioned the iron tools, which prompted increased agricultural productivity during the Warring States period. We have seen, in the story of the wily Feng Xuan who sings to his "Longsword" and advises his Lord Mengchang (pp. 66–67), that peasants borrowed money from their lords as well as from private moneylenders.

The Money Economy of the Warring States Period

Money, in the form of miniature agricultural tools and weapons, began to circulate widely all over the realm sometime around the year 500 B.C.

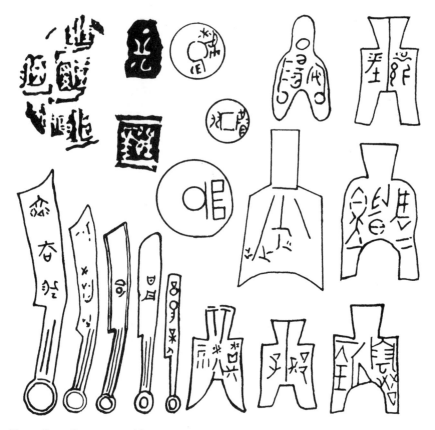

THE ODD SHAPE OF MONEY

Money was introduced in three places in the world between the seventh and fifth centuries
B.C.: the kingdom of Lydia (in modern Turkey), India, and China. While the Greeks of
Lydia and the Indians used round coins, as did the Chinese on occasion, only Chinese coins
took the shape of miniature knives and shovels, which were objects of utility and value.

In the years of the Shang and the early Zhou, rulers had used cowrie
shells and cloth as currency, while their subjects probably bartered for
any goods they could not themselves produce. Barter remained the primary means of trade, especially among commoners, but the new types of
money enjoyed limited use, especially for paying taxes.

Both Xunzi and Mencius reported that peasants paid taxes with money
in the shape of a spade or a knife, and graves have been excavated that
contain either precious metals or models of precious metals (made of less
valuable materials and labeled "gold").

Opposing excessive taxes on merchants, Mencius advocated lower taxes at the same time that he defended prices determined by the market. Like Mencius, Xunzi characterized the reign of the ideal king as one whose "officials shall examine the goods but levy no tax" at markets and borders. The merchant class grew as trade among the different regions increased. Neither Mencius nor Xunzi looked down on the merchants; both saw trading as a legitimate occupation necessary for the smooth functioning of society, although not equal in status to that of a scholar. Xunzi described the many goods the central states imported:

> In the far north there are fast horses and howling dogs; the central states acquire and breed them and put them to work. In the far south there are feathers, tusks, hides, pure copper, and cinnabar; the central states acquire them and use them in their manufactures. In the far east there are plants with purple dye, coarse hemp, fish, and salt; the central states acquire them for their food and clothing. In the far west there are skins and colored yaks' tails; the central states acquire them for their needs.

This thumbnail sketch of the economy suggests a well-developed network for trade with the borderlands in four directions.

Xunzi also commented on the increasing degree of specialization among regions as some produced a certain type of weapon or cloth. Archeologists have since discovered stone workshops and blacksmith shops from the period. Specialization occurred on an individual level as well. Zhuangzi told of a family who made their living bleaching silk but who were able to sell a secret formula for hand salve for a hundred measures of gold. As specialization increased, so too did the size of urban areas, and the cities of the Warring States often had a separate, walled section for economic activities, in addition to the political center with the ruler's palace.

The Chaotic Pace of Change

The pace of change never slackened during the centuries from 770 B.C., when the Zhou shifted their capital to Luoyang, to 256 B.C., when the Zhou fell to the Qin. Only one aspect of life held constant: fighting. The rulers of different regions fought to expand the areas under their control, either seizing territory from their political rivals or encroaching further on the border peoples. The war machines they built demanded enormous resources from the citizens of each state. Because subsistence agriculture practiced on large quasi-independent estates did not produce sufficient surplus, rulers began to tax individual households. Improve-

ments in tools and irrigation allowed some households to develop occupational specialties while others continued to farm to meet their tax obligations. Money circulated in ever-increasing quantities, as trade networks
developed and cities grew. Obsessed as they were with the costs of constant war, contemporary observers were blind to the many advantages
the fighting brought them. War forced rulers to extract more from their
people, prompting a host of economic changes and feeding a long-lasting economic boom.

The social changes of the time may have been the most far-reaching.
At the beginning of the period, people, even those like the plotting Lady
Li, could be confident that a king's sons would succeed him, but their
certainty was misplaced. Regional rulers displaced the Zhou kings, ministers displaced regional rulers, and later on, even the ministerial lineages
fell from power. On the battlefield, well-born chariot warriors were replaced by men who rose up in the infantry and the cavalry. Such dramatic social change prompted anxiety among those who had to live
through it, much as it produced genuine opportunity for talented men
(but not women) of low birth to rise. Families with means sought to guarantee their sons' social place by sending them to study with the increasing numbers of private tutors.

Guan Zhong, Sunzi, Confucius, Mozi, Zhuangzi, Mencius, Xunzi—
the list of thinkers during these centuries testifies to the stimulation of
their times. No period in later history would produce such diverse cur-
rents of profound thought. Almost all possible positions found a propo-
nent, each one as articulate as the next. Where Mozi used logic, Zhuangzi
used humor and analogy. Where Confucius engaged in dialogue with his
students, the multiple voices of *The Way and Integrity Classic* spoke in
cryptic poems. Different as these thinkers' positions were about service
to the state, or man's original nature, or the existence of the spirits, or the
virtues of music, they concurred on one point. They lived in a terrible
time, one far different from the ideal age of the sage kings, a time to
which they all hoped to return.

The Legalist teachings practiced in the Qin state that Xunzi found so
repellent marked a real departure from all the positions this chapter has
followed. Disdaining the time of the sage kings, the Legalists proposed
a radically new way of organizing the state and its subjects—a way that
allowed its adherents to unite the realm for the first time, in 221 B.C., as
we see in the next chapter.

The Spring and Autumn period and the succeeding Warring States
period established a negative example to which no one wished to return.

The thinkers and their descendants failed to realize that the terrible age that spawned them was in fact one of the most intellectually lively, economically vibrant, and socially diverse times—even if it was politically chaotic and incessantly violent. The possibility that disunity, even with its high price, could be good for the realm seems never to have occurred to them; and they subsequently devoted their every effort to preventing the return of such a chaotic, but vital, age.

CHRONOLOGY

359 B.C.	*Shang Yang initiates Qin reforms*
221–207 B.C.	QIN DYNASTY
221–210 B.C.	*Reign of Qin Shi Huangdi*
217 B.C.	*Death of Mr. Xi, buried at Shuihudi*
207 B.C.–A.D. 220	HAN DYNASTY
207 B.C.–A.D. 9	FORMER (WESTERN) HAN
206–195 B.C.	*Reign of Liu Bang (Emperor Han Gaozu)*
200–100 B.C.	*Invention of paper*
after 168 B.C.	*Death of Lady Dai, buried at Mawangdui*
145–ca. 90 B.C.	*Lifetime of Sima Qian, author of* Records of the Grand Historian
140–87 B.C.	*Reign of Emperor Wu*
124 B.C.	*Founding of Confucian academy*
81 B.C.	The Salt and Iron Debates *composed*
A.D. 9–23	WANG MANG INTERREGNUM, THE XIN ("NEW") DYNASTY
A.D. 25–220	EASTERN (LATER) HAN
A.D. 27–97	*Lifetime of Wang Chong, author of* Balanced Discussions
A.D. 45–ca. 120	*Lifetime of Ban Zhao, female author of* Lessons for Women
A.D. 142	*Founding of Celestial Masters Daoist Sect*
A.D. 184	*Yellow Turban Daoist uprising*
A.D. 192–220	*Regency of Cao Cao*

C H A P T E R   3

THE CREATION OF EMPIRE

(221 B.C.–A.D. 200)

In 221 B.C., the Warring States period came to a sudden end when the
kingdom of Qin defeated all its competitor kingdoms and unified the
empire—roughly two-thirds of the area of modern China—for the first
time. The Qin ruler then crowned himself China's first emperor. Indeed,
the English word for China (which came via Latin and Sanskrit) derives
from the name of the uniting dynasty, the Qin. The Qin were able to
conquer their rivals not because of any new technologies but because they
found a new way to organize their state. To draw a modern analogy, one
could say that the armies of the regional kingdoms all fought with the
same hardware—crossbows, bronze weapons, and armor—but that the
Qin had the advantage of new software—namely a bureaucracy organized on the basis of merit. The Qin founder followed the teachings of
Legalist ministers who advocated the abolition of all privileges of the
nobility.

In twentieth-century America, the word *bureaucracy* carries largely
negative connotations of inefficiency. In third-century B.C. China, however, bureaucracy provided a new form of government far more efficient
than the aristocratic rule of the Warring States period. The Qin ruler
used this new type of government to build a powerful fighting machine.
The state created by the Qin survived for a mere fourteen years, but its
immediate successor, the Han dynasty, ruled China for the next four hundred years. Although the Han founders denounced the rule of the Qin
as brutal, the Han dynasty took over many Qin-dynasty organizational
techniques. One of the greatest challenges for the modern analyst is to
assess the accomplishments of the Qin dynasty without being blinded by
overly critical Han-dynasty sources.

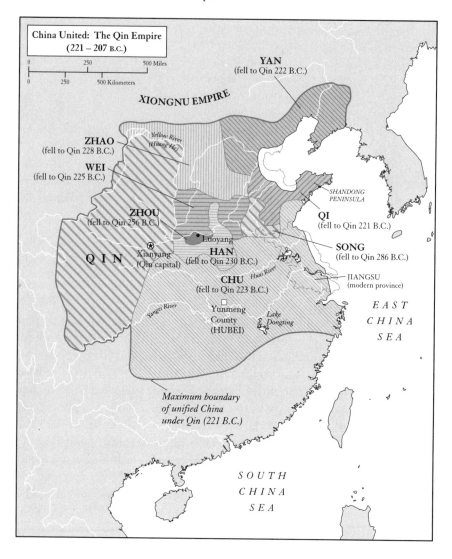

China United: The Qin Empire
(221 – 207 B.C.)

0   250   500 Miles

0   250   500 Kilometers

XIONGNU EMPIRE

YAN
(fell to Qin 222 B.C.)

Yellow River
(Huang He)

ZHAO
(fell to Qin 228 B.C.)

WEI
(fell to Qin 225 B.C.)

SHANDONG
PENINSULA

ZHOU
(fell to Qin 256 B.C.)

QI
(fell to Qin 221 B.C.)

Luoyang

QIN

Xianyang
(Qin capital)

HAN
(fell to Qin 230 B.C.)

SONG
(fell to Qin 286 B.C.)

JIANGSU
(modern province)

CHU
(fell to Qin 223 B.C.)

Huai River

Yangzi River

Yunmeng
County
(HUBEI)

Lake
Dongting

EAST
CHINA
SEA

Maximum boundary
of unified China
under Qin (221 B.C.)

SOUTH
CHINA
SEA

Before the unification of China, thinkers had struggled to understand
human nature and to define the best type of government. After 221 B.C.,
they addressed a fundamentally different set of questions—the same set
that would challenge scholars and rulers for the next two thousand years.
What role should the state play in the economy? How should the government recruit talented officials? What should scholars opposed to certain policies do? Unlike later generations who asked these questions,
though, the people of the Qin and the Han had the unique sense of being the first people to face such problems.

With the founding of the empire, Chinese society assumed the contours it would retain for the next two thousand years. During the Warring States period, social commentators envisioned a society of two classes: the privileged aristocracy and the laboring masses. But after 221 B.C., observers ranked society into four groups: scholars, peasants, artisans, and merchants. (A convenient way to remember this ranking is by the first letter of each group: SPAM). This ranking reflected Legalist prejudices in favor of producers, namely peasants and artisans, over merchants, whom they felt manufactured nothing and so contributed little of value to the economy. Of course, merchants had much more money and much more freedom than did peasants, and most cultivators would have gladly switched places with any merchant.

This breakdown diverged from social reality by omitting some social groups, such as slaves, doctors, and religious specialists, but even so, it shaped many people's thinking. This classification also overlooked women, probably because everyone assumed women could be classed with their husbands. Still, the four hundred years of Han rule produced several notable women; some were empresses, but one woman made a name for herself as a historian.

Under the influence of the different historians of the Han dynasty, the conception of the dynastic cycle gradually took shape. Indeed the Han dynasty fit the model perfectly. Founded by a strong leader, who was succeeded by a strong woman, the dynasty enjoyed two hundred years of competent leadership. Then in A.D. 9, an interloper named Wang Mang, who was from the clan of the empress, tired of being regent. He seized power and founded a dynasty, which he called Xin, meaning "new." Within fifteen years, other members of the Han family had regained power, but at the cost of weakening the dynasty. Destruction of their great capital at Changan forced them to move 320 kilometers (200 miles) east to Luoyang, in Henan province, where the dynasty lasted another two hundred years. But the shift to Luoyang marked the beginning of decline and the erosion of the tax base. Empresses managed to wrest control from a series of weak emperors, and eunuchs came increasingly to the fore—so much so that students studying the Confucian classics organized protests against them. A series of peasant protests, many proclaiming the teachings of the newly founded Daoist church, rocked the empire in A.D. 184, a disaster from which the dynasty never recovered.

Still, the founders of the Han had much of which to be proud. They, in combination with the Qin, had developed a formula that allowed them to rule for four hundred years and to create a sophisticated civilization, with extensive cities and lengthy trade routes, that could rival and even surpass the great empires of their day, whether the Roman or Kushan in north India.

THE LEGALIST STATE

The philosophers of the Warring States, most notably Xunzi, had remarked on the unusual strength and Legalist policies of the state of Qin at the turn of the third century B.C. In an age that prized eloquence, the Legalist thinker Han Fei (280–233 B.C.) stuttered, so he wrote directly to his ruler about his philosophy of government. In doing so, he became the first thinker to record his own ideas—unlike earlier thinkers whose students compiled their teachings after their deaths, often in a question-and-answer format. Han Fei envisioned the role of the ruler in much the same terms as *The Way and Integrity Classic*. The ruler was to remain detached from the everyday business of government; if he applied an unbending standard to judge his officials and his people, his kingdom would become stronger than its rivals.

Although the Chinese term for Legalist, *fajia*, literally means "law experts," Legalist thinkers did not advocate rule of law in the modern Western sense. They did not believe in a law that could be used to challenge their rule. Instead, they believed in a law that treated all men equally. Only the systematic application of the law, Legalists felt, could control people, whose essential nature was evil.

The Architect of Qin Success: Shang Yang's Reforms

In 359 B.C., a powerful prime minister named Shang Yang initiated a series of reforms to build a strong Legalist state. These are described in a book bearing the name, *The Book of Lord Shang*, which was written after his death. Since the seventh century B.C., the Qin kingdom had occupied the former homeland the Zhou dynasty abandoned when it moved to Luoyang, but it did not rise up above its rivals until Shang Yang's term in office. His policies strengthened the fiscal basis of the Qin state, enabling it to finance a fighting force far stronger than that of any other contemporary state.

Legalist teachings differed from all other Warring States–period philosophies in their disdain for the past, voiced in this passage from *The Book of Lord Shang*:

> Former generations did not follow the same doctrines, so what antiquity should one imitate? The emperors and kings did not copy one another, so

what rites should one follow? . . . As rites and laws were fixed in accordance with what was opportune, regulations and orders were all expedient, and weapons, armor, implements, and equipment were all practical.[1]

This skepticism about the past allowed Legalists to reject all that the Confucians valued, especially ritual, which Legalists viewed as a series of expensive and pointless ceremonies.

Sima Qian's *Records of the Grand Historian* gives a detailed description of the measures Shang Yang took to reorganize the Qin state:[2] "He commanded that the people be divided into tens and fives." The registration of individual households marked the culmination of a trend taking place in other kingdoms of the Warring States period. By abolishing all intermediaries between cultivators and the state, the Legalists extended the earlier attempts of Warring States–period rulers to establish a direct link between subject and ruler.

As part of this reform, Minister Shang established population registers to record who lived together in different households.

> He commanded that . . . they supervise each other and be mutually liable. Anyone who failed to report criminal activity would be chopped in two at the waist, while those who reported it would receive the same reward as that for obtaining the head of an enemy.

The registers listed the members of groups of five and ten who bore mutual responsibility should anyone in their group commit a crime. Once a man reached sixteen or seventeen years of age and a height of 1.5 meters (5 feet), he was obliged to perform military service, fulfill his labor obligations, and pay taxes on his land. Because the Legalists drew no distinction between the army and society, they expected all men to serve in the army.

Minister Shang is credited with establishing private ownership of land. In fact, land continued to be viewed as the property of the ruler, but the link between land ownership and military service provided people with a stronger claim to the land than when they had worked on estates in earlier ages. The institution of the population registers marked a sharp break with the past, with officials keeping detailed records of their subjects for the first time. These registers shaped popular consciousness as well, because many people thought the gods kept a set of parallel registers on which they recorded each person's allotted life span.

"Any family that had more than two adult males who did not divide the household would pay a double military tax," continued Historian Sima Qian. This clause documents the deep antipathy of the Legalists toward cherished Confucian beliefs. Where Confucians advocated that sons live together in harmony with their parents, Legalists required that an extended family break apart into separate households, a trend that may have been occurring anyway.

"Those who had achievements in the army would receive an increase in rank in proportion to their accomplishments." This simple statement represented a startling departure from past practice. The entire population of the Qin state was divided into twenty different ranks, each with its own perquisites in the form of permitted clothing, land, slaves, or housing. All hereditary titles—even those of the royal family—were dropped in favor of this new ranking based strictly on performance. The Legalists did not subscribe to the Confucian belief that only gentlemen should serve as officials or even that one should reward virtue. They felt instead that strict standards of personal achievement should replace subjective judgment and hereditary privilege. In the army, for example, soldiers gained promotions strictly on the basis of how many severed heads they submitted. Those who submitted more heads rose faster than those who submitted fewer heads. "Those who devoted themselves to the fundamental enterprises and through their farming and weaving contributed much grain and cloth would be freed from tax and corvee." Here, the historian Sima Qian summarizes the economic thinking of the Legalists. Because all farmers also served as soldiers, the agricultural sector provided the lifeblood of the state. The farmer-soldiers of the Qin staffed the Qin armies, completed all the public works, and produced the food for everyone in the state. Anyone who did not produce food must, then, play a less important role in society. This rigid blueprint of the economy minimized the importance of merchants and scholars.

"He collected the small district towns together into large counties and established officials for them." Minister Shang Yang divided society into a series of interlocking units, the smallest of which was the groups of five or ten households. These units formed larger units of counties (*xian*), which provided the population with the services of local government. County officials organized the army, carried out public works, collected taxes, and administered justice. The Qin state reached up from the county to the center, and it reached down to the very lowest unit of land, an individual's fields.

"For the fields he opened up the footpaths and set up boundaries." Although the meaning of "opened up" is not clear, it is likely that the Qin eliminated the grid paths through agricultural land. Later historians thought these reforms made the sale of land possible. "He equalized the military levies and land tax and standardized the measures of capacity, weight, and length," continues Sima. The standardizing impulse extended to different measures of weight and length, which varied from place to place.

The Qin first implemented these measures within their own borders, but in 316 B.C., the Qin state began a series of conquests that accelerated under the leadership of young King Zheng (259–210 B.C.) who came to the throne in 246 B.C. at the age of thirteen. In 237 B.C., when the king turned twenty-two, he took power into his own hands and led his kingdom through fifteen years of all-out war that culminated in the unification of China in 221 B.C.

China's First Emperor

On taking power, King Zheng decided that he needed a new title: "I have raised troops to punish the rebellious princes and thanks to the sacred power of our ancestors, all six kings have been chastised as they deserve, so at last the Empire is pacified. Now unless we create a new title, how can we record our merit for posterity?"[3] As part of his effort to unify China, the Qin ruler required that the six defeated kings move to his capital accompanied by the noble families of their kingdoms. The title he took, *Shi Huangdi,* literally meant First August Emperor. *Di* ("emperor," "highest deity") contrasted with the word *wang* ("king") that earlier regional rulers, including the founders of the Zhou, had used to refer to themselves.

Once he had assumed his new title, the Qin emperor implemented various policies to shore up his power. He toured his empire five times between 220 and 210 B.C., in an effort to show himself to his people and to make offerings to the spirits. In line with Shang Yang's teachings, the First August Emperor emphasized farming as the mainstay of the economy. He unified all measures and imposed a standard currency on the empire. A circular coin with a square in the middle replaced the different monies of the Warring States period, which had taken the shape of knives, shovels, or shells. This new currency had the advantage that it could be threaded together to form strings, which became the major unit of accounting in subsequent periods. In addition to implementing a unified system of units for length and volume, the new dynasty also specified a national standard gauge for vehicles so that roads could be a uniform width and carts could travel freely throughout the empire.

After unifying the empire, the Qin divided all the territory under its control into regional units called commanderies (the initial thirty-six were increased to forty-two), and the commanderies were further subdivided into counties. The administrative structure of the commanderies replicated that of the central government. Governmental functions were divided into three: civil matters having to do with taxation and the registration of the population, military affairs, and the supervision of governmental officials. The top officials in the central government were the chancellor, who headed the bureaucracy; the imperial secretary, who drafted the emperor's orders; and the grand commandant, who was in charge of the military. Similarly, each commandery had three main officials; first, the administrator who collected taxes, updated population registers, and heard legal disputes; next, an oversight official who ensured that the administrator followed all imperial regulations and laws; finally, a commandant who recruited and trained the militia. The law of avoidance, which held that no official could serve in his home area, was already in effect at the time, but clerks were recruited locally.

Perhaps the most striking standardization was that of the script. Scribes in earlier centuries had used Large Seal script to write, and many regional variants of the same character had come into use in the years of the coexisting Warring States. The Qin reformers introduced a new, simpler script called Small Seal script, and they discouraged the use of different variants for the same character. (The Small Seal script they used was largely abandoned in the succeeding dynasty, when it was replaced by the characters in use today.) Because the Qin forbade any writing in regional or popular variants, the rulers ensured that linguistic unity would continue even when the empire was no longer unified. Chinese characters continued to be used without significant change until the introduction of simplified characters after 1949.

The Qin dynasty also organized the population in massive public works projects. In the twelve years before the Qin emperor's death in 210 B.C., laborers built a network of roads over 6,800 kilometers (4,000 miles) long which rivaled the road system of the Romans, estimated by Gibbon at 6,000 kilometers (3,740 miles).[4] These men dug irrigation canals, and some 300,000 men built extensive walls of pounded earth along the northern border of China by stringing together existing walls. The Great Wall one sees today was built in the fifteenth, sixteenth, and seventeenth centuries, not during the third century B.C., but the Qin did establish a precedent for massive wall building. They also sent large numbers of troops to distant areas—to the Ordos region of modern Mongolia and to Vietnam—in what turned out to be unsuccessful and unpopular campaigns. One of the largest public works projects was constructing the tomb of the first emperor.

Building a Final Resting Place for the Qin Emperor

Fearful of death, the Qin emperor expended great efforts, especially at the end of his life, to obtain an elixir that would allow him to join the ranks of the immortals in heaven. He also devoted enormous energy to the construction of his tomb. Later sources give the improbably high figure of 700,000 for the number of men who worked on his tomb, which was intended to replicate the universe since it would serve as his permanent resting home. The historian Sima Qian provides a fascinating description of the tomb as it looked when it was first built:

> From the time the First Emperor took the throne, work was begun on his mausoleum at Lishan [24 kilometers or 15 miles northeast of Changan]. After he had won the empire, more than 700,000 conscripts from all parts of the country labored there. The laborers dug through three subterranean streams which they sealed off with bronze in order to make the burial chamber. This they filled with models of palaces, towers, and the hundred officials, as well as precious utensils, and marvelous rarities. Artisans were ordered to install mechanically triggered crossbows set to shoot any intruder. With mercury the various waterways of the empire, the Yangzi and Yellow Rivers, and even the great ocean itself were created and made to flow and circulate mechanically. The heavenly constellations were depicted above and the geography of the earth was laid out below. Lamps were fueled with whale oil so that they might burn forever without being extinguished. . . . Finally, trees and grass were planted on the mound to make it look like a mountain.[5]

For fear that any of the workers might disclose its exact location under the large hill, all artisans and laborers who had worked on the project were imprisoned inside the tomb while still alive. When the emperor died in 210 B.C., his second son, whom the sources describe as seriously unbalanced, succeeded him. He ordered that his father's concubines be buried with him in his tomb, the site of the world-famous terra-cotta warriors.

The Terra-Cotta Army

In the 1970s, a group of peasants were digging a well near Xian when they uncovered the first group of terra-cotta warriors and some bronze weapons. Subsequent excavations in three different pits have produced some 7,300 figures spread out over an area of 2 hectares (5 acres). These figures make up the model army of the Qin founder, who led a force including infantry, cavalry, and chariots. As stunning as this find is, it does not include the main chamber of the emperor's tomb, which has yet to

Thousands of these lifelike sculptures were buried in the tomb, east of the modern-day city of Xian, of the first emperor, who unified the empire in 221 B.C. These life-size statues replaced the sacrificial human victims of earlier times. The terra-cotta army buried in the first Qin emperor's tomb gives a startlingly lifelike impression of an army on the move. It includes foot soldiers, archers, charioteers, and cavalry. Although the bodies were mass-produced with identical legs and torsos, the faces differ, possibly because each soldier sat to have his portrait done in clay. Originally painted a wide range of hues, the statues are now all the same terra-cotta hue.

be excavated. Sometimes called the eighth wonder of the world, the life-like soldiers of the terra-cotta army seem frozen in their precise formations.

(Left) This archer kneels, ready to stand and begin shooting his arrows, which no longer survive. Like his contemporaries, he refrained from cutting his hair; he viewed it as a gift from his parents and he thought his filial duty was to preserve it. Because of the exigencies of battle, he used an elaborate system of tight braids (right) to bind his hair.

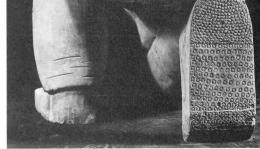

This close-up of the underside of the archer's foot reveals a raised surface designed to provide greater traction.

Although designed to be viewed in large groups, the statues contain surprising details. Their hair is bound with elaborate ties so that it would not interfere in battle, and the soles of their shoes had raised bumps for increased traction. The facial features of each figure differ, leading some to suggest that individual soldiers sat for their portraits. But the absence of any facial scars or torn clothes means that each figure, though different, is idealized. Their bodies were mass produced. The soldiers stand on trunk legs, which have been separately fired from their torsos, as have their heads and hands. Traces of pigment reveal that all the soldiers were originally painted a variety of bright colors before being placed in the tomb. Ranging in height from 1.75 to 1.86 meters (5 feet 8 inches to 6 feet 1 inch, slightly taller than the real population), the soldiers wear seven different kinds of uniforms, depending on their unit. Infantry stand separate from charioteers, while each soldier is equipped with actual bronze weapons. The consistent dimensions of the bronze arrows and crossbow triggers indicate that they too were mass produced. Once completed, the statues were placed on brick floors. Dirt walls, covered with a wooden roof, stood over them. After they had been covered with dirt and mats, no one could detect their formations, which remained the emperor's secret—to be used only in battles he might have to fight in the underworld.

When the Qin founder died in 210 B.C., he named his more popular first son to succeed him, but a powerful eunuch named Zhao Gao (?–207 B.C.) succeeded in placing the second son on the throne and forging a letter ordering the first son to commit suicide.

The founder of the Qin was the first Chinese emperor to name a eunuch to an important advisory post, but we know that the Zhou-dynasty rulers—and possibly even the Shang kings—had entrusted the care of their wives and concubines to castrated men, who enjoyed unequaled access to the ruler and to the women's quarters. Court officials looked down on the eunuchs, whose smooth faces, flaccid bodies, and high voices made them conspicuous.

In 208 B.C. the same eunuch, Zhao Gao, ordered the great Legalist chancellor Li Si put to death. The eunuch then took over as chancellor. The following year, as a series of rebellions ranged throughout the empire, the eunuch forced the second Qin emperor to commit suicide. A third emperor, a young boy, assumed the throne, arranged for the murder of the eunuch, and surrendered to the rebel forces in 207 B.C. only forty-six days after taking power.

According to the historians of the Han dynasty, the greatest opposition to Qin rule came from those at the bottom of society who were forced to do military or labor service. The official history of the Han dynasty tells the story of how a group of laborers, delayed by rain, decided to revolt. "Now if we flee, we shall die," they said. "If we undertake a great plan, we shall die. It's death either way. But we could risk death for a kingdom."[6] Because absconding from labor service brought death, as did rebellion, they reasoned that they might as well rise up against the harsh rule of the Qin.

The Han scholar Jia Yi (201–169 B.C.), who was born after the end of the Qin dynasty, rendered the following famous verdict on the years of Qin rule:

> Qin, with its originally tiny territory and a force of only one thousand chariots, nevertheless summoned to itself the eight regions of the world and made its peers pay court to it for more than a century. Later, after it had converted everything within the six directions into its home and made the Xiao and Han passes into its strongholds, a single fellow created trouble, whereupon its seven ancestral temples straightway toppled, its ruler died at the hands of men, and it became the laughing stock of the world.
>
> Why? Because it failed to display humanity (ren) and righteousness (yi) or to realize there is a difference between the power to attack and the power to consolidate.[7]

Jia Yi's analysis seems to have much to recommend it. Opposition to the Qin sprang from all quarters. The nobles and rulers of the defeated six kingdoms numbered some one hundred twenty thousand people whose aristocratic ranks were removed and who were forced to move to the Qin capital, where the emperor could keep close watch over them.

Reasons for Doubting the Historical Record

We must be cautious, though, in using later sources to study the Qin. In one of the most infamous incidents recorded by later historians, the Qin emperor launched a large-scale book burning in 213 B.C. that sought to destroy all dissenting points of view. The famous Confucian classics, including *The Book of Songs* and *The Book of Documents*, were banned, as were the historical annals of earlier kings. Only books on agriculture and divination were permitted.[8] Still, we must remember that book-making technology remained in its early stages. Because most classical learning, and certainly *The Book of Songs*, continued to be orally transmitted from teacher to student, a book burning would not have had much effect. Later sources also allege that, one year later, the emperor sentenced to death four hundred sixty scholars who opposed his rule. Some sources say the men were buried up to their necks and then trampled by horses, but the phrasing strongly suggests a later interpolation added after the Qin had fallen.

Jia Yi's Confucian viewpoint, with its emphasis on humanity and righteousness, provided the Han dynasty with the perfect justification for the overthrow of the Qin. As a piece of historical writing dictated by political considerations, the story of the rebelling laborers further contributed to the myth. In the Grand Historian Sima Qian's account of the Zhou conquest of the Shang (described in chapter 1), the last Shang king, surrounded by beautiful women and luxuries, could do no right, while the first Zhou king could do no wrong. The same kind of stereotyping shaped later accounts of how the Han dynasty leaders overthrew the Qin.

A tomb excavated in 1975 provides a surprising corrective to received wisdom about Qin brutality. The legal materials from the Shuihudi tomb reveal that men called up for service who failed to report or who absconded were liable to be beaten, not killed, as the Han historians falsely maintained in their account of the dynasty's founding.[9] The officials in charge of a group of laborers could be fined one shield if the laborers were six to ten days late; a suit of armor if over ten days late. We must conclude that the Han-dynasty historians overstated these punishments to discredit the previous and fallen Qin dynasty.

A New Slant on Qin-Dynasty Rule: The Finds at Shuihudi

Located in Yunmeng county, Hubei province, the Shuihudi tomb held a Qin-dynasty official who died at the age of forty-five in 217 B.C., five years after the unification of the empire. The stagnant water in which the tomb was submerged preserved the contents of the official's tomb in much the same way as standing water in German and Danish peat bogs kept Iron Age corpses in excellent condition. Beginning as a scribe, Mr. Xi worked his way up the bureaucracy to the rank of prefectural clerk, eventually gaining the right to hear criminal suits. Although the Shuihudi tomb lacks anything as dramatic as the terra-cotta warriors, it contained 1,155 bamboo documents, including both legal writings and divination manuals Mr. Xi must have intended to use in the netherworld. The presence of these texts suggests that he fully expected to hold the same kind of clerical position in the underworld bureaucracy as he had held in the Qin-dynasty bureaucracy during his lifetime.

Before the invention of paper in the second century B.C., people used bamboo or wood as writing materials. They cut slips of the same size—approximately three popsicle sticks long—in which they punched holes at regular intervals. They then strung the slips together so that they formed something like a modern placemat. Wood or bamboo texts took up much more space than paper or silk rolls; one estimate put the records of the Han dynasty at two thousand wagon loads in A.D. 25.[10] The scholars who have reconstructed the texts at Shuihudi first arrayed the bamboo slips into groups depending on their length and then reconstructed the order on the basis of their content. To make their task even more complicated, the scribes who wrote the texts at Shuihudi treated each group of bamboo slips like a piece of paper. They wrote on the back and front of each slip, and they divided their text into separate blocks spanning ten or more slips, so that an individual slip could contain discontinuous phrases from two or three separate paragraphs.

The Shuihudi cache illuminates daily life at the lowest level in China. One of the bamboo texts specified how to choose which days were lucky for certain activities and which were not. Some of the activities, like apprehending criminals or sentencing wrongdoers, directly impinged on the work of local officials, while others, like choosing a good day to build a wall or to wed, affected everyone. Many of the entries in this book warn against marrying on an inauspicious day and risking getting the wrong type of wife: a wife with a long tongue (who talks too much), a stingy wife, a sickly wife, an ugly wife, or perhaps worst of all, an infertile wife. One possibility mentioned by the daybook is divorce, but always divorce instigated by the husband, never by the wife.

As an official needed to consult a daybook, he also needed to check legal reference books. Mr. Xi took several such books with him, including selections from the Qin code relevant to his administrative duties and a book in question-and-answer format explaining terms and phrases to be used by judges. The collected statutes pertained directly to Mr. Xi's tasks, which included overseeing government granaries and labor service, performed both by free men and by criminals. The answers in the judge's handbook also occasionally cite the Qin statutes. Because these are the only sections of the Qin code to survive today, they allow us to judge whether Qin law was as brutal as later historians suggested.

Contrary to the writings of the Han historians, and contrary to the expectations of modern scholars, the provisions from the Qin code stress close adherence to a rigorously delineated series of judicial procedures. Since the Legalist code specified particular punishments for particular crimes, the handbook included model cases elucidated by question and answer. These examples instructed officials how to determine whether a person killing someone in a fight had done so accidentally, which would bring a charge of manslaughter, or deliberately, which constituted murder. The law distinguished between weapons that one might pick up in the heat of the fray, like an awl, and those that one had to unsheathe, like a knife. Another example described a fight between two women, one of whom subsequently miscarried. The judge was charged with determining the age of the fetus and whether the fight had caused its death. Parents could kill a deformed baby at the time of the birth, explained the manual, but not a healthy baby simply because they had too many children. This manual also held that spontaneous confessions had greater value than those coerced by beatings or torture.

The Shuihudi materials also described a system of punishments that strike modern readers as grisly, although they were no more so than the crucifixions done in the contemporaneous Roman empire. Decapitation, which was thought to divide a person's head from the body even in the afterlife, constituted the most severe punishment. Those who committed lesser offenses were sentenced to hard labor: men were required to build walls and women were forced to pound grain. The records refer to some of those sentenced to hard labor as "complete" or "intact," meaning they had not been mutilated. The less fortunate had one foot cut off or the nose severed. Because any damage to the body (a gift from one's parents) caused great shame, tattooing, head shaving, and beard shaving were all prescribed for lesser offenses. Actual sentencing occasionally diverged from Legalist teachings that all stood equal before the law. The Shuihudi materials show that because privileged people could pay fines and avoid these grim punishments, they received less onerous punishments than commoners or slaves.

As instructive as they are, the Shuihudi materials remain prescriptive rather than descriptive. They explain how the legal system was supposed to function, not how it actually functioned. Even so, the Shuihudi materials depict a legal system that stressed careful procedures usually marked by unvarying punishments for specific crimes—they show, in short, a legal system far different from that suggested by Han-dynasty denunciations of the unjust rule of the Qin.

The Founding of the Han Dynasty

The absence of peasant uprisings during his reign suggests that the Qin emperor must have enjoyed a measure of popularity with his subjects. As soon as he died and his unpopular second son succeeded him, many of the former regional states broke away once again. The rebels may initially have hoped to restore the emperor's first son to power while leaving the Qin dynasty in place. As the situation at court deteriorated, the rebels, who included both bona fide peasants and low-ranking officials, began to denounce the cruelty of the Qin and to call for the founding of a new dynasty. The rebel who would defeat all his rivals to become the founder of the Han, Liu Bang (reigned 206–195 B.C.) was one of only two

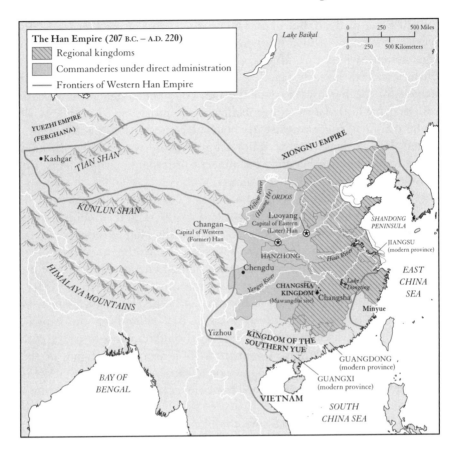

The Han Empire (207 B.C. – A.D. 220)
Regional kingdoms
Commanderies under direct administration
Frontiers of Western Han Empire

emperors born into a commoner family. (The other founded the Ming
dynasty). The Grand Historian Sima Qian describes him as a man whose
oafish ways antagonized everyone he met, but also as a man whom local
innkeepers allowed to drink for free since their receipts unaccountably
went up whenever he was around. During the years of the Qin, he passed
an examination and won a low-level appointment as a neighborhood head
who supervised one thousand households.

As he sought to increase his popular support, Liu Bang attacked the
Qin for its brutal laws. When his forces won the decisive battle and entered the Qin capital, he proclaimed an agreement with the assembled
leaders of the community:

> You elders have long suffered under the harsh laws of Qin. . . . I make an
> agreement with you that the law shall consist of only three sections: He who
> kills others shall die; he who harms others or steals from them shall incur ap-
> propriate punishment. For the rest, all other Qin laws should be abolished.[11]

So Liu Bang pledged, but in fact he retained most of the Qin laws. His service as a neighborhood head gave him some experience with the Qin legal system, whose careful procedures must have impressed him. Sima Qian described the early Han legal reforms saying, "When Han arose it lopped off the harsh corners of the Qin code and retreated to an easy roundness, whittled away the embellishments and achieved simplicity."[12] As his comment suggests, the early Han rulers modified rather than eliminated the Qin legal system. They allowed those who had been found guilty to pay fines rather than be subject to stipulated punishments, the most gruesome of which they canceled.

One major departure from Qin policies concerned the treatment of the nobility. Where the Qin emperor had required all the nobility of the vanquished kingdoms to reside in his capital, the Han founder created a new nobility. He gave nine of his brothers and sons the title of king and the lands necessary to sustain them, and named one hundred fifty of his most important followers to the rank of marquis. Two-thirds of his territory remained in the hands of his sons and other relatives. Only one-third of his empire, the crucial western half containing the capital, remained under direct administration. We should remember that the core of the Han-dynasty empire lay in the region around Changan, or the modern city of Xian in the province of Shaanxi, while the coastal areas and much of south China remained backwaters largely populated by non-Chinese peoples.

As with their Qin predecessors, the Han-dynasty government at both the central and local levels had three major divisions: one branch supervised the collection of taxes, one the army, and the third, government officials. The central authorities presided over some one hundred commanderies, which were in turn divided into fifteen hundred counties. Local authorities were in charge of registering the population, collecting taxes, maintaining waterways, and dispensing justice. Local officials also recommended literate men of good character for government positions.

After Liu Bang had defeated his rivals and assumed the title of emperor, he asked prominent Confucians to design new rituals for his court. He hoped to create an aura around himself that would discourage his former drinking companions from being too familiar. Although occasionally willing to take the advice of ritual specialists, the future emperor did not slavishly follow all of Confucius's teachings. At one point in the struggle to gain power, his main rival Xiang Yu (233–202 B.C.) captured Liu Bang's father and threatened to boil him alive unless the son surrendered. Liu Bang replied that because he and Xiang Yu had taken an oath of brotherhood, his father was also Xiang Yu's father. As he put it,

"My father is your father too. If you insist on boiling your own father, I hope you will be kind enough to send me a cup of the soup." Shockingly to Confucians, he did not allow familial ties, even the all-important bond between parent and child, to interfere with his ambition to rule the empire. (Xiang Yu subsequently adhered to the terms of his oath and freed the father.)

The first years of the Han were difficult ones as the Han emperor attempted to suppress rebellions within China—usually by members of the nobility—and to quell a powerful enemy to the north, the Xiongnu people. The Xiongnu may have been the eastern branch of the Hun tribes who invaded Rome centuries later. The Xiongnu had warred with the Qin, but the Chinese armies succeeded in pushing them back into the Ordos region of modern Inner Mongolia. But after a new ruler in 209 B.C. succeeded to the position of *shanyu*, as the Xiongnu called their leader, the Xiongnu successfully attacked the Han, enticing the first Han emperor to lead his army north in 201 B.C. The Xiongnu trapped the emperor and his forces in a walled city for seven days. In 198 B.C., the hostilities ended when the Chinese signed a peace treaty with several humiliating clauses. The Chinese agreed to present gifts of textiles, foodstuffs, and wine to the Xiongnu, who were designated a brother, or peer, state of the Han. They also promised to send a Chinese princess to marry the Xiongnu leader. In exchange, the Xiongnu promised only that they would not invade China.

The Reign of Empress Lü

In 195 B.C., the dying Liu Bang named his docile fifteen-year-old son Huidi (reigned 195–188 B.C.) to succeed him, confident that Huidi's mother, the Empress Lü (reigned 188–180 B.C.) would guide the empire with the help of the chancellor. The Grand Historian Sima Qian recounts how she became engaged to Liu Bang, a man so poor he could not afford the fee required to sit at the more expensive tables at a banquet. The father of the future empress told people's fortunes on the basis of their facial features, and Liu Bang's face was so unusual, Sima Qian reports, that the fortune-teller decided to give his daughter to Liu Bang in marriage. Liu Bang went on to fulfill his father-in-law's predictions by founding the Han dynasty, and his wife, Empress Lü, matured into a powerful woman.

Although some of her husband's associates did not trust her, the emperor's advisors agreed that her son should succeed to the throne, partially because they thought she would help the new emperor to rule. When Huidi died in 188 B.C., Empress Lü placed an infant on the throne;

and when he died, she replaced him with another, so she was able to rule as ostensible regent until her death in 180 B.C. Historians hold her responsible for the deaths of four princes with stronger claims who could have succeeded to the throne.

As a woman ruler, Empress Lü was subject to unusual pressures, like those from the Xiongnu, whose ruler wrote her an unusually frank letter in which he said:

> I am a lonely widowed ruler, born amidst the marshes and brought up on the wild steppes in the land of cattle and horses. I have often come to the border wishing to travel in China. Your majesty is also a widowed ruler living a life of solitude. The both of us are without pleasures and lack any way to amuse ourselves. It is my hope that we can exchange that which we have for that which we are lacking.

The empress's reply strongly indicates her disapproval of his proposal:

> My age is advanced and my vitality weakening. Both my hair and teeth are falling out, and I cannot even walk steadily. The *shanyu* ruler must have heard exaggerated reports. I am not worthy of his lowering himself. But my country has done nothing wrong, and I hope that he will spare it.[13]

Deeply offended, the empress realized China did not have the power to launch an attack, and the peace, with its onerous terms for the Chinese, resumed.

Although Empress Lü named many of her relatives to office and killed her rivals, including her husband's child by another wife, she continued to rule in the name of the Han dynasty. The years of her reign brought much needed stability to the Han. Empress Lü found it convenient to keep up the facade of the Han dynasty even as she—and not the Han founder's heirs—exercised power. After her death in 180 B.C., two elderly powerful court officials, who had served the founder of the Han, succeeded in dismissing her relatives from office. They appointed a new emperor to rule; he was the son of the Han founder by a concubine and could not challenge their power. Because these elderly officials took no measures against the Liu family members to whom the Han founder had awarded ranks, the central government continued to administer only one-third of the empire while the regional kings—all but one of whom were related to the dynastic founder—ruled the remaining two-thirds.

The first three reigns of the Han dynasty spanned fifty years, during which the emperors modified the Qin legal system only slightly. Very little data survive about the distribution of income in Han-dynasty China. Among the wealthiest families were those local kings and marquises who had received titles and lands from the Han founder. Another extraordinary archeological discovery, this time from the city of Changsha in Hunan province (800 kilometers, or 500 miles, southeast of Xian), reveals just how prosperous these families were.

THE WORLD OF THE REGIONAL RULERS: THE MAWANGDUI FINDS

Many Chinese include the southern city of Changsha on their lists of the so-called four ovens, or the four hottest cities in China. Always humid, with temperatures regularly over 35 degrees Celsius (100 degrees Fahrenheit), Changsha's climate damages, rather than preserves, all artifacts it encounters. Imagine then the surprise of archeologists who excavated three Han-dynasty tombs in the small hamlet of Mawangdui during the Cultural Revolution. Tomb number 2 belonged to the marquis, a man named Li Cang, who figured among the original supporters of the Han founder. First created in 202 B.C., the Changsha kingdom included most of modern Hunan, northwestern Guangxi, and northern Guangdong provinces. Named chancellor to the regional king in 194 B.C., and given the rank of marquis, Li Cang then ruled for seven years before his death in 186 B.C. Although he was the highest-ranking of the three tomb occupants, his tomb sustained the most damage and is notable primarily for its seals, which made it possible to identify the other tombs. Tomb number 1 belonged to his wife, Lady Dai, who died near the age of fifty sometime after 168 B.C. Her son, who died near the age of thirty in 168 B.C., was buried along with his personal library in tomb number 3.

Lady Dai's tomb offered the most breathtaking find of all, a perfectly preserved corpse. Archeologists offer this striking description:

> In this coffin was a female corpse wrapped in twenty coats of embroidered silk and brocade. The deceased lady was 1.54 meters tall [5 feet] and weighed 34.3 [75 lbs] kilograms. The appearance of the corpse was intact, the body soft, the muscle elastic, the light yellow complexion and black hair and eyelash clearly visible, the drum in the left ear complete, and the solid blood was yet in the artery. It is a wonder that the corpse was so well preserved from decay for more than two thousand years.[14]

In 1975, when the first major exhibit of Chinese archeological finds came to Washington, D.C., the National Gallery showed an unforgettable film of the Mawangdui find in which astonished physicians poked over and over again at the flesh of Lady Dai. Each time her supple flesh bounced back.

The level of preservation stunned the film's audience, but as the site report explains, the four interlocking coffins formed a micro-

Lady Dai's Tomb

This top-down view of Lady Dai's tomb shows how her interlocking coffins created a wooden apartment for the dead, occupying approximately two-thirds the area of a squash court (6.7 meters by 4.8 meters or 21.9 feet by 15.7 feet). The contents of her coffin complex, individually numbered by the archeologists who excavated her tomb, reveal what a rich woman needed in the afterlife. The rectangular space at the top contains her sitting room, and three other side coffins contain storage rooms. In the sitting room food has already been laid out for her first visitors. One can even see the chopsticks (383, 391) intended for their use—evidence that the Chinese used chopsticks to eat in the Han and not just to take food from serving trays as they had earlier.

environment that protected all the grave's contents. Twenty layers of shrouds provided further protection for her body. Lady Dai's skin was fully preserved as were the contents of her stomach, which contained over one hundred muskmelon seeds. An X ray revealed that she had sustained a fracture in one leg. In addition to Lady Dai's intact corpse, archeologists found magnificently embroidered silks, whose once-brilliant colors have since sadly faded. All these items were listed on bamboo slips found in the grave.

Lady Dai's tomb permits a singular glimpse of Chinese conceptions of the afterlife in the centuries before Buddhism came to China. Like the tomb of the Qin emperor and that of the low-ranking official at Shuihudi, hers provided a home for one of her souls after her death. Written sources from the period differ in the details, but overall they concur that people had two kinds of soul: the superior spirit-soul (*hun*) that could travel to the land of the immortals and the inferior body-soul (*po*). The inferior body-soul might reside in the tomb, but it could also travel to the netherworld unless sufficient preventive measures were taken. The three side chambers of Lady Dai's tomb held many goods for the use of the body-soul: 154 lacquer vessels, 51 ceramics, 48 bamboo suitcases of clothing and other household goods, and 40 baskets holding clay replicas of 300 gold pieces and 100,000 bronze coins.

The Cuisine of the Han Dynasty

The plates in Lady Dai's tomb contained a variety of meat dishes and cups for beer. The grave inventory mentions two kinds of beer, one an unfermented malt drink with low alcoholic content, perhaps for women, and the other, a stronger brew fermented with yeast. The meat would have complemented the beer perfectly since the people of the Han did not eat their main staple of steamed grain when they drank beer. (Even today few people choose to eat rice when drinking alcohol.) Elsewhere in the tomb, archeologists found the remains of rice, wheat, barley, and two varieties of millet as well as soybeans and red lentils. The tomb inventory lists seven kinds of meat, prepared in thirteen different ways, suggesting that Lady Dai was going to feast in her next life on much of the same foodstuffs wealthy people ate in this world.

Although Lady Dai could afford an expensive diet, the foods she ate divided into the same categories of dishes and starch used by the people of Anyang. The grave inventory provides recipes for several versions of the most popular dish in the Han, a stew of vegetables and meat cooked in a pot until it gained the consistency of a thick soup. The suggested variations include beef and rice stew, dog meat and celery stew, and even

The walls of the sitting room are covered with fabrics, some of which have been torn, and a tray of food for the dead woman is in the foreground. On the tray are six dishes, cups, and food.

deer, fish, and bamboo shoot stew. Many modern seasonings were also listed: salt, sugar, honey, soy sauce, and salted beans. The cooks of the Han took particular pleasure in cutting their meats precisely, as one anecdote suggests. A man imprisoned in Luoyang recounts that he recognized his mother's stew by the shape of the meat cubes: "When my mother cuts the meat, the chunks always come in perfect squares, and when she chops the scallions, the pieces always come in sections exactly one inch long."[15] Like Lady Dai, this man ate meat stew frequently, but many ordinary people had to make do with just grain and vegetables.

Lady Dai's sitting room, the north chamber of the tomb, contains home furnishings in use during the Han dynasty, including curtains on the wall and tatami-like mats on the floors. On one side, the room contained a painted screen, an armrest, and a wooden cane that she had to use when she walked; the other held figurines who would dance, play music, and attend to her needs, including the food she would eat at her party.

Han Views of the Afterlife

Inside three outer coffins was a fourth coffin, on top of which lay a T-shaped banner formed by three different textiles. The banner can be divided into horizontal scenes. The narrow, lower section shows Lady Dai standing, propped up by her cane, with two men kneeling before her and three women standing behind her. This scene depicts her body-soul as she will live in her underground tomb. Below her is a scene of a feast, complete with large ritual vessels standing on the ground. Here attendants flank a lower table with a shelf. The bowl with the chopsticks standing upright marks this as an offering to the dead, and indeed her wrapped corpse is the rounded object lying on the lower table. Her relatives hoped that her body-soul could remain in her tomb, as the banner depicts, and not travel to the underworld shown at the very bottom, which holds two earth goats flanking the intertwined fish.

The top section, all analysts concur, shows the realm of the immortals, whose entrance is guarded by two hatted figures—the gods of destiny who keep records of each individual's allotted life span. In the upper left hangs the moon and its characteristic residents, a toad and a rabbit, and in the upper right is the sun with its corresponding raven. (The ten blank disks underneath the sun may illustrate its different stations.) The figure floating at the top of the banner, seated on the snake, poses the greatest mystery, with some arguing she represents the Queen Mother of the West, a goddess who presides over the realm of the immortals. Others contend, more convincingly, that she represents the immortal Lady Dai will become, with the two birds to the left and the three to the right representing the same five figures who surrounded her in the two other scenes below. Gone is her cane, and she appears as a much younger woman.

PORTRAIT OF LADY DAI

This 2.05-meter- (6-foot-) long T-shaped banner lay on top of the interior coffin containing Lady Dai. In the center is a woman with a cane. X rays of Lady Dai's legs showed a healed fracture, suggesting she was lame. This banner is quite possibly the earliest known portrait of a historical personage in Chinese history.

The three scenes, then, show three different phases after death: the laying out of the corpse, existence in the underworld, and release into immortality. Although no texts explain the relationship among the three, it seems most likely that they are related in the same way that different bands on earlier bronzes had been. That is, they depict different, nearly simultaneous activities, not a chronological sequence. Lady Dai's spirit-soul would ascend to the world of the immortals, while her body-soul would reside in her grave without traveling to the dreaded underworld. The T-shaped-banner, then, illustrates all the possibilities for Lady Dai's afterlife, but it does not explain how one ascends to the realm of the immortals, perhaps the most pressing question of all.

Because Lady Dai prepared forty-eight suitcases but no reading matter for her journey to the underworld, she may have been illiterate. In contrast, her son's tomb contained a library of books, maps, and treatises—the earliest manuscripts written on silk found thus far in China. Each text had to be hand copied in the age before printing. Awkward as writing on bamboo slips was, it was much easier than writing on silk. Because a slip of the hand could destroy a whole page, one had to use just the right pressure on the brush.

A Library in the Second Century B.C.

The tomb of Lady Dai's son contains manuscripts of text already well known to scholars, such as The Book of Changes (Yijing), a version of a book closely related to Intrigues of the Warring States, and two copies of The Way and Integrity Classic. These excavated books permit us to examine texts as they circulated in the centuries before Christ. Although the Mawangdui editions reverse the two halves of The Way and Integrity Classic, the tomb texts overlap with the transmitted text to a surprising degree, suggesting ancient Chinese copyists scrupulously copied the classics each time they reproduced them.

If the Mawangdui manuscripts have increased the confidence of the scholarly community in the accuracy of transmitted texts, the discovery of so many previously unknown texts has also forced scholars to reassess the intellectual world of the Han. Before the discovery of the tomb, scholars had calculated that of 677 books listed in an imperial library catalogue from the year 0, only 23 percent survive today, revealing that many books had been lost.[16] Confirming this view, tomb number 3 introduced previously lost texts on law, fortune-telling, and even sexual techniques, which are of even greater interest than the books already known to scholars.

When the historian Sima Qian's father, Sima Tan, listed the important schools of the Han dynasty, he mentioned the Huang-Lao school, a philosophical school whose texts did not survive to the present. Scholars knew that Huang, literally "yellow," referred to the Yellow Emperor, one of the legendary kings of yore, while Lao stood for Laozi, the putative author of *The Way and Integrity Classic*. Because the new texts in tomb number 3 mention both figures, many modern scholars see them as the missing Huang-Lao texts.

The Philosophy of the Huang-Lao School

Of the texts newly discovered in the tomb, a series of short texts appended to *The Way and Integrity Classic* have commanded the most attention because they reconfigure political philosophy. Unlike Confucius, who looked down on law as the tool of lesser rulers, and unlike *The Way and Integrity Classic*, which derided law as an unnecessary encouragement to criminals, several short Mawangdui texts award law a more important position. Modern commentators sometimes refer to these short untitled texts as *The Classic of Law*. These texts, possibly by one author, possibly by multiple hands, envision a world in which rulers must govern their states in accord with nature, or the Way. *The Classic of Law* begins by saying:

> The Way (*dao*) brings forth law. Law is the mark that indicates success and failure and distinguishes the crooked from the straight. Therefore one who holds fast to the Way can produce laws but dares not transgress them.[17]

These texts make further demands on the ruler, who is to balance punishments with rewards, who can undertake only just wars, and who is required to live on a reasonable budget. Still, for all its statements about the need for rulers to adhere to the Way and to follow the law, *The Classic of Law* offers no specific mechanism to check a ruler who does not adhere to its teachings.

Along with *The Classic of Law*, tomb number 3 contained a variety of other texts giving guidance in various areas of life. Some offered explicit sexual advice to couples, usually from the male author's point of view. Detailed drawings of female anatomy accompanied instructions for bringing one's sexual partner to a climax. Startlingly frank, "Prescriptions for Nourishing Life" instructed readers how to heighten sexual pleasure, while a work entitled "Joining yin and yang" listed different sexual positions, and enumerated female reactions to them—including the five noises women make when excited. Like the Huang-Lao texts, these sex manuals seem to have dropped from sight soon after being written, to be recovered only when tomb number 3 was excavated.

The deceased also buried fortune-telling books along with three maps in his tomb. The smallest map shows the tomb area, but the two other maps show larger areas: a topographic map covers the borderlands between the Han territory, as ruled by the king at Changsha, and the kingdom of the Southern Yue peoples; the other shows the garrisons the Han troops used in a 181 B.C. attack on the Southern Yue. Ruled by a Chinese leader, the Yue lived by fishing and agriculture. The Chinese called this region Nanyue, meaning Southern Yue, but the people who lived there reversed the two words. They pronounced the word Yue as Viet, and the compound as Vietnam, which is still the word used today. The lands they occupied included the southern Chinese provinces of Guangdong and Guangxi in addition to modern Vietnam.

Linguistic evidence suggests the Southern Yue peoples originally occupied the central Yangzi River valley and that the Chinese settlers pushed them south, sometime between 1000 and 500 B.C. Modern Chinese has several words for *river*. Curiously, only one refers to the rivers of the south, *jiang*. Sometime in the first millennium B.C., the Chinese began to use this loanword from Austro-Asiatic to refer to the central Yangzi valley, the ancient homeland of the Viet peoples. Even today the Vietnamese believe their ancestors once lived along Lake Dongting in the central Yangzi valley. The Chinese residents in north China adopted Austro-Asiatic loanwords for *tiger* and *ivory* to name things foreign to them but present in the south, and they adopted a foreign word for the new weapon of the crossbow, which they first encountered when the Qin tried to conquer the Viet peoples.[18]

The maps in the tomb of Lady Dai's son indicate that he served as a military official in charge of defending borders against the attacks of the Southern Yue peoples. Just as Lady Dai expected to receive her guests, he fully expected to continue fighting in the next world. The maps remind us that the Han Chinese continued to expand the territory under their control, often at the expense of non-Chinese speakers like the Yue, who left no records of their defeats.

Li Cang, the Marquis of Dai, buried in tomb number 2, had assumed the position of chancellor at the request of the local king, the only regional king not related to the Han founder. When Li Cang died in 186 B.C., a new chancellor was named—not by the local king but by the central government. In 157 B.C., when the king died, the central government replaced him with a member of the imperial family. What was happening on the periphery also occurred elsewhere in the empire as the Han took measures to centralize its power. The emperor who took the most effective measures to do so, Emperor Wu, began to rule in 140 B.C. By the time he died in 87 B.C., he had established Confucian institutions and precedents for all his successors.

THE HAN DYNASTY UNDER EMPEROR WU

When Emperor Wu took the throne in 140 B.C., he was a mere fifteen-year-old boy, and actual power lay in the hands of the dowager empress and the chancellor. Empress Dou, the mother of his predecessor, died in 135 B.C., and the chancellor, who was also Emperor Wu's uncle, died in 131 B.C. From that date on, Emperor Wu took power into his own hands, never allowing anyone to acquire the power that his uncle and his grandmother had enjoyed. Because Emperor Wu had the good fortune to live until the age of sixty-eight, he had time to take lasting measures to strengthen the central government. As he eliminated checks on imperial power, he conquered new territory and established a Confucian academy. He did not, though, succeed in securing sufficient revenues to support these reforms, and his successors continually struggled with inadequate revenues.

Patronizing Confucian Scholars

Emperor Wu's Confucianism deeply reflected the influence of his advisor Dong Zhongshu (175?–105? B.C.), who believed that the emperor served to link heaven with his subjects. If he governed well, heaven would continue to support him, but if he violated heaven's intent, heaven could send various portents to warn him of his misconduct. These portents could appear in the form of eclipses, floods, droughts, or any other calamity. The philosopher went on to explain that all human history could be understood as the manifestation of a larger pattern. Complementary yin and yang forces alternated with each other, so that light, activity, and heat predominated at some times, and dark, inactivity, and cold in others. Once one force had become predominant, it began to wane, while the other ascended. Each phase of change was marked by one of five different elements: wood, fire, earth, metal, and water. The book *Luxuriant Gems of the Spring and Autumn* (*Chunqiu fanlu*) attempted to explain the rise and fall of previous rulers in terms of this five-phase theory. Although traditionally attributed to Dong Zhongshu, it was actually written down long after his death, sometime in the third to sixth centuries A.D.

Emperor Wu may have turned to Confucian scholars like Dong Zhongshu as an alternative to the Huang-Lao school. Dong Zhongshu urged the emperor to ban all members of non-Confucian schools, and he encouraged the emperor to support the study of Confucian classics. In the years just before or just after the empress's death, the emperor named five scholars to the position of Erudite Scholars, each of whom specialized in a different Confucian classic: *The Book of Changes, The Book of Documents, The Book of Songs, The Book of Rites*, and *The Spring and Autumn Annals*. The selection of these five books as the most important texts marked the first step in the formation of the Confucian canon. When the emperor named fifty students to study with the Erudite Scholars in 124 B.C., he created an imperial academy, whose students could enter the government. It grew quickly, enrolling three thousand students in the next seventy-five years. Emperor Wu also established schools in each locality; students in these schools could join the local government, attend the imperial academy, or be recruited into the central bureaucracy.

The Institution of Civil Service Examinations

The Han dynasty continued to recruit officials largely by recommendation, but it required its officials to take examinations after they arrived in the capital in order to place them in appropriate entry-level positions in the bureaucracy. Whenever the central government decided to hire staff at the local level, it asked local officials to recommend talented young men. After entering the bureaucracy as low-ranking clerks, these men could work their way up the bureaucratic ranks. During Emperor Wu's reign, this system offered the advantages of on-the-job training, but in later centuries it proved susceptible to manipulation as powerful families gained control of the nomination process.

At the same time that Emperor Wu strengthened the bureaucracy, he took strong measures to curtail the power of the regional rulers empowered by the Han founder. Starting in 127 B.C. he required that when a given ruler died, his lands were to be divided among all his sons—not passed down intact to the oldest son as had previously been the case. Like the Qin founder, he required these families to move to a new city close to the capital, and he forbade members of some families to live together. Emperor Wu broke with earlier practice, too, in his consistent refusal to appoint the sons of these powerful families to high office. Emperor Wu chose his own appointees instead.

Foreign Affairs

As Emperor Wu consolidated his power within the empire, he also sought to extend the territory under Han control. The peoples of the Southern Yue, with whom Lady Dai's son had fought, continued to trade with the Chinese, especially with merchants from Sichuan province. The Chinese exported iron arms and tools, silks, lacquer goods, and bronze mirrors, buying horses, yaks, cows, and slaves in return. In 109 B.C. Emperor Wu's armies conquered these lands, but the Chinese held them only until the first century, when they again slipped beyond Chinese control.

The troops of the Han faced a more difficult challenge to the north, where the Chinese continued to make annual payments to the Xiongnu according to the peace agreements they continued to renegotiate. Just after taking the throne, Emperor Wu sent an envoy to visit another tribal people, the Yuezhi, with whom he hoped to secure an alliance against the Xiongnu. But the envoy never reached the Yuezhi. He was taken prisoner by the Xiongnu, with whom he stayed for over ten years. When he returned to the capital, he told of the extensive riches of the region, especially of the extraordinarily rapid horses of Ferghana that supposedly sweated blood. The Han and Xiongnu subsequently engaged in many battles, with neither side achieving a decisive victory.

In 99 B.C. the emperor sent a general named Li Ling (d. 74 B.C.) with a small force into battle against the Xiongnu. General Li Ling fought bravely, as the Grand Historian Sima Qian vividly described:

> . . . Li Ling's troops numbered fewer than 5,000 when he led them deep into the territory of the nomads. They marched to the khan's court and dangled the bait in the tiger's mouth. They boldly challenged the fierce barbarians, in the face of an army of a million. . . . For a thousand miles they retreated, fighting as they went, until their arrows were exhausted and the road cut off. The relieving force had not arrived. Dead and wounded lay in heaps. But when Li Ling rallied his men with a cry, his soldiers rose to fight, with streaming tears and bloody faces.[19]

When his troops could fight no longer, Li Ling surrendered, rather than commit suicide, the more honorable course of action. Another commander, Su Wu (d. 60 B.C.), had also been taken prisoner, but he refused to surrender and lived as a prisoner among the Xiongnu after surviving a suicide attempt. During the years they were imprisoned, the two men met occasionally. Li Ling always tried to persuade Su Wu to capitulate, but Su Wu remained steadfast. Only in 81 B.C., after the Han and Xiongnu signed a new peace, did Su Wu return to the capital, while Li

Ling continued to live among the Xiongnu as an exile who had betrayed the Chinese cause.

As Sima Qian later wrote in a letter to a friend, he had known Li Ling when he was young. Because the historian believed the general must have had a reason for surrendering, he defended him before the emperor. But the emperor interpreted his remarks as treasonous and sentenced Sima to be castrated. Unable to pay a fine and gain his freedom, he too could have taken the more honorable course and been put to death. But he chose instead to be castrated. He explained why:

> If I concealed my feelings and clung to life, burying myself in filth without protest, it was because I could not bear to leave unfinished my deeply cherished project, because I rejected the idea of dying without leaving to posterity my literary work.

That work became *Records of the Grand Historian*, the first work of history to recount events in a logical way while describing the motivations of individuals. Although employed as an astrologer at court, as his father had been, Sima wrote his history privately. Continuing the work of his father, he covered the years from the legendary past to events within his own lifetime. In the chapters above I have cited Sima's work frequently because it often provides the only surviving description of events, always in the characteristically crisp prose of the Grand Historian.

The Creation of Autocracy

Sima Qian's tragic encounter testifies to the power of Emperor Wu. After the dowager empress had died and he permanently disabled the post of chancellor, Emperor Wu ruled with no significant checks on his power until his death in 87 B.C. During his reign, he dismissed and sentenced to death some five chancellors, undermining the authority of what had been the highest position in the bureaucracy. Rather than appoint men of high-ranking families to office, Emperor Wu chose instead to promote men of low birth, who remained entirely dependent on him for their success.

In 87 B.C., Emperor Wu promoted the stepbrother of his wife, a man named He Guang (d. 68 B.C.) to serve as regent. In the years after Emperor Wu's death, Regent He Guang succeeded in gathering so much power into his own hands that he outranked the emperor. He placed one child emperor on the throne, only to remove him and replace him with another. In subsequent reigns, various people, whether officials, empresses, or eunuchs, named themselves regent and used the same stratagem of ruling through a figurehead child emperor. Since the child bore some kind of blood tie to the Han founder, the Han dynasty was able to continue.

Economic Problems during the Han Dynasty

Almost every measure Emperor Wu introduced, whether sending troops far afield or establishing a Confucian academy, required funds, yet officials soon found that the revenue from the land tax could not meet the empire's growing financial needs. Following the precedent of the Han founder, Empress Lü had set the land tax at one-fifteenth (6.67%) of agricultural produce, and it was subsequently lowered to one-thirtieth in 168 B.C. In 119 B.C., to provide a supplementary source of revenue, Emperor Wu created government monopolies for two of the most profitable sectors in the economy: salt and iron.

In the case of the salt and iron monopolies, the government established some fifty foundries, with staffs of convicts or conscripts ranging from several hundred to a thousand. They used the most sophisticated technologies of their day—blast furnaces to produce iron and tipped drills to get at the underground salt pools. Because the government controlled the production of iron, which was used to make farm implements, cooking pots, scissors, and weapons, it was able to charge artificially high prices for the products over which it had monopolies. The profits generated from the monopolies provided an important source of revenue for the central government. The salt and iron monopolies were so successful that in 115 B.C. the central government also assumed control of the production of copper and bronze and took the right to mint coins from the commanderies, which had each been minting their own currency. In 98 B.C. the government created its fourth monopoly over a drink often translated as wine: a fermented beverage made from grain.

The long years of fighting the Xiongnu and the heavy tax burden exacerbated by the exactions of the monopolies took a heavy toll on the populace. In 86 B.C., the year after Emperor Wu's death, the central government formed a commission to investigate the sufferings of the people, and in 81 B.C., the sixty Confucian scholars who were summoned to the capital to propose solutions severely criticized the creation of the monopolies. A rare account of debates at court concerning the monopoly system, called *The Salt and Iron Debates*, records the opinions of the critics—who were the Confucians—and the defenders of the monopoly system. Occurring in 81 B.C., the debates were recorded between ten and thirty years after the fact.

Two groups participated. On one side was the architect of the new monopolies, called the minister; on the other stood the learned men, a group of critics who deplored the disappearance of a simpler lifestyle and economy. The learned men criticized the creation of the monopolies as well as government policies encouraging trade with the peoples outside China. They felt that government officials should refrain from trade, remove themselves from the monopolies, and return to a simpler economy in which everyone was largely self-sufficient.

The minister vigorously defended the trade policies of the government:

> Thus, a piece of Chinese plain silk can be exchanged with the Xiongnu for articles worth several pieces of gold and thereby reduce the resources of our enemy. Mules, donkeys and camels enter the frontier in unbroken lines; horses, dapples and bays and prancing mounts, come into our possession. The furs of sables, marmots, foxes and badgers, colored rugs and decorated carpets fill the Imperial Treasury, while jade and auspicious stones, corals and crystals, become national treasures. That is to say, foreign products keep flowing in, while our wealth is not dissipated. Novelties flowing in, the government has plenty. National wealth not being dispersed abroad, the people enjoy abundance.[20]

This spirited defense of trade with the Xiongnu provides a useful picture of foreign trade during the first century B.C. For silk, the Chinese obtained a wide array of goods, including animal skins, rugs, and rare stones.

The learned men rejected the government's argument totally. They saw no possible benefits of trade, simply asserting "Trade promotes dishonesty." Even though the surviving record has been doctored in favor of the learned men, the minister's defense of trade reflects accurately the extensive commerce the Han-dynasty Chinese had with outsiders. Indeed, the monopolies continued unchanged after the debates and provided an important source of revenue for the central government in subsequent dynasties as well.

The Developing Market Economy

A satiric essay by Wang Bao (active in 61–54 B.C.) echoes the scholars' concern that the traditional social and economic order had changed too quickly during the years after Emperor Wu's death. In the essay, a slave named Bianliao refuses to go and buy wine for the guest of his widowed mistress.

Although the text does not explain how Bianliao became a slave, it does call him "bearded," an indication that he was of non-Chinese ancestry. Other sources reveal that there were several paths to slavery during the Han dynasty. In some cases, people from neighboring kingdoms were captured in battle and subsequently enslaved; these slaves may have looked slightly different from their Chinese owners, but over time they could absorb Chinese ways. In other cases, people who became deeply indebted were forced to enslave themselves or their family members to pay off their debts. Some convicts performed forced labor for specified periods. Slavery was not necessarily a permanent condition. Slaves who made enough money could buy themselves out of slavery, and their masters could also free them. One estimate is that the total number of slaves was 1 percent of the entire population, which the earliest extant census put at 58 million in A.D. 2.[21]

All that the fictitious Bianliao says about his past is, "When my master bought me, Bianliao, he only contracted for me to care for the grave and did not contract for me to buy wine for some other gentleman."[22] The angry guest asks the widow why she has not yet sold the slave, and she explains that she could not find a buyer. The guest then agrees to purchase the recalcitrant slave, who asks the guest to list all his duties in the contract because he will "not do anything not in the contract."

The resulting contract with its many clauses mocks the excessively detailed contracts in favor at the time. The text specifies all the slave's tasks, from morning sweepings to midnight feedings of the horse and cattle, and assumes he will continue to work for the widow. The slave lives on a farm where livestock is raised and where different crops—melons, eggplants, onions, garlic, beans, and fruit—are grown, presumably for the widow's household to eat. The contract also requires the slave to hunt deer, wild ducks, and turtles, testimony to the extensive wildlife of this era.

Although the slave is instructed to gather crops and to hunt wild animals, the widow's farm is not self-sufficient. Many of the slave's tasks involve going to market:

> Behind the house there are trees. He should hew them and make a boat, going downriver as far as Jiangzhou and up to Jianzhu. On behalf of the storehouse assistants he shall seek spending money, rejecting the strings of cash which are defective. He shall buy mats at Mianting, and when traveling between Du and Luo he should trade in the small markets to get powder for the ladies. When he returns to Du he shall carry hemp about on his pole, transporting it out to the side markets. He shall lead dogs for sale and peddle geese. At Wuyang he shall buy bitter sauce, and he shall carry lotus on his pole from the Yang family pool. When he travels to market assemblies he shall carefully guard against the practice of theft. When he enters the market he may not squat like a non-Chinese, loll about, or indulge in evil talk or cursing. He shall make many

knives and bows, and take them into Yizhou to barter for oxen and sheep. The slave shall teach himself to be smart and clever, and may not be silly and stupid.

Although we have nothing with which to compare it, this contract, with its sardonic close, seems to list many more tasks than a normal contract would. While Wang Bao exaggerates the detail of a contract, he has no reason to distort the economic activity taking place around him.

His literary exercise reveals the existence of a widespread network of markets, ranging from larger ones to smaller "side" markets that met only seasonally. Although not all the place names can be identified, the slave was expected to travel to many places within the modern province of Sichuan, and Luo may refer to the capital of Luoyang, hundreds of kilometers away from modern Chengdu. The slave also went to Yizhou, a town near modern Kunming in Yunnan, where he traded knives and bows for livestock. A money economy coexisted with a barter economy, at least in Sichuan, although perhaps not in Yunnan, a peripheral region that is home to many non-Chinese minorities even today. The slave also

STREET LIFE TWO THOUSAND YEARS AGO

Like China's markets today, the Sichuan market shown on this Han-dynasty tile has both permanent shops and temporary stands on which merchants lay out goods for sale.

used money, copper cash he was to examine for counterfeit. Although a market network existed, it traded largely in luxury goods like the face powder the widow's household required. Most people continued to grow, or to hunt, the food they ate.

When the new owner finished reading the contract, the stunned slave bemoaned his initial refusal to obey his new owner's request to purchase wine. Traditional views required the slave to obey a guest's request with alacrity, but as Wang Bao's spoof shows so tellingly, this new-style slave would do only what his contract requires.

This essay, written in the middle of the first century B.C., reflects a growing sense that Han-dynasty society was divided into two groups: estate owners, here represented by the widow, and those who worked the land, like the slave Bianliao. Although divided, Han-dynasty society was fluid. Nobles could be stripped of their property and reduced to slavery while slaves could purchase their freedom and rise in society.

Even at the founding of the dynasty, large disparities of income had existed between those who had received large grants of land from the new emperor and those who worked the land for them. In the following centuries the gap widened, as powerful families began to amass even larger estates; they accomplished this often by buying land from poorer farmers and tenants, some of whom lost their land when they could not pay their debts. Because the owners of these estates enjoyed enormous influence on the local level, it was easy for them to evade taxes, and government revenues from agrarian taxes declined. The loss of revenue prompted the proposal of a government measure in 7 B.C. to limit the largest estates to a maximum of three thousand sixth-acres with a slave population of two hundred. Because large landowners opposed it, the measure never took effect, but when the regent Wang Mang seized power in A.D. 9, he justified his move as necessary in order to lessen the power of the large estate owners.

The Wang Mang Regency: A Break in Han-Dynasty Rule

Wang Mang founded the Xin ("new") dynasty, calling for a return to the golden age of the same ancient Zhou dynasty about which Confucius had written. Wang Mang tried to take several punitive measures against the large estate holders. Claiming that he wanted to help the poor, he forbade the sale and purchase of all land, and he limited the size of individual landholdings, ordering those with excess land to cede property to the landless. He also freed all slaves. But the redistribution of land and the abolition of slavery proved impossible to implement, allowing estate owners once again to augment their landholdings and obtain slaves.

Although his measures antagonized the estate holders, Wang Mang's reign came to an end when he lost the support of those who worked the land. A massive flood of the Yellow River delivered the fatal blow to his short-lived government. The Yellow River is one of China's two largest rivers (the Yangzi is the other). Its course runs 4,300 kilometers (2,700 miles) in total, starting in the high mountains to the west and traversing the yellow clay soil, or loess, plains of north China as it makes its way to the sea. For the last five hundred miles of its course the level of the river drops only one foot per mile. Yet, as it flows, the river deposits particles of yellow silt in the riverbed, which causes the river's level to rise year after year. Only the construction of high dikes of mud and stone can block its course and prevent annual flooding. When the dikes give way, the resulting floods can inundate an area several hundred kilometers wide. This is what happened in A.D. 11.

The river's original course had been south of the Shandong peninsula, reaching the sea near what is now the modern city of Tianjin. But during the floods the river formed two arms, one flowing south of the Shandong Peninsula and the other flowing north. The resulting flooding displaced thousands of peasants who rose up against the central government. Because the rebels painted their foreheads red in hopes of gaining the increased energy of red blood, they were called the Red Eyebrows. A loose coalition of powerful landowning families joined together to suppress the rebels, and after they had defeated both the rebels and the imperial troops, they agreed to place a distant heir of the Han founder on the throne. The coalition forces killed Wang Mang in A.D. 23, but they gained full control only in A.D. 25, when the new emperor ordered the capital moved to Luoyang, which served as the capital until A.D. 190.

THE RESTORATION OF THE LATER HAN

The new capital of the Later Han (sometimes called the Eastern Han because Luoyang was east of Changan) was smaller than Changan but still a world-class metropolis. Its walls surrounded an area of 10 square kilometers (3.91 square miles), or three times the area of New York's Central Park. The area of Luoyang that lay outside the walls covered an additional 24.5 square kilometers (9.4 square miles).[23] Only Changan, with an area of 33.5 square kilometers (13 square miles), and Rome, with an area of 13.8 square kilometers (5.3 square miles), outranked it. The walls surrounded the imperial palace, inns, canals, markets, and schools. Its residents included 10,000 women and eunuchs of the imperial household, 5,000 imperial guards, and 50,000 students at the Confucian Academy and their dependents. If Luoyang had the same number of residents as Changan, 400,000 other commoners lived in the smaller city as well. With a population approaching 500,000, Luoyang had one of the largest urban populations in the world at that time. (Rome had one million.)

The newly restored dynasty was able to govern only with the cooperation of influential families who had supported its return to power. Accordingly, it took no measures against the families who amassed enormous estates and who regularly placed their sons in office, often by recommending them to local officials. As the Han dynasty entered its third and fourth centuries in power, eunuchs came to play an increasingly important role. Apprehensive about the eunuchs' influence in the Qin dynasty, the early Han emperors had largely succeeded in keeping them from exercising power for the first two centuries of the dynasty. This pattern changed in A.D. 92, however, when the reigning emperor enlisted the support of a eunuch against a powerful faction, and eunuchs often appear as major players in the political intrigues of the second century.

After A.D. 25 peace was restored, and some of China's greatest literary talents lived in the new capital. One of the most famous writers of the Han, Wang Chong (27–97), did not come from a long-established family. As a young student, Wang frequented the bookstalls of the new capital. Although he could not buy books, his memory was so powerful that he could remember any book that he scanned. He studied with one of the great writers of his time, the poet and historian Ban Biao (d. 54).

Wang Chong's Skepticism

In a long work entitled *Balanced Discussions*, completed circa A.D. 50, Wang Chong described many contemporary religious beliefs and then denounced them for lacking any logical basis. Although critical in approach, *Balanced Discussions* contains much information about the practices Wang examined, practices followed by the majority of his contemporaries. For instance, since the people of his time feared digging into the ground and disturbing the spirits of the earth, they made a figurine out of dirt to which they performed ceremonies asking forgiveness. Wang Chong clearly explained his opposition:

> If one examines this more closely, then one realizes that it is empty trickery. How can one test it? Now, the earth is like a human body, with everything in the empire forming one body with head and feet at different ends some 10,000 third-miles apart. People live on the surface of the earth, much as lice live on a person's body. Much as lice eat and steal human skin, people pierce the earth and steal the

earth's body. If some of the lice understood and wanted to propitiate the person, and they gathered together to propitiate and ask for pardon from what they were going to eat, would the person know? Much as the person could not know the sound of the lice, so too can the earth not understand the speech of people.[24]

This passage perfectly embodies Wang Chong's approach. After equating the presence of people on the earth with the presence of lice on the body, he argued that, as we would never notice lice performing a ceremony, similarly the earth gods would not notice any human activity.

Wang Chong devoted an entire chapter of his book to "Daoist Untruths," which provides an unrivaled description of Daoist practices during the first century. Like the original followers of Zhuangzi, Han-dynasty Daoists continued to refine their breathing techniques, to urge their followers to adhere to a strict diet, and to make potions—all in the hopes of attaining immortality. Laozi, the putative author of *The Way and Integrity Classic*, was among those who these Daoists believed had gained immortality. Wang Chong resoundingly rejected the Daoists' claims to be able to fly to the realm of the immortals:

> If the Daoists and students of immortality could first grow feathers and plumes several inches long so that they could skim over the earth and rise to the terraces of high buildings, one might believe that they could ascend to heaven. Now there is no sign that they are able to fly even a small distance, so how can they achieve the goal of flying high?[25]

As he proceeded point by point to demolish the Daoists' claims, he painted a picture of a small community of individuals aiming to achieve the status of invincible "pure men," an aim beyond the reach of a larger lay community. Wang Chong's description, the best source about Daoism at the time, mentions several teachers and holy men, but no organized religious community.

A Literary Family: The Accomplishments of the Ban Family

Wang Chong's teacher Ban Biao was well known for the size of his private library and for the success of his talented children. One daughter, Ban Zhao (ca. 45–120), became the most famous woman writer of the Han dynasty. Chinese girls read her *Lessons for Women* and the imitations it spawned until the twentieth century. Ban Zhao had twin brothers. One twin was a famous general who fought in northwest China; the other, Ban Gu (A.D. 32–92), perfected a new literary genre, the rhapsody (*fu*), which strung together countless adjectives and brilliant nouns to make a verbal picture of a place, often a city. In one famous rhapsody, two men debated the virtues of the two Han-dynasty capitals and concluded that Luoyang outranked Changan. In praising the new capital, the poet was also praising the reigning emperor, who he argued surpassed the rulers of the former Han. His favorable attitude toward the reigning emperor qualified him for another literary pursuit, the writing of officially commissioned history.

When his father died in A.D. 54, Ban Gu resolved to complete his father's history of China, which began where the Grand Historian Sima Qian had left off, during Emperor Wu's reign. Ban Gu undertook his father's task without official support. Later, when a contemporary charged him with distorting the record, he was thrown into jail, only to be released by Emperor Ming (reigned 58–75). The emperor was so impressed by his draft that he granted Ban Gu privileged access to court archives. This set an important precedent: because the historians chronicling events at court received the sponsorship of the reigning emperor, they could not criticize their patron—unlike Sima Qian's far freer independent effort. When the historian Ban Gu died in A.D. 92, the emperor commissioned his brilliant sister Ban Zhao to complete his unfinished history, a testament to the remarkable literary talents of this woman.

Ban Zhao: China's Most Famous Female Scholar

Little is known of Ban Zhao's own life. In the introduction to *Lessons for Women*, she explained that forty years after her marriage at the age of fourteen, she had decided to write down what she felt every woman should know. Ban Zhao described the unequal treatment accorded to females from the moment they are born until they marry and die.

Fearful that the newborns might not survive the first days of life, Han-dynasty families delayed presenting them to the ancestors until the third day. If a family was unable to raise a child, it could abandon the newborn before three days had passed. Ban Zhao's account of how girls should be raised begins on the third day after birth. "On the third day after the birth of a girl the ancients observed three customs: first to place the baby below the bed; second to give her a potsherd with which to play; and third to announce her birth to her ancestors by an offering."[26] Ban Zhao explained that "now to lay the baby below the bed plainly indicated that she is lowly and weak, and should regard it as her primary duty to humble herself before others." The potsherd represented hard work, while the announcement to the ancestors reminded the infant of her obligation to serve them.

The theme of subservience to men and others shapes *Lessons for*

Women. Women are to serve their husbands, obey their in-laws un-flinchingly, and avoid any conflicts with their sisters-in-law. Ban Zhao listed four qualities women should have: "1. womanly virtue, 2. wom-anly words, 3. womanly bearing, and 4. womanly work." The modest woman remained chaste while watching her every motion, spoke with care, maintained a high standard of personal hygiene, and devoted her-self to weaving, sewing, and food preparation. Ban Zhao's counsels of re-straint deny women any opportunity to speak their minds or to question anyone in their families, but Ban Zhao's ideal woman was educated. She begins her book by instructing the young women in her family to copy down her instructions, evidence that they were literate.

In one telling passage, she complained that the husbands of her day "only know that wives must be controlled and that the husband's rules of conduct manifesting his authority must be established." Accordingly they teach their sons to read. Here, Ban Zhao's objections contain a mov-ing plea for equal education:

> Yet only to teach men and not to teach women—is that not ignoring the es-sential relation between them? According to the *Rites*, it is the rule to begin to teach children to read at the age of eight years, and by the age of fifteen years they ought then be ready for cultural training. Only why should it not be that girls' education as well as boys' be according to this principle?

Few women received the kind of education Ban Zhao had, but that re-mained her ideal. Yes, women were to serve their husbands and their families, but not as ignorant servants. Women should not scold their hus-bands, Ban Zhao argued, but neither should husbands beat their wives. Both husband and wife bore a responsibility to sustain a harmonious and intimate "marriage relationship."

Ban Zhao's own family was exceptional in that with its extensive im-perial connections, it had sufficient wealth to educate her, even though she would leave home when she married. Other families abandoned their daughters rather than provide them with marriage costs, and a second-century adage held, "A thief will not enter a household with five daugh-ters" because such a family would have no possessions worthy of a robber's notice.[27] While low-born families may have dreaded the birth of daugh-ters, the highest-born families could use daughters to further their am-bitions.

The Political Influence of the Consort Families

Powerful families often married a daughter to the emperor in the hope that she would give birth to the crown prince or be named dowager empress should the emperor die childless. If the emperor died young and a member of the consort's family held the all-important post of regent, the empress's family could appoint a child to the throne and so gain a controlling voice in the governing of the empire. Court intrigue marked the last two centuries of the Han-dynasty history during which consort families often chose the new child emperor, while their daughters ruled as dowager empresses. Ban Zhao herself served as tutor to the young Empress Deng while her husband was alive, and advisor to her once she became dowager empress in A.D. 106, a position Deng held until her death in 121 (Ban Zhao died at the age of seventy-five in A.D. 120).

Palace officials kept detailed records of how the emperor's staff judged candidates for him to marry. In 147, a woman named Maid Wu wrote a report following her visit to a potential bride for the Emperor Huan (reigned 146–168).[28] After she and a male official visited the girl's family and examined her, Maid Wu took the girl into a private room, where "sunlight came through the shell windows and shown upon Ying's face, which radiated a brightness like the morning cloud or snow." The girl Ying objected to Maid Wu's request to examine her naked body, but Maid Wu explained: "It is a palace rule which must be complied with. Please let a poor old woman see it. Loosen the belt knot and I shall be very careful." Then she described the girl's body:

> Her skin was white and fine and so smooth that my hand slipped as it touched it. Her belly was round and her hips square. Her body was like congealed lard and carved jade. Her breasts bulged out, and her navel had enough depth to permit a half-inch pearl to go in.

Her report attempts to be strictly clinical, yet the girl's beauty so moves her that she creates her own idiom—not the written language of the classics—to describe it.

During the interview the girl says nothing until Maid Wu asks her to thank the emperor, to which the girl replies, "Long live the Emperor!" Maid Wu completes her report as follows:

> Her voice was like a wind moving through a bamboo grove, very pleasant to the ear. She had no piles, no bad marks, no moles and no sores, or defects in the mouth, the nose, the armpit, the private parts, or the feet.
>
> I am a stupid humble woman and cannot express properly what I saw or felt. I make this secret report, properly sealed, knowing that my life depends on Your Imperial Pleasure.

This unusual document, which came from the empress's file in the palace archives, leaves much unsaid. Maid Wu's report focuses almost entirely on the girl's appearance. Except for her voice, the reader learns nothing about her mind or her temperament. The list of potential defects catalogues common ailments from which the girl is happily free.

Maid Wu's report makes it sound as if the new empress, whose full name was Liang Nüying (d. 159), was chosen solely on the basis of her beauty and her demeanor. In fact, she had a far more important qualification. A member of the powerful Liang family who dominated court politics for much of the second century, she was the younger sister of the reigning dowager empress and the regent Liang Ji (d. 159), who arranged for her to marry the emperor.

The Power of Empresses in the Later Han Dynasty

The new empress's husband, Emperor Huan, ascended to the throne in 146 while still a boy of only fourteen. Like many of the emperors of the Later Han, he was chosen by a consort family—in his case, the Liang family. His wife's older brother Liang Ji served as regent to his predecessor and to him. At the peak of his power, Regent Liang Ji commanded so much respect that visitors came to see him even before they visited Emperor Huan.

The suffocating power of his in-laws frustrated Emperor Huan, and he gained his opportunity to challenge them in 159, when his first wife, Liang Nüying, died. In a secret plot with five eunuchs concluded in a privy, he launched a coup and unseated the Liang family. This move was unpopular with many of those living in the capital, including students. In what must be among the earliest student protests in world history, the students resident in the capital, whom one source puts at thirty thousand, took to the streets to chant the names of the members of families they supported and the eunuchs they opposed.

Refusal to Serve in Government

After his unpopular coup in 159, which had depended on eunuchs to succeed, Emperor Huan invited five men to serve as officials in his new government, but all declined on the grounds that government service could only contaminate men of virtue. These men's refusal to accept office evoked the precedent of Confucius and his disciples who had not held office. A sixth man gave the following explanation:

> Now if I seek a salary and look for advancement, this would follow my ambitions. Yet there are thousands of women in the imperial harem, and how shall their number be reduced? There are tens of thousands of horses in the impe-

rial stables, and how shall their number be diminished? The attendants at the imperial court are powerful oppressors, and how can they be removed?[29]

For him, holding office meant having to censure the emperor. As long as critics of the emperor were punished, he saw no way he could serve in the emperor's government.

A few years earlier, a man named Wu Liang (78–151) who shared the same view of government service died in a small town in rural Shandong province. As his three sons and grandson explained in his epitaph, they "personally followed the path of sonly duty and spent everything they had to construct his shrine."[30] Other families made the same decision to spend family resources on a shrine for a deceased relative, and one may speculate about their motives. Did they simply seek to pay tribute to the dead? Or did they build a shrine and publicize the costs in the hope of establishing a reputation as loyal Confucians? By the second century most men received government appointments after being recommended by locally prominent families. The presence of such a monument could only enhance their reputations.

Although Wu Liang's brother and his nephew both held low-ranking posts, he refused to serve as an official. His epitaph explains:

> He studied widely and examined the texts in detail. He inquired into the roots of texts, and there was no book that he did not read. The departments of the prefecture and the district invited and summoned him to official posts, but he declined on the grounds of illness. He contented himself with the poverty of his humble home and was pleased with the righteousness that he learned every morning.

Like the men who refused Emperor Huan's summons, Wu Liang did not believe he could sustain a virtuous life as an official.

A Pictorial History of the Empire: Wu Liang's Tomb

The building of shrines initiated a boom in stone carving during the second century A.D. Wu Liang's shrine, the most complete shrine of these, has been the subject of intense study since the eleventh century when literati first examined rubbings taken of the images on its many blocks. Although the stone carvings survive, their original order has been lost, prompting many analysts to reconstruct the shrine by analyzing the logic linking the different sections. One recent analysis argues that Wu Liang designed the shrine to express his political views. Like the Grand Historian Sima Qian, Wu Liang began with the creation of human beings and extended his narrative through to the present. Different scenes, labeled

THE FAMOUS HAN-DYNASTY TOMB OF WU LIANG

This is one of the first examples of two-dimensional art in China. Found in the tomb of a scholar who refused to participate in what he saw as a corrupt government, it shows an emperor trying and failing to retrieve a bronze tripod from a pond. According to legend, only just rulers could possess this tripod. Here the first Qin emperor tries to get the tripod, but when the rope snaps, three henchmen on the left, and three henchmen on the right, tumble backward.

with detailed cartouches, explain who is being shown. The artist always selected a moment that represented the high point of the narrative. The founder of the Qin, the epitome of an evil ruler, tries to fish out a tripod from the water, where it had sunk with the fall of the Zhou. Because these tripods belonged only to the legitimate rulers of China, a dragon bites the rope, and the emperor's men are shown falling down at the moment the rope snaps.

Wu Liang's scope exceeded that of the Grand Historian. Like Sima, he depicted all of human history, but he went beyond him to show the land of the immortals, presided over by the Queen Mother of the West and her counterpart the King Father of the East, in the west and east gables of the shrine. The gables suggest the shrine was intended as a home both for his body-soul that would remain in the tomb, and for his spirit-soul that could travel to the realm of the immortals.

143

The Rise of the Organized Daoist Church

Uncertain of his support from the righteous scholars, Emperor Huan tried instead to tap support from members of a new religious movement, the Daoists. Daoist beliefs underwent a major transformation during the second century. In the previous century, the putative author of *The Way and Integrity Classic*, Laozi, had attracted followers who hoped they could attain immortality, as reported by the skeptic Wang Chong in his denunciation of Daoist beliefs. Starting sometime in the second century, Daoists began to believe that Laozi was a deity who could appear to his followers as a prophet and who could bring them salvation.

Even as a boy under the control of the regent Liang Ji, sometime between 146 and 149, Emperor Huan had founded a temple to Laozi. In 166 the emperor made a personal visit to the temple, where he made offerings to the deity Laozi. One source mentions that the emperor also prayed to the Buddha, a foreign deity from India who was often associated with Laozi during this early period. (See the next chapter for a full discussion of Buddhism.) Daoism, or the worship of Laozi, offered an alternative to Confucian teachings, which stressed one's obligation to father children so that they could worship one's ancestors.

The emperor's efforts to depict himself as a devout Daoist did not prevent a series of uprisings against the Han dynasty. Many of these peasant leaders claimed to have seen Laozi, who foretold the beginning of a new utopian era. The best documented and the most influential of these groups was based in the Hanzhong region in the mountains near the northern Yangzi River. They were known by two names: either the Celestial Masters or Five Pecks of Rice, which was the offering they asked from their followers. They dated their founding to A.D. 142 when their leader, a man named Zhang Daoling (originally Zhang Ling) had a vision of the deified Laozi who appointed Zhang to be his earthly representative. As described in a later source, Zhang Daoling was to found a purer religion in which the priests worshiped only clean gods and refused to accept money, hence the offerings of rice. The god and his earthly representative wrote up their pact on a piece of iron that they smeared with the blood of a white horse.

Much in Zhang Daoling's vision broke with earlier Daoist practices. Where earlier practitioners had taught only selected adepts breathing exercises, sexual techniques, and medical potions—all to enhance that individual's ability to attain immortality—Zhang shifted the focus of Daoist religion away from those few individuals to a larger lay community, who did not actively seek immortality. Zhang established a hierarchy for his church, in which the already initiated were called "libationers," a title suggesting they had the social honor equivalent to that of the elders who took the first drink at a village feast. The libationers presided over a section of the laity, who made offerings to the priesthood and promised to give up the worship of unclean gods who accepted meat offerings. In exchange, Zhang promised them good health. Zhang's biography in a later history explains, "They all taught the people to be sincere and not to lie. If anyone was sick, he had to confess his wrong-doings."[31] These Daoists linked illness with bad behavior: anyone who fell sick must have violated their teachings, and the libationers heard confessions before instructing the ill how to recover.

The Five Peck Daoists were active in Sichuan, a region that houses many non-Chinese minorities even today. Zhang Daoling grew up in Jiangsu, where he studied the traditional Daoist arts of making potions to seek immortality. Only after his move to Sichuan did he receive the revelation that allowed him to found a new Daoist church. The Chinese state often appointed local governors to serve as the hereditary rulers of such border states, and they did the same with the Five Peck Daoists, so that first Zhang Daoling, then his son, and then his grandson served as the local representative of the Chinese government.

Important continuities linked the practices of the Five Peck Daoists with earlier Daoist teachers like those described by Wang Chong. The Five Peck Daoists worshiped the Dao, in the person of the deified Laozi, and their members recited *The Way and Integrity Classic* as a means of curing illness. Another group of Daoists, called the Yellow Turbans, was active at the time in the area between the Yellow and the Huai rivers on the eastern coast of China, but they differed from the Five Peck Daoists in that they rebelled against Han-dynasty rule.

The Yellow Turban Revolt

The minimal information known about the Yellow Turbans reflects the point of view of official historians who saw these Daoists as dangerous insurrectionists, named for the yellow cloths they tied around their heads. The Yellow Turbans shared many practices with the Five Peck Daoists. Both groups considered illness a sign of wrongdoing, and both encouraged the confession of sins. The Yellow Turbans gave patients holy water as a cure; if the patients did not recover, their sins were assumed to be too great to be absolved.

A series of epidemics had broken out in the years leading up to 184, which may account for the Daoists' stress on curing illness. The Yellow

Turbans established their own religious hierarchy with a leader, a second tier of thirty-six adepts, and further divisions under the adepts. They claimed to inaugurate a new age, which they called the "Era of Great Peace (*taiping*)." (The Taiping rebels of the nineteenth century would use the same term some 1,700 years later.) The year 184 fell on the first year of the sixty-year cycle in the Chinese calendar, an auspicious year that they prophesied marked the beginning of a new epoch.

The Yellow Turbans found support at different social levels, spanning the peasants in the countryside, whose crops had been damaged by recent flooding of rivers, and eunuchs within the palace. The Yellow Turbans planned their rebellion for the third month of 184, but government officials discovered their plot ahead of time. The arrest of one adept, who had been in communication with some palace eunuchs, prompted all the adherents to rebel ahead of schedule. One source reports that 360,000 insurgents from 8 provinces joined the movement. The central government dispatched its own imperial troops, and it recruited the armies of several independent generals, including one named Cao Cao (155–220). The Daoist rebels proved no match for the combined forces, who captured and killed all the important leaders by the end of 184. Although a few rebel groups held out briefly, the Yellow Turbans disappeared as quickly as they had formed, leaving the Five Pecks as the only surviving Daoist group.

The Yellow Turban uprisings rattled the palace leadership. Emperor Huan was the last emperor to act on his own, and his decision to use eunuchs to attack the consort family of the Liangs ushered in decades of conflict between eunuchs and consort families in which the child emperors played no role at all. After Emperor Huan died in 168, three more emperors came to the throne, but each one was placed there by powerful consort families, who tangled with the eunuchs at their peril. In one memorable incident in 189, the eunuchs managed to wrest power from a consort family and to decapitate the reigning regent, tossing the severed head to those questioning their authority. The following year, the anti-eunuch forces, backed by a regional army, captured the emperor, forced the dowager to name a new emperor, moved the capital back to Changan, and took over the regency. In 192, Cao Cao, the general who had suppressed the Yellow Turbans, became regent. General Cao Cao went on to become one of the most famous generals in Chinese history and one of the leading protagonists of the great Chinese novel, *Three Kingdoms* (written in the fifteenth or sixteenth century), yet he never gained control of more than one-third of the empire. When Cao Cao died in 220, the Han-dynasty puppet-emperor was still in place, but he was forced to abdicate by Cao's son, who proclaimed himself the founder of a new dynasty. Three centuries of disunity ensued.

The Legacy of the Han Dynasty

Much remains unclear about the fall of the Han dynasty. The standard explanation argues that the empire experienced a massive shortfall of funds at the end of the second century, when the entire agrarian population became impoverished. Official sources describe the amassing of huge estates by dominant families in the countryside during the last two centuries of the dynasty, yet it seems they continued to pay their taxes for much of the period. The government was able to raise more funds by selling offices in the second century. Certainly the emperors had sufficient funds to maintain enormous households staffed by eunuchs, slaves, and palace women. Openly hostile sources estimate that Emperor Huan had six thousand women in his harem, and descriptions of the power struggle in 189 record the generals as killing some two thousand eunuchs.

It seems just as likely that economic growth continued during the first and second centuries A.D. but that the center found it increasingly difficult to tap that growth. Economic growth often prompts a widening of the gulf between rich and poor. The revolt of the Yellow Turbans might in fact have signaled an economic upsurge in the countryside, a surge the center could not tax. The many clauses of the fictive contract with the slave Bianliao, like the tomb tile from Sichuan, testify to the presence of an extensive market system that supported both a barter and a money economy.

The Qin and Han dynasties, like the Greek and Roman empires of Europe, left the imprint of a unified state in the minds of their citizens. They used the same standardized measures (with some regional variations), they wrote the same characters, they spent the same money, and they revered the same emperor. In the centuries immediately following the fall of the Han, as in those following the fall of Rome, leaders tried to reconquer the territory of the bygone empires. In this respect, the difference between China's and Europe's histories is striking. After three centuries of disunity, the Chinese restored the empire and stayed unified more often than divided. Europe, of course, remained divided, and it was for only brief stretches, as under Charlemagne, that any monarch could even claim to unite the European continent.

Even in areas not subject to government supervision, one can see a surprising degree of uniformity during the Qin and Han dynasties. Many of the most splendid archeological finds from the period are tombs, which show a common vision of the underworld. The Qin emperor's tomb, and the Qin clerk's tomb at Shuihudi in central China, testify to the belief that the deceased will continue their work—whether fighting enemy troops or drafting documents—even in the underworld. Lady Dai's lavish burial in a region farther south, in Changsha, equipped her with many supplies to remain in her tomb. But she was not certain that she would, and her T-shaped banner showed her both staying in her coffin and rising to the land of the immortals. Three centuries later, in eastern China, in Shandong, Wu Liang built a shrine for himself that could house both his body-soul, which would remain in the tomb, and his spirit-soul, which would travel, he hoped, to the upper gables of his shrine where the immortals dwelled.

Wu Liang belonged to a network of powerful people whose amorphousness frustrates social historians. His family must have owned land, and its male members sought official posts—unless they, like Wu Liang, felt government service would tarnish rather than contribute to their reputations as worthy scholars. They built the shrine to their father in hopes of further enhancing their reputations. Families like the Wus enjoyed a high rank in their localities, as did the families who supplied the emperors with their consorts. But what was the source of their power? Certainly not the civil service examinations, which did not become a standard means of recruitment until several centuries later. Nor could their position rest on aristocratic titles, which the Qin had abolished and which had died out by the end of the Han.

These landed, scholarly families stood at the top of a social model that had become widely accepted by the end of the Han dynasty. Peasants and artisans made something, so they ranked second and third, while merchants, who produced nothing, ranked at the bottom of the society. Merchants often sought ways to place their sons in the ranks of the privileged, and they must have had better luck than either peasants or artisans. By the end of the Han, women played the same subordinate roles they had at the beginning of the Qin. Even so, the brilliant literary career of Ban Zhao and the political success of the various dowager empresses proved women could break out of their traditional roles when given the opportunity.

During the four hundred years of Qin and Han rule, Chinese society assumed the contours it would retain for the rest of the imperial era, with a powerful, landed stratum of educated families at its top, but with movement among different social layers. The market economy of the Han and the government's role in regulating it also persisted. The one realm in which momentous change would come, and it came soon after the fall of the dynasty, was spiritual. The religious world of the Han, with its Confucian and Daoist poles, would be forced to admit a new, foreign religion, a religion whose first adherents had already entered China during the Han, but whose missionaries would become influential only after the dynasty's close.

FACING WEST

(A.D. 200–1000)

CHRONOLOGY

ca. 500 B.C.	*Lifetime of the historical Buddha*
65 A.D.	*Earliest mention of the Buddha in a Chinese document*
220–589	SIX DYNASTIES PERIOD OF DIVISION
ca. 300–ca. 350	*An Lingshou converts more than 200 nuns to Buddhism*
300–400	*Numinous Treasure (Lingbao) and Mao Shan schools of Daoism formed*
300–400	*Buddhist cave paintings done at Kizil, Kucha*
310–349	*Fotudeng propagates Buddhism in China*
311	*Fall of Luoyang to troops led by Shi Le*
344–413	*Lifetime of Kumarajiva, translator of Buddhist texts*
386–534	NORTHERN WEI DYNASTY OF THE TABGACH (XIANBEI) PEOPLE RULES NORTH CHINA
399–414	*Faxian travels to India and back to China*
485	*Equal field system of land redistribution promulgated by Northern Wei*
547–550	*Yang Xuanzhi compiles* Record of the Monasteries of Luoyang
502–557	LIANG DYNASTY RULES SOUTH CHINA
before 589	*Yan Zhitui,* The Family Counsels of Mr. Yan

CHINA'S RELIGIOUS LANDSCAPE

(200–600)

No one in the year 200 could have predicted how much China's religious landscape would change by the year 600. One of the new religions, Daoism, had roots going back to at least the fourth century B.C., but a lay community took shape only in the years after Zhang Daoling's vision of A.D. 142. The other religion to spread in this period, Buddhism, was founded in India. Despite its origins as a foreign religion, Buddhism won more Chinese followers than did Daoism. Buddhist teachings of chastity required the family-loving Chinese to live in monasteries, to forgo marriage, and worst of all, to violate their obligation to carry on the family line. Buddhist religious texts were written in Sanskrit, a language that could not have been more different from classical Chinese. Still, Buddhism offered a far more optimistic view of the afterlife than did the indigenous Chinese view of harsh underworld jails for most of the dead, with the realm of the immortals reserved for only a few. By the year 600, China had become a predominantly Buddhist country with a landscape dotted with thousands of monasteries.

Many reasons underlay the Buddhists' success. Most important, they were willing to absorb elements of preexisting religions. As in other countries, Buddhist missionaries assimilated many local deities as guardians, and especially in the early years, they drew on a largely Daoist vocabulary to introduce their teachings. Although the Buddhist and Daoist clergy attacked each other, sometimes bitterly, the Chinese populace saw no contradiction in continuing to worship Buddhist, Daoist, and local deities at the same time.

During these centuries of political disunity, Buddhist missionaries gar-

China Divided: The Six
Dynasties Period (220–589)

XIONGNU CONFEDERACY

Liao River

YIN SHAN

*Yellow River
(Huang He)*

Dunhuang

⊛ Pingcheng

Wuwei

NORTHERN WEI

Liangzhou

Luoyang

Changan

Huai River

Nanjing

Yangzi River

EAST
CHINA
SEA

SOUTH
CHINA
SEA

0   250   500 Miles
0   250   500 Kilometers

nered far more support from China's different regional rulers than did
their Daoist rivals. Local kings patronized Buddhists rather than Daoists
in the hope of fulfilling the Buddhist ideal of the *cakravartin* (literally
"wheel-turning") king, who governed well because of his pious acts. They
provided public funds to finance the construction of large imperial
monasteries and the translation of Buddhist texts into Chinese. All over
China, local governments excavated huge cave complexes, some hewn
out of rock, others dug out of sandstone, in order to express their devotion to the new religion. On the walls of these caves, artists painted some
of China's most striking religious and secular scenes.

Long-lasting political instability marked the centuries of China's conversion to Buddhism. For the three centuries after the fall of the Han dynasty, often called the Six Dynasties (220–589), no regime succeeded in
conquering more than half of China's territory. In many periods, one
government prevailed in the north while another ruled the south.

THE FIRST BUDDHISTS IN CHINA

The earliest Buddhists, who were foreign merchants from Central Asia and India, first arrived in the Chinese capital sometime near the beginning of the Christian era. In Luoyang, these traders established small, self-contained communities of believers who remained largely isolated from the Chinese.

From its inception in India, Buddhism had been associated with trade. In his attempts to win followers, the Buddha (ca. 500 B.C.) focused on cities rather than the countryside, for there he found merchants who provided crucial financial support. The first Chinese converts saw the Buddha as a particularly powerful foreign god who could help them if they prayed to him. We have seen (in chapter 3) how Emperor Huan worshiped the Buddha at the same time that he worshiped the deified Laozi, as did many Chinese during the second and third centuries. Like the deified Laozi, the Buddha was thought to have attained immortality. Early sources state that he could fly from one place to another and that he emitted light. This belief in miracles underlay many early conversions.

The earliest mention of Buddha in a Chinese document occurs in the dynastic *History of the Later Han*. The emperor issued an edict in A.D. 65 praising a prince in Pengcheng, a city in northern Jiangsu, for his respectful performance of "the gentle sacrifices to the Buddha,"[1] whom he worshiped alongside the Daoist deity, Laozi. The officials who drafted the edict already knew some of the specialized vocabulary of Buddhism. They used awkward Chinese transcriptions to convey the Sanskrit terms for lay believer and monks, and referred to "gentle sacrifices," at which no animals were killed. Foreign monks were already active in Luoyang at the time. In A.D. 148 the famous missionary An Shigao from Parthia, southeast of the Caspian Sea, arrived in Luoyang, where he began to work on translating Sanskrit texts into Chinese. Some of his translations survive today in the Buddhist canon, a gigantic compilation of Buddhist texts. The language of the early translations tends to be simple, with a limited vocabulary, as if the Chinese authors transcribed the oral teachings of their foreign preachers.

The written records of the time, whether from the official histories or from the Buddhist canon, remain biased toward the activities of the highborn and the literate, many of whom lived in the capital. Because such sources reveal little about the activities of ordinary people, archeologists have devoted much effort in recent years to uncovering the traces of early Buddhism in widely separated places.

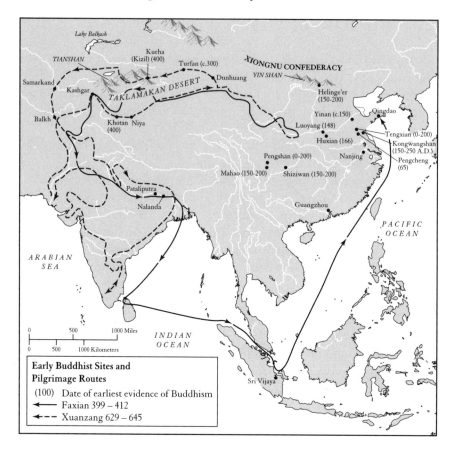

Early Buddhist Sites and Pilgrimage Routes

(100) Date of earliest evidence of Buddhism

→—— Faxian 399 – 412

←- - - Xuanzang 629 – 645

Early Buddhist Art at Kongwang Mountain (Kongwangshan)

Of all these early Buddhist sites, the most interesting—and the most puzzling—must be Kongwang Mountain, near the coast of Jiangsu. Although it lies some ten miles from the China Sea today, it probably
overlooked the sea at the time it was built, in the late second or third century. Its coastal location suggests that the first Buddhist missionaries from
India may have traveled to China by boat. Local stonemasons carved reliefs on the surface of the rock and slightly modified the outlines of free-
standing rocks to make statues. The rock reliefs show some classic scenes
from the Buddha's life, such as the nirvana scene in which the dying Buddha lay on his side surrounded by his disciples.

The Mount Kongwang artists used symbols that had meaning both in
Buddhism and in indigenous Chinese religion, like the large elephant
carved into the side of a cliff. Because an elephant appeared to the Bud-

dha's mother before she gave birth, the elephant had clear Buddhist associations, reinforced at Mount Kongwang by the lotus flowers carved onto his feet. To the Chinese the elephant was an auspicious sign, whose appearance signaled Heaven's approval of the emperor's rule. To the Buddhists, the beautiful lotus flower emerging from dirty water represented the possibility of salvation even for sinful humans.

No written materials survive from this unusual site, and the mixing of indigenous and Buddhist elements has caused some to suggest that the elephant was a survival from an earlier temple to an ocean god, which the Buddhists later took over. Frequently, new proselytizing religions incorporated artistic elements from the preexisting belief systems. We see this pattern with the advent of Buddhism to Mount Kongwang. Buddha came into China quietly, often in the company of indigenous deities, and early devotees probably did not recognize him as an alien god.

The Successors to the Han Dynasty

The Buddhist missionaries who came to China in the third century found a confused political situation. The Han dynasty was succeeded by three regional kingdoms: one in the north led by General Cao Cao, one in the south, and one in the west in today's Sichuan province. Although engaged in war, General Cao Cao had a bureaucracy to staff, and later historians trace the creation of the system of nine grades to his administration. In principle, a local official, called the impartial judge, was supposed to assign each candidate for office a rank from one to nine, depending on his accomplishments and his moral standing. Candidates were then assigned official posts commensurate with their ranks. Men born to good families were assumed to have the requisite moral standing. Once the impartial judge had categorized the families of his region, his task became far simpler, since he could assign to sons ranks that were identical to those of their fathers. Even in the system's early years, contemporary critics pointed out that men of talent but low birth could not get government appointments, unlike those of high birth but no talent. Their comments suggest that the pattern established during the Han dynasty persisted: as long as officials received appointments on the basis of recommendation, the sons of powerful families had a significant advantage over those from less-prominent families.

The Nine-Grade system survived the many changes of power occurring from the third to the sixth centuries. In 265, General Cao Cao's heirs lost power to one of the dominant families under them. The Sima family founded the Jin dynasty, who ruled for barely half a century before they too were subsumed in the War of Eight Princes (290–306), a long and costly civil war among eight different rulers. North China then entered a long period of division, during which no less than sixteen different states ruled in separate areas, with the Jin retaining control of the former Han-dynasty capital at Luoyang. Although the site of many battles, Luoyang remained an imposing city in the early fourth century. Magnificent imperial roads, with reserved lanes for the ruler and his highest ministers, divided the city, while the mother-of-pearl blinds on the splendid buildings of the palace shimmered in the changing light of day.

The Fall of Luoyang

In 311, the previously unthinkable occurred. The Xiongnu, the northern people who had defeated the Han dynasty, conquered the former capital, Luoyang, in what was easily the most dramatic political event of the time. Like the sacking of Rome in 410, the loss of Luoyang shocked its residents, who saw themselves as the center of civilization. Like the citizens of Rome, those living in Luoyang forgot that the unlettered people of the steppes had cavalry far swifter and an army far more powerful than their own.

A letter by a Persian merchant, who wrote in his native dialect to an associate in Samarkand, records his shock that "those Huns [Xiongnu] who were yesterday the Emperor's vassals" have kidnapped the emperor himself:

> And, Sir, the last Emperor—so they say—fled from Luoyang because of the famine. And his fortified residence (palace) and fortified town were set on fire. . . . So Luoyang is no more.[2]

This letter, along with four other complete letters and a few fragments, came from a mailbag abandoned in Dunhuang, where it was found at the beginning of the twentieth century. At least one of the letters was in an envelope addressed to Samarkand, some 3,220 kilometers (2,000 miles) to the west. These important letters describe communities of foreign merchants, from both India and Persia, in several major Chinese cities.

The Appeal of Buddhism to the Northern Rulers

The ruler who conquered Luoyang, Shi Le (274–333) belonged to one of the tribes in the Xiongnu confederation. Although he understood spoken Chinese, he could neither read nor write the classical language. Born to a Xiongnu chieftain, he was kidnapped around the age of twenty-five and sold into slavery to the Chinese. Assigned to tend the stables of a Chinese official, he escaped and joined a gang who successfully robbed different places in north China. His retinue grew into an army. In 310, just as his followers were about to take Luoyang, one of his generals introduced him to the Buddhist missionary Fotudeng (d. 349). The leader asked him about the miracles of Buddhism. The monk's biographer, writing in the early sixth century on the basis of earlier materials, explains that the monk realized that the ruler would not understand the complexity of Buddhist doctrine:

> Thereupon he took his begging bowl, filled it with water, burned incense, and said a spell over it. In a moment there sprang up blue lotus flowers whose brightness and color dazzled the eyes.[3]

The ruler was impressed, and he subsequently granted the Buddhists the right to build monasteries, a decision that allowed them to gain an important foothold in the north.

Because of Fotudeng's privileged relationship with the ruler, much material survives concerning his proselytizing activities and his magical abilities. He was able to bring rain on command, and he used Indian medicine to cure the ill. His biographer credits him with the ability to predict the future because, after he smeared his palm with dust, events in other places came into view. One does not have to believe that these events actually occurred to understand their importance; the news of Fotudeng's miracles fostered the spread of Buddhism.

Buddhism offered non-Chinese rulers an alternative to Confucianism, which empowered literate Chinese officials. Several years after Fotudeng had won over the ruler Shi Le, one official, a Mr. Du, complained that too many people had joined the clergy. He urged the ruler to forbid the Chinese to convert and to himself refrain from worshiping Buddha. Mr. Du's suggestion was rejected, and one high minister explained why:

> Du's argument is that Buddha is a deity of foreign lands and is not one whom it is proper for the emperor and the Chinese to worship. We were born in a border region, and though We are unworthy, We have complied with our appointed destiny and govern the Chinese as their prince. As to sacrifices, we should follow our own customs, equally [with those of the Chinese]. Buddha being a deity of the Rong people to the west is the very one we should worship.

In short, non-Chinese like Shi Le were drawn to Buddhism simply because the religion did not originate in China.

The Ordination of Women

Fotudeng attracted students of both sexes to the clergy. *Lives of the Nuns* gives biographical information about sixty-five women who became nuns in the fourth to sixth centuries. Most were well-born; fifty-three could read and write. One woman founded a nunnery after Fotudeng met her father. When the girl, named An Lingshou, explained that she did not want to marry, her father, like many other fathers, objected: "You ought to marry. How can you be like this?" She explained, "My mind is concentrated on the work of religion, and my thought dwells exclusively on spiritual matters. . . . Why must I submit thrice to father, husband, and son, before I am considered a woman of propriety?" Her response has a curiously modern ring, for she objects to the three submissions all women were asked to perform: to their fathers and elder brothers when young, to their husbands in middle age, and to their sons when elderly. To her father's charge of selfishness, she replied, "I am setting myself to cultivate the Way exactly because I want to free all living beings from suffering. How much more, then, do I want to free my two parents!"[4]

This dialogue, which must have taken place in homes all over China, rehearses the main themes of the conflict between the individual's obligation to the family and the Buddhist call for salvation. An Lingshou denies any selfish motivation by arguing that she seeks to bring salvation to all, including her parents. The Buddhist doctrine of the transfer of merit, by which someone could give merit he or she had accumulated to someone else, underlay An Lingshou's argument. A monk or a nun could transfer the merit they accrued by joining the clergy to their families, while their families could accrue merit by supporting the clergy.

In An Lingshou's case, such arguments did not persuade her father. Fotudeng then spread sesame oil and safflower onto her father's palm, where he saw a woman in monastic robes preaching about Buddhism. Fotudeng explained that this was his daughter in a former life, and her father finally granted his consent.

Joining a nunnery offered Chinese women a rare alternative to family life, and the Buddhists succeeded in recruiting many nuns. An Lingshou herself is said to have converted more than two hundred nuns and to have established five or six monasteries. The other women in *Lives of the Nuns* are also torn between their vocation and their obligations to their families. Some care for ailing parents or mourn three years after their deaths; some resist marriage while others marry and bear children before joining a nunnery. All these women faced a major difficulty in that the rules governing the ordination of nuns, which differed from those for monks, had yet to be translated into Chinese, an event that finally occurred in the 370s or 380s, when a group of Sri Lankan nuns taught the Chinese nuns the correct vows for women. Anyone ordained before that date could not be certain that she had followed the correct procedures.

The Difficulties of Translating Buddhist Concepts

Like all nuns, all other Chinese Buddhists needed to have usable, workable translations of the original Indian texts. Although Buddha had preached in his own dialect of Magadhi, his teachings were transmitted orally and first written down in Sanskrit only during the first and second centuries A.D. Religious teachings can be very difficult to translate accurately, especially when the translator is bridging a gap between two dissimilar languages like Sanskrit and Chinese. The two languages each had a long literary tradition stretching back to at least the second millennium B.C. They belong to different language families: Chinese, a group of languages normally written in characters, belongs to Sino-Tibetan, while Sanskrit, which has an alphabet, is Indo-European. In Chinese, nouns have only one case, verbs one tense. (One has to use particles of completion or the addition of words like "yesterday" and "tomorrow" to show tense.) The ancient religious language of Sanskrit preserves many archaic conjugations and declinations so that verbs have different endings for the past, present, and future, and for first, second, and third person—singular, two-person, and plural.

The different cultural assumptions of the two societies posed a different challenge to translators. Because Indians talked about sex much more freely than the Chinese, the cautious translators dropped any mention of kissing and hugging. Buddhism offered women greater freedom than they enjoyed in family life, yet the Chinese translators changed the original "husband supports wife" to say "husband controls his wife," while "wife comforts the husband" was altered to become "wife reveres her husband."[5]

A far more confusing strategy adopted by the Chinese translators was to use Daoist equivalents for unfamiliar concepts. Buddhist texts used an overwhelming number of new terms, all crucial to an understanding of Buddhist teaching. Because early translators feared that a Chinese readership would not be able to understand such unfamiliar teachings, they opted instead to translate an unfamiliar Buddhist term into a familiar Daoist term. One can understand the logic of their decision. Nirvana literally meant extinction or the dying out of a fire in Sanskrit, but in Buddhism it took on the specific meaning of gaining enlightenment, as the

Buddha did when he died surrounded by his disciples. The early translators thought the nearest Chinese equivalent was *wuwei* ("letting things follow their own natural course," the most important teaching of the Daoist text, *The Way and Integrity Classic*), yet the word *wuwei* hardly conveyed the difficult concept of nirvana. Only someone with an extensive knowledge of Buddhist teachings, and even of Sanskrit perhaps, could make sense of such a translation, yet very few Chinese managed to master Sanskrit.

Another concept that proved difficult to translate was *karma*. (American slang, too, has distorted the meaning of this term so that it has the sense of aura or vibes, as in "she has good karma.") Early Buddhist teachings held that each individual was constantly in flux. As one scholar explains, "One is born as the self of today, a self that has transcended yesterday, as a result of one's own acts up to and including yesterday, and that in the same way one will change into the self of tomorrow."[6] One is the ceaselessly changing product of all of one's actions. As one changes from day to day, one's essence changes on death as well. Depending on what one had done in the course of one's life—and all of one's previous existences—one could be reborn as an animal or as a person. This view of a soul constantly in flux ran directly counter to the traditional Chinese view that one's self remained constant, even when traveling to the underworld. Lady Dai of the Mawangdui T-shaped banner looked basically the same, whether alive or in the realm of the immortals. Although early Buddhist teachers tried to teach this subtle idea of karma, the Chinese tenaciously clung to their view of an underworld to which one traveled in one's own body.

Kumarajiva and the New Translations

Private individuals sponsored the first translations of Buddhist doctrine, which had a curiously archaic feeling. In many cases a non-Chinese monk, who was from Central Asia or from India, came to China where he lived with a group of Chinese devotees. After he explained a text to them, they did their best to transcribe his translation. The next generation of translators was able to achieve a much higher level of accuracy and readability because of the imperial funding they received. In the first large-scale, publicly financed translation project of its type, the regional ruler brought the brilliant Central Asian monk, Kumarajiva (344–413), to Changan, where he managed a translation bureau starting in 401. He and his collaborators produced thirty-nine different texts in over three hundred chapters, many of which are still read today. Kumarajiva was very much the product of Central Asia, which provided many important translators and interpreters of Buddhism for the Chinese.

BUDDHISM IN CENTRAL ASIA: THE EXAMPLE OF THE KUCHA KINGDOM

As a boy, Kumarajiva was trained by a monk in Kucha (or Kuche), an oasis state in Central Asia, where his father, born to a high-ranking ministerial family in India, had emigrated so that he could study Buddhism full-time. Although Kucha is now part of China's Xinjiang Autonomous Region, it was an independent kingdom during Kumarajiva's lifetime and came under direct Chinese rule for a brief period only during the seventh century. Even today one hears little Chinese in Kucha; most of the inhabitants, who belong to the Uighur people, speak a Turkic language.

The ruler of Kucha married his devout younger sister to Kumarajiva's father. When Kumarajiva reached seven, his mother decided to pursue her religious vocation and to become a nun, but her husband opposed her decision. On the sixth day of her hunger strike, he acquiesced, with the result that both mother and young son joined the Buddhist clergy.

During Kumarajiva's lifetime, Kucha had a population of ten thousand monks in a town of some one hundred thousand inhabitants. Just outside of Kucha are China's earliest Buddhist caves, in the small town of Kizil. There artists, quite possibly trained in India or using sketchbooks from India, painted with vivid lapis lazuli blues and malachite greens, pigments that remain startlingly fresh even today. They showed scenes from the Buddha's former lives, the so-called jataka tales. These classical Indian animal fables stressed the virtue of people and animals who sacrificed themselves to save other living beings.

Early Buddhist Art at the Kizil Caves

The Kizil caves testify to the sudden increase in Buddhist activity in the region. One of several cave complexes in the area, the Kizil caves strike all visitors with their stunningly preserved, vibrantly colored paintings. There workmen dug out caves from the hillside of conglomerate. Once the walls were even, artists prepared an undersurface of hair or textile to cover the conglomerate, which they then covered with plaster. Since they waited for the plaster to dry before painting on it, strictly speaking these paintings do not constitute frescoes, which are painted on wet plaster.

Carbon-14 testing dates the first human occupation of the Kizil caves to the first century B.C., but the earliest cave, which has both a wall oven and a window, shows no uniquely Buddhist features.[7] At the site, a small stream, picturesquely named the Spring of Tears, trickles down the face of a nearby rock. Even today one can hear the singing of a cuckoo at Kizil, a rare sound in densely settled China.

The first signs of Buddhism at Kizil date to the fourth century A.D., during Kumarajiva's lifetime, when the paintings were done. One of the earliest caves, cave 38, is also one of the most beautifully decorated. It has been carbon-dated to 320 ± 80.[8] Cave 38 now has two rooms: a central room with an arched ceiling, and a back room around a central pillar. Originally a third anteroom existed, but it has collapsed, probably because of an earlier earthquake, a reminder of how fragile the caves are. The people who dug these caves probably never imagined that they would survive over fifteen hundred years. Another threat, this one man-made, has damaged the caves, including cave 38. The most beautiful ceiling paintings all have gashes where collectors removed portions of them, often to take to Germany or Japan, in the early years of the twentieth century.

When one enters cave 38 today, one sees a niche for an image of the Buddha cut into a blank wall with holes going up to the cave ceiling. Wooden sculptures of trees and rocks were originally placed in these holes to create Mount Sumeru, the Buddhist mountain at the heart of the cosmos. The passageway to the left and right of the central pillar leads to a back room, where the Buddha is painted lying down in a nirvana scene. (One can see his halo on the back wall on the left-hand side.) The central pillar serves as a support for the cave, and it is the Chinese version of a stupa, a column built over the Buddha's relics. Worshipers in India circumambulated around stupas to express their devotion to the Buddha. Similarly, Buddhist devotees in China walked through the passage around the central column of the cave.

Turning around to face the door, one sees a picture of the Maitreya Buddha, the Buddha who presides over a future paradise. The most striking paintings in the cave appear on the spine of the arched roof in this central room. The artist has painted the universe in the Indian way. Four wild geese fly around the sun and moon gods. Unlike the Chinese sun god with his raven (seen in the Mawangdui T-shaped banner), this depiction of the Indian sun god shows him as a spinning spoked wheel. Between the sun and the moon stand two flaming Buddhas, two wind gods, and a two-headed garuda, with snakes in both mouths. The garuda, a legendary bird from India, became a protector of the Buddhist law after his conversion.

Among the earliest Buddhist art along the Silk Road are the paintings on the walls of the caves in Kizil, in northwest China, a small kingdom whose residents spoke Tokharian, a lost Indo-European language. The paintings there are so Indian in style that scholars debate whether Indian artists came to the site to paint or whether local artists copied the motifs from pattern books brought from India.

This view is looking straight up at the ceiling of the cave. Along the center axis of the ceiling the artist has painted the Buddhist universe. The blank areas originally contained paintings that were removed by German explorers at the beginning of the century and taken to Berlin.

On both sides of the ceiling appear the characteristic lozenges of Kizil. Like postage stamps, their uneven borders fit together to form an intensely colored background of blue, green, white, and tan. Each diamond contains a scene showing the dramatic high point of a legend about the Buddha. The *avadana* stories, sometimes called cause-and-effect stories, are allegories in which the haloed, seated Buddha appears, with a figure on the side. Appearing in the alternate bands are the *jataka* stories, which tell about Buddha's activities in earlier lives.

The *jataka* stories are based on ancient Indian legends, to which Buddhist interpreters have added an extra layer of interpretation to emphasize the sanctity of all life. In one famous scene, a monkey uses his body as a bridge for two other monkeys. This illustrates the story of the mis-

Early Buddhist Teachings

The paintings at Kizil provide a glimpse of how the early Buddhist missionaries spread the message of Buddhism. They used techniques developed in India of giving popular folk tales a Buddhist twist.

In this example, a monkey uses his body as a bridge for two other monkeys. This illustrates the story of the playful monkeys who stole food from the king's garden. When the king ordered his men to pursue them, the monkeys ran to a river, which they could not cross until their king made a bridge from his body for them. After they crossed, he fell into the river and died. Buddhists reinterpreted this story about the monkeys' ingenuity to say that it showed the king's willingness to sacrifice himself for his fellow monkeys, proving he had been the Buddha in a former life.

chievous monkeys who stole food from the king's garden. When the king ordered his men to pursue them, the monkeys ran to a river, which they could not cross until their king made a bridge out of his body for them. After they crossed, he fell into the river and died. The Kizil picture shows the hunter crouching at the bottom of the lozenge, where he aims his bow at the monkeys (see the accompanying illustration). The

Buddhists reinterpreted this story about the monkeys' ingenuity to say that it showed the king's willingness to sacrifice himself for his fellow monkeys. The monkey king, the story explained, was the Buddha in a former life.

MERCHANT SUPPORT FOR EARLY BUDDHISM

The early Buddhist missionaries received important financial support from merchants, who often traveled together with them. This painting from Kizil depicts a scene in which the Buddha uses his hands as torches to light the way for the merchant who stands beside him, his ox laden with trade goods. This picture underlines the importance of merchants to the Buddhist establishment.

Although the *jataka* stories number in the hundreds, a few were painted over and over again. Many of these, which tell of various animals saving merchants from the perils of long-distance travel, underline the enduring link between commerce and Buddhism in its formative stages. One of the diamonds in cave 38 shows a Buddha figure lifting his hands, which have been transformed into torches, above his head to light the way for the merchant who accompanies him. Educated Buddhists would have explained the tales as their listeners gazed at the beautiful ceiling paintings.

Halfway down the wall, the arched ceiling joins the wider cave wall, leaving an underlip about one foot across. There, artists painted a waterscape including ducks, water snakes, and seashells, which vividly conveys the liveliness of aquatic life. The jewels with three upward prongs and one downward prong are *mani* jewels, a symbol of purity, that can clear turbid waters. They make it possible to see dangers lurking in the water, like the monsters with tubed bodies and animal faces. Below this band, on the wall underneath, is a row of seated Buddhas. Other caves duplicate the layout of cave 38 at Kizil, with its central column, Mount Sumeru, preaching Maitreya, and nirvana scene, but none with the same exquisite artistry.

Cave 38 was dug sometime around the year 400. The high quality of the painting suggests that a royal donor may have financed its construction, but no records survive. The Kucha king did pay for the digging of an enormous cave at the turn of the fifth century. In the face of the mountain stood a giant Buddha, now gone, that stood 16 meters (52.5 feet) tall. Around him were five stories of Buddhist images, also missing, although

ANIMALS IN BUDDHIST ART

Chinese art of the day rarely shows animals, but this Central Asian painting of A.D. 400 depicts a waterscape with ducks, water snakes, and seashells, and vividly conveys the Buddhist view that all living things are precious.

the holes for the posts that held up the wooden frames are still visible. This monumental art made a statement about the Kucha king's power to all who visited, for the cave was visible from the main northern trade route around the Taklamakan Desert, whose dry climate helped to preserve the cave paintings. Everyone would have followed the course of the Muzat River, literally the ice river, named for its source in the snow-capped peaks of the Tianshan Mountains. Other Buddhist cave sites, whether those near Kizil or elsewhere in Xinjiang, have similar geographic settings. Surrounded by the reddish-gray rocky desert, they overlook verdant green oases on both sides of a crystal-clear stream. The great translator Kumarajiva grew up in this setting.

Kumarajiva and the Teachings of the Lesser and Greater Vehicles

Kumarajiva studied Buddhist texts in Sanskrit and spoke Tokharian, an Indo-European language, at home. As a boy he may have learned some Chinese from merchants who came to Kucha. Kidnapped by a ruler who sought to tap his religious powers, he resided in north China, in the city of Liangzhou, Gansu, for seventeen years, where he mastered Chinese. In 401, when he arrived in Changan some 500 kilometers (300 miles) to the west, he had become a believer in the Greater Vehicle tradition.

Practitioners of the Greater Vehicle (Mahayana) coined the pejorative but easy-to-remember Lesser Vehicle (Hinayana) name for the earlier teachings, which dated back to the first centuries of Buddhist teachings. By Kumarajiva's time, Buddhists in both India and China subscribed to new beliefs, which they called the Greater Vehicle. These two labels subsumed many teachings, but it is possible to sketch the major differences between them. The Lesser Vehicle school held nirvana possible only for the few who joined the Buddhist clergy, while the proponents of the Greater Vehicle offered salvation even to those who remained in the laity. In line with the Buddha's original teachings, the Lesser Vehicle discouraged the worship of Buddhist images; the Greater Vehicle encouraged the building of massive images, like the one the Kucha king paid for at Kizil. Also, the teachers of the Lesser Vehicle regarded the Buddha as a great teacher, but very much a human being; those in the Greater Vehicle saw the Buddha as a divine being capable of great miracles.

Starting in 401, Kumarajiva summoned skilled translators and knowledgeable monks from all over north China to join his project. Working in groups, with a clear procedure of initial drafts and cross-checking, they eschewed the use of inexact Daoist terms for Buddhist ideas and introduced a new vocabulary of loanwords from Sanskrit. Although initially confusing to the inexperienced Chinese reader, this vocabulary enabled people to talk about Buddhist teachings with far greater precision than before. The enormous number of translations done by Kumarajiva made it possible for Chinese to understand the differences between the teachings of the Lesser and Greater Vehicles. Other rulers sponsored translation projects like Kumarajiva's, and the number of texts available in Chinese increased dramatically in the years after 400.

Contact between India and China

As Kumarajiva's biography reveals, the overland trade routes linking India and China received much traffic during this period of political instability. Chinese sources mention pilgrims going to India as early as 260. One pilgrim, Faxian, left a detailed record of his search for the Sanskrit originals of monastic regulations in the flourishing oasis states between China and India. Departing in 399, he traveled for thirteen years on an established tourist route including the region of India where the Buddha preached, the site of the Buddha's first sermon, and the place where he achieved nirvana. Frustrated in his search for written texts by the prevalence of India's oral traditions, Faxian at last found documents in Pataliputra, on the Ganges River. He stayed for three years, paying scribes to record the lectures of Buddhist teachers.

Faxian set off on the return journey by boat alone. In Sri Lanka, he visited an image of the Buddha made out of jade and decorated with the seven precious substances that was 6.6 meters (22 feet) tall. In the first personal insight of his entire narrative, he admits to homesickness:

> All at once, as he was standing by the side of this jade figure, he beheld a merchant present to it as a religious offering a white silk fan of Chinese manufacture. Unwittingly Faxian gave way to his sorrowful feelings, and the tears flowing down filled his eyes.[9]

The Chinese fan had made the long journey all the way to Sri Lanka, where the monk sees it being given by a merchant to a monastery, possibly in thanks for a safe trip, a transaction that must have been repeated countless times along the trade route.

Faxian remained in Sri Lanka for two years, during which time he acquired more texts, and then he joined a merchant boat carrying two hundred passengers. When his boat was engulfed in a terrifying storm on the way to Indonesia, Faxian prayed with all his might to a bodhisattva named Avalokitesvara, who had been depicted with male features in India but in Chinese Buddhism became a female deity with the name Guanyin. Bodhisattvas were beings who had given up their own chance for enlightenment so they could help humankind attain salvation. Buddhists credited bodhisattvas with miraculous powers, including the ability to protect a ship at sea.

The storm passed, and the ship landed somewhere in Java or Sumatra, where the monk waited five months for a ship going to China. This last leg would prove to be the most difficult of all. Carrying two hundred people, his ship held rations for a trip of fifty days to the southern port of Guangzhou. After a month at sea, the ship was caught in a storm, and again Faxian prayed to the bodhisattva Avalokitesvara. The next morning his travel companions, all high-caste Brahmans from India, consulted with each other:

> It is because we have got this Buddhist monk on board we have no luck, and have incurred this great mischief. Come, let us land this monk on any island we meet, and let us not all perish for the sake of one man.

A merchant then threatened to report the men if they hurt the monk. Faxian uses a loanword from Sanskrit, *danapati* (literally "lord of alms," or "donor"), to refer to the man who spoke up on his behalf, and the men let the monk go unharmed. Just as groups of merchants supported monasteries, an individual merchant had provided Faxian with his travel expenses.

After the ship had traveled seventy days with no sight of land, it shifted course. The crew began to cook with salt water, and they divided the last of the freshwater among the passengers. They traveled for another twelve days before touching shore. They sent Faxian, apparently the only Chinese speaker on board, to determine their location. When he returned, he reported that they had landed at Qingdao, a port on the southern coast of the Shandong peninsula, 1,600 kilometers (1,000 miles) off course. No wonder the trip had taken so long.

The Silk Road

The romantic term *silk road* has fired the imagination since the German geographer Ferdinand Paul Wilhelm Freiherr von Richtoven (ancestor of the World War I flying ace, the Red Baron) first coined it in the 1870s to describe the ancient trade route between Rome and China. As early as

This figurine from the eighth century of a merchant dozing on his camel shows how goods were transported along the Silk Road. Although many people conceive of the Silk Road as if it were a highway like I-80 stretching all the way from Rome to China, very few people actually traveled from one end point to another. Most merchants (like the one depicted here) traveled only from one trading depot to the next, where they exchanged goods with other merchants, who then took the merchandise on to the next trading depot.

the Roman Empire, the writer Pliny ranted against the luxurious lifestyle of his fun-loving contemporaries, claiming that enormous quantities of Chinese silk had entered Rome. As further evidence for the link between China and the silk trade, the Latin word for silk, *serica*, derives from the Greek name for China, Seres.

Yet, contrary to this image, no single Silk Road stretched all the way from Rome to China. The most frequented routes out of China led to India, where Faxian traveled, or to Persia. While it is unlikely that any individual traveler went all the way from Rome to China, a few individual pieces of Chinese silk may have made the journey after being traded from one merchant to another. Recently, an unusual find of silk at Uzbekistan has prompted some to date the earliest export of Chinese silk to ca. 1200 B.C. (Because the Chinese removed the gelatinous protein sericin from the silk they unraveled from cocoons, while those who used a different type of silkworm did not, archeologists can distinguish Chinese silk from lesser imitations.) The discovery of Caucasian corpses in northwest China's Xinjiang province indicates that a route to China from Eurasia was open as early as 1200 B.C. The presence of the geographic features—river valleys skirting deserts, oases, mountain passes—that made overland travel so feasible has prompted some to speculate that the routes from China to Europe were open as early as 20,000 B.C.

The Chinese textiles that traveled all the way to Europe in ancient times remain the exception rather than the rule. When Zhang Qian traveled west for the Han emperor Wu in the second century B.C., the Chinese still dominated the world silk trade because only they knew how to process silkworms. Legend has it that the Chinese lost their monopoly when a Chinese bride smuggled the first silk cocoon out in her hair when she traveled to marry a Central Asian prince. By the fourth or fifth century A.D., silk was made in Persia, India, and Byzantium, as well as China. The Byzantine emperors took measures to develop their own silk industry, and they became very successful exporters of silk to Europe.

THE SECRET OF MAKING SILK

One legend told that the Chinese lost the secret of making silk when a Chinese bride smuggled the first silk cocoon out in her hair as she went to meet her husband, a Central Asian prince. In this painting of the legend on a wooden panel, the attendant on the left points to the cocoon hidden in the princess's hair. By the fifth century, the Chinese had indeed lost their monopoly on silk, as silk production had begun in both India and Byzantium.

Analysis of over one thousand pieces of silk found in European churches has produced only one definitively Chinese piece, indicating that much of the so-called Chinese silk in Europe was actually made in Byzantium.

Chinese Exports of Silk to India

Even after the Chinese lost their monopoly, they retained a competitive edge because their superior technology produced more densely woven silks with more complex weaves. The Chinese began to produce export silks with special motifs aimed at the Indian market. Although no ancient Chinese silks have survived in India's hot climate, the Buddhist pilgrims' diaries reveal extensive use of silk. Faxian saw "canopies of embroidered silk" at festivals held in Pataliputra, while his successors traveled with hundreds of rolls of Chinese silk that they used as spending money, as was done in China itself at that time. Buddhist believers also draped silk from stupas as a way of honoring the Buddha. Yijing, a monk who visited India in the late seventh century, kept a piece of silk as "a cloth kept for defraying the cost of medicine (in case of necessity)." He also recorded the use of silk strainers, made out of two layers of fine silk, to keep insects out of water and so to prevent the monks from killing the insects. The irony of the situation was not lost on Yijing, though. He realized that silkworms had to die when silk was processed. If one allowed them to break the cocoons, the moth would live, but the damaged cocoon could only be used to make an inferior grade of silk. Yijing ingeniously explained that, as long as the monk had not ordered the killing of the moths, he could freely use silk donated by others.

The Seven Treasures

In addition to silk, Buddhist devotees made offerings of the Seven Treasures to honor the Buddha. The term had originally denoted the equipment of a ruler in India: a wheel (a traditional symbol of rule), an elephant, a horse, a gem, a queen, a householder, and a minister. By the third century A.D., the term took on new, more tangible meanings. The seven treasures could include gold, silver, lapis lazuli, crystal, coral, pearls, and agate. When Faxian explained that the tall jade statue of the Buddha in Sri Lanka was draped with the seven treasures, he did not elaborate, but he probably saw gold and silver, mixed with blue, pink, and clear stones. Although the components varied depending on availability, and people substituted cheaper items like glass beads, the genuine gems originated in India, from where they were shipped to China. Sri Lanka was one of few sources in the world for pearls, and Afghanistan was the sole producer of lapis lazuli, a semiprecious stone prized for its deep blue color.

Although the Chinese could produce glass of a lower quality with a higher silicon content, they continued to import foreign glass, some beautiful examples of which have been found in archeological excavations. Not realizing that the difference between the two types of glass was a matter of degree, the Chinese used two different words for glass, *liuli* and *boli*—both loanwords from the Sanskrit. Buddhist texts often refer to the seven treasures, and *The Lotus Sutra*, quite possibly the most influential Buddhist text in China, urged believers to decorate urns for the Buddha's relics with the seven treasures. Indeed, the seven treasures have often been found in conjunction with Buddhist relics, either made of real bones or artificial bones.

Religion and trade remained closely entwined on the many Silk Roads stretching westward out of China. Buddhist monks like Faxian traveled on merchant ships in the company of businessmen who paid their way, and monasteries could not survive without the presence of a large business community who made regular donations in the hope of transferring merit to themselves and their descendants. The Chinese had silk to export, while the Indians offered different gems, semiprecious stones, and glass. They also offered relics. The two-way flow of goods supported the Buddhist clerics, and Buddhist texts urged devotees to demonstrate their faith by donating exactly the goods Indian and Chinese merchants traded. When a wave of conquests cut off the trade routes between China and India at the end of the tenth century, the great age of the Silk Roads came to an end, having lasted over a thousand years. Many of the great oasis city-states of the past dwindled and returned to the sands, only to be rediscovered in the early years of the twentieth century.

THE NORTHERN WEI DYNASTY (386–534)

China experienced a bewildering series of governments during the early years of contact with India and Central Asia, and the only government in north China to retain power for over a century was established by a non-Chinese people, the Tabgach. When the Tabgach first appear in the Chinese historical record in the second century, they belong to a Xiongnu confederacy in the long band of the steppe stretching from the Liao River in Manchuria to the Gansu corridor in the west. The first Chinese sources refer to them as either by the name of the tribe, the Xianbei, or by the name of the most powerful clan within the tribe, Tuoba, as the Chinese transliterated the word Tabgach. The Tabgach included different tribes from the steppe who spoke both Turkic and Mongolian languages, but who had no written language of their own. In the 311 battle for Luoyang, the Chinese histories record that the Tabgach allied with the losing Chinese side.

An early Chinese description describes the Xianbei as tribesmen who both hunted and herded and who lived in temporary dwellings with domes, probably a kind of yurt. The Xianbei chose their leader for his bravery and judgment, this source notes, commenting that the position could not be inherited. Terming this type of rule tanistry, a modern analyst defines it as rule of the tribe "by the best qualified member of the chiefly house."[10] What this meant in practice was that all contenders for power had to prove their ability to lead by defeating their rivals in battle. A competent leader could attract thousands of followers, both from his own tribe and others, while an incompetent ruler could quickly be deposed. Under the system of tanistry, because there was no clear line of succession, a son could replace his father, but so could a brother or an uncle. Whenever a leader died, his sons and brothers would organize campaigns against each other until a new leader could be selected, often at a meeting of the tribal elders.

Written descriptions of the Tabgach reveal other important differences from the Chinese. Unmarried women shaved their heads, but married women grew their hair and put it up under hoods that hung down to their shoulders. The Tabgach men adopted an even more distinctive hairstyle. After they married, they shaved the front of their heads, a custom that different steppe peoples sustained until the seventeenth century when the Manchu conquerors required their Chinese subjects to adopt the same practice. Unfortunately, since the men wore hooded helmets, their hairstyle is not visible on surviving figurines. Some Chinese sources report that the men braided their hair, but figurines of the Xianbei have a bulge under their hoods, probably from a top-knot, not braids.

As in other nomadic societies, women knew how to tend the herds and how to hunt because the men left them in charge when they went to battle. As a result of their sharing men's work, tribal women generally enjoyed more power than their counterparts in sedentary society. The Tabgach women participated in all decisions but those concerning war, the Chinese sources report.

As the Tabgach gradually shifted their base from the Yin Shan Mountains in Inner Mongolia to northern Shanxi province, they derived more of their income from taxing the Chinese peasantry, and they adopted a Chinese law code. A new ruler, known only by his Chinese name, Tuoba

Gui, took power in 386, the traditional date for the founding of the Northern Wei dynasty. Following the custom of the nomads, the young state established no permanent capital because the capital was wherever the ruler pitched camp. In 396, Tuoba Gui assumed the Chinese title of emperor, and in 398 he began to build a permanent capital in northern Shanxi at Pingcheng. Establishing a precedent for all Northern Wei rulers, there he forcibly resettled over three hundred thousand Chinese, who included officials, tribesmen, and craftsmen. One thousand square kilometers (620 square miles) were set aside for farmers on which they were to grow crops for the new capital's residents, but the need for a reliable food supply was not fully met.

This artificial city, which had little commerce and no coinage of its own, served as home for the Tabgach ruler and his military staff. Visitors to the palace described workers making metal, herdsmen tending animals, and a thousand slaves weaving fine cloth. Whenever the Tabgach forces defeated an enemy army, they enslaved the defeated men and their families. Most of the captives were sent to work the fields around the capital, but some were assigned to the palace where they produced difficult-to-obtain goods. The Tabgach also forcibly recruited slaves from among the relatives of criminals. When a man was convicted of a capital crime, such as treason, the state seized his family property and en-

WHAT THE TABGACH LOOKED LIKE

These figurines show the equipment of the Tabgach soldiers of the Northern Wei, who ruled north China from 386 to 534 and whose rulers patronized Buddhism. They covered themselves from head to toe in armor, and, like the Persians, they covered their horses' upper bodies too.

slaved his relatives. The younger men in the family were sometimes castrated and then assigned to duties at court. Some slaves came from poor families who had been forced to sell their own children in famines or to pay off debts.

The Tabgach rulers continued to worship their own gods of the steppe in addition to making contributions to Buddhist teachers. They controlled the Buddhists by creating a separate section of the central government bureaucracy to supervise Buddhist monasteries. Breaking with the pattern of support for the Buddhists, one ruler, Taiwu (reigned 424–452), met a Daoist practitioner Kou Qianzhi (d. 448), who told him about a series of revelations he had received. At his urging the emperor underwent a Daoist investiture ceremony and adopted a Daoist reign title, the "Perfect Ruler of Great Peace." Although his Daoist advisor had studied Buddhist teachings in Changan with a student of Kumarajiva, the emperor attacked both Buddhist clergy and other indigenous deities, whom he called "little gods," in 446. Little is known about the identities of these local deities, but a group of eighteen poems suggests they were largely gods who presided over rivers, mountains, tides, and other natural sites. The effects of the suppression were short-lived, and the new ruler reinstated Buddhism to its former favored position in 454. He also initiated a huge cave-digging project at Yungang, outside the city of Datong, Shanxi. Here enormous statues of Buddha were carved, statues that rose 8 meters and 16 meters (26 and 52 feet) high. By the middle of the fifth century, the Northern Wei had defeated most of their rivals to take control of north China.

Dowager Empress Feng and the Equal-Field System

Although the new capital in Pingcheng seemed more foreign than Chinese, some of the Tabgach were drawn to Chinese ways. Those who married the children of socially powerful Chinese clans gave birth to a mixed aristocracy who could speak both Chinese and Tabgach, who rode on horseback, and who supported Buddhism. A female member of this mixed aristocracy came to power with the death of her husband the emperor in 465. Empress Dowager Feng exercised considerable influence on the young new emperor, gained even more power following the young man's death in 476, and ruled unchallenged as regent to her step-grandson until her own death in 490.

As soon as Empress Feng gained power she began systematically to appoint Chinese to office and just as systematically to lessen Tabgach influence. She poured state funds into building Buddhist monasteries, which she guaranteed a steady income by two means. Some tax-paying peasants were instructed to pay their crops directly to monasteries instead of to government officials, while condemned criminals sometimes had their sentences commuted so they could work for the monasteries. She also gave the monasteries large stretches of mountain lands not previously under cultivation; to clear these lands required the services of this captive labor force.

Starting in 477, the dowager empress passed a series of measures that reveal the seriousness with which she sought to transform Tabgach tribal rule into a Chinese bureaucracy. These new policies also reflect the persistent problem of how to tie the Chinese farming population to the land. Because the nomadic Tabgach did not pay land taxes, the Northern Wei needed to persuade Chinese to settle on farms, to cultivate agricultural land, and most important, to pay land taxes to the state. For nearly a century, their capital at Pingcheng had been home to a large, mixed population of bureaucrats and artisans who did not grow their own food. During that time, the Northern Wei rulers always had difficulty recruiting farmers to feed the capital.

In 485 a new system of land reform was proclaimed throughout the area under the control of the Northern Wei. The state awarded land to all those of tax-paying age. When a boy reached the age of eleven, he was eligible for half a grant; he received the rest when he became fifteen. At the age of seventy, the elderly retained their land but no longer had to pay taxes. Like boys under fifteen, the handicapped were eligible for half a grant. Detailed regulations specified that each free male was to receive forty third-acres of farmland and twenty third-acres of mulberry tree land. If excess land was available, each free male was eligible for another forty third-acres of farmland. The regulations also specify how much land was to be allotted to free females, slaves, and cows. The generous provisions for slaves and livestock meant that powerful landowning families could retain control over large areas of land nominally given to their slaves and cattle.

Distinctions were drawn between farmland and mulberry tree land. Because farmland required a shorter-term investment, it reverted to the state when the farmer stopped working, to be redistributed. But the land on which peasants planted mulberry trees for silkworms was awarded on a permanent basis. There peasants might have to wait long periods for mulberry trees to mature. To encourage this investment, the mulberry tree land was a permanent grant. It could even be bought and sold.

The earlier policy of forcible resettlement prompted the design of the equal-field system. By the time of Empress Dowager Feng, Northern

Wei officials realized they could not tie people to the land permanently, so they tried giving farmers incentives, like land grants, to stay in place. Clearly the architects of this plan hoped to stem the tide of people leaving the land, to which the edicts refer indirectly. One edict from the time stipulates that during famines certain families may leave their land to seek food while others must remain behind, evidence that too many families were leaving their fields. Officials also tried to control the farming population by dividing them into groups of 5, 25, and 125, which were responsible for making sure that each member paid his taxes and performed his labor obligation—which they could do only if they stayed in place.

From the first years of the new policy, high officials had problems enforcing it. In 487, one official in Shandong complained that "day by day, cultivators dwindle. Day by day, more fields are abandoned,"[11] suggesting the equal-field system had not taken effect in his area. During the famine year of 487, officials were instructed to compile new household registers for those families who had left their land and gone farther south to seek food. It seems most likely that the equal-field system first took effect in the region immediately surrounding the capital, while officials in outlying areas may not have been able to implement its complicated stipulations, which required a powerful state bureaucracy.

Although Empress Dowager Feng emulated certain Chinese practices, the promulgation of the equal-field system had no precedent in the history of earlier Chinese dynasties. When the Empress Dowager died in 490, her step-grandson continued her policies.

The Adoption of Chinese Ways

In 493, Emperor Xiaowen (reigned 471–499) implemented a series of measures designed to make his empire Chinese, the most remarkable of which was to establish a new capital in Luoyang, which had lain in ruins since 311. Even in shambles, Luoyang represented the past glories of Chinese civilization. To rebuild the city required ten years, and by the time workers doing labor service had completed their task, the emperor had died. During this decade of capital building, the emperor promulgated other ambitious edicts as well. The royal family dropped their own family name of Tabgach and adopted Chinese family name Yuan instead. They ordered officials to take Chinese names, to speak Chinese at court, and to wear Chinese clothing. Following the earlier Chinese precedent, the emperor also appointed impartial judges who ranked Tabgach families according to a nine-grade system that determined which offices they could hold.

Although these measures encouraged the Tabgach to emulate the Chinese, many Tabgach resisted the policies. Emperor Xiaowen ordered *The Classic of Filial Piety* to be translated into the language of the Xianbei, an indication that many continued to speak their native tongue. Women persisted in wearing non-Chinese clothing, and various officials in the north expressed their opposition to building a new capital at Luoyang, so far from their traditional homeland. In 496, several trusted senior advisors rose up in a rebellion that had to be suppressed. Most upsetting to the emperor, his son opposed the decision to relocate the capital and tried to move his own household north. His angry father imprisoned the prince in Luoyang, denied him his title, and then forced him to commit suicide in 497. When the father died prematurely only two years later, a sixteen-year-old boy became the new emperor, with the help of a regent to guide him.

Although historians have traditionally interpreted Emperor Xiaowen's policies as a step along the inevitable process of becoming Chinese, modern analysts see the emperor's reforms differently. They argue that the emperor's moves to suppress native Tabgach ways masked a move against the military, a group who retained significant power at the Northern Wei court. The Chinese model of government granted the emperor more power than did the traditional power-sharing practices of the steppe, and Emperor Xiaowen wanted all the power he could get. His predecessor's attack on Buddhism can be seen in the same light. Rather than reflecting a genuine conversion to Daoism, it seems much more likely that the emperor wanted to weaken those who had associated with the Buddhist establishment, and turning to Daoism allowed him to do so.

The history of the Northern Wei might have been very different had Emperor Xiaowen lived for another thirty years. Under his strong leadership and pro-Chinese policies he could have united all of China. Instead, with his death in 499, the dynasty entered three decades of discord. Regents propping up child emperors plotted against generals who sought to depose them. The government in Luoyang lost control of the armies on the northern borders. When they were not losing battles to invaders from previously unheard-of Erzhu tribes, the troops mutinied. The Northern Wei came to a miserable end in 534 at the hands of military leaders who saw no need to maintain the pretense of supporting the powerless emperor any longer.

The Growth of Buddhism under the Northern Wei

Even during the difficult years for the dynasty, Buddhist establishments continued to receive unprecedented support from the different factions vying for power. Sometime around the year 547, after the Northern Wei had ended and Luoyang was no longer capital, Yang Xuanzhi, an official who had held a position in the archives of the Northern Wei, compiled his *Record of the Monasteries of Luoyang.* His factual description of the largest monasteries provided a frame for his narration of the sad events leading to the fall of the dynasty.

His book opens with a description of the magnificent Monastery of Eternal Peace, built by the powerful Empress Dowager Ling in 516. Yang gave the height of the monastery's wooden pagoda as 270 meters (900 feet), with a gold pole on top that raised it another 30 meters (100 feet), for a total of nearly 300 meters (1,000 feet), the height of the Eiffel Tower.[12] Other sources suggest it may have been half as high, still tall for a structure of the time. In 528, the leader of the Erzhu tribes amassed his troops at this monastery, and from this base they defeated the troops of Dowager Empress Ling, conquered the city, and named a new emperor. When the Erzhu leader invited all the officials to come and meet their new sovereign, his troops killed over two thousand courtiers, and they threw the dowager empress and the child emperor into the Yellow River, where they died. Luoyang lay in ruins, yet it remained the capital until 534, when a fire laid waste the Monastery of Eternal Peace.

In 518 a prince of the Northern Wei complained, "Today there is no place that does not have a Buddhist sanctuary." Many of these monasteries were built in the years after 500. According to a Buddhist history written around the year 600, three types of monasteries existed during the Northern Wei. The state built the largest ones, such as the Monastery of Eternal Peace, which received regular government support, housed officially ordained monks, and conducted all Buddhist observances for the emperor. There were forty-seven of these. Royal princes and other highborn families built another 839 monasteries, which would also have enjoyed a steady income. The final category comprised the small chapels and shrines throughout the countryside whose only income came from commoners and whose clergy were not officially ordained; thirty thousand places of worship fell into this category. Figures for the total number of Buddhist monks in China vary, but they never exceeded 1 percent of the population.[13]

The Persistence of Tabgach Identity

Even after the fall of the Northern Wei, the Tabgach did not lose their ethnic identity. When warlords could not agree on a new emperor, the Northern Wei broke into two succeeding regimes, with the Eastern Wei occupying Luoyang. The Chinese and the Tabgach remained sufficiently distinct that the Eastern Wei ruler, a general named Gao Huan (d. 547), tried to keep the Chinese in the capital of Luoyang, so that they could staff the bureaucracy. The Tabgach stayed in north Shanxi, where they filled the ranks of the army. This general, the power behind the puppet Tabgach emperor, could speak both Chinese and Xianbei and claimed to be Chinese, although he was probably of Xianbei descent. He addressed the soldiers in Xianbei, saying:

> The Chinese are your slaves, the men farm for you, the women make your clothing, so they bring to you what you eat and what you wear, allowing you to be warm and full, why do you want to oppress them?

To the Chinese, he spoke in Chinese:

> The Xianbei are your clients, you give them a measure of grain and a bolt of cloth, and they fight for you and enable you to have peace and order, why do you hate them?[14]

Two generations after Emperor Xiaowen's efforts to make the Xianbei Chinese, they retained their own language and identity, and apparently, their hostility toward the Chinese.

A Chinese Official's Memoir

We can see the continuing influence of steppe culture on north Chinese life in the memoir of a Chinese official, Yan Zhitui (531–after 590), who wrote *The Family Counsels of Mr. Yan* sometime before China was re-unified in 589 by the Sui dynasty. Yan's book of advice is directed to his children and reflects his experience as an official under four different dynasties. In such difficult times, the only strategy for survival, he felt, was complete mastery of both spoken and written Chinese, the necessary tools for officials in whichever government came to power. Accordingly he urged his sons to speak Chinese correctly and to study hard. Yan did not, however, think his sons should learn the Xianbei language, for it was a secondary pursuit that would only distract them from their core studies.

The Family Counsels of Mr. Yan describes many differences between the regions north and south of the Yellow River. People in these areas spoke differently, had different manners, and treated women differently:

> In the south the husband must cut a good figure in public, however impoverished the family may be. He would not scrimp on his carriages or clothes, even if his extravagance causes his wife and children to suffer hunger and cold.
>
> In the north of the Yellow River it is usually the wife who runs the household. She will not dispense with good clothing or expensive jewelry. The hus-

band has to settle for old horses and sickly servants. The traditional niceties between husband and wife are seldom observed, and from time to time he even has to put up with her insults.[15]

Yan Zhitui attributed the difference in women's standing to the influence of the Tabgach. In the north, where the Tabgach had ruled, women had more power than in the south, which never came under Tabgach control. Yan Zhitui writes frankly about many topics, including female infanticide:

> I had a distant relative in whose household there were many concubines. When any were pregnant and the time of delivery drew near, janitors and servants were set to watch. As soon as the birth pains were noticed, the watchers waited at the door and peered through the windows. If a girl were born, it was snatched away at once; though the mother screamed and cried, no one dared to save it; one could not bear to listen.[16]

Yan is equally critical of those families who sell their daughters to the families into which they will marry.

Even after the fall of their government in 534, the influence of the Northern Wei continued to be felt. They were the first non-Chinese people to govern a large piece of Chinese territory and to wrestle with the problem of creating a government that could control both the settled Chinese population and the nomadic tribesmen. Although Dowager Empress Feng and Emperor Xiaowen had tried one policy—the wholesale adoption of Chinese-style government—with little success, future rulers from the steppe could learn much from their efforts.

During the century of Tabgach rule in the north, south China witnessed a series of Chinese dynasties culminating in the Liang (reigned 502–557). Although modern Chinese think of Nanjing on the Yangzi River as central China, during the fifth and sixth centuries, northerners viewed it as south China. At the time, the political and cultural center of China still remained very much in the north, while everything south of the Yellow River constituted a peripheral area.

The Move South

Among the Chinese of the north, South China harbored a fearsome reputation as an uncivilized, malarial place far from the capital. Few Chinese speakers would have chosen to live in the south, but the fall of Luoyang to the steppe peoples forced the first reluctant migrants to go there. In spite of the Chinese habit of writing about the south as if they were the first people to live there, the region was already occupied when they arrived. The original residents may not have spoken Chinese, and, because they did not write Chinese, they left no records, meaning we know all too little about these indigenous peoples.

The northerners realized that because the many tributaries of the southern rivers, including the Yangzi, crisscrossed the landscape, travel by boat was much easier in the south than in the north. The annual rainfall in some areas of the south was two or three times what it was in the north, and the climate was hotter, too. From a modern vantage point we know the climate of the south was perfect for the cultivation of rice. But the migrants fleeing the north viewed south China with apprehension. The hot, wet climate provided the perfect home for illnesses, including malaria and other dangerous fevers. Before the lowlands of the south could be cultivated, dikes had to be built around the rice fields so they could be flooded and drained as needed during the growing season. The transformation of the swamps of the south into rich rice paddies took long centuries and a great toll on those who settled there.

RELIGIOUS LIFE IN SOUTH CHINA

Although we cannot estimate the numbers of Chinese who fled to the south, there were constant pressures to move, from the forced resettlement and labor gangs of peacetime to the dangers of battle during war. Many descendants of northern Chinese aristocrats moved to Nanjing, which became a regional capital for the first time after the fall of the Han. A number of these northern migrants continued their study of Daoist practices.

In south China, where Daoist teachers were most active, Buddhist and Daoist practitioners had frequent contact and influenced each other deeply. Both religious traditions changed dramatically during this period. For the Buddhists, the teachings of the Greater Vehicle superseded those of the Lesser Vehicle, while Daoist visionaries developed two new schools—the Numinous Treasure (Lingbao) and the Mao Shan—on the basis of new revelations. Although Buddhists and Daoists attacked one another, they also borrowed from each other, so much that it can be difficult to decide whether a given practice was originally Buddhist or Daoist. Members of both religions avoided animal sacrifices, incorporated local deities, and built monasteries for their clergy. Daoist images from the sixth century look curiously like their Buddhist counterparts, and Daoist devotees request blessings for seven generations of family members, language borrowed directly from the Buddhists.

Like many of his émigré subjects, the Liang emperor was interested in Daoism, and as a young man he studied with one of the great Daoist teachers of the age, Tao Hongjing (456–536), who devoted himself to the collection and editing of a series of revelations recorded by his wife's ancestors more than a century before. Because the men studied these texts on Mao Shan mountain, this new Daoist sect took the name of the mountain.

The Teachings of the Mao Shan Daoists

Just as Zhang Daoling had organized a new branch of Daoism, the Five Pecks, after his revelation of teachings from the divine Laozi, the Mao Shan Daoists introduced their new teachings, saying they were what the immortals had taught the visionary Yang Xi (fl. 364–370) in his encounters with them. The Mao Shan adherents continued some of the practices of the Five Pecks Daoists, such as curing the ill, but they tried to distance themselves from practices that had given the Daoists a bad name, specifically certain sexual rites. The Mao Shan Daoists believed in a totally new divine order with seven levels housing both divine immortals as well as the spirits of the dead. The lowest level lay under the earth, as did the level above it, which housed candidates for immortality.

The lowest level in the Mao Shan system, where the souls of the dead went to be judged, replicated the indigenous Chinese view of the afterlife, which held that souls of the dead would go to a series of courts in the underworld, where their future would be decided and where they would most likely remain forever. The Mao Shan Daoists offered a slightly more optimistic view of the afterlife for they claimed the authority to intervene with the officials of these underworld courts. They also taught that the dead could lodge underworld suits against people who had wronged them when they were still alive. If the targets of the suits had already died, then their living relatives could suffer as well. One of the early Mao Shan Daoists, an official named Xu Mi (303–373), began to suffer a series of misfortunes culminating in the early death of his wife. When he investigated by petitioning the underworld officials, he discovered that his uncle had served as an official and had unjustly killed someone below him in rank. The wrongfully killed man had sued his uncle in the courts of the underworld, with the result that Xu Mi's wife had died. Xu's family was able to escape further punishment only because Yang Xi, the visionary who had first seen the immortals, intervened on his behalf. The Daoists' claim to intercede on behalf of the dead in the underworld courts brought them many adherents.

Learning from Teachers

The Mao Shan Daoists offered adepts a way to escape these grim underworld prisons by ascending to levels above. Disciples could join the higher ranks of the immortals by experiencing a series of revelations through texts transmitted by teachers. Mao Shan teachers charged disciples considerable sums, sometimes as much as a length of silk and two gold rings, for each text they transmitted. Moreover, they stressed the importance of transmission at the hands of certified teachers, and threatened to punish those who made illicit copies. The disciples had to take oaths every time they received a new revelation or text from their teachers. The high fees, secrecy, and oaths of the Mao Shan Daoists paint a picture of a secret brotherhood of adherents, who kept Daoist teachings alive over the centuries.

Another Daoist movement took shape in south China during the fourth century, the Numinous Treasure (Lingbao) school, whose practitioners drew much from contemporary Buddhism to develop a more open school of Daoism. The Numinous Treasure teachers and many lay practitioners saw Buddhism and Daoism as complementary teachings. Like the Greater Vehicle in Buddhism, the Numinous Treasure school offered salvation to everyone through the teachings of a Buddha-like savior. Also like the Buddhists, the members of this school created a clerical structure with monasteries and successive series of vows for the laity and clergy to follow. The Numinous Treasure teachings remained distinctly Daoist in their promise of immortality, which they ingeniously interpreted to mean a posthumous immortality. After the body died, they taught, the soul would travel to a netherworld where it would be purified by smelting. Neither the Mao Shan nor the Numinous Treasure teachers emphasized *The Way and Integrity Classic* or *Zhuangzi*, the two most famous Daoist classics in the West.

The Religious Policies of Emperor Wu of the Liang

As a young man, Emperor Wu of the Liang studied with Tao Hongjing, the great compiler of the Mao Shan scriptures, but in 504 he urged the royal family and his officials to give up Daoism for Buddhist teachings. In 517 he ordered the destruction of Daoist temples, although he continued to correspond with Tao Hongjing. The emperor's measures against Daoism do not seem to have weakened the Daoist church, but his actions in support of Buddhism provided the monasteries in the south with a solid source of support.

In 527, Emperor Wu claimed he wanted to become a monk. He made sacrifices at a monastery, but then returned to the throne after his ministers paid the monastery a large fee. Two years later, a devastating plague prompted the emperor to repeat his performance, and again his ministers ransomed him for a hefty price. He then hosted a feast for fifty thousand monks and laymen. These and other extravagant performances expressed the emperor's wholehearted devotion to Buddhism but stopped short of his joining the clergy. Many of his subjects shared his desire to be a devout Buddhist without becoming a monk or a nun.

Critics of the Buddhist Establishment

By the middle of the sixth century Buddhism had become an enormously successful transplant to Chinese soil. Contemporary sources, which may exaggerate, put the number of Buddhist monks and nuns at an astonishing two million living in some thirty thousand monasteries. The clergy, who did not work or serve in the military, were widely perceived as a drain on the resources of the state, and many doubted their knowledge of their own religion.[17] This aroused the ire of the emperor of the Zhou dynasty (557–581), which succeeded the Qi dynasty in the north. In 574 he ordered all Buddhist monks to return to lay life and all Buddhist texts and statues destroyed. He also ordered the laicization of the Daoist clergy.

There were criticisms of the Buddhist establishment from within as well. Even devout monks and nuns could not extend their knowledge beyond the few pages of texts they had memorized. Instead of devoting themselves to the study of Buddhism, monasteries, engaged in commerce, made loans at usurious rates, and sheltered criminals, according to their critics. These critics saw the decay of the Buddhist establishment as a sign of the irreversible degeneration that characterizes the final Buddhist era. This era would end, they believed, with the coming of a savior who would reform both the church and the state.

The critics had stumbled on an important truth that shapes our understanding of Buddhist history. The surviving sources describe only the most literate members of the clerical elite, or some fifteen hundred monks and nuns. These people constituted a tiny percentage of the clergy.[18] They worked in the imperially sponsored, richly endowed monasteries of their age, while most of their colleagues staffed simple shrines and depended on the laity for irregular contributions.

The differences between the teachings of Daoism and Buddhism were best understood by the highly educated who had studied their texts carefully. Most devotees, and many in the Buddhist and Daoist clergy, would have found it difficult to explain the subtle differences in the teachings of the two religions. They would have all acknowledged the power of holy men to cure the ill, predicted that the world as people knew it would be destroyed in an apocalypse, and prayed to deities, including the Buddha and Laozi, for miracles. These beliefs had begun to take shape during the second century A.D., in a period when few monasteries had been built and the clergy had not expanded greatly. By the end of the sixth century, both the Buddhist and Daoist religious establishments had become fully established in Chinese society—so much so that the court tried to move against them both in 574. Yet a short-lived imperial suppression could do little to shake the hold of either. Both had become major forces in Chinese society some four centuries after their first appearance in China.

These formative centuries saw the heightened migration of Chinese settlers to the south, where they began to dredge the swamplands. The longest lasting government of the period was that founded by the Tabgach, the steppe people who united north China under the Northern Wei dynasty and bequeathed the equal-field system to their successors. Because the equal-field system tied the Chinese population to the land at the same time that it increased land revenues, the system lasted into the eighth century, well beyond the time the empire was reunified.

Although the Chinese then and historians since have depicted the long period of division between 220 and 589 as a blot on China's record of unity, we need to reconsider this view. The amount of territory controlled by the different dynasties discussed in this chapter, including the Northern Wei, equaled that of many European nations. The kingdoms seem small only when compared to later empires. As was so often the case in traditional China, disunity pushed people to innovate. During these centuries Daoist adepts experimented with new formulas and medicines while intrepid Buddhist pilgrims and merchants discovered and frequented the overland Silk Route and maritime routes to Central Asia, India, and Southeast Asia. As Yan Zhitui pointed out, north and south China developed different cultural identities that persisted even after the empire was reunified in 589, the subject of the next chapter.

CHRONOLOGY

581–604	*Reign of Emperor Wendi*
589–618	SUI DYNASTY
ca. 596–664	*Lifetime of monk Xuanzang, traveler and translator of Buddhist texts*
618–907	TANG DYNASTY
624–755	*Equal field system in effect*
624–755	*Household registration system in effect*
626–649	*Reign of Emperor Taizong*
626–649	*Issuing of the Tang Code*
640	*Tang-dynasty troops take Central Asian oasis of Turfan*
690–705	*Zhou dynasty interregnum of Empress Wu*
712–755	*Reign of Emperor Xuanzong*
before 755	*Fictional tale of Li Wa set in Changan (written by Bai Xingjian, 776–827)*
755	*An Lushan rebellion*

C H A P T E R 5

CHINA'S GOLDEN AGE

(589–755)

In 589 the Sui dynasty reunified China and ruled for three decades. The Sui rulers were succeeded by the Tang, who ruled for nearly three centuries. These were the years of China's Golden Age, the peak of China's cultural glory. Even today, the word for Chinese in Cantonese means "people of the Tang," and Chinatowns all over the world are called Tang-people-streets (*Tangrenjie*). The empire flourished during this time when its populace was more open to and more enthusiastic about foreign influence than it would ever be again. Many Chinese of high and low social status intermarried with non-Chinese, often Turkic, people. Anything Indian or Central Asian was all the rage. Learned monks traveled through Central Asia to reach Indian teachers, merchants accompanying them brought back exotic trade goods, and even the Chinese who stayed home wore non-Chinese fashions as they composed poems set to the latest foreign tunes.

The Tang was an age not just of cultural openness but of political strength. The central government had more power over its inhabitants, who numbered some sixty million, than did any other premodern dynasty. The Tang issued a law code so influential that it was later adopted in Japan, Korea, and Vietnam by rulers who sought to replicate the strength of the Tang. Local officials closely monitored the population of the empire, regularly redistributed land, and strictly supervised markets. We can see the government's reach in the central capital of Changan, where it built a planned city with walled subdivisions. The commercial markets were strictly separated from the rest of the city, and market officials set prices for basic commodities every ten days. We can see the government's reach as well in the distant desert oasis of Turfan in mod-

China United: The Sui and Early Tang Dynasties (589–755)

ern Xinjiang, in the northwest of China. There the Tang state established a complex system of household registration and land redistribution, enforcing it every three years.

The Tang was also, unusually, an age of women. Some ruled through their husbands or sons, while one, Empress Wu, became the only woman in Chinese history to assume imperial power in her own name. Short stories and paintings of the time allow glimpses of the lives of more typical women as well. Historians have traditionally held a woman—an imperial concubine famed for her beauty—responsible for the end of China's Golden Age because her affair with a Central Asian general triggered one of the most destructive rebellions in Chinese history.

How the Sui Dynasty Brought the Empire Together

The task of reuniting the empire proved far easier than anyone could have predicted given the preceding two hundred fifty years of disunity.

The founder of the Sui dynasty, Yang Jian (reigned 581–604) was born into a powerful military family and spent the first twelve years of his life under the care of a nun in a monastery. A more traditional military education followed, and he became a general under one of the regional rulers, the Northern Zhou. In 566 he married a woman of mixed heritage, whose ancestors included both Xiongnu and Chinese families. She did not accept the Chinese tradition of taking concubines and insisted that he have no children but those she bore. In 578, Yang Jian's eldest daughter was married to a crazed Northern Zhou prince who subsequently succeeded his father as regional ruler. The ruler insisted that Yang Jian's daughter commit suicide, presumably so that he could remarry, and only a plea by Yang Jian's wife saved the girl. Then the ruler fell ill and died. It was at this point that Yang Jian decided to seize power, first posing as the regent of the child emperor and then founding his own dynasty in 581, when he began his reign as Emperor Wendi. In 589, the new dynasty, the Sui, conquered the south.

The Sui dynasty, like the Qin, did not rule for long. The people of the North and South had grown apart, and the influence of the Turko-Mongol population was much stronger in the north than in the more refined, aristocratic south. The first Sui emperor took measures to try to eliminate those differences. He insisted that all, regardless of background, be treated equally before the law, and he promulgated a new streamlined law code. When his third son violated spending limits by building a palace of jade and precious stones, the emperor ordered that he be stripped of his offices and placed under house arrest, for the law applied to all, even to imperial princes. The first Sui emperor also tried to heighten his subjects' support for his rule through Buddhism.

Patronizing Buddhism

In 580, the Sui founder rescinded the ban on Buddhism (and Daoism) passed by the previous Northern Zhou dynasty in 574. During the ban, many devotees had resolved to take measures to protect the teachings of the Buddha, then and in the future. They knew that the authorities' support for Buddhism would remain inconstant, and they believed they were witnessing a sign of the shift to the Final Age of the Doctrine, when all religious life would disappear. Only after the world had been destroyed would a new Buddha come to this earth.

In the Residing-in-the-Clouds (Yunju) Monastery, which is located in the township of Fangshan just a short drive from modern Beijing, the modern tourist can visit one of the most tangible expressions of this impulse to protect Buddhism. Leaving the modern monastery, one hikes into the hills for about half an hour before reaching nine caves with a balustraded path in front of them. The center cave, the Thunder-Sound Cave, is both the largest and the oldest, dating back to the early seventh century. Lining the walls of the cave, which is the size of a large room with a high ceiling, are 146 stone tablets bearing Buddhist texts. The 4 pillars of the cave bear carvings of 1,000 Buddhas, each labeled with its own name, a characteristic motif of the Sui dynasty.

The monks who dug this cave (and the neighboring caves in subsequent ages) commissioned copies of important Buddhist texts to be incised in stone. They placed the stone tablets inside the caves and then walled them up. The monks at the Yunju monastery continued this practice through the tenth century, when they stopped using the caves and began to bury the stone copies in the ground. A total of 4,200 stones have been found in the 9 caves, and over 10,000 were buried in the monastery grounds. Although some of

A BUDDHIST TIME CAPSULE

War and chaos in the late Sui dynasty drove many to believe that the end of the world was at hand. In the Thunder-Sound Cave at Fangshan, near Beijing (shown here), sacred art and a vast Buddhist library were hidden. The cave was then sealed and camouflaged in hopes that the treasures would survive the destruction before the Buddha's second coming.

the stones have been damaged by wind and rain, or by the many rubbings taken by avid collectors of calligraphy, the high level of preservation testifies to the efficacy of the precautions taken by the monks, who believed that the caves and the stone copies would survive the apocalypse.

The Sui founder saw himself as a grand donor to Buddhism who built a national network of monasteries and ordered the chanting of Buddhist prayers during the three months of the Buddha's birthday. His capital housed one hundred twenty new Buddhist temples, one of which supervised all the monks in China, translated Buddhist texts, and established standards for the clergy. The emperor's most dramatic gesture in support of Buddhism came in the year of his sixtieth birthday, in 601: he ordered stupas built all over the empire to house relics of the Buddha, sent monks and nuns out from the capital to celebrate their opening, and closed government offices for one week's holiday. Here he was consciously emulating the ancient Indian king Ashoka (reigned 209–232 B.C.) who served as a model of Buddhist kingship.

Yang Jian's son, Yang Guang (reigned 604–617), also supported Buddhist monasteries generously. His father arranged his marriage to a southern woman and sent him to a southern city, where he ordered Buddhist scriptures to be recopied and Buddhist monasteries and a new library built. He also sponsored vegetarian feasts and corresponded with Zhiyi (538–597), the founder of the Tiantai school of Buddhism. Zhiyi reconciled the many different teachings of previous Buddhists, while emphasizing the potential for each individual to realize his or her own Buddha-nature.

In 604, Yang Guang succeeded his father, possibly after foul play directed at his brothers. Traditional historians have always cast him in the role of the bad last emperor who caused the downfall of his dynasty. They criticize him for the extravagant rebuilding of a capital at Luoyang. Yet they also credit him with digging waterways that ensured a reliable grain supply between the capital and the rice-producing south.

The Sui-dynasty canal linked a series of preexisting waterways and harnessed several rivers to make a link between the Sui capital and the grain-producing areas of the south. The emperor used much conscripted labor to build these waterways, which served a political purpose in unifying the north and the south. China had not been under the rule of one dynasty since the fall of the Han in 220. During the long centuries of disunity, cultural patterns between the north and south had diverged, especially since the north was more often under non-Chinese rule than was the south. The reunification of China by the Sui has been likened to Charlemagne's reunification of Europe in 800, with this important difference: while Europe broke apart again after Charlemagne's death,

China remained unified for much of its subsequent history. Public works projects like the Grand Canal helped to keep China together in the centuries after the Sui reunification of 589.

The Fall of the Sui Dynasty and the Founding of the Tang

After 609, the second Sui emperor began a series of campaigns outside of China, to the south to modern Vietnam, to the north against the Eastern Turks, and to the northeast against modern Korea. The campaign against Korea ended in failure, rebellions broke out in China, and the emperor was killed. In 618, one of the rebel generals, Li Yuan (reigned 618–624), declared the founding of a new dynasty, the Tang. Like the Sui emperors, he belonged to the north Chinese aristocracy and was of mixed Chinese and Turkic ancestry. By 624, the Tang had secured control of the empire.

The Tang ruled China in name for nearly three centuries, though its grip was much weakened after 755, when the An Lushan rebellion forced the center to cede much power, including the power to tax, to local rulers. The Tang enjoys a reputation as China's most glorious dynasty partially because of the enormous territory the dynasty succeeded in conquering and ruling. The Tang dominion stretched far into Central Asia, including much of the modern Xinjiang Autonomous Region in northwestern China. After the Tang lost political control of the northwest, a thousand years passed before a Chinese dynasty, the Qing, regained control in the eighteenth century. The Tang is famous, too, for the many great poets, essayists, and artists who lived at the time. Finally, the Tang stands as a high point in Chinese history because under its rule the machinery of government functioned efficiently, at least until 755.

Although one would be hard-pressed to detect power struggles in the smooth narrative of the official history, problems of political succession plagued the Tang dynasty from its very founding. Two sons of the Tang founder began to contend for power starting in the 620s. In 626, one of them, Li Shimin (reigned 626–649), killed one brother, the heir apparent, and watched one of his officers slay another at the Xuanwu gate of Changan. He then forced his father to step down, and he ruled as Emperor Taizong for over twenty years.

The empire had witnessed its share of power struggles, what with the Sui overthrowing the Northern Zhou, and the Tang overthrowing the Sui, but the Xuanwu Gate incident violated Confucian norms in a way that the other transfers of power had not. The second Tang emperor had, after all, murdered one brother, arranged for the killing of another, and deposed his father. There were few checks on the emperor in this world, unless he was deposed, but popular belief held that the dead could be tried in another tier of courts, under the earth, for crimes that had gone unpunished while they were alive.

The Tang Emperor's Journey to Hell

A legend arose that the emperor was summoned before Yama, King of the Dead, who then assigned a lower official to conduct his case. That official explained that the emperor had been charged by his two younger brothers and that he could return to the living if he answered one question:

> His Majesty Taizong, Emperor of Tang, is asked why, in the seventh year of Wude, 626, he slew his brothers in front of the Palace and imprisoned his loving father in the women's apartments? An answer is requested.[1]

The emperor was appropriately terrified. If he could not answer the question, he would not be allowed to return to the living. The story ends with his interrogator composing a concise answer for him: "A great Sage will destroy his family in order to save the kingdom." In other words, he sacrificed his family for the good of the empire. Even though the emperor is allowed to go free, this tale shows that the jurisdiction of the courts of the dead—and norms of justice—extended even to him. The emperor consciously cultivated an image of himself as a model king who ruled according to Buddhist ideals; the story of his underworld trial reveals, however, that the emperor could not control what his subjects thought of him.

At the end of the tale, the emperor returns to the world of the living after being urged to publish copies of Buddhist texts and to do good deeds, indications that the Buddhists recorded this version.

In fact, Emperor Taizong enthusiastically patronized Buddhism. Originally he had banned all foreign travel, forcing the famous monk Xuanzang (ca. 596–664) to escape from China through the northwest border. But when Xuanzang returned from a sixteen-year journey to Central Asia and India, the emperor welcomed him back and showered him with many presents. Xuanzang was China's most famous Buddhist pilgrim and an accomplished translator of texts from Sanskrit to Chinese.

The Tang Code

Emperor Taizong also presided over one of the great projects of the Tang, the issuing of a new legal code. The Tang Code is the first Chinese law code to survive in full. It has two sections: the first enunciates general principles of criminal law; the second lists specific offenses and punishments.[2] The Tang Code was revised every ten to fifteen years and was regularly supplemented. Subsequent Chinese dynasties adopted the Code in part or in full, as did China's neighbors, including the Japanese, the Koreans, and the Vietnamese. They embraced the Tang Code for what it symbolized, not for its contents. Even if all the provisions of the Code did not apply to their societies, they wanted their new dynasties to be just as glorious as the Tang.

Aiming for an automatic administration of justice, the compilers of the Code granted the local magistrate, who heard all disputes first, no discretion. His job was simply to decide which article of the law applied and then to sentence the culprit. Higher officials reviewed severe punishments, and the emperor himself had to approve all instances of the death penalty. In many instances, though, an offense did not fall under a specific provision, and the magistrate could decide which provision of the Code best fit the crime. To give one example of how the Tang Code worked, in the case of robbery, the magistrate had to decide whether force had been used and whether government documents, Buddhist images, articles connected to national sacrifices, or weapons had been stolen. The magistrate determined guilt after collecting testimony from different people and extracting confessions from the accused. The punishment varied depending on his determination.

Punishment also varied depending on the social status of the violator. The compilers of the Code divided Tang society into three social groups: the privileged, commoners, and inferior people. The privileged consisted of imperial relatives and high officials; the inferior people were personal retainers, bondsmen, and slaves. As in the Northern Wei dynasty, people became slaves in different ways. Emperors frequently awarded successful generals hundreds of slaves from among the prisoners they took from enemy forces. Some men and women were sentenced to slavery when a close relative was convicted of a crime, and some sold themselves or their children into slavery to pay off debts. Other inferior people, who were not officially slaves, performed unclean tasks thought to be polluting, like tending tombs.

The vast majority of Tang citizens had the status of commoners. Although inferior classes received heavier punishments than commoners for the same crimes, the Code also calibrated penalties with the age, sex, and mental and physical condition of the offender. Those younger than seven and older than ninety could not be sentenced to death. In general, women were given lighter sentences, and magistrates could be jailed for executing a pregnant woman. The Tang Code recognized three categories of disabilities as cause for leniency: (1) the maimed who had no vision in one eye, were deaf, had tumors, or suffered other malfunctions; (2) the seriously crippled who were dwarfs, could not speak, or had deformed backs; and (3) the totally helpless who were blind in both eyes or who could not use two or more limbs.

The Code reflected Legalist thinking in its insistence on the appropriate punishment for the crime, but it also espoused Confucian values in that the penalty for killing one's father was much heavier than for killing a stranger. A son could be punished for hitting his father, but a father remained free to hit his son. Likewise for husbands and wives. Finally, we know that there were variations in how the Tang Code was enforced. Evidence from the oasis community of Turfan in northwest China indicates that at least one provision of the Code, that fixing monthly interest on debts at 6 percent, was routinely disregarded in the second half of the seventh century.

Hoping to avoid a succession dispute, Emperor Taizong, who sponsored the Tang Code, named his heir just after he took the throne. An early choice was not necessarily a wise one, for the son he chose had mental problems. Moreover, the son's homosexual affair with a palace entertainer angered his father, who had the lover killed. The prince refused to speak Chinese and insisted instead on speaking Turkish and wearing Turkish clothes, revealing how close the Tang ruling house still was to its Central Asian roots. With the discovery of a plot the heir had organized to kill his brother, the heir was killed, and another son chosen to succeed the emperor.

That son ruled as Tang Gaozong (reigned 649–683), but he remained in the shadow of his wife, Empress Wu, who was content at first to rule through her husband, and after his death, through his son. Then in 690, she seized power outright. Because she was the only woman to found her own dynasty, the Zhou, and because she directly challenged the Confucian ideal of women obeying their husbands, all her contemporaries and all the traditional historians who wrote about Empress Wu saw her as a violation of the natural order. Their accounts are therefore highly suspect.

Rule by a Woman: Empress Wu

Wu Zhao took power after an unusual series of events. At the age of thirteen, she was a low-ranking concubine in Emperor Taizong's entourage. Her father was a scholar-official; her mother was a devout Buddhist descended from the Sui ruling house. In 649, when Taizong died, Wu Zhao should have shaved her head and entered a nunnery, as did all his other concubines who had not borne children, but she did not. She apparently had already met the new emperor before his father—and her husband—had died. Historians debate the year she returned to the palace, but she definitely gave birth to the new emperor's son in 652. Some historians think the heir apparent and Wu had sex even before his father died, which would have constituted incest between a son and his father's concubine. Many historians explain Wu's arrival in the palace as a maneuver of the empress—the new emperor's wife—who hoped Wu could entice the emperor away from a favorite concubine.

Once Wu had arrived in the palace, her next challenge was to get rid of her main patron and her main rival, the emperor's first wife; she succeeded in 655. Her task was made easier since she had given birth to the emperor's son three years earlier while the original empress remained childless. Once Wu had secured the title of empress for herself and ensured that her son was heir apparent, she was reputed to have cut off the arms and legs of her two adversaries, the empress and another concubine, and dumped the bodies into a wine vat. Empress Wu's accession to power was also aided by her husband's ill health. After he suffered a paralyzing stroke, she became de facto ruler of China in 660. She did not crown herself empress until 690, seven years after his death.

Empress Wu had to have the acquiescence of the bureaucracy in order to take over the government. Some of the most famous and most upright officials of her day supported her. During the long years she ruled as shadow empress, Empress Wu had succeeded in creating her own corps of secret police, many of whom were her relatives, and in placing them in positions of power. These men, later labeled cruel ministers in the official history of the dynasty, reported any criticisms to her, and they carried out gruesome punishments of her opponents.

Empress Wu's greatest innovation was her use of a particular form of Buddhism to legitimate her rule as a woman. The emperors of the Sui and Tang who preceded her had all patronized Buddhist monasteries and had financed the carving of Buddhist caves at several sites. The most imposing of these carvings are at Longmen, just outside Luoyang, on the banks of the Yi River. Patrons of Buddhism began to carve Buddhist images in the sandstone there starting at the end of the fifth century.

Today a visitor can see more than one hundred thousand images in over thirteen hundred different caves and niches, which stretch along both sides of the river for a kilometer or so. Many of the niches are just a meter high, but some reach up several stories. Even though many of the statues' heads and hands have been cut off and stand today in museums around the world, the size of the Longmen caves makes them one of the most impressive Buddhist sites in China. The largest cave, the Ancestor Worshiping Cave,

Buddhist Art at Longmen Caves

Following an Indian art tradition, Chinese sculptors carved giant statues of Buddha out
of solid stone all over China. The Longmen caves, outside of Luoyang city in Henan
province, are the most famous of all these Buddhist grottoes, and the Ancestor Worshiping
Cave shown here is the largest cave complex at Longmen. These rounded figures mark the
peak of Tang-dynasty Buddhist sculpture. Each of the statues assumes a different posture,
and each bears a facial expression suitable to his age and position. The central Buddha—
17 meters (55 feet) high, the largest at Longmen—towers above the others and has a ma-
jestic yet gentle face.

contains an image of the Absolute Cosmic Vairocana Buddha that stands
17 meters (55 feet) high. It took fifteen years to build this enormous cave,
and construction was complete by 675, when Empress Wu was still empress. In 672, she donated to the cave the cost of her cosmetics for one
year—some twenty thousand strings of copper cash.

The Longmen complex contains another imposing cave, the Three
Buddha niche, which was never completed. This cave differs from the
others in that the middle Buddha is the Maitreya Buddha, the Buddha
of the future who will rule over the world after it has been transformed
into a paradise. This cave dates to the reign of Empress Wu, who ar-
dently supported the cult of Maitreya because of its links to a female ruler.

Empress Wu became infatuated with a drug and cosmetic merchant
sometime in the late 680s. In order to continue to meet him clandestinely,
she arranged for her son-in-law to adopt him and then she named him abbot of the White Horse monastery outside Luoyang. The two began the
massive project of building Bright Hall, over 90 meters (295 feet) high, in
Luoyang; such a building substantiated the empress's claim to be a ruler
worthy of the traditions of the ancient and glorious Zhou dynasty.

In 690, this monk, purportedly the empress's lover, wrote a new commentary to a minor Buddhist text, *The Great Cloud Sutra*, that told of a female goddess (Heavenly Lady Pure and Radiant) who retained her female form, rather than allowing herself to be transformed into a man, so that she could better help all living beings. The text predicted that seven hundred years after the Buddha's death she would be reborn as a princess in a small kingdom in south India, where she would be loved by her people for her great beauty. Because of her devotion to the Buddhist teachings, her country would prosper and be transformed into a paradise, and kings of neighboring states would submit to her. After her death, she would be reborn in the Pure Land of Amitabha Buddha, as the Buddha prophesied:

> You shall reign over the territory of a country with the body of a woman. . . .
> The people shall prosper; there will be no weaknesses, nor sorrows from ill-
> nesses, nor afflictions, nor fears nor calamities; all propitious events will be
> completely realized.[3]

In spite of the differences between this fictive ruler and herself, Empress Wu and her monk-lover used this text to justify her accession to the throne. Two months after Empress Wu received this sutra, she established her own "Zhou" dynasty, a reference to the time of Confucius, and brought the Tang to an end. She, like the Sui emperor, ordered a monastery to be built in each prefecture in China, where monks would lecture on *The Great Cloud Sutra*.

The empress pursued other Buddhist policies, banning the slaughter of animals and the catching of fish. In 693 she proclaimed herself the traditional great ruler of Buddhism, and in 694 she claimed to be the Maitreya Buddha who presides over a future paradise, but nothing suggests that her subjects accepted her claims. Wild sexual rumors about her persisted even in the last years of her life when she fell in love with two half-brothers. She was alleged to have taken so many aphrodisiacs that she sprouted new teeth and eyebrows. Finally, in 705, she was deposed in a palace coup, and the Tang dynasty was restored.

After seven years of infighting at the court and the murder of the emperor in 710 by supporters of Empress Wu, the Tang dynasty regained a stable footing; in 712, the Emperor Xuanzong took over the office he was to hold until 756. Historians see him as one of China's most talented emperors. He restored the Tang dynasty after the Empress Wu interregnum, ruled over a large territory for over forty years, and brought efficiency to government institutions during his long reign. His was a reign of great contrasts: near the end of his life this very talented emperor also very nearly caused the downfall of his dynasty during the An Lushan rebellion, the subject of the next chapter.

DAILY LIFE IN THE CAPITAL

During the Tang dynasty, the city's population may have reached one million people, with some five hundred thousand inside the city walls and as many outside. They all knew that they lived in a planned and highly regulated city. Changan (now Xian, Shaanxi) was built by the founder of the Sui dynasty as a political statement; it was rebuilt by the Tang for the same reason. Both dynasties sought to construct a symbol of their power. Changan was a large city, with the outer walls stretching 9.5 kilometers (5.92 miles) long along the east-west axis and 8.4 kilometers (5.27 miles) along the north-south axis. Five meters (5 yards) high, these walls were made of pounded earth covered with bricks; they formed a perfect rectangle.

Inside the city, more walls divided it into over one hundred smaller quarters, largely for security purposes. The state compiled household registers for residents in each quarter; it used these to collect taxes and recruit soldiers. The quarters were separated by internal walls with gates that closed and opened according to curfew. Local officials maintained a complicated system of drum towers that announced the time. Special regulations governed the precise time and order in which gates were to be opened in the morning and closed at night. After the evening drum sounded, all gates were closed and locked, and no one was allowed out on the streets, which were patrolled by soldiers on horseback.

Changan's layout was unconventional in some ways. The city designers, who, like the royal families they served, came from a mix of Chinese and Central Asian backgrounds, felt free to modify classical prescriptions about how a Chinese city should be built. Ancient texts described the model city as one surrounded by a square wall, with the emperor's palace at the center of the city, the market to the north, and the temple to the imperial ancestors and the shrine of the earth to the south. One scholar has neatly summed up the logic of the plan: "The ruler, facing south in his audience hall, receiving his officials and conducting public business, literally turns his back on the market and thus symbolizes the lowly position which official ideology assigned to commerce."[4]

South of the palace was the home of the central government of the Tang, which divided the tasks of governing among six ministries, called the Six Boards: Revenue, Civil Appointments, Rites, Works, Punishments, and War. These remained in use until the twentieth century. The emperor met with the heads of the Six Boards to discuss important matters of state. Other sections of the government were responsible for drafting and reviewing documents.

The Changan planners placed the palace flush against the north wall

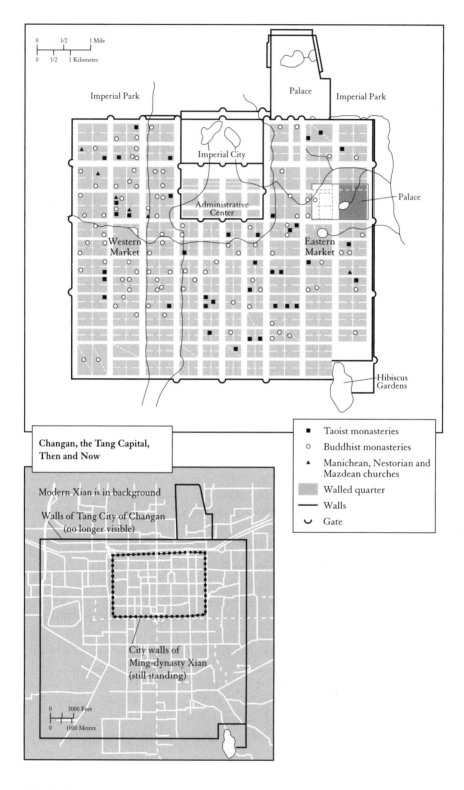

0   1/2   1 Mile
0   1/2   1 Kilometer

Imperial Park

Palace

Imperial Park

Imperial City

Administrative
Center

Palace

Western
Market

Eastern
Market

Hibiscus
Gardens

Changan, the Tang Capital,
Then and Now

Modern Xian is in background

Walls of Tang City of Changan
(no longer visible)

City walls of
Ming-dynasty Xian
(still standing)

0   3000 Feet
0   1000 Meters

■   Taoist monasteries

○   Buddhist monasteries

▲   Manichean, Nestorian and
      Mazdean churches

      Walled quarter

──   Walls

∪   Gate

and allowed sufficient space for two markets to the south of the palace. The emperor and the imperial family lived in the palace in the north of the city; this was not open to the public, but almost everything else in the city was.

Changan is one of the few Chinese cities to retain its original layout. The visitor to Xian today can see the city walls from the Ming dynasty, rebuilt most recently with Japanese funding. The city retains its gridded street map, but the modern city within the walls takes up just one-seventh of the Tang city's area—approximately the area originally covered by the emperor's palace. The enormous area of the Tang city left plenty of room for gardens and orchards, which do not survive in today's urban crush. Buddhist and Daoist monasteries were spread evenly around the city.

The center of the foreign quarter was the Western Market, around which clustered Changan's sizable foreign population—sometimes estimated at one-third of the city's total population. Non-Chinese residents built religious institutions dedicated to the religions of their homelands. The Persian-speaking merchants continued to worship at two kinds of temples devoted to religions they brought with them from Iran. They sacrificed live animals at Zoroastrian fire altars, and they sang hymns about the forces of light triumphing over the forces of darkness at Manichaean temples. Travelers from Syria embraced their own form of Christianity, Nestorianism, which held that Christ had two different natures: the human from his mother Mary and the divine from his father the Lord.

Very few buildings from the Tang remain—just two brick pagodas to the south of the city, Little Goose and Big Goose pagodas—for the people of Changan did not build permanent monuments. Almost always made of wood on pounded earth foundations, buildings went up with lightning speed, as they were meant to last a generation or two at most. In 643, one official reception hall was built in only five days. In the heavily forested China of the Tang, wood was cheap and widely available. One can still see the extraordinary joint-work characteristic of Tang-dynasty wooden buildings in Nara, Japan, but only because those wooden structures have been lovingly preserved while their Chinese counterparts have long since disappeared.

The visitor to Changan in the seventh century would have been struck by the high number of Buddhist temples: ninety-one in 722. Resident monks conducted funerals, prayed for the dead, and celebrated the various holidays of the calendar, including Buddha's birthday in the fourth month and the festival of the dead in the eighth. Because Buddhist teachings also stressed helping others, even strangers, the monks offered many services to the city's inhabitants, including free dispensaries, pawnshops, hostels, and public baths. The city hired Buddhists to run hospitals, and awarded them bonuses if less than one-fifth of their patients died.

A City of Different Social Classes

The emperor's city above all, Changan was built as testimony to the glory of his dynasty. It was, second, a city for officials, some of whom lived luxuriously indeed. One high official even owned a house equipped with a system of fountains that rained down on the roof in the summer and cooled those inside. The officials, who commanded enormous sums of disposable wealth, patronized the popular musical troupes of Central Asian women who played new instruments, like the pipa, similar to a guitar, and who performed at parties seated on platforms carried by camels. The city also hosted those who hoped to become officials, the exam candidates. Of the five to seven thousand candidates who arrived each year to take the examinations, some came with large allowances while others had to scrimp.

Preparing for the Examinations

Photographs taken in the nineteenth century show the examination halls as long rows of rooms constructed to keep secret the identities of those writing the examinations. In the Tang period, the role of the exams differed markedly. Because the government used them to recruit men of good character, examiners had to know the candidates. Those taking the examinations made a practice of regularly visiting their examiners, giving them samples of their writing (called warming-the-exam papers) and trying to impress them. The exams themselves tested types of writing that only those brought up in good families could be expected to know. Poetry was a regular part of the advanced degree, and the poems the candidates wrote had to follow a rigid form, not unlike an English sonnet, to get full points. The examiners were much more interested in mastery of the form, which indicated the right background, than in originality of the poem. The importance of poetry in the curriculum of the educated gentleman prompted an explosion in poetry writing. Some of China's most famous poets lived during the Tang period.

In subsequent centuries the examinations would become a means of recruiting talent rather than men with suitable family background. In the Tang, those men who failed the exams could still be appointed to office, though they might not rise as high in the bureaucracy as those with the prestige of having passed the examinations. Most of those who passed the Tang examinations, however, came from exactly the social class the system was designed to protect: the scholar-officials.

CHANGING IDEALS OF FEMININE BEAUTY

The eighth century witnessed a dramatic change in ideas about feminine beauty. At the beginning of the century, beautiful women had thin bodies like these four women. The two women on the right wear shawls of Central Asian origin as was quite the fashion in the eighth century.

WHEN FAT WAS BEAUTIFUL

By the mid-eighth century the contours of the ideal beauty had widened considerably. These four billowy women have the look of full-blown Tang beauties. Their entire bodies are rounded and no waist shows underneath their generously cut dresses. This was the Precious Consort Yang look that so many aristocratic women aspired to.

Once they had taken the exams, all the candidates awaited the posting of the results. Those who succeeded were given a banquet and had their names inscribed on the walls of a Buddhist pagoda. At this time, high officials would bring their marriageable daughters out for show; the

FREEDOM OF MOVEMENT FOR COURT WOMEN

Five beautifully dressed court women (all sisters of Precious Consort Yang) wear loose trousers as they sit astride their magnificent steeds, one with her daughter riding in front of her. The aristocracy of the Tang dynasty was descended from the Turkic-speaking peo-

girls would walk or ride, hoping to attract the attention of a successful candidate.

Fashionable women wore the tight dresses so characteristic of Central Asia, with equally trendy shawls draped over their shoulders. This freedom of movement was a far cry from the sequestered lifestyle of upper-strata women in later centuries, whose bound feet would have hindered their walking and who rarely ventured outside the house. Paintings of the time give a strong sense of the relative freedom northern women enjoyed. The women depicted ride with great ease; one mother is teaching her daughter how to handle the reins.

The Life of Merchants

Underneath scholars in the SPAM model came merchants, who were banned from the civil service exams in the years before 755. Although the SPAM model ranked merchants below peasants and artisans, merchants were much better off than those who worked with their hands. A

ples of the steppe, whose women enjoyed much greater freedom than did their sedentary sisters. By the twelfth century, when this copy of an eighth-century painting by Zhang Xuan was done, Chinese women had begun to bind their feet, and it must have been difficult for women viewers used to riding in sedan chairs to conceive of women riding on horseback as they do here.

normative scheme, the SPAM model did not describe the social reality of China. Many envied merchants' wealth. After all, their riches made Changan bustle, and they brought goods all the way from Persia and India to the east and Japan to the west. Sumptuary laws restricted the size and types of decoration of merchant houses, but those involved in the lucrative trade certainly had the means to circumvent these laws.

Government officials did not limit themselves to policing the merchants' lifestyles. Far more important, they subjected the two markets of Changan to strict supervision. Changan's two markets were very big, each about one kilometer (.6 miles) square. They lay at the center of two systems of transportation, one of imperial roads and one of canals. The Eastern Market specialized in locally produced goods, like salt, tea, silks, precious metals or jewels, slaves, grain, timber, and horses. The wine shops and brothels of the red-light district were in this market, where exam candidates stayed.

The government regulated the houses of prostitution. The prostitutes, who had been abandoned by their husbands or parents or had been kidnapped, worked for madams whom they called their fictive mothers. These women trained the recruits to sing, dance, and play drinking games. Restricted to the district, the women could leave only if their customers posted a bond. Men could pay a fee to obtain the exclusive services of an individual woman, and families seem to have patronized certain madams.

Officials restricted trade to authorized markets. The two markets in Changan each had a market director, who, with his staff, enforced a host of government regulations. The market office could punish merchants for any offense against public order. The markets opened only at noon and closed promptly at sundown. The market supervisor was supposed to check weights and measures, the quality of goods on sale, and the quality of money in circulation. Because of a chronic shortage of bronze coins (made out of copper, lead, and tin), bolts of silk served as the main currency and were sometimes supplemented by silver coins brought in from Iran.

The market supervisor was charged with preventing such unfair trading practices as cornering the market for commodities, price-fixing, or deceiving the public. Every ten days, after reviewing prices, he issued new ones for three grades of each basic commodity. Every time someone sold livestock, slaves, or land, they had to apply to his office for a certificate of sale. These regulations indicate enormous government control over commerce. Fragments of the ten-day price lists have been found in a northwest Chinese oasis, indicating that a high level of control was actually maintained.

Although Changan was at the end of the Silk Road, with its extraordinary level of trade in the most exotic goods, government officials remained suspicious of all those involved in long-distance trade. Many were foreigners, and Tang sculptures of the time show camels with riders of distinctly un-Chinese features, mustaches, and hairy eyebrows.

Viewing all merchants as potential spies, the government maintained strict surveillance over them as they went from one city to the next. They had to show their travel documents at every checkpoint they went through, and they had to prove ownership of all the animals and slaves in their caravans.

Commoners

The merchants endured a high degree of government supervision, but the life of the common people in the city was just as regulated and not nearly as comfortable. Little documentation remains concerning the lives of working people in the city. They ate simply, often only two meals a day. Families shared one or two rooms. Pawnshop records from Luoyang reveal that the poor were often forced to pawn their possessions to borrow money, on which they made installment payments every two weeks. They usually pawned clothing or bolts of silk, but sometimes the items were rugs or copper mirrors.

Thousands were employed in menial jobs running shops, maintaining gardens, cleaning streets, tending horses, and peddling goods. Inadequate grain supplies posed another difficulty for the common people. Throughout the seventh century frequent canal blockages prompted the emperor to order the capital shifted from Changan to Luoyang, a city slightly to the east and located on a better section of the canal system. The resulting moves must have burdened everyone in the city, especially the working people who had to do the carting.

The life of the common people did have its compensations. They could get medicine from Buddhist clinics not widely available elsewhere in the empire. The lunar New Year marked the coming of spring and was a time of great celebration. The fifteenth day of the first month was the lantern festival, and in 715 the emperor erected a structure 45 meters (150 feet) high laden with 50,000 lanterns for the pleasure of the city's inhabitants. On this day people did not have to go to work and they feasted, eating meat for perhaps the only time each year. The rest of the year they ate a diet of wheat and millet gruel, supplemented by vegetables. They also went outside the city on temple visits, which provided welcome respite from the drudgery of their daily lives.

"The Tale of Li Wa"

A short story written in 795, but set in pre-755 Changan, allows a glimpse of what life was like for the different social groups in the city. The brother of the poet Bai Juyi, Bai Xingjian (776–827), wrote "The Tale of Li Wa," quite possibly as a "warming" exercise to impress his examiner with his literary talents. It is the story of a young examination candidate who goes from riches to rags and back again to riches. Like many examination candidates, the protagonist Yuanhe is the son of a governor, who gives him beautiful clothes, a carriage, and spending money for his trip to the capital to sit for his examinations. At the beginning of the story he falls in love with a girl he glimpses near the Eastern Market. The Li Wa of the title, she lives in the red-light district. A friend explains that she is a prostitute.

The scholar pays a call on Li Wa and meets her madam, who poses as her mother. He is so taken with the girl that he hopes to stay the night when her madam remonstrates, "The drums have sounded. You had better go right away so that you will not violate the curfew."[5] Li Wa urges him to stay, and he asks his servants to give the mother two rolls of silk, the currency of the time. His gift is refused, he spends the night, and then moves in with the two women for about a year, during which time he exhausts his spending money. All is well until they trick him into going along on an outing to visit the Spirit of the Bamboo Grove, ostensibly to pray for a child. Li Wa and the madam feign a family emergency, promise to return, and part with the scholar. When he returns to the house to meet them, a servant tells him they have moved away.

The young man's troubles begin at this point, as he learns what life is like for those who do not have any money. He is forced to pawn some clothes to pay for his lodgings and is so sad that he becomes terribly ill, so ill that he is left for dead at a funeral shop. The employees of the shop nurse him back to life, and he begins to learn their mourning songs. He soon becomes the best professional mourner in the city, a lucrative career but one that is polluted because it is associated with death. Luckily, no one at the shop realizes he is an official's son, and his large disposable income makes him the social equivalent of a merchant.

His employer is so confident of his talent that he challenges his main rival to a funeral competition, which tens of thousands attend. The market supervisor is not consulted about this spontaneous competition, but one detail suggests extensive governmental control nonetheless: "Even the governor of the Metropolitan District became aware of the proceedings, having heard about it from the chief of police, who had in turn got it from the constable of the quarter." The scholar sings a solo so moving that the owner of the other shop acknowledges his defeat by simply returning home. The scholar's father, the governor, happens to be in Changan, and when he meets his son, he horsewhips him and leaves him for dead. This development is certainly difficult for the Western reader to accept: How could any father be so heartless? But in the society of the Tang with its rigid divisions, the son has violated all mores by assuming the status of a polluted, inferior person, and his father has no choice but to kill him.

The young man is severely wounded but does not die. His friends from the funeral home try to save him, but his wounds are so repulsive they give him up for dead, and he becomes a beggar. Like the other homeless people of the city he sleeps outside at night and goes to the market during the day. One snowy day he goes out to beg and again meets the girl Li Wa. She takes him in, arranges to buy her freedom from the madam, and sets to work nursing his wounds. His recovery begins, and one year later he resumes studying for the examinations, in which he succeeds brilliantly. At the end of the story he has become an official, is reconciled with his father, and marries the prostitute, who bears him four sons.

The story vividly captures the degree of surveillance under which the people of Changan lived. The nightly curfew is strictly observed. But life in the city has its pleasures, as the young scholar discovers to his peril. As long as a visitor has money, he can enjoy elaborate meals, performances, and the company of prostitutes. Any of the city's residents could visit the shrine of the Bamboo Grove, and many of them attend the funeral competition, an outpouring of the city's commercial spirit that does not quite fit the Tang Code's highly regulated picture of commerce.

At first glance this seems to be a story about social flux, but it is really about the lack of social change in Tang society. The official's son does everything he can to change his status, from singing in a funeral house to begging on the streets, but at the end of the story he remains a member of the official class and assumes his rightful place as an official. The prostitute does change her status. She begins as a member of a polluted profession and ends as the wife of a high official, but the author takes great pains to emphasize that this type of social change was rare: "How remarkable that a woman of the courtesan class should manifest a degree of loyalty and constancy such as is rarely exceeded by the heroines of antiquity! How can such a story fail to provoke sighs of admiration!" It is not surprising that on occasion beautiful women were able to marry out of their social class. In this respect, Tang China was no different from other traditional societies.

DAILY LIFE IN RURAL AREAS

As the life of those who lived in cities was highly regulated, so too was rural life. At its founding, the Tang dynasty established a common and uniform system of household registration, land allocation, taxation, military conscription, and labor service. The dynasty faced a real challenge in determining how to administer law throughout its huge empire, and the compilers of the Tang Code and other laws decided to treat the three hundred prefectures and fifteen hundred counties of the empire as if they were all the same, regardless of their geographical location or differences in climate. In theory, a peasant in the northwest, where there was a shortage of arable land, was entitled to the same allocation of land to support his family as a peasant in the south of China, where there was much land. They were to pay the same taxes, perform the same military and labor obligations (twenty days of service per year), and follow the same laws.

But before 589 the empire was not even united, and cultural changes persisted after reunification. Because the Tang dynasty had 17,000 officials and 50,000 clerks to govern a population of probably 60,000,000 people, the average county of 25,000 to 30,000 people was governed by just one magistrate, aided by 4 assistants and some clerks. These ratios meant that institutions designed to be applicable throughout China had to be formulated in broad general terms. It was the generalized, adaptable, and flexible nature of Tang law that made it so successful. The Tang Code specified that a magistrate could make decisions by analogy. When an offense did not fall exactly under the provisions of one article, the magistrate was free to adapt the law to find a solution.

The level of control described in the code could be attained only if the central government and its agents had detailed knowledge of each household and its individual members. The household registration system was the source of this knowledge.

> The household registers are to be drawn up every three years. One copy is to be retained in the county, one sent to the prefecture, and one copy sent to the Board of Finance. Provision for the necessary writing materials—paper, brushes, colored wrappers, and rollers for the scrolls—should be provided by charging one cash per individual member included in a given register. . . .
>
> The tax registers should be compiled annually. The village headman should scrutinize the declarations from the people under his jurisdiction and enter in them the ages of household members.[6]

Officials carried out inspections to count all members of a household and to determine which young men had just come of age and were eligible for military and labor service. They also classified the elderly and the crippled, who qualified for different degrees of tax exemption. On the basis of the information contained in the registers, officials divided the population into nine grades, which determined each man's level of taxation and labor service.

These registers also served as the basis of the land redistribution called for in the Tang Code, the equal-field system. The equal-field system divided all the land in the empire into two categories: personal share land and perpetual holdings. Each married couple was entitled to a grant of personal share land from the state. These grants were adjusted every three years, depending on the size of the household. In return for the land each household was obliged to pay taxes in grain and cloth and to perform labor service. On their deaths the personal share land was to revert to the state. Raising silk and silkworms required long-term investment in mulberry tree orchards, however, so government officials created the second category: perpetual holdings.

Silk continued to be an important commodity during the Tang dynasty even though the secret of making silk had already spread beyond China's borders. Silk had different uses. Most people paid some of their taxes with bolts of silk. During the Tang dynasty silk was a currency equal in importance to silver bars and copper coins, and of course, it continued to be used for the clothes of the very wealthy, which were often decorated with elaborate foreign designs. In some areas where mulberry trees could not grow, other types of land were classed as perpetual holdings. The government granted this land to households forever, so that when the parents in a family died, their children inherited their perpetual holding land.

The equal-field system, a legacy of the land policies of the earlier Northern Wei dynasty, was designed for an economy in which land was underused and money undeveloped as a means of exchange. As the Tang economy began to develop, the equal-field system proved inflexible. Many people, including the imperial family and all their relatives, remained exempt from paying taxes. Monks and nuns, registered on separate household registers, paid no taxes and performed no labor service. And because commercial taxes were very light, merchants who did not own land went largely untaxed. Many people falsified their registration, so that government registers showed too few people and too little land throughout the empire. A chronic shortage of funds resulting from these inefficiencies plagued the Tang dynasty.

Although the first century and a half of Tang rule are often seen as a period when the central government enjoyed unprecedented control over both rural and urban life, central government records, long available to historians, reveal persistent shortfalls in expected revenues. We must remember that even in the early years of the Tang, the equal-field system never paid for itself, and therefore, could not have gone unchanged.

A spectacular archeological find in northwest China provides a unique glimpse of the equal-field system at work. The Tang had conquered much of the northwest by 640. Since they governed Turfan just as they governed all the other prefectures in the empire, it was subject to all the regulations of the Tang Code. The finds from the Astana graveyard in northwest China, near the modern city of Turfan in eastern Xinjiang, shows the Tang state in action.

The Astana Tombs

The Astana graveyard lies in the Turfan depression, a hot, dry place with temperatures averaging 38 degrees C (100 degrees F) in the summer. Its climate is ideal for preserving textiles, wood, leather, food, and paper. In

1959, some farmers dug an irrigation channel through the Astana grave-yard, and archeologists subsequently found over ten thousand fragments of documents dating back to the seventh and eighth centuries. Because paper was scarce at Astana, it was used over and over again. The local people equipped the dead with paper hats and shoes, which they made from wastepaper. Scholars have painstakingly reconstructed some two thousand original documents from the sections of shoes and hats. Because these documents were not deliberately placed in the graves, but survive only by accident, they provide a genuinely random sample of the documents used in daily life. Family letters, police reports, official documents, texts of regulations, and contracts all appear.

The Turfan documents reveal that local people observed the provisions of the Tang Code to a surprising degree. Just as in Changan, market officials drew up price lists every ten days. Officials compiled household registers. They also redistributed land, but because of the land shortage in the oasis, each individual received much less land than government regulations specified. The Tang Code forbade the sale of land (except to meet funeral expenses), but people certainly rented and probably sold land, both their personal share land and their perpetual holdings (mulberry trees did grow in Turfan). People in Turfan lived in a largely subsistence economy, often using barter. Even so, they had contracts drawn up for even the lowliest of transactions: the loan of a gown, the exchange of camels, the purchase of a shirt.

Moneylender Zuo's Tomb

The contracts from one tomb at Astana provide a vivid picture of rural society under Tang rule. In 673, a moneylender and soldier named Zuo Chongxi was buried at the age of fifty-seven, with thirteen legible contracts dating from 660 to 670. Unlike other contracts from Turfan, the thirteen contracts in Moneylender Zuo's tomb were deliberately buried with him. With one contract Zuo bought a fifteen-year-old slave; with another he purchased ninety bundles of hay, presumably for his herds of sheep and camels. Seven contracts were for loans of money or silk cloth, which served as an alternate currency. And he used four more to rent land from the poor. Presumably only a fraction of the contracts he held during his lifetime, these thirteen include examples of the major types of contracts used in Turfan under the Tang: those for buying and renting land, for acquiring or exchanging goods, and for incorporating new sources of labor into the household, either as slaves or family members.

The contracts are similar in format: they begin with the date, name the parties and goods involved, specify when ownership will change hands, and spell out the consequences should either party break the agreement. They repeat long sections of text, testifying to the prevalence of legal boilerplate in the seventh century. The mixture of fixed legal language with personal interpolations indicates that scribes, and possibly ordinary folk, had a rough command of simple legal terminology. At the end of the contract came the names of the parties involved, the guarantors, and the witnesses. Because he was lending money and in the superior position, Moneylender Zuo did not draw his finger joints, but the borrower and his guarantors did. Tracing one's finger joints, much like drawing a cross in the West, was the way illiterate people indicated their assent in Tang contracts.

Most of the contracts in Moneylender Zuo's tomb are one-time agreements with different individuals, but three contracts are with the same farmer, Zhang Shanxi. In 668, Moneylender Zuo and Farmer Zhang signed a contract in which Zuo lent Zhang twenty silver coins, at a monthly interest of two coins, or 10 percent. The exact value of these coins is unknown, but silver coins from Iran have been found at Astana. The interest rate of 10 percent a month was much higher than the 6 percent allowed by the Tang Code. The frequency of contracts at Turfan setting the monthly rate of interest at 10 percent, sometimes 15 percent indicates that the government lacked the means to enforce the interest rate stipulated by law.

Farmer Zhang and Moneylender Zuo signed the contract in the third month, just at the time of the first planting, when many cultivators were short of money. Zhang promised to pay the money back whenever Zuo asked for it, and he put up his household possessions and one vegetable field as security. Two years later, in 670, in the second month, Moneylender Zuo agreed to rent a different vegetable field from Zhang, for which he would pay rent twice a year, in the sixth and ninth months, for three years. In the fourth year he was to make a cash payment of thirty silver coins. He made no payment at the time of signing. Contrary to prevailing stereotypes, the tenant, Moneylender Zuo, was demonstrably better off than his landlord. Only one month later, Moneylender Zuo lent Zhang forty silver coins, at a monthly interest of four coins, again 10 percent. Although we do not know whether Zhang paid Zuo back, Zhang seems to have been getting deeper and deeper into debt. Moneylender Zuo must have lent money to Zhang and rented his land with the hope of ultimately taking it over.

These documents show that Moneylender Zuo was involved in a wide variety of transactions involving contracts, but they reveal little about him as a person. Fortunately, his tomb contains several objects and documents that supplement the information to be gleaned from the contracts. Moneylender Zuo was buried with a crude figure of a woman labeled "Wife Heduan." Heduan was the Chinese transcription of the Turkish word for queen, *kutoun*. Was Moneylender Zuo married to a Turkish woman? Could he have been Turkish himself? We cannot be sure.

One of the documents in the tomb is an inventory listing the goods accompanying Zuo to the netherworld: 5 slaves, 30 pecks of silver, 50,000 piculs of different grains, and 10,000 pieces of white silk. Large quantities of silk are frequently mentioned in documents of this type; the silk was seen as a means of climbing to heaven. These inflated figures probably refer to paper facsimiles of the goods in question, which were burnt at the time of the funeral. This inventory begins by summarizing Moneylender Zuo's good deeds: he built a statue of the Buddha and two attendants, and he sponsored the writing or recitation of *The Yulanpen Sutra*, a Buddhist text.

Moneylender Zuo's relatives included this inventory in his tomb because they thought he would need the listed goods in the underworld. They also believed he would need a record of his Buddhist acts, presumably to tilt the balance in his favor when he was being judged by the gods of the underworld. Another document from his tomb testifies to the widely held belief in underworld justice. It is a letter addressed to the deceased moneylender stating that five hundred silver coins were stolen from the moneylender's household in 667, and that the moneylender assumed a man named Fen She had taken the money. The author of the letter, the accused Fen She, denies the charge and explains that he ran away rather than be beaten for the theft. The letter concludes with the following claim: "He knew the dead man would realize who had taken the money, once he had met his soul on the twenty-ninth day of the fourth month of the fourth year of the Xianheng reign [673] and seen those who had been freed."[7] All innocent people would have been allowed to go free in the underworld, Fen She claims, and he fully expects to be included in their ranks. We have no way of determining whether Fen She was as innocent as he maintains.

Fen She buried his letter in the moneylender's tomb for the same reason that Moneylender Zuo buried the thirteen contracts. Both men believed in the existence of the netherworld courts, and both men wanted to go before the judges of the dead armed with correct documents. Moneylender Zuo hoped to collect on all his unpaid contracts left over from his lifetime, and Fen She wanted to defend himself against any charges Moneylender Zuo might bring against him in the netherworld courts. This was the netherworld court system that tried the Tang emperor for murdering his brothers. The widespread belief in the court system—from the people of Changan to the people of Turfan—shows how widely the people of the Tang shared the same assumptions.

The Shared World of Changan and Turfan

Residents of the empire, whether they lived in Changan or in Turfan, lived in a Chinese world extraordinarily open to foreign influence. They were serious devotees of a religion originating in India. As the Sui and Tang emperors had patronized Buddhism and used it, like Empress Wu, to legitimate their rule, so too did Moneylender Zuo sponsor the reading of Buddhist texts and the carving of Buddhist sculptures. The citizens of the Tang empire traded with foreigners, and they also married them and adopted their customs. Moneylender Zuo's wife was probably Turkish, and so was the wife of the founder of the Sui, who would not allow him any concubines. So were many people in the Tang imperial family. Remember the son of Emperor Taizong, the seemingly crazed prince who insisted on speaking only Turkish. The people of the Tang lived in a culturally mixed world filled with foreign art, music, and fashions.

They also lived in a world governed by regulations. Officials supervised all markets carefully, stipulating what hours they could open and where they were located. Regulators monitored prices and checked weights and measures. They kept just as close a watch on rural residents, tallying members in their households and redistributing land at regular intervals. They collected taxes in kind, and made sure that citizens performed their labor and military duties. The Tang rulers were able to sustain an extraordinary degree of uniformity throughout their empire.

CHRONOLOGY

618–907	TANG DYNASTY
755	*An Lushan rebellion*
763	*An Lushan rebellion suppressed*
after 763	*Equal-field system falls into disuse, two-tax system implemented, salt monopoly revived*
772–846	*Lifetime of Bai Juyi, famous poet and official*
779–831	*Lifetime of Yuan Zhen, author of "The Story of Oriole"*
800–1000	*Lay associations active in Dunhuang*
819	*Han Yu (768–824) denounces worship of Buddhist relics at Dharma Gate Monastery*
838–847	*Japanese monk Ennin travels to China*
845	*Short-lived imperial suppression of Buddhism*
880	*The rebel Huang Chao captures Changan*
885	*Tang emperor held prisoner by eunuchs and military governors*
907	*Last Tang emperor killed*
907–960	FIVE DYNASTIES PERIOD OF DIVISION
921	*Dated manuscript of the story of Turnip's visit to the underworld*
945	*Widow Along sues to get her land back*
after 1000	*Dunhuang cave sealed*
1900	*Library cave at Dunhuang discovered*
1907	*Aurel Stein visits Dunhuang*

THE AN LUSHAN REBELLION AND ITS AFTERMATH

(755–960)

The rebel An Lushan dealt the Tang dynasty a blow from which it never recovered. Although it lasted for another century and a half, the Tang survived in name only. The dynasty steadily ceded power at the center to eunuchs and in the provinces to military governors. Indeed, the An Lushan rebellion may be seen as the major turning point in pre-modern Chinese history. Before the uprising, the central government enjoyed great power and controlled the tax system. In fighting the rebellion, however, the central government granted important powers to provincial rulers. Among these were the authority to collect taxes, only a small part of which the provincial governors forwarded to the center. The weakness of the center in relation to the provinces continued until the end of dynastic government in 1911.

In the ninth century, the court made several attempts—all ultimately unsuccessful—to regain power and to increase revenues. In 907, twenty-five years after military governors had gained actual control, a general killed off the last boy emperor of the Tang and founded a new dynasty. With the demise of the Tang dynasty, its once-glorious capital in ruins, the empire broke apart into autonomous regions. A rare cache of manuscripts from the cave site of Dunhuang reveals how the populace came to terms with a world in which regional rulers exercised nearly total autonomy and in which household registers no longer existed.

THE AN LUSHAN REBELLION

Although Emperor Xuanzong (reigned 712–756) is credited with restoring the Tang dynasty after Empress Wu's interregnum, and although he

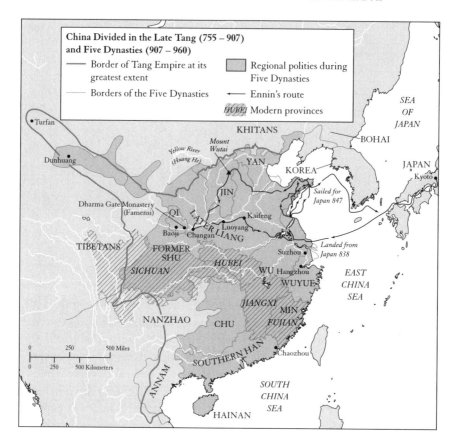

China Divided in the Late Tang (755 – 907)
and Five Dynasties (907 – 960)

—— Border of Tang Empire at its
greatest extent

----- Borders of the Five Dynasties

Regional polities during
Five Dynasties

←— Ennin's route

HUBEI Modern provinces

ruled over a prosperous and powerful empire for more than forty years, his own reign ended ignominiously when his once-loyal general An Lushan rose up against him. Sometime in the 740s, as Emperor Xuanzong was nearly sixty, he fell in love with the wife of one of his sons. She left her husband and temporarily became a Daoist adept, and her husband subsequently remarried. The sources do not reveal whether they divorced, but divorce existed in eighth-century China, and the breakup of their marriage did not incur the criticism one might expect. After a brief period of ostensible devotion, the woman joined Xuanzong's household and was given the title Precious Consort Yang (Yang Guifei).

The emperor and his consort were very close, but she was also drawn to a part-Turkish, part-Sogdian general named An Lushan, whom she adopted as her honorary son in 751. The Sogdians spoke a dialect of Middle Persian and originally hailed from the region surrounding Samarkand in modern-day Uzbekistan. An was a surname assigned to non-Chinese originating from Samarkand, while Lushan was the Chinese pronunciation of the name Rokshan ("light," which is the masculine form of the modern English name Roxanne, also of Persian origin). The general's Chinese name is used here, although many would have called him by the Persian equivalent. Later historians presume that the foreign general and Precious Consort Yang had an affair, but there is no clear evidence that they did.

In the decade leading up to 755, An Lushan became so involved in court intrigue that one faction at court plotted to murder him for his disloyalty to Emperor Xuanzong. Meanwhile, the emperor continued to support him and in 754 even proposed naming him chief minister; his enemies, however, argued that his illiteracy disqualified him. The emperor compromised by appointing him Commissioner of the Imperial Stables, a position that allowed An to purchase many new horses for his army. This was a dangerous position to give to someone whom others suspected of plotting a revolt.

The situation at court worsened, and in 755, when the emperor summoned An Lushan to attend the wedding of one of his sons, General An refused. The emperor sent an envoy, but the general refused him even

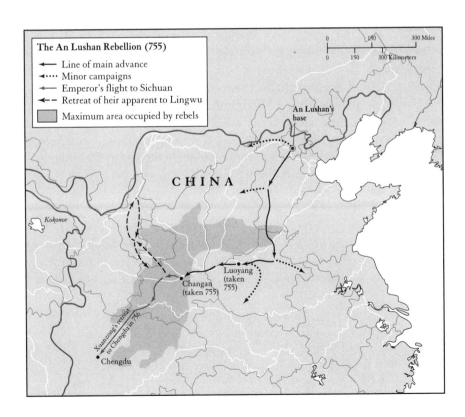

The An Lushan Rebellion (755)

→ Line of main advance
◄···· Minor campaigns
← Emperor's flight to Sichuan
◄-- Retreat of heir apparent to Lingwu

Maximum area occupied by rebels

An Lushan's base

CHINA

Kokonor

Changan (taken 755)

Luoyang (taken 755)

Xuanzong's retreat to Chengdu in 756

Chengdu

0   150   300 Miles
0   150   300 Kilometers

the most basic courtesy of standing in his presence. Four months later the general rebelled. The advantage lay with his powerful army, and his forces took the eastern capital of Luoyang with ease. A few months later, after a particularly disastrous defeat, the emperor, accompanied by a few troops and Precious Consort Yang, fled Changan for Sichuan. Blaming Precious Consort Yang for their predicament, the troops mutinied and refused to go on unless the emperor killed his beloved concubine. Giving in to the mutineers' wishes, the emperor ordered his chief eunuch to strangle her.

Visual and Literary Depictions of the An Lushan Rebellion

The disastrous end to the emperor's love affair with Precious Consort Yang has caught the imagination of many poets and painters. An early landscape painting, "The Emperor Minghuang's Journey to Shu" (a tenth-century copy of an eighth-century painting), shows the emperor's forces on their way to Sichuan. The sharp mountains are painted with the vivid blues and greens typical of Tang-dynasty mineral paints.

Here too one can see the freedom of the women in the emperor's entourage. The emperor's horse is in the foreground, with its mane tied into three bunches. Although some of the women's hats have veils, their faces are uncovered and they are wearing riding trousers. Women of equivalent status in later centuries would always be veiled, wear robes, and be restricted to sedan chairs. It is hard to make out the soldiers' faces, but they seem to be smiling, although the shadowed, somber tones of the painting convey the tragedy of her death. A different painting, now held at the Metropolitan Museum of Art in New York City, shows Precious Consort Yang's riderless horse, a far more poignant image than any concrete depiction of Precious Consort Yang's death.

One of the most popular poems in Chinese, Bai Juyi's "A Song of Unending Sorrow," was written some two generations after Precious Consort Yang's death. Very pleased by the success of his work, Bai Juyi proudly told the story of a singing girl who was able to charge more money for her services because she could recite the poem in its entirety.

The poem told the story of the emperor's love for Precious Consort Yang:

> . . . It was early spring. They bathed her in the Flower-Pure Pool,
> Which warmed and smoothed the creamy-tinted crystal of her skin,
> And, because of her languor, a maid was lifting her
> When first the Emperor noticed her and chose her for his bride.
> . . . And the Emperor, from that time forth, forsook his early hearings

THE IMPERIAL FAMILY IN FLIGHT

As the rebel forces of An Lushan attacked the Tang-dynasty capital in A.D. 755, the imperial family escaped on horseback across mountains into Sichuan province. The women in the imperial household knew how to ride and are depicted wearing trousers and on horseback with the men, in this eleventh-century copy of the eighth-century painting, "The Emperor Ming-huang's Journey to Shu," held in Taipei.

And lavished all his time on her with feasts and revelry,
His mistress of the spring, his despot of the night.

The emperor, so besotted with his love that he cannot attend meetings is, of course, the stuff of stereotype. But the poem challenges other stereotypes:

. . . And, because she so illumined and glorified her clan,
She brought to every father, every mother through the empire,
Happiness when a girl was born rather than a boy.

The father of a daughter who died young, Bai may exaggerate the popularity of Precious Consort Yang, but she was extraordinarily popular, because she embodied changing views of feminine beauty.

THE RIDERLESS HORSE

Blaming her for the disaster, soldiers forced the emperor to kill his beloved Precious Consort Yang. Here a painter, working five centuries later, depicts her solitary horse, a poignant symbol of the fallen Tang dynasty that never regained its former glory.

Like the anonymous painting of "Emperor Minghuang's Journey," the poet tells of her death indirectly:

> The Emperor's eyes could never gaze on her enough—
> Till war-drums, booming from Yuyang, shocked the whole earth . . .
> The imperial flag opened the way, now moving and now pausing—
> But thirty miles from the capital, beyond the western gate,
> The men of the army stopped, not one of them would stir
> Till under their horses' hoofs they might trample those moth-eyebrows . . .
> Flowery hairpins fell to the ground, no one picked them up,
> And a green and white jade hair-tassel and a yellow-gold hair-bird.
> The Emperor could not save her, he could only cover his face.
> And later when he turned to look, the place of blood and tears . . .[1]

"A Song of Unending Sorrow" alters historical fact to suit the poet's purpose. In the poem, the consort dies trampled by horses; in actuality, the emperor ordered his chief eunuch to strangle her. Bai Juyi describes the two lovers as if they were roughly the same age; in fact, the emperor was some forty years older than his young bride.

Emperor Xuanzong continued to rule for a few months after the death of Precious Consort Yang, but one of his sons deposed him in 755 and granted him the title of retired emperor. After eight years of fighting and considerable concessions to the regional military commanders, the Tang forces were finally able to defeat General An's army in 763.

The Costs of Suppressing Rebellion

Internal schisms surfaced following the rebels' early success in 755, and after the assassination of their commander An Lushan in early 757, the rebel forces split into two factions, one led by An Lushan's son, the other by a rival general. The new emperor Suzong (reigned 756–762) was able to regain Changan only with the help of Uighur mercenaries. After a long stalemate, the rebellion finally ended in 763, following the suicide of the rebels' leading general. Still dependent on hired Uighur troops from Central Asia, and unable to defeat the rebels decisively, the court was forced to give them a blanket pardon. The uncertain peace was short-lived. At the end of 763, Tibetan troops entered Changan for two weeks of pillaging and then withdrew, only to attack the capital every autumn for the next twenty years. The emperor's troops were powerless to stop them because, by the eighth century, the kingdom of Tibet had become China's most powerful neighbor in Asia. Its troops would continue to plague the Chinese until the ninth century, when Tibet fell into disunity.

The violence of the rebellion and its suppression destroyed the cities that lay in the rebels' path and wrecked the equal-field system. During the years it took the court to put the rebels down, the government had neither the manpower nor the funds to carry out the triannual land and population surveys the equal-field system demanded. The number of registered households in the Tang Empire dropped from nine million in 755 to two million in 760—not because the population diminished but because the system of household registration was not enforced. After the rebellion, the tax base of the empire was less than one-third of what it had been.

The rebellion forced the emperor to share power with the military governors who ruled both the frontier provinces and those in the interior. These newly empowered governors commanded their own armies, which they funded from the tax revenues of the areas they governed. In 763, at the end of the rebellion, the court named four rebel generals to serve as the military governors of Hebei, one of the richest provinces in China's heartland. When these newly appointed military governors seceded by refusing to pay taxes, the center lost over one-quarter of the empire's population and the tax revenues they produced. Hebei and Henan were the first areas to drop off, but over the next century and a half, as more and more provinces followed suit, the Tang succumbed to a diminution it was powerless to combat.

The desperate court appointed special commissioners for taxation, whose task was to raise revenues in any way possible. They tried selling offices, speculating with the money supply, and taxing trade; they soon found that the salt monopoly could produce the highest revenues with the least manpower. Salt was produced in only a few areas, either along the coast or in Sichuan, where salty brine could be mined. In both places, saltwater was poured into large pans where it was allowed to evaporate. As long as the state maintained direct control over the area of production, it could buy up all the salt produced there and sell it to merchants. The populace at large could then buy the salt, a crucial element in their diet, from these merchants. The merchants who distributed the salt all over the empire were responsible for collecting the salt tax for the state. This was a genuine and lucrative innovation. In 779, the salt monopoly produced half the central government's revenues.[2]

The state continued to collect the tax on agricultural production but it was forced to develop a new method of taxation. In 780, it launched the two-tax system, a twice-yearly collection of taxes in summer and autumn, as the replacement for the defunct equal-field system. Each province was assigned a quota, which the military governors paid to the center, and then local government officials distributed the tax burden among the local population as they saw fit. Unlike the equal-field system, which had assigned tax obligations in goods—grains, cloth, or labor—all quotas in the two-tax system were calculated in money, either bronze coins or silver specie. Although most people continued to pay taxes using commodities like grain or cloth, the use of money gradually increased, and the use of cloth as currency declined.

During these difficult years, the civil service examinations continued to be held, even though the central government hired far fewer new officials than it had in the years before the An Lushan rebellion. Some of China's most talented writers—Bai Juyi (772–846), Yuan Zhen (779–831), and Han Yu (768–824)—were born, received their examination degrees, and pursued bureaucratic careers in the tumultuous years after 755.

The Poet Bai Juyi (772–846)

The turmoil of the last years of the eighth century forced Bai Juyi and his brothers to live with relatives, sometimes near the capital, sometimes in the southern cities of Suzhou and Hangzhou. Bai's father, who had attained only the rank of assistant governor at his death in 794, left behind him a widow with three sons and no means of support. The most obvious means of advancement for a young man in these straits was the civil service examinations. In 799, Bai passed the local examinations and so earned the right to sit for the national exams, but still he faced many obstacles.

Bai had a choice between an examination on the five classics, which stressed memorization and resulted in lower placement in the civil service, or the more prestigious literary examination. His father and grandfather had passed only the classics examination. Bai opted for the literary examination, which tested both one's knowledge of the classics and one's literary ability. The candidates were asked to write essays on a given topic incorporating words from a line of poetry; the examination tested knowledge of allusion as well as the ability to compose essays of substance in a strictly regulated format.

The other obstacles were social. Those grading the examinations knew all the candidates, and the chief examiners often rewarded the sons of powerful official families with high scores. Even though Bai's father and grandfather had been officials, he saw himself as being outside the privileged classes. Unlike the students studying at the capital, whose long residence gave them many chances to establish good relations with their examiners, those passing the provincial examinations arrived in the capital in the tenth month and sat for the exams a mere two months later.

After Bai's arrival in the capital, in the hope of advancing his prospects he wrote a fawning letter to an elder statesman in which he explained, "I am a man of undistinguished birth. At Court I have no powerful connections to help me on; at home I have no influential friends to commend me. Why then have I come to the Capital? In the hope that my powers as a writer will serve me. I am dependent therefore on fair treatment by my examiner. Fortunately Gao Ying, of the Board of Rites, is to be the examiner, and there is no juster man than he."[3] This letter did not win Bai a patron, but he was right about Gao Ying, who hoped to end all the practices by which candidates sought to ingratiate themselves with their examiners, including warming-the-exam papers and letters like the one Bai sent. For once, the exams were graded on the basis of merit, not social connections, and in 800 Bai received a first-class literary degree.

This degree was no guarantee of a post, and Bai proceeded to take a second examination at the capital, the Placing Examination. First he had to prove that his father was not a merchant or craftsman and that he had never been arrested for a crime. Then Bai gained the right to sit for an examination that required him to demonstrate mastery of an even more arcane literary form: the judgment. On the basis of his full command of the archaic pseudolegal vocabulary as well as his genuine literary flair, Bai won a very low-ranking and low-paid post in the Palace Library that required him to go to the library only one or two times a month. It was at this time that Bai published a collection of one hundred judgments on different topics, which were then sold in bookstores, presumably to other examination candidates.

One of these model judgments provided a spirited defense of merchants' right to sit for the examinations. Given that the Tang Code explicitly barred all merchants and artisans and their descendants from taking the civil service examinations, Bai's answer marks a surprising departure from the received wisdom of his time:

> When all the candidates are known to one, how can one possibly reject the ones with the most outstanding talents. Since the only valid objection to merchants is that they are petty and low, how can you reject one of them who proves to be excellent and outstanding? If you found gold among gravel, you surely would not refuse to pick it up just because it was found mixed up with worthless material.
>
> . . . There is ample proof to be found in past experience that it is possible to select officials from among the children of mean traders.[4]

His position is clear: even the children of merchants should be allowed to serve if they can prove their talent. Bai's reply reflects the social changes occurring in China after the An Lushan rebellion and its destruction of the dynasty's tax base. The financial demands of the central government were so great that officials developed new means of raising money, like the salt commission; and because they needed the expertise of merchants, they eased the ban on merchants sitting for the exams. Even an Arab merchant took the civil service examinations in the early ninth century.

The Rise of the Eunuchs

At the same time that the new tax system strengthened those who collected the taxes, particularly military governors and finance commissioners, the changes at court after 755 also empowered eunuchs. Unlike earlier periods in which eunuchs were drawn from war captives, most Tang-dynasty eunuchs came from the indigenous peoples in the poor districts of the south and southwest, whose prefects captured the boys and sent a certain number to the emperor every year. The province of Fujian supplied so many boys that some called it a eunuch factory. Once the boys arrived in the capital, they joined the Palace Domestic Service and were adopted by senior eunuchs, whose family names they took. Their responsibilities were ostensibly limited to the women's quarters, but some served as messengers to—and possibly spies on—military commanders.

After the An Lushan rebellion, eunuchs gradually gained control of the emperor's personal army, the only forces available to the center not commanded by the military governors. Eunuchs managed to insinuate themselves into high positions, often by placing their adopted sons (including some who were not eunuchs) into different offices in the capital and outside it, and by forming factions with others. The ninth century saw the formation of a Eunuchs' Palace Council, whose members coordinated the different realms of eunuch activity, primarily within the domestic quarters and the forces controlled by the eunuchs. Its members advised the emperor on issues of state and so posed a direct threat to the regular court ministers. Because eunuchs were able to report to the emperor directly, they also served as his personal spies.

The official histories, the source of so much of what we know about court politics, provide little information about the eunuchs' activities. The officials who drafted these histories were regular bureaucrats who were suspicious of the eunuchs and had little contact with them. We can overcome their silence with a rare day-to-day account of the brief reign of the Emperor Shunzong, who ruled for only six months in 805. Han Yu, one of the great prose stylists of the Tang, drafted this text. Han Yu, dissatisfied with the convoluted prose of his contemporaries, sought to restore the elegance of Chinese prose by following the classical masters. Employing a new prose style called the "literature of antiquity" (*guwen*), he hoped to revive the teachings of both Confucius and Mencius (discussed in chapter 2).

The Reign of Emperor Shunzong

Han Yu's historical account of the Emperor Shunzong's reign records that just before acceding to the throne, the future emperor suffered a stroke that left him unable to speak and "unable to make decisions." This disability made him an ideal front man for scheming politicians, two of whom engineered his accession in 805, in spite of opposition from another faction. The edicts they forged in his hand purport to show his concern for the people of Changan.

In 805, the emperor issued an edict abolishing the palace marketing system, through which eunuchs supplied the palace with goods from the city's markets. The eunuchs were accused of setting unfair prices without regard for the actual market price. Han Yu mentions an incident from an earlier reign in which a eunuch seized a handful of brushwood from a farmer whom he paid only a few feet of silk, hardly the value of the wood. The eunuch then tried to requisition the farmer's donkey to take the wood to the palace. The desperate farmer then beat the eunuch. The emperor heard about the incident and awarded the farmer compensation, but the palace marketing system persisted.

This same incident prompted Bai Juyi to write a poem:

> An old charcoal-seller
> Cutting wood and burning charcoal in the forest of the Southern Mountain.
> His face, stained with dust and ashes, has turned to the color of smoke.
> The hair on his temples is streaked with gray: his ten fingers are black.
> The money he gets by selling charcoal, how far does it go?
> It is just enough to clothe his limbs and put food in his mouth.
> Although, alas, the coat on his back is a coat without lining,
> He hopes for the coming of cold weather, to send up the price of coal!
> Last night, outside the city,—a whole foot of snow;
> At dawn he drives the charcoal wagon along the frozen ruts.
> Oxen,—weary; man,—hungry: the sun, already high;
> Outside the Gate, to the south of the Market, at last they stop in the mud.
> Suddenly, a pair of prancing horsemen. Who can it be coming?
> A public official in a yellow coat and a boy in a white shirt.
> In their hands they hold a written warrant: on their tongues—the words of an order;

They turn back the wagon and curse the oxen, leading them off to the north.
A whole wagon of charcoal,
More than a thousand catties!
If officials choose to take it away, the woodman may not complain.
Half a roll of red silk and ten feet of damask,
The Courtiers have tied to the oxen's collar, as the price of a wagon of coal![5]

The poet vividly captures the human toll of the palace marketing system and also confirms the widespread use of cloth as currency. The official pays far less than the real value of the charcoal, and he does so in cloth. The reader does not have to be familiar with obscure literary allusions to understand Bai's criticisms of the palace marketing system. Because Bai Juyi often used such vivid, direct language, he became one of China's (and Japan's) most beloved poets.

Although the abolition of the palace marketing system drew public favor, it was not enough to keep Emperor Shunzong in power. The faction in control of the army persuaded the emperor to name his successor, and soon after this he abdicated. The ninth century saw eight more changes of emperor, each like that of Emperor Shunzong, engineered by eunuchs working in concert with political factions.

Bai Juyi and his friend Yuan Zhen were also affected by these developments. After Emperor Shunzong abdicated, the new emperor held a Palace Examination in which the candidates wrote an essay on a single topic set by the emperor. Yuan Zhen came first in the competition, Bai Juyi, second. The two men had first met five years earlier, when they had both passed the Placing Examination and won identical posts in the palace library. Like Bai, Yuan Zhen was a gifted literary stylist, and he and Bai became very close friends. Theirs was to become one of the most famous and best documented friendships in Chinese history. Also like Bai, Yuan Zhen did not see himself as belonging to the top social echelons though he was descended from the rulers of the Northern Wei dynasty. The two men considered themselves outsiders in the bureaucracy who had won their positions on the basis of merit, not social position. Yet, like their colleagues, their fortunes depended on which faction was in power. The sudden ups and downs of their careers characterized those of many of the highly born aristocrat-bureaucrats around them.

Yuan Zhen and "The Story of Oriole"

Yuan Zhen wrote a short story about a broken-off love affair between a young examination candidate and the daughter of a high-ranking family, Oriole (Yingying), that reveals the heavy influence of political ambition on the decisions of young men of his time. The narrative begins with a description of Zhang, a young man who, unusually, is a virgin at the age of twenty-two. The scholar meets Oriole at the monastery where she is staying with her widowed mother and brother. When a rebellion breaks out, the young scholar protects the girl's family, and the mother invites him to visit her so that she can thank him. She also insists that her daughter appear, which Oriole reluctantly does, wearing no makeup and a simple dress. Zhang falls immediately in love with Oriole and subsequently enlists her maid's help in winning the girl. The maid suggests that he propose marriage, but he tells the maid that his suffering is so great that he will not live long enough to conduct a proper engagement. He then gives the maid a poem for Oriole, who asks to meet him in the middle of the night. When the two meet, she rebukes him at great length for making an unsolicited advance, and she withdraws.

Oriole later sends her maid to Zhang's room at night to announce her mistress's arrival. This change of heart, described in just a few words, comes as a surprise and is one of the least understood reversals in Chinese literature. The astute reader detects Oriole's longing for Zhang in the length and timing of her speech in which she so vehemently denounces his overture. When she changes her mind and decides to make an advance, she adopts a helpless stance thought to be attractive in women: Oriole "was meek and coy, and so languid that she appeared as though she could not support her limbs." When she arrives, she rests on her maid's arm, and, when she leaves in the morning, she does so again with the maid's assistance. Oriole and Zhang fall in love and spend every night together for a month.

Suddenly, Zhang leaves Oriole in order to take his examinations in the capital. After he fails on his first attempt, he writes of his decision to stay in the capital, so breaking off their relationship. In response, she sends him a letter in which she gives eloquent voice to her emotions:

> You say that you are staying at the capital so that you may prosecute your studies; this is the way of advancement and it is as it should be. My only complaint is that this bids to make permanent what started out only as a temporary separation. But it is my fate; there is no use talking about it. . . .
>
> As we shared mat and pillow, profound was our abiding faith; and I in my simple and unsophisticated mind believed I had found a support for the rest of my life. Little did I think that the meeting with my Prince would fail to result in solemn wedlock, and that I would only incur the shame of self-surrender without winning the privilege of openly waiting upon you with your cap and kerchief. This regret will torture me to the end of my life. I can only sigh over it in secret but may speak of it to no one.

If in the capaciousness of your kind heart you should deign to fulfill the secret hopes of this infinitesimal speck of life, I shall live forever, come when
death may. But even if you should choose to be like a man of the world, who
scorns the voice of the heart and discards things he considers of no conse-
quence for the sake of what he considers to be of real moment, and decide to
look upon a former love merely as an accomplice in sin and to regard the most
solemn vows as something to be lightly broken—even then my love shall en-
dure as the cinnabar endures the fire and I shall, though my bones be consumed and my form dissipated, follow the dust of your carriage with the wind
and dew.[6]

The story ends with Oriole's refusal to meet with Zhang when he comes
to the town where she lives. In the intervening years, they have both married new mates.

The narrator, ostensibly Zhang's friend, concludes the tale by saying,
"The people of the time who knew the story all gave credit to Zhang for
his readiness to rectify his mistakes. I have myself spoken of this affair on
many occasions so that those who hear it will not commit the same mis-
take." This didactic comment makes it sound as if Zhang is the more sympathetic character in a morality tale about the evils of premarital sex, but
in fact, all readers find the blameless Oriole the more compelling of the
two lovers. Yuan Zhen, a great prose stylist, succeeds in realizing one of
the most sympathetic and strong women in Chinese literature. Writers in
subsequent centuries often returned to this intense story of thwarted love.

Yuan Zhen's Autobiography

Critics have long debated why Yuan Zhen wrote this story and whether
it was drawn from his own life. In 809, after the death of his wife, Yuan
wrote an autobiographical poem entitled "A Springtime Outing: A
Dream" in which he discusses, obliquely, an affair he had in his youth.[7]
The poem gives broad hints that Yuan Zhen himself is Oriole's lover, the
selfish Zhang.

> Years ago I dreamed of an outing in spring
> An outing in spring, and what did I find?
> I dreamed I entered a deep, deep cavern
> And there achieved my lifelong desire.

When the poet meets the girl of his dream,

> I approach at length the curtained door
> And hesitate, feeling fearful still.

> I take time to peek in the rooms west and east—
> Everywhere rare objects set out in view:
> The partition painted bright green,
> The hump-hooks gilt and purple.

After this richly sexual opening, the poet describes his own wedding in flat language devoid of emotion:

> When the right time came, I got married.
>
> I was just twenty-three at the time,
> On the auspicious occasion of our wedding night. . . .
> The Wei Clan was just at its most prosperous
> Having entrée gave much pleasure.

Yuan then himself participated in an arranged marriage in order to further his career: his wife belonged to the well-positioned Wei family. In light of this poem and "The Story of Oriole," we can surmise that Yuan first had an affair with the so-called Oriole, broke off with her, and then married into a prominent family. Initially he did well at court, especially after he came in first in the Palace Examination,

> Especially since I, in my prime
> From early times did my duty.
> Imperial notice placed me first among the outstanding.
> I offered counsel in the palace, setting out right and wrong.

But then Yuan Zhen fell out of favor with the powerful eunuchs:

> At thirty I again came up to court,
> No sooner came up than down I fell again.

Yuan Zhen wrote this poem in 809, after a political setback that brought a reprimand and the order to leave the capital immediately for a distant city in Hubei.

Yuan's story and poem tell us much about life among the educated classes after 755. It suggests that men engaged in premarital sex—often with prostitutes—as did some women. Having had an affair seems to have posed no obstacle to subsequent marriage, which for most couples was arranged by their parents or other senior relatives. Oriole's mother tolerated the young couple's affair in the hope that they would eventually wed. But the decision to do so involved more than love, for the narrator opted to marry a different girl from a more influential family. We do not know who the real-life Oriole was, though she may have been a cousin of Yuan Zhen's. We do know, though, as Yuan came to realize, that his calculated marriage backfired. When he was exiled to Hubei, he was left with neither high political position nor his original love.

Bai Juyi in Exile

Bai Juyi's career suffered as well when a political enemy was named Chief Minister in 811. A Chinese proverb warns, "Disaster does not come alone," and indeed disaster did not come alone for Bai that year. His mother, who had made several previous suicide attempts, drowned herself. Fulfilling his mourning obligations at his family home, Bai was troubled by problems with his eyes, in an age in which corrective lenses did not exist. The final disaster was the most upsetting. His only child at the time, a three-year-old girl named Golden Bells, died suddenly:

> Girls are a burden, but if one has no son
> It is strange how fond one can grow, even of a girl!
> . . . The clothes she was wearing are still hanging on the pegs;
> The rest of her medicine is still at the side of her bed.
> I bore her coffin down the long village street;
> I watched them heap the small mound on her grave.
> Do not tell me it is only a mile away;
> What lies between us is all Eternity.[8]

Bai Juyi and Yuan Zhen managed to conduct their subsequent careers, punctuated by spells of exile, as if they were part of a normally functioning bureaucracy, but occasionally events occurred that gave the lie to the myth of dynastic power. In 815, Bai returned to the capital from exile to take up a low post. One early summer morning the Chief Minister was assassinated as he was on his way to court. As soon as he heard the news, Bai drafted a memorial demanding that the court take immediate measures to find the murderer, while the authorities had already posted handbills all over the city offering a reward for information about the murder. His enemies seized on this pretext and had Bai banished to Jiangxi. The chief councillor's murderer was never found, evidence of the instability of the times and the weakness of the Tang dynasty. After this incident, chief ministers traveled the streets of the capital only under armed escort. Yuan Zhen himself served for a brief time as Chief Minister but also suffered the reversals of factional infighting.

In the last years of his life, Bai Juyi became interested in Buddhism.

WORSHIP OF BUDDHIST RELICS

Of all the treasures buried in the secret crypt of the Dharma Gate Monastery, this relic—thought to be a joint from the finger bone of the Buddha—was the most precious. Housed in seven interlocking boxes made from gold, silver, and precious jewels (left), this 4-centimeter- (1.5-inch-) tall relic (right) was taken out of the monastery and displayed every thirty years, when it attracted a large number of worshipers.

In 815 he converted to the Southern School, which taught that one could suddenly reach enlightenment through meditation. Among his friends were many monks, and Bai often wrote about the Indian sage Vimalakirti who was a good Buddhist in spite of having lived a luxurious life. At the same time that Bai was drawn to Buddhism, many officials criticized it. In 819, Bai's friend Han Yu most famously denounced Buddhism as a foreign religion.

Imperial Worship at Dharma Gate Monastery

One particular Buddhist observance at a monastery outside Changan attracted Han Yu's ire. Dharma Gate Monastery (Famensi) had a long history. Its proponents claimed it was founded in the third century B.C. at the time of the great Indian king Ashoka, who distributed the Buddha's relics all over the world, but the first reliable date for the monastery is 555, when the regional ruler who controlled Changan worshiped the Buddha's relics there. The monastery had a precious relic, which it claimed was a joint from the finger bone of the Buddha and which it exhibited at intervals of thirty years. In 629, the Tang founder sponsored an elaborate procession that carried relics from the monastery to the capital and back again. On the new high-speed highway from Xian to Baoji, a traveler can make the 119-kilometer- (74-mile-) trip in less than three hours, but it takes several days by foot.

The eighth procession in 819 deeply dismayed Han Yu, prompting him to write an official document, or memorial, to the emperor in protest. He cited the reactions of the crowds of worshipers as the relic passed among the monasteries of the capital:

[They] burn the crowns of their heads and roast their fingers in groups of tens or hundreds. They untie their clothing and scatter coins from morning till evening. They do so in mutual emulation, fearing only to fall behind. Young or old, they ceaselessly rush to sacrifice their patrimony. If an end is not called to these manifestations forthwith and further transfers of the relic from monastery to monastery take place, then there will certainly be some who shall consider severing their arms or pieces of their bodies a form of veneration.[9]

To persuade the emperor of the severity of the problem, Han Yu fastened onto the Buddhist practice of devotees demonstrating their detachment from their bodies by mutilating themselves. What in Buddhist eyes seemed the ultimate demonstration of faith particularly repulsed Han Yu. If he had limited himself to criticizing the blind faith of the masses, his memorial might not have had any repercussions. But it was construed as an attack on the emperor himself. It resulted in his immediate demotion and exile to the distant and wild Chaozhou prefecture in modern Guangdong province.

Critics of the Buddhist Establishment

Han Yu also argued that the tax-exempt Buddhist establishment was draining the resources of the state and many concurred with him. Throughout the ninth century, the state had struggled with the problem of diminishing tax returns. The country had experienced a long period of deflation, and taxpayers had difficulty meeting the assessments of the two-tax system implemented after the An Lushan rebellion as these payments were to be made in cash, not grain (see pp. 228–29). Also, many mines had closed down after the rebellion, and the number of coins minted annually fell to one-third of the number before 755. Many officials blamed the shortage of coins on excessive use of copper to make Buddhist statues, although the underlying problem was more complex.

The very high percentage of copper (83 percent) in the coins minted by the Tang meant the metal in the coin had greater value than the coin itself. One could derive a profit by melting the coins and using the copper to make other goods—including Buddhist statuary but more often utensils and tools. Because of the inherent value of the metal in the coins, it was profitable to export them, and large quantities of coins flowed out of China to the Persian Gulf.

The shortage of bronze coins at the local level forced people to use barter for their transactions. Han Yu notes this in a memorial of 822 to the emperor: "Apart from the prefectural town itself, those who buy salt with ready cash will be less than two or three out of ten; most of them will employ miscellaneous goods or grain and barter them to obtain salt."[10] As the currency shortage persisted, Buddhist monasteries drew the suspicion of those who thought the resources in Buddhist hands would have been put to better use had they been circulating in the economy. An eyewitness account by a Japanese pilgrim, Ennin, testifies to the wealth controlled by the Buddhist establishment in the 840s.

Ennin's Trip to Mount Wutai

Ennin left Japan in 838 and traveled to China's most famous Buddhist mountain site, Mount Wutai, Shanxi province, in 840. As he traveled the terraced hills, he described the many monasteries clustered around the five peaks that gave the pilgrimage center its name. It was a place of natural beauty, as Ennin tells us:

> There are rare flowers of strange colors blooming all over the western slope. From the valley to the summit there are flowers everywhere, like a spread-out brocade. Their incense is fragrant and perfumes men's clothing. They say that in the present fifth moon it is still cold, and the flowers are not fully out, but that in the sixth and seventh moons the flowers will be even more luxuriant. To see the colors of these flowers is a new experience for man.

Mount Wutai was home to the cult of the bodhisattva of wisdom, Manjusri, and many of the sights there were places where he had appeared to his followers. Ennin recounts many such miracles, including one at a temple where maigre (vegetarian) feasts were regularly held for Buddhist devotees. There a donor had repeatedly refused the request of a pregnant woman for extra food for her unborn child. When the woman left the hall, she was transformed into the bodhisattva Manjusri. From that day on, Ennin reports, all were given their fill. "Those who enter these mountains naturally develop a spirit of equality. When maigre [vegetarian] feasts are arranged in these mountains, whether one be cleric or layman, man or woman, great or small, food is offered to all equally."[11]

As the tales about Manjusri's miracles spread throughout China, images of Mount Wutai also began to circulate. Ennin received such a picture from a traveling companion who asked him to take it with him to Japan, where he could continue to worship Manjusri.

Ennin was still in the capital of Changan when the emperor, on the advice of several Daoist adherents, issued a series of imperial edicts designed to reduce the wealth and power of Buddhist monasteries like that at Mount Wutai. The fifteenth day of the seventh moon was an important Buddhist festival during which laypeople made offerings at monasteries to their deceased relatives in hopes that the food would reach them

in the underworld. Ennin reports that, at the emperor's order, these offerings were removed from the Buddhist monasteries and taken to Daoist halls of worship.

Attacks on Buddhism

This and other anti-Buddhist measures witnessed by Ennin were the culmination of several years of state pressure. Blaming Buddhist monasteries for hoarding wealth and seeking to enlarge the tax rolls, the emperor took his first measures against the Buddhist establishment in 842 by ordering monks and nuns to return to lay life or to begin paying taxes. Two years later the government shut down some small monasteries and then

ordered all monks and nuns under the age of fifty to return to lay life.
In 845 the emperor ordered all tax-exempt Buddhist monasteries to close
and forced all Buddhist monks and nuns to return to lay life, as they
would then have to pay taxes. He allowed a certain number of monasteries—four in both Changan and Luoyang, and a few in other loca-
tions—to remain open, with the number of monks in residence reduced
to 20, 10, or 5, depending on the monastery's size.

> All other Buddhist monks and nuns in the capital, along with Mazdeans and
> Nestorians, were secularized. . . . The rich possessions and lands belonging to
> the temples were confiscated, and the materials of the condemned buildings
> were employed in the construction and repair of public buildings and post sta-
> tions. Bronze images, bells, and chimes, were melted down to make coins.[12]

The Buddhist community, numbering some 300,000 tax-exempt people
in a total population of 60,000,000, posed an easy target, but even so, the
much-weakened central government was unable to enforce these measures outside the capital. Even Ennin, a foreigner, reported that the Tang
was losing battles to Uighur troops at the same time it moved against the
monasteries. Only two years later, in 847, a new emperor took the throne
and lifted the ban on Buddhism (though not on the Persian religion of
Mazdeism, also called Zoroastrianism, and the Christian sect of Nestori-
ans). The emperor ordered all damaged temples to be rebuilt and new
monasteries to be built as well. The short-lived attempt to suppress Buddhism did not solve the central government's twin problems of money
shortage and declining revenues.

Continued Worship at Dharma Gate Monastery

In 873, for the first time since the events that so disturbed Han Yu in
819, an imperial procession went to Dharma Gate Monastery to arrange
for the transport of the relics to Changan. The emperor accompanied the
finger relic back to Dharma Gate Monastery at the end of the year. The
relic was reburied inside its casket under the pagoda of the tomb with
the expectation that it would be exhumed in another thirty years, but the
dynasty was so weakened in 903 that the relic remained untouched, never
to be displayed again.

The region around Dharma Gate Monastery, to the west of Xian, is
prone to earthquakes, and in 1569 a particularly severe tremor destroyed
the Tang pagoda. It was rebuilt and survived for centuries until a series
of terrible rains in 1981 caused half the monastery to collapse in a mud
slide and exposed the underground vault dating to the Tang dynasty.
Archeologists leveled the pagoda and excavated the underground cham-

An earthquake in 1981 at the Dharma Gate Monastery (Famensi), outside the city of Xian, cut a pagoda in two, causing half the pagoda to fall away (left). A secret crypt with Silk Road treasures was revealed. See the pagoda after restoration (right).

ber, which consisted of a vault leading to a set of seven interlocking boxes of extraordinary workmanship and beauty, each made of a different rare material. The gold with silver inlay may seem most striking to us today, but the people of the Tang thought glass and crystal exotic too. Inside the smallest box was a gold cylinder, slightly larger than a lipstick case. The cover could be lifted off to expose the contents—the relic of the Buddha's finger bone.

As dramatic as this find was—and no one expected that these treasures of the Tang would survive undamaged and undisturbed for over eleven hundred years—the accompanying goods proved even more breathtaking. The textiles from the crypt, containing large quantities of gold thread, constitute the single most important find of luxury textiles from the Tang dynasty. Among them was a red jacket with splendid embroidery that might have been worn by Empress Wu. Also found were many gold and silver implements used in monastery rituals.

The Last Years of the Tang Dynasty

A series of uprisings began in 874 that ultimately led to the collapse of the Tang dynasty. Lacking any explicit ideology, the rebels' goals were simply to loot cities and to avoid paying taxes. A failed examination candidate named Huang Chao (d. 884) eventually emerged as the rebels' leader. In 880 he took Changan and declared himself the founder of a new dynasty, but the rebels were unable to form a stable regime. The rebels withdrew from the ravaged city of Changan in 883, leaving a powerless central government behind them.

After 885, the emperor was held prisoner by eunuchs and military governors. This allowed the fiction that there was a Tang dynasty to continue, but in 904 the most successful regional commander, a former rebel named Zhu Wen, captured the emperor. Zhu had the entire imperial entourage—down to the lowliest servant—put to death, and he floated the dismantled buildings and palaces of Changan down the Wei River to his capital at Luoyang. In 907 he killed the last Tang boy-emperor and founded the Liang dynasty, whose dual capitals lay at Luoyang and Kaifeng. The ruined Changan would never again serve as the capital of the empire. Zhu Wen ruled in the name of the Liang dynasty until 923, when the Shatuo Turks founded the Later Tang dynasty, which ruled north China until 937. Between 907 and 960 a succession of regional kingdoms prevailed in the north and south, each in turn replaced by a new regime led by its generals. Historians now call this period the Five Dynasties, which came to an end when one general, Zhao Kuangyin, founded the Song dynasty in 960.

The Legacy of An Lushan

The choice of a date for the end of the Tang dynasty is arbitrary. Whatever year one chooses, be it 885, 904, 907, or 937—and historians have traditionally preferred 907—the Tang dynasty lost most of its power in 755, the year of the An Lushan rebellion. The uprising forced the dynasty to cede power to its regional commanders in the suppression effort. Unable to update household registers, Tang officials could not implement the triannual redistribution of land called for by the equal-field system.

When the Tang dynasty developed the new two-tax system and the salt monopoly in response to the rebellion (see p. 228) the direct bond between the central government and the producer was snapped. The government no longer maintained any records concerning the landholdings or output of any individual cultivator. Instead, it made a series of deals with regional commanders establishing the amount of revenue each province owed. This loss of direct government control over revenue was lasting. In later dynasties, as we shall see, certain emperors and prime ministers attempted to regain the same degree of direct control over the economy as the Tang, but their efforts always failed.

The central government's withdrawal from direct management of the economy after 755 marks a major turning point in Chinese history. Before the rebellion, despite some evasion, the central government knew how much land everyone had and who worked it. After the rebellion, the central authorities lacked those records and were forced to rely on locally powerful families to collect taxes for them. They were permanently weakened as a result.

The weakening of the central government in the years after 755 also affected the historical record. As the central authorities continued to cede power to the outlying regions, the sources from the capital reveal less about life in the outlying regions. A cache of primary documents discovered circa 1900 at Dunhuang, in modern Gansu province, offers a rare glimpse of day-to-day life in the ninth and tenth centuries and provides a valuable supplement to the dwindling records of the center.

THE DISCOVERY OF THE LIBRARY CAVE AT DUNHUANG

In the 1880s, the local people of Gansu began to explore the site of the Caves of a Thousand Buddhas. The caves, which had been neglected for centuries, were located outside the oasis of Dunhuang. This was an important monastic center along the Silk Road, where travelers could stop before leaving China and beginning their long trip around the Taklamakan Desert. At the cave site were found hundreds of cave temples that had been dug out from the crumbly conglomerate face of a cliff, reinforced with pillars, and covered with mud and straw and then a plaster layer. Starting in the fourth century, local artists painted mostly Buddhist and occasionally secular scenes on the dry plaster surface. Sometime around 1900, a local religious practitioner known as Daoist Wang took up residence at the caves, and in the course of his explorations, he noticed a gap in the plaster of one of the caves. When he tapped on the wall, he found it was hollow, and behind the damaged wall was the library cave of Dunhuang.

"The sight disclosed within made my eyes open wide. Heaped up in closely packed layers, but without any order, there appeared in the dim light of the priest's flickering lamp a solid mass of manuscript bundles rising to a height of nearly 10 feet [3 meters]. They filled, as subsequent

THE LIBRARY CAVE AT DUNHUANG

The discovery of the Dunhuang caves—and the unedited, primary materials in the library cave—marked one of the greatest discoveries in the history of China. This photograph, taken by the British explorer Aurel Stein in 1907, shows the small door on the right-hand side that led to the library cave. The bundles on the floor have already been removed from the cave.

measurement showed close on 500 cubic feet [14.24 cubic meters]," reported Sir Aurel Stein (1862–1943), the naturalized British explorer who became world famous following his discovery of the library cave in 1907.[13] The cave contained 13,500 paper scrolls, most about 30 centimeters (1 foot) high and 4.5 to 6 meters (15 to 20 feet) long.[14] Almost all the scrolls were Buddhist texts in Chinese, but some were in Sanskrit, Tibetan, or other Central Asian languages such as Khotanese, Uighur, and Sogdian. These languages were spoken in the area spanning northwest China and the modern republics of Tadjikistan and Uzbekistan, and colonies of merchants from these different oases settled in Dunhuang to conduct trade.

After protracted negotiations, Stein purchased 7,000 scrolls from Daoist Wang for 4 silver horseshoes. Later, he wrote a letter to a friend in which he estimated the total cost of the documents at 130 pounds. Stein admitted the price was low, even by the standards of his day, and that "the single Sanskrit Ms. [manuscript] on palm leaf with a few other 'old things' are worth this."[15] Stein had extensive experience examining and purchasing Sanskrit manuscripts in India, but because he could not read

246

Chinese, many of the scrolls he sent to London to be stored there were duplicates.

One year later, the great French Sinologist Paul Pelliot (1878–1945) arrived at the site, fearful that Stein, or other Chinese, would have removed all the important scrolls. But the early twentieth century was a time in China when Western learning was in vogue, and few Chinese realized the value of the scrolls. When Pelliot saw the cave, he wrote to his Parisian colleagues that he was stupefied by the quality of the scrolls Stein had left behind:

> The results [of the research done to date on China] we can admit or reject by contrasting books with one another, but always books, written after the fact; we never deal with original documents, with independent sources that were not destined to be public documents. This time we can see in private notes, decrees, letters, what was done in a Chinese province from the seventh to tenth centuries—real life—religious life and civil life—whose characteristics we have only known vaguely and according to dogmatic writings. For these reasons, and for still others, since Daoist Wang made available the greatest discovery of Chinese manuscripts in centuries, I rejoice to have the unmerited good luck that these manuscripts were willing to wait for me for eight years.[16]

Pelliot understood the importance of what he had found, and in an unusual flight of imagination, credits the inanimate documents with waiting for him.

The discovery of the Dunhuang cave, like the deciphering of the dragon bone writing, opened up the study of a new period of Chinese history. Why were the scrolls placed in the cave? Although Stein said the scrolls were "heaped up in layers, but without order," a Chinese scholar at Beijing University has reexamined the original photographs Stein took. They show that, in addition to some piles of wastepaper, many of the scrolls had been tied up in bundles of a dozen or so. The bundles were then wrapped in cloth, with labels on the covers.[17]

Several documents from the library cave indicate that because the library at a monastery located in Dunhuang was missing many Buddhist texts and because it could not afford to hire copyists, the monk-librarians there wrote to other monasteries in the region asking them to donate their duplicates. The bundle labels use the traditional Buddhist bibliographic categories to catalogue the library's texts.

No one has successfully explained why the library cave was sealed up sometime after 1000. Monastic centers to the west of Dunhuang were conquered around that time by Islamic peoples who destroyed local monasteries. Perhaps the monk-librarians at Dunhuang aimed to pre-

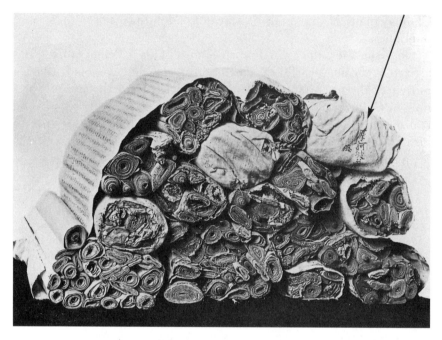

HOW TEXTS WERE CATALOGUED IN THE TENTH CENTURY

This photograph shows the documents from the Library Cave at Dunhuang in their original bundles, which held some twelve scrolls. The label on the bundle on the upper right is still visible. It gives the traditional Buddhist library classification—the equivalent of a modern library call number—for the scrolls within.

serve Buddhist teachings by placing the entire contents of their library—including all the scraps from lost texts—in a cave. Like the monks at Fangshan who carved Buddhist texts in stone (see chapter 5), those who walled up the cave did not live to see it reopened, and the Dunhuang library remained sealed until around 1900, when Daoist Wang detected the hollow wall.

Many of the scrolls in the cave begin with a dedication in which the donor explains why he or she had commissioned a copy of whichever Buddhist text followed. Such texts take up one side of the scroll, but because paper was recycled, the margins and the backs display all kinds of written materials, including literary works, contracts, government documents, copying exercises, and even students' doodles. As Pelliot noted, all were preserved by accident in the Dunhuang cave. It is these unofficial sources, the scribbled notes and scrawled exercises, that allow scholars to reconstruct daily life in Dunhuang in the last years of the Tang dynasty.

Dunhuang in the Years after 755

Like other places under Tang rule after 755, Dunhuang was ruled by a military governor; but it differed from Central China in important ways. Living in an oasis along the Silk Road, Dunhuang's residents depended on irrigation to grow their crops, and families had less land to farm than did the residents of Central China. Located some 1,100 kilometers (700 miles) due west of the Tang capital, Dunhuang was a frontier garrison populated by Chinese and non-Han peoples. It fell to the Tibetans in 787 and stayed under Tibetan rule until 848, when a Chinese general, Zhang Yichao (799–872), reclaimed it. Although he officially swore fealty to the Tang dynasty, sent tribute to the capital, and was named military governor in return, he ruled the area on his own, collecting taxes and staffing his own army. The ruling authorities in Dunhuang paid lip service but little else to Changan. Zhang was succeeded by his son, and then in 923, by the Cao family, who continued to rule as military governors after the fall of the Tang dynasty.

A tenth-century source describes Dunhuang at the time the Cao family ruled it:

> In this valley there is a vast number of old Buddhist temples and priests' quarters; there are also some huge bells. At both ends of the valley north and south, stand temples to the Rulers of the Heavens, and a number of shrines to other gods; the walls are painted with pictures of the Tibetan kings and their retinues. The whole of the western face of the cliff for a distance of two *li* (two third-miles), north and south, has been hewn and chiseled out into a number of lofty and spacious sand-caves containing images and paintings of Buddha. Reckoning cave by cave, the amount of money lavished on them must have been enormous. In front of them pavilions have been erected in several tiers, one above another. Some of the temples contain colossal images rising to a height of [48 meters] 160 feet, and the number of smaller shrines is past counting. All are connected with one another by galleries, convenient for the purpose of ceremonial rounds as well as casual sightseeing.[18]

This observer was struck by the splendor of the Caves of a Thousand Buddhas, which lay 24 kilometers (15 miles) to the southeast of the town of Dunhuang. The complex contained temples to Buddhist gods, like the four guardian deities called Rulers of the Heavens, and to other gods as well. The paintings of the Tibetan kings must have been on the back walls of the cave, where the donors often had their pictures painted. The pavilions described in front of the caves were no longer standing in 1900, when over five hundred caves were discovered, but many of the images inside the caves were found intact.

PORTRAIT OF A DONOR AT DUNHUANG

A wall painting from the Yulin caves near Dunhuang shows the military governor of
Dunhuang who ruled from 945 to 974, Cao Yuanzhong, with his wife, Lady Zhai. They
financed the digging of new caves at Dunhuang (including the cave with the mural of
Mount Wutai) as well as the printing of books and the carving of woodblock prints honoring Buddhist deities.

Thirteen monasteries were located in this town of only fifteen thousand people. The population fell into three distinct groups, each with a
different relationship to the monasteries. Monastic dependents were
bound to the monastic lands on which they labored. Also living in the
monasteries were those who had taken their vows, shaved their heads,
and become monks and nuns. Not living on monastic grounds were the
laypeople of Dunhuang, who joined in mutual aid associations with
monks and nuns. These associations mirrored Dunhuang society, with
different groups for the wealthy, the middle strata, the working poor,
and even women servants.

The monasteries at Dunhuang had landholdings and ran a variety of moneymaking enterprises, including oil presses and flour mills. A list of work assignments for one hundred ninety monastic dependents mentions such religious tasks as temple repair, bell ringing, and sprinkling water on the temple courtyards. These laborers also transported grain; tended monastic herds of camels, horses, and sheep; ground flour; pressed oil; cultivated gardens; raised fruit trees; and manufactured paper and felt. Monasteries regularly made loans of grain and money on which they received interest, and the laity donated wheat, millet, oil, flour, hemp, bran, beans, cloth, felt, and paper.

During the ninth and tenth centuries, slightly less than a tenth of the population lived in the monasteries as monks and nuns. Separate census documents record that most of these clergy were locally recruited. A list from 865–70 gives the names, ages, and villages of two hundred seventy nuns in three nunneries. All but two were from Dunhuang. Some of these nuns were in their teens, with the two youngest only thirteen years old. Some of them lived to be seventy, suggesting that celibacy may have been easier on women than married life with the ensuing dangers of childbirth. Their knowledge of Buddhist doctrine and the number of vows they had taken determined whether these nuns were classed as full-fledged nuns or novices. A document from 896 explains that forty nuns were expelled because they were too young or did not follow the monastic rules. Some of these expelled girls were the daughters of local farmers and low government functionaries, whose families had chosen to send them to the nunnery rather than paying dowries.

Those resident in the monasteries—both the dependents and the clergy—came from local society, and they continued to have regular contact with the laity. Groups of fifteen or twenty people formed lay associations, or mutual help societies, that helped members to offset unanticipated large expenses, like funerals, or, in the case of merchants, long-distance trips. Monks often served as head or officers of these associations. These associations also sponsored vegetarian feasts on holidays like the Buddha's birthday, or the ghost festival on the fifteenth day of the seventh month when the spirits of the dead were thought to return to the world of the living for a visit. The Japanese Buddhist pilgrim Ennin witnessed this festival in Changan in 845.

During these festivals, monks preached about Buddhist teachings or told stories with Buddhist themes to the laity. One of the most interesting documents from the library cave is the manuscript of one of these lectures, dated 921, which was performed during the ghost festival.[19] In it, the narrator tells the story of Turnip (Mulian), a boy who traveled to the underworld to save his unrepentant mother. This story spawned many successors, including a popular Beijing opera. The Dunhuang version is especially interesting because it shows how the narrator tried to persuade laypeople to give up their traditional ancestor worship for Buddhist practices.

Turnip's Visit to His Mother in the Underworld

At the beginning of the story, Turnip was about to go to another country on a business trip, a common occurrence in the oasis communities along the Silk Road. Before leaving, he gave his mother money to pay for vegetarian meals for monks and beggars who came to their house, but his mother kept the money for herself and lied to her son on his return. After she died, Turnip, a filial son, mourned her and his father for the requisite three years, and then became a monk. He took a new name, the Sanskrit Maudgalyayana (but let us continue to call him by his childhood nickname, Turnip). He began a course of meditation, but was unable to find his mother. In Heaven he did find his father, who explained, "Throughout her life, your mother committed a large number of sins and, at the end of her days, she fell into hell" (l. 193–94). With this introduction, the narrator establishes the basic plot, Turnip's search for his mother. He also hints at the main tension in the narrative: Can a child be filial to parent who was not a good Buddhist?

And so Turnip begins his long search for his mother through the many compartments of hell. Some of the sections he visits predated the introduction of Buddhism, while others, the realm of the god Yama, the King of Hell, and his overlord, Ksitigarbha Bodhisattva, clearly came with Buddhist teachings from India. As he searches, Turnip meets a group of wandering ghosts who were mistakenly summoned because the underworld bureaucracy mistook them for someone else of the same name and same surname, a recurring error of the underworld bureaucracy.

Turnip steadfastly continues his search for his mother until, at last, he is forced to ask the Buddha for assistance to reach the worst hell of all, where his mother is. There the dead "were made to crawl up the knifemountains and enter the furnace coals. Their skulls were smashed to bits, their bones and flesh decomposed; tendons and skin snapped, liver and gall broke. Ground flesh spurted and splattered beyond the four gates; congealed blood drenched and drooked the pathways which run through the black clods of hell." (l. 683–88). Original Buddhist teachings may have held that the body was a temporary home for one's soul, and that one's disembodied soul floated somewhere until it found its next home, but

Buddhist missionaries were unable to dislodge the indigenous Chinese view that one traveled in one's own body to the underworld. Turnip's is a hell where all retain their earthly bodies and where all sorts of gruesome punishments are visited on those bodies.

When Turnip finally locates his mother, she too is suffering grisly bodily punishments. Because the none-too-bright Turnip never grasps that his mother's own deeds have brought this punishment on herself, he once again blames his failure to be a good son for her plight. He is shocked to find that his daily offerings of food have not reached her. Other people in the underworld have warned him that traditional offerings to one's dead ancestors are useless, and his mother echoes their comments:

> "Though you diligently sacrificed to me while you were at home,
> It only got you a reputation in the village for being filial;
> Granted that you did sprinkle libations of wine upon my grave,
> But it would have been better for you to copy a single line of a sūtra."
> (l. 848–851)

Her comment, while betraying her characteristic ingratitude, also conveys one of the story's most important teachings: the dead will benefit more if their living kin pay for Buddhist texts to be copied, or give donations to the monastery, than if they perform the traditional rites for the dead. After many more travails, Turnip finally succeeds in getting his mother reborn as a person. The tale ends with the reformed mother and her always virtuous but slightly stupid son going off to heaven together.

Although this narrative ostensibly tells how the Buddha destroyed the underworld, the sufferings of the dead stay with the listener much longer than the memory of their liberation. The tale's most vivid passages all concern the tortures inflicted on the dead, and the accompanying illustrations, now lost, must have been just as graphic. The residents of Dunhuang took the text's grim message to heart and formed lay associations that would allow them to make contributions to the monasteries so their kin would not suffer in the underworld.

Lay Associations

Although Turnip's relationship with his mother shapes this narrative, an unusual group of documents reveals that many people in Dunhuang had extensive contact with those outside their families. Some fifty charters specifying the rules and goals of lay associations survive. Because the people joining one association agreed to make the same monthly donation, they often joined with people of equivalent social level, but from different families. These charters show that people could not depend on their families to help them out in all crises, and even though family ties bound families like Turnip's tightly together, ties outside the family were also significant.

The most prominent members of Dunhuang society, whether officials or scholars, joined together to raise money for large-scale building projects, usually the digging out and decoration of a new cave. The charters of these groups were written in beautiful characters and discuss Buddhist doctrine at length.

The middle-level charters ask their members for much smaller offerings:

> The following announcement is about the one-day ceremony to pray for good fortune, which will be held as usual. Everyone should bring a couple of pancakes and one measure of millet. Everyone seeing this announcement please go to assemble in front of the gate to Dabei monastery between five and seven A.M. on the fourth day of the month. The two who arrive latest will be fined a beaker of wine. Those who do not show up at all will be fined half a jar of wine. This announcement should be circulated quickly from one to another. . . .[20]

The members of this association are hoping to generate merit by sponsoring a ceremony to pray for good fortune, a much more reasonable expenditure than digging out a cave. It was inconceivable that the most socially prominent would carry grain and pancakes and stand in front of a temple to wait for fellow association members as this charter asks them to do.

Some of the associations limited their membership to women. One association formed in 959 began its charter with an explanation of the different roles of family and friends: "Our parents give us life, but friends enhance its value: they sustain us in time of danger, rescue us from calamity. In dealing with friends, a single word may serve as a bond of faith." On feast days and the first day of each month, each member was to give oil, wine, and white flour. Discipline was important, the charter continues:

> If in the club there is anyone who disregards precedence in small things and great, in unruly fashion creates disturbance at a feast, and will not obey the verbal instructions of her superior, then all the members shall repair to the gateway and fine her of enough alcohol for a whole feast, to be partaken of by the rest of the company.[21]

This sounds to be a lively group of women, who, at one moment, might start to brawl, but who, at another, would share wine with each other. Fifteen women signed their names—in very rough brush strokes—to this document.

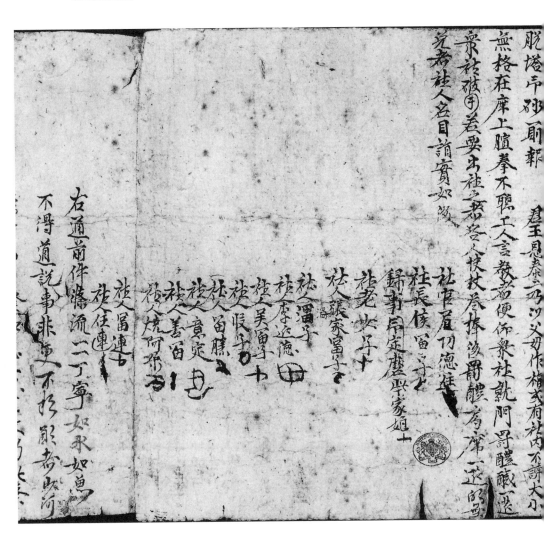

A WOMAN'S ORGANIZATION FORMED IN 959

Fifteen women signed this document stating the rules for their lay association, which met every month for a party. The scribe who drew up the document used colloquial language, which the women may have dictated directly, and then listed the fifteen members' names. Each woman made her mark under her name. Some drew an X, others a circle, and others a more individual signature. The signatures testify to a range in writing ability, but clearly none of the women could sign her own name.

All these charters testify that the people of Dunhuang sought to protect themselves from unexpected danger by joining with friends who were not family members. All kinds of disasters could befall an individual or a family, and they formed associations to try to protect themselves from those dangers. An unusual set of court documents confirms what the charters suggest: that Dunhuang society was fluid, that a woman in a well-off family could suddenly find herself in poverty, and that the descent into poverty could begin with the death of a family member.

The Widow Along's Change in Social Status

In 945, a widow named Along sued a squatter for encroaching on her family's land. The records from the suit include a contract drawn up by the widow's son with his deceased father's brother, depositions from the widow, the squatter, the uncle, and the presiding judge's decision.[22] Pieced together, they record the following events.

The widow was originally well-to-do. She and her husband owned several houses. After he died, she and her son were left with thirty-two sixth-acres of land. Then her son committed an unnamed crime and was exiled to the neighboring town. The court arranged for his uncle to tend the widow's land, and they drew up a contract. Because the widow was short of money after her son left, she was forced to sell twelve sixth-acres to her neighbor, leaving her with only twenty sixth-acres. Her son never returned.

Her brother-in-law supported her from the proceeds of the land, but he left at one point to fight some bandits on horseback. *Bandits* was a catch-all term for any threat to the peace, and he does not specify who the bandits were. When he came back, a squatter was occupying the widow's remaining land. The squatter had been raised by more unnamed bandits, who had kidnapped him when he was a small child, but he managed to escape with two horses. He gave one to the local officials, who paid him grain and cloth, and they gave him title to the widow's remaining twenty sixth-acres. He stayed for only one or two years and left because he found the life too difficult. A nephew of the squatter then came and took over the widow's land.

After ten years, the widow sued to get her land back. In weighing the conflicting claims to the land, the deciding official considers the testimony of the widow, her brother-in-law, and the squatter, as well as the contract her deceased son signed entrusting his uncle with the land. He does not include a copy of the family's household register or the document giving the squatter the rights to the land. No one even mentions the government land registers. Because of the widow's difficulties in supporting herself after her son's death, the court awarded her the land and the water so that she could live out her old age.

Although the court awarded her part of her original landholdings, she had clearly fallen from the privileged position she enjoyed when her husband was alive and her son was living with them. When her husband was alive, the widow might have had enough money to join the socially prominent in a lay association sponsoring the building of new caves. After he died, she could have joined the pancakes and wine association, but after she lost her land, she would have been hard-pressed to make any contributions at all. What if the court had not awarded her the land? If her brother-in-law had not been able to support her, she would have had to join the ranks of the household servants who joined together in hopes of protecting the little wealth they had.

This judge's decision shows what happened after the equal-field system fell into disuse. Personal share land became entirely heritable, with the state making no claim to taking the land back on the death of the previous owner. This was just one court case, from Dunhuang, but what happened in the far northwest was happening all over China. Once the Tang stopped regularly updating its registers, neither it nor its successors could use them to chart landholding. Regional governments had to develop new means of taxation, whether monopolies or the two-tax system, to substitute for the equal-field system.

People were forced to adjust to the new fiscal system. They could not depend on the state to provide them with land or to redistribute land at three-year intervals. They could join together in lay associations with people of similar incomes and hope their friends would support them in times of need, but they had entered a new age in which the wealthy, like Widow Along before her husband's death, could buy land from others, and in which the poor, like Widow Along after her son's conviction, were vulnerable to the depredations of others.

Women were surprisingly independent. When married, they might derive their identities from their husbands and their sons, as Turnip's mother did; but if death and illness came to their menfolk, they could suddenly face life alone. Luckily, Widow Along's brother-in-law was willing to support her after her son left, and he helped her to sue for the return of her land. Other women were not as fortunate. Like the women of the Dunhuang lay associations, they looked to other women to provide them with entertainment—including feasts and possibly brawls—and to sustain them in time of danger.

Because the library cave was sealed up, the Dunhuang documents do not disclose what happened after 1000. Just as those who closed the library feared, waves of invaders, some Muslim, some not, conquered northwest China, destroying Buddhist monasteries and any human depictions they found. The fighting cut off the trade routes, and China turned away from India and Central Asia. No longer would Buddhist missionaries travel back and forth, and no longer would the Chinese follow Central Asian fashions and study Indian religion. The Chinese saw these nomadic peoples as a threat, and they looked down on them as uncivilized. With the closing off of the trade routes, China was no longer open to Indian and Central Asian influence. The age of the Silk Route had ended.

III

FACING NORTH

(1000–1600)

CHRONOLOGY

COMING TO TERMS WITH
MONEY: THE SONG DYNASTY
(960–1276)

In 960 a powerful general reunited China and founded the dynasty that was to rule for three hundred years of enormous prosperity and equally wrenching economic change. Though not as rapid as Europe's thirteenth-century commercial revolution, China's commercial revolution had consequences that were just as far-reaching. In Europe, before the revolution, most cultivators worked or gave a share of their crop to pay off their rent obligations to the landholders. By the fourteenth century they paid their rent in the money they received for their crops. Money came to circulate in both cities and the countryside, with urban residents able to use money year-round and many farmers doing so on a seasonal basis. In China, at the beginning of the market revolution, most cultivators were self-sufficient, growing their own foodstuffs, and buying only salt, if that. By the end of the revolution they had specialized, growing cash crops, making handicrafts, or weaving cloth, all to sell at market. With the proceeds they were able to buy their food for the year, often with money. A national market developed in which certain goods were traded across all of Song territory.

THE FIRST COMMERCIAL REVOLUTION
AND ITS EFFECTS

The effects of this expanding market were not limited to material life. As concubines and prostitutes joined the new commodities being traded, the practice of footbinding spread from courtesans to women of all social groups, though unevenly by region. Both high- and lowborn were

Legend:

Song-dynasty China (960–1276))

- Area controlled by Southern Song (1127–1276)
- Area lost in 1126
- Border of Northern Song (960–1126)
- Li Qingzhao's route
- Modern provincial boundaries
- Border of modern China

lifted out of a self-sufficient economy and launched into a market economy, complete with its dizzying upturns and downward plunges.

Government officials were hard-pressed to keep up with the rapidly changing economy whose direction they tried to control. They attempted to develop policies that would benefit the countryside, but their failure to understand the need for a stable currency prevented any success. They minted ten times as many bronze coins annually as the Tang had, but because they continuously lowered the coins' proportion of copper, thus increasing the value of older coins, the private melting down of coins persisted. In this time of rapid economic growth, merchants developed the world's first paper money to facilitate their long-distance transactions. By 1023, the central government had taken over the production of paper money. Although scarce, the evidence we have of increased occupational specialization and expansion of markets points to a booming economy whose participants desperately needed a stable currency but whose government did not produce one.

At the same time government officials faced the problem of providing an effective currency, they also had to stave off alien regimes to the north. For the three hundred years of the dynasty's reign, these northern regimes and the Song stood as threats to each other. The next chapters discuss the conquests of the Liao, Jurchen, and Mongols, campaigns that were very expensive to the Song dynasty and drained its treasury.

The extraordinary cultural brilliance and wealth of the Song were unmatched by any other contemporary state anywhere in the world. After the fall of north China in 1127 to the Jurchen, many powerful families devoted themselves to local society, investing in temples, schools, and bridges, and paying obeisance to the new sages of Neo-Confucianism. And as peasants and merchants struggled to make sense of the times they were living through, they began to worship deities who could perform economic miracles. By the end of the Song dynasty, the Chinese religious landscape had expanded to include these popular deities and the new sages of a Confucian revival.

The Shift South

The tumult of the two centuries between the An Lushan rebellion of 755 and the founding of the Song caused mass migrations that could only be detected after the reestablishment of unified central power. In 742, 60 percent of China's population of sixty million lived in the wheat and millet producing regions of the Yellow River, with the remaining 40 percent in the south. By 980, the proportions had reversed: as the population neared one hundred million, 38 percent lived in the north and 62 percent in the south, in the rice-growing region of the Yangzi Valley.[1] The proportion of those living in the south continued to increase throughout the Song dynasty and in later periods as well. China's center of gravity, where the bulk of its population lived, had shifted permanently to the south, where it would remain for the rest of the imperial era and where it still is today.

During the Tang, the malarial swamps of the south had been a dreaded destination of political exiles, including the prose stylist Han Yu. But as the settlers learned how to drain swamps and the threat of illness receded, more people moved down from the hills to the lowlands. Because rice cultivation required the ability to flood seedlings and drain paddy fields, rice was more difficult to grow than wheat. The new settlers were able to use new gates and waterwheels to flood and drain the rice fields as needed, allowing them to take advantage of the south's greater rainfall to harvest rice.

They also planted new, improved types of rice. New strains of double-cropped rice entered China from Vietnam in the early years of the Song. Requiring a much shorter growing season, these foreign strains could produce two crops a year. Unfortunately, the new strains rotted easily and tasted bad. Over time, farmers were able to develop hybrids with indigenous strains to make a better double-cropped rice, and the resulting increase in production freed some of the working population from having to grow their own food. It was those workers who were able to produce goods for market.

The effects of these economic changes varied by region. In regions that remained outside the market network, farmers continued to grow their own foodstuffs. Those who were drawn into the market network began to plant specialized crops, such as lichees, lotus roots, or tangerines, or to make handicrafts for market, such as cloth, thread, or baskets. They then used the proceeds to supplement the goods they could grow at home. Those most involved in the market economy bought all their own food at markets while devoting themselves full-time to producing market goods.

Regional Variations in Economic Change

The enormous disparity among regions can be glimpsed most clearly in the iron-producing industry of the eleventh century. In 1078, China's annual output of iron was at least 113,375 metric (125,000 English) tons, a sixfold increase since 806. The 1078 figure breaks down to 1.4 kilograms (3.1 pounds) of iron per person, a rate of production attained in Europe only in 1700. Much of the Chinese iron went to the capital of Kaifeng, which had a population approaching one million. There thousands of workers used the iron to produce swords, armor, and other weapons in large-scale workshops. Still more iron was consumed by the state workshops making tools, nails, locks, and musical instruments. The smelters supplying these workshops in the capital were substantial, resembling enterprises in Europe at the beginning of the Industrial Revolution.

At the end of the eleventh century, the poet Su Shi (1037–1101) described how iron was produced at one of the major smelters supplying the capital in northern Jiangsu near Xuzhou. Over three thousand men worked full-time at thirty-six different foundries, owned by very wealthy families whom Su Shi calls "the great surnames" without specifying the source of their wealth. The scale of production, some tens of thousands of tons, was so great that the forests in the immediate area, the source of fuel for the smelting, were stripped bare by 1100. With wood no longer available, the smelters were forced to burn coke in blast furnaces, an innovation occurring in Europe only in the early eighteenth century.

Outside the capital, local demand for iron was limited to implements needed by blacksmiths and farmers, and production remained small scale. Bao Cheng (999–1062), an official so famous for his honesty that he later became a legendary magistrate in the underworld, wrote a report in the 1050s about the iron industry in the province of Shandong near Qufu. All the smelting, gathering of fuel, and mining took place in the winter when no farming could occur. Such time was limited, and Judge Bao wrote, "I pitied each and every household of the Jiang and Lu clans. Indeed they were poverty-stricken. Year after year they had no leisure time from agriculture to begin smelting."[2] The men who worked in the mines and smelters came together for a month or so at the time of iron production. The rest of the year they farmed the land because the market network of Shandong was not sufficiently developed to allow them to engage in full-time work. If the men could collect sufficient fuel, they could support a small blast furnace. If not, they had to forge wrought iron into tools.

We owe this glimpse of Song iron production to two men, Bao Cheng and Su Shi, who typified the officials who governed in the first one hundred years of the Song. Both passed the civil service examinations before being appointed to their posts.

THE FOUNDING OF THE SONG

The founder of the Song, Zhao Kuangyin (reigned 960–976), himself a general, was particularly aware of the dangers the military posed to stable regimes. He had served under one of the successor regimes to the Later Tang, the Later Zhou, whose capital was also at Kaifeng, and in 960 he overthrew the boy ruler on the throne. He then proceeded to unify the empire, taking the middle Yangzi in 963, Sichuan in 965, Guangdong in 971, Anhui, Jiangxi, and Hunan in 975. After he died in 976, his younger brother succeeded him and conquered Jiangsu and Zhejiang in 978, and Shanxi in 979.

One of the first challenges the Song faced was regularizing the various currencies in use throughout its new empire. Copper, iron, and lead coins of varying weights and composition circulated in different regions. When the Song unified China, it established a standard for copper coins and then began to issue coins in large quantities. The unit of currency was the string, with originally one thousand coins per string, but more often seven or eight hundred in practice. Over time, the Song also lowered the amount of copper in each coin from a high of 83 percent to a low of 46 percent.[3]

The varying number of coins per string and the varying ratios of copper, lead, and tin in each coin make direct comparisons uncertain, but Song production of coins was of a different order of magnitude from production during the Tang. The Tang generally produced from one hundred thousand to two hundred thousand strings per year, with the annual average somewhere around ten coins per head. In contrast, the number of coins minted annually in the Song ranged from 1,000,000 to 1,500,000 in the first half of the eleventh century, and reached a high of 6,000,000 strings in 1080.[4] These figures break down to 60 coins per head, and by the year 1080, had increased to an average of 200 coins per head.[5] This output of coinage would not be matched by succeeding dynasties, testifying to the rapid growth of the Song money economy.

By the eleventh century, some 6,000,000,000 coins had been cast, yet the insatiable demand for coinage continued, largely because the coinage was not stable. Song-dynasty monetary officials failed to see that, each time they issued coins with a lower percentage of copper, they enhanced the value of the previous generations of coins. Consumers, who could test the coins to determine their metallic composition, melted down the older coins or hoarded them. By continuously lowering the amount of copper in the bronze coins, monetary officials undermined the currency system—this during an age of economic growth when the populace desperately needed a stable currency.

Once the empire had been reunified, the second Song emperor tried to recapture the area around Beijing from the Liao, a powerful nomadic state (described in the next chapter), but two successive campaigns failed. These losses set a precedent that all Song rulers would struggle with. Unable to defeat these powerful nomadic peoples, they had to buy peace, for which the nomadic peoples charged a high price. In 1004, the first of many peace agreements was signed, requiring the Song to pay 100,000 ounces of silver and 200,000 bolts of cloth each year to the Liao. The Liao demanded tribute in silver, whose value was fixed, and not in uncertain bronze coins. Over the course of the next three centuries, although different northern peoples fought and defeated the Song, tribute payments to the north continued. The government was hard-pressed to meet these financial obligations, but they probably served as a stimulus to the economy, since many of the northern peoples used this money to buy goods from Song merchants.

When the Song founder took power in 960, it was the fourth change of rule since the Later Tang had been overthrown in 936. The new emperor realized the threat his own military posed to the stability of his regime. Accordingly, he persuaded the generals who supported him to retire in exchange for generous pensions, and he structured his government so that the military were subordinate to civilian officials, not separate from them as they had been in the Tang and the successor states of the Five Dynasties. The military governors, who had become so powerful after 755, were replaced with civil officials.

The Bureaucratic Families of the Song

Since the seventh century, the number of officials recruited via the civil service examinations had been increasing steadily. In the Tang, a number of officials were still appointed on the basis of recommendation, but during the Song, civil service examinations became the primary means of recruiting officials, and the practice of appointing officials who had not taken the examinations died out. This shift to recruitment by open examination did not mean that officials came from all social levels. To the contrary, only the wealthiest of families could afford the extensive preparation required by the examinations; accordingly, those who passed the examinations were generally the sons of socially prominent families, many of whom claimed descent from the great clans of the Tang.

The civil service examinations in the Song were structured to benefit those with family ties to officials already in the bureaucracy. The *yin*, or shadow, privilege was granted to the male kin of officeholders. Depending on one's rank, one's sons, grandsons, nephews, sons-in-law, brothers, and cousins could sit for an easier examination with a higher pass rate—often close to 50 percent—than the open examinations. A degree granted on passing these restricted examinations did not have the same prestige as success on the open examinations, but it allowed entry into the lower levels of officialdom. The talented relatives of officeholders could always opt to sit for the open examinations and take the faster route of advancement in the bureaucracy if they were successful, but the system of the shadow privilege meant they did not have to risk the open examinations unless they wanted to.

For the dynasty's first century, some one hundred powerful families specialized in taking the civil service examinations and pursued various strategies to heighten their chances of success on the exams. To maximize the benefits from the shadow privilege, their sons intermarried with other families in this group, who were then able to confer the shadow privilege on them. If the wife of a man died, he would often marry her younger sister so that he could maintain his ties to her family. These hundred families formed a congenial group, whose members, based in the capital at Kaifeng or the nearby city of Luoyang, saw each other often.

These new bureaucrats developed a nagging sense of growing apart from their less-successful kin who remained at home. Some, like the reformer Fan Zhongyan (989–1052), formed charitable estates, setting aside property and specifying that the income it produced be used to help family members with unexpected expenses, usually connected to births, weddings, or funerals. Others, like the famous writer Ouyang Xiu (1007–1072) and the poet Su Shi's younger brother Su Xun (1009–1066) drew up genealogies in which they listed all relatives descended from their own great-grandfather; these were the family members they were obliged to mourn. Contemporary observers attributed the many mistakes the two men made in their lists to their long absences from the family home. Ouyang Xiu never lived in his ancestral home and visited only briefly for funerals; Su Xun did spend some time at home, but one year after completing his genealogy, he moved away, never to return. Family graveyards played an important role in sustaining the links between prominent family members in the capital and the less successful who remained in the countryside. The grave-sweeping ceremony of the Qingming festival, when relatives gathered at the graves of the dead, gained in popularity during the Song.

These officials behaved like the members of a well-connected club, whose sons regularly took and passed the exams (either open or restricted to those with the shadow privilege), whose daughters married the sons of equally important families, and whose sons succeeded each other in the highest positions of state. Of course, these families had occasional disputes, and factions formed among the bureaucracy, but the disputes were amicably resolved with no lasting animosities until the reign of Emperor Shenzong (reigned 1068–85). At this time the factional disagreement became so violent that it caused the permanent dissolution of this harmonious world.

THE NEW POLICIES:
SUPPORTERS AND OPPONENTS

The pressure from the rival empires on China's northern border created steady fiscal pressure on the Song, who had to pay high annual indemnity charges to the alien regimes in the north. The government also needed to raise money to support its army of one and a quarter million men, whose costs were enormous. In 1065, defense expenditures took 83 percent of the government's annual cash income.[6] With the accession of a new emperor in 1068, officials split into two camps with sharply divided views of how to resolve the fiscal crisis. One group, the historicists, were led by the great statesman Sima Guang (1019–1086), who advocated incremental reforms. The other group, the classicists, advocated radical reforms to restore the legendary age of the sage kings.

Sima compared a successful dynasty with a house and saw the people as the state's foundation. Ritual and law formed the building's pillars, and ministers, officials, generals, and soldiers served as different parts of the house. Maintaining a dynasty, then, required regular upkeep on the individual parts, not tearing the house down and building a new one. Such reforms, Sima felt, should be modeled on the policies of the immediate predecessor governments of the Tang and the Five Dynasties. To that end, he compiled a history of China up to 959, *The Comprehensive Mirror for Aid in Government*, that is still read today for its elegant, simple prose. Sima Guang was also the first historian to include differing interpretations of the same events under the category "examining the differences."

This approach was too gradual for the opposing faction of officials, led by Wang Anshi (1021–1086), who served as chief councillor (the equivalent of prime minister) from 1070 to 1073, and 1075 to 1076, and whose policies continued to shape state policy until 1086. The classicists' stated goal was to return to the hallowed age of the pre-Confucian Sage Kings, and the only way to do so, they argued, was through a campaign of massive and radical reform. The two groups disagreed fundamentally over the pace of reform as well as the causes of the financial crisis the empire faced. Wang Anshi argued that officials had lost the Dao, or way, of creating wealth, and he claimed that only those who understood the Dao, or his interpretation of the classics, should serve in the bureaucracy. He worked to create a national school system to teach his curriculum, and he thought that the civil service examinations should test only his interpretation of the classics.

Although much of the debate with the historicists was phrased in terms of the Dao, or way, and how to recover it, the underlying disagreement between the two groups concerned money. Suspicious of money, the historicists wanted to limit the government's economic activities. They held that the money economy could not grow, and they thought that the traditional relationships among the wealthy and the poor needed no alteration. Wang Anshi and his followers took a diametrically opposed stance: the government should intervene to hasten economic development, create prosperity, and draw in the higher tax receipts the government so desperately needed. Wang also believed that the traditional relationships between rich and poor required massive alteration.

Wang Anshi and his followers were infatuated with the potential of money in a way that only the first generation to encounter it could be. They loved its many advantages. Unlike cloth and grain, it could not spoil and could be stored forever. It was liquid. Best of all, it could be produced—either by minting metal coins or even more expeditiously, by printing paper money.

The Introduction of Paper Money

The world's first paper money emerged in Sichuan, which remained a separate currency zone even after the reunification of the empire under the Song. Facing a shortage of bronze coins, the government stipulated that only iron coins could be used in Sichuan, but iron was too bulky a metal to serve as a currency. To buy 500 grams (1.1 pounds) of salt required 700 grams (1.5 pounds) of iron, and 28 grams (1 ounce) of silver was worth over 40 kilograms (90 pounds) of iron.

The currency situation was further complicated by government regulations that forbade the use of any bronze coins, even as officials continued to assess tax obligations in bronze coins. The exchange ratio of iron coins to bronze also varied, with the official exchange rate stipulating one bronze coin to ten iron coins, but the real rate closer to four. Peasant rebellions erupted at the end of the tenth century, revealing the level of discontent among the common people.

In response to this chaotic situation, Sichuanese merchants developed the world's first paper money to facilitate their long-distance transactions, and the local people made deposits of iron with merchant houses and used their deposit slips as promissory notes. This paper money gradually replaced the cumbersome strings of iron coins.

Sometime at the turn of the eleventh century the central government granted sixteen of these merchant houses a monopoly of the notes, but the difficulties persisted. Because the merchants occasionally failed to pay the value of the notes, the government took over the monopoly in 1023 when it founded the Bureau of Exchange Medium. The government initially proposed that the paper money be traded in every three years, but gradually these regulations were relaxed and the money circulated for longer periods. The region of circulation had extended beyond Sichuan to include all of north China by the end of the eleventh century. Although the initial offering had been backed by a cash reserve of 29 percent, the percentage of backing of the later issues shrank and led to widespread inflation.[7] Even though the value of notes with a face value of one thousand had fallen to 940 or 960 coins in the 1070s, Wang Anshi and his followers continued to see money as the solution to the empire's fiscal crisis.

Many of the reforms Wang instituted, the New Policies, were linked to money. He wanted to put all government employees, even those in the lowest positions, on cash salaries to replace the pay in kind they had previously been receiving. Wang established a new section of the bureaucracy, the Tea and Horse Agency, that went into business trading Chinese tea for Tibetan horses. Merchants were recruited directly into this agency, and promotions were made on the basis of how much money each official earned.

The most representative of the New Policies was called the Green Sprouts reforms, intended to relieve the chronic debt of the poor peasants. They always had to borrow money to buy seed to plant; when the harvest came in, they had to sell their crops at low prices, earning barely enough money to pay back the moneylenders. If they could break out of this cycle of debt, Wang argued, they would extricate themselves from the clutches of the local moneylenders, or engrossers, as he referred to them. As they became more prosperous, they could serve the empire better by paying taxes and performing military service. In the Green Sprouts reforms, Wang instituted what were called ever-level granaries; the granaries loaned grain to cultivators when they were short, to be repaid after the harvest. These loans were supplemented by the Green Sprouts loans made to peasants at planting time and to be paid back, with no interest, after the harvest. Wang hoped that these loans would enable cultivators to pay their taxes.

But the goal of the program shifted almost as soon as it was implemented. Within months of making the loans, officials recognized the enormous revenue potential if they levied interest, and they started to charge 20 percent to 30 percent interest on the loans. Initially these officials raised much money, and in keeping with Wang's view of merit, they were promoted on the basis of the amount of revenue they took in. Soon the state encountered difficulty in collecting loan payments from poor families, the intended beneficiaries of the program. Officials responded by giving one- and then two-year extensions, but within ten years so many peasants were in arrears that the entire Green Sprouts program, once so profitable, was losing money. The most successful loans were those made to the rich and to moneylenders, the very groups the program was intended to eliminate.

Sima Guang viewed the program with great apprehension because he did not share Wang's optimism about the state of the rural economy. He thought there was insufficient coinage in circulation to allow the rural poor to pay back their loans in money, and he was right. The continuing shortage of bronze coins kept the price of money artificially high. Peasants had to trade too much grain to get the cash to repay the state. Those who did not yet produce for market and had less ready access to cash were hurt the most.

The collapse of the Green Sprouts loans forced the poor farmers who had borrowed money from the state and had fallen behind in their payments to borrow more money from the only source still available: the wealthy moneylenders and big landlords who continued to dominate the countryside. Under Wang Anshi, the state had attempted to intervene in the rural economy, but it lacked the resources to do so. In 1086, after the emperor Shenzong had died, the new emperor retracted the policies, leaving the same stratum of rich landowners intact in the countryside. In 1101, another emperor, Huizong (reigned 1101–1125) reinstituted the New Policies. These shifts and countershifts raised the level of factional hostility in the government, with the classicists appointing only other classicists in the Wang Anshi mold, and the historicists appointing only other historicists. These political shifts had little effect on the powerful families of the countryside, who had been the target of so many of Wang's reforms and whose hold on rural power continued unabated.

Portrait of a Marriage I: A Wealthy Landlord and His Wife

Although written sources have little to say about the material lives of these rural moneylenders, archeological sources are revealing. In 1951 Chinese archeologists excavated a tomb in Baisha, a town lying on a trade route 75 kilometers (47 miles) southeast of Luoyang, the former capital

This portrait in the sitting room of their tomb shows Master Zhao and his wife attended by four servants. Behind the man and his wife are screens with waves on them; behind the servants is a wall covering with pseudo-writing on it. The couple sit on chairs, a new innovation in home furnishing during the eleventh century, which are modeled and attached to the surface of the painting.

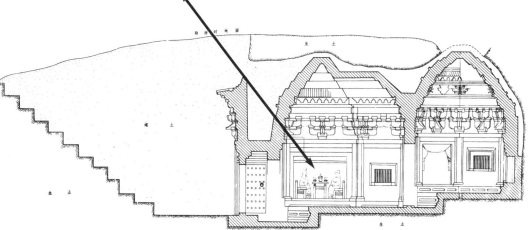

PORTRAIT OF A MARRIAGE FROM A TOMB

Master Zhao, a wealthy landowner, and his wife, had a lavish tomb constructed for their burial (shown here in cross section), complete with a portrait of themselves in the front sitting room (see above). They were buried in 1099 in the back bedroom, along with their contract granting them possession of the land their tomb occupied.

on the Yellow River.[8] One document and one painting found there refer to the deceased, who died in 1099, as Great Master Zhao. They do not use an official title for him. The size and elegant construction of the tomb, combined with this form of address, suggest that Master Zhao was a big landholder and possibly a prosperous merchant or an engrosser, to borrow Wang Anshi's term for those wealthy families he saw as leeches on the countryside.

Great Master Zhao was buried with his wife. Their tomb took the form of a facsimile miniature house, with a front room and a back room, two halls, and a main dining room. The architectural details are exquisite. The roof beams rest on elaborate wooden joints, and the multilayered brickwork forms an intricate vaulted ceiling. Joined by doors, the rooms have mock windows with mock drapes, and the door at the end of the tomb is even half open to allow a servant-girl to peer out. Such half-views of figures were all the rage in eleventh-century painting.

Their tomb contains few funeral goods: one gold ingot, porcelain pots, and a few pieces of iron, which were thought to drive spirits away. Rather than bury miniature models of the grave goods they desired, Great Master Zhao and his wife commissioned elaborately detailed paintings depicting their domestic arrangements, down to the couple's cat. The halls are decorated with men and women bringing the Zhaos the goods they would need in the afterlife—strings of money, skins of wine, and bags of grain. Guards stand outside their door, while a troupe of musicians performs.

As painted on the wall of the front room, the couple sit on chairs at a table and watch the musicians. Their portrait shows them across from one another, feet on footrests, drinking wine, with a brazier underneath the table. This cozy scene depicts all the latest trends in home decorating among the newly rich. Screens showing waves breaking on top of waves were popular at the time, as were tables and chairs. Instead of using one's bed as a daytime table and reserving tables for home altars, as had been common in previous dynasties, Master and Mrs. Zhao have a separate table and chairs for meals. Although a contemporary observer noted that in the Northern Song, women from literati and official families did not sit in chairs, Mrs. Zhao's being depicted in a chair indicates that her family did not observe the restrictions governing the socially conservative. Behind the couple are four servants: the woman behind Great Master Zhao is carrying a dish of peaches, the man in front of her a spittoon, and the women to their left a jar; the last woman has her hands in her sleeves. The writing on the wall covering behind them looks like calligraphy, but its meaningless squiggles, interrupted by a few genuine characters, are actually a mere imitation of real writing.

For the Zhaos are not scholars. They have luxurious living quarters, staffed with many servants, and they derive their pleasure from drinking and eating, listening to music, and enjoying each other's company—not from reading. The only legible writing in the tomb paintings is a label on a bag of grain saying the year and Great Master Zhao. This grain is either rent or repayment of a loan owed to the Zhaos—just the type of exaction so opposed by Wang Anshi.

The tomb contains only one written document, a deed for the purchase of their tomb plot, which was placed in the back room with the skeletons of the deceased couple. More than half the document, written on a brick tablet with a cover, is illegible, but because it follows a model given in a contemporary burial manual, its contents can be reconstructed. The text gives the identity of the deceased, the location of the funeral plot, and the amount of money paid for it: 99,999 strings of cash. Besides the enormous wealth this amount conveys, it carries a symbolic meaning. Three is a number of light, and nine, the product of three threes, is a strong counter to the forces of death. This deed specifies the consequences should any spirits of the dead return to the world of the living, and like a real-world land contract, it gives the name of the guarantor and the witness.[9] Any soul previously buried in the tomb is enjoined to stay far away from the deceased or face punishment by the officials of the underworld bureaucracy. The living put in a final good word for themselves and close by citing the law of the spirits.

This contract shows an extraordinarily legalistic view of the underworld: even the spirits of the dead are bound to recognize the terms of this contract. The burial manual that contains this text recommends the burial of two copies of the text: one for the deceased, to keep on his or her person should his or her claim to the tomb land be challenged, and one for the owners of the land, the gods of the earth, to keep in their netherworld files. Forty-four copies of this contract, or close variants, have been excavated from all over China, spanning the eighth to the nineteenth centuries. Many of the examples are from the twelfth to fourteenth centuries, when it was most common to bury such contracts in tombs.

Portrait of a Marriage II: A Bureaucrat and His Poet Wife

If we can judge from their funeral portrait, the Zhaos enjoyed a convivial marriage. They had their cat painted but no children, suggesting that they may have been childless. They left a lasting visual record of their marriage, but no written record. In contrast, the great eleventh-century poet Li Qingzhao (1084–ca. 1151) left a memoir of her marriage. Written in 1132, it is an afterword to her husband's study of his collection of rubbings, *Records on Metal and Stone*.[10] She and her husband had a convivial but childless marriage. She met her husband, who was born into one of the great bureaucratic families of the Song, when he was still a student of twenty-one and she was eighteen. Her husband, Zhao

Mingcheng (1081–1129), had the same family name as the Zhao couple of the Baisha tomb, but they were not related. Since she too was from a powerful family, theirs was a typical marriage for people in their social group.

The two newlyweds devoted themselves to collecting books, artworks, and antiquities. Rare for their time, they were intellectual equals. Li describes the friendly competition the couple had:

> I happen to have an excellent memory, and every evening after we finished eating, we would sit in the hall called 'Return Home' and make tea. Pointing to the heaps of books and histories, we would guess on which line of which page in which chapter of which book a certain passage could be found. Success in guessing determined who got to drink his or her tea first. Whenever I got it right, I would raise the teacup, laughing so hard that the tea would spill in my lap, and I would get up, not having been able to drink any of it at all. I would have been glad to grow old in such a world.

Is Li hinting at her childlessness by using the sexually suggestive image of spilling tea in her lap? Gradually the couple becomes more preoccupied with ownership as they labor to correct any flaws in their growing collection of books.

The reigning emperor, Huizong, like Li Qingzhao and her husband, devoted himself to collecting, but his was a collection of paintings numbering over six thousand. A serious painter himself, well known for his distinctive calligraphy, he founded the first imperial Academy of Painting, a branch of the government that granted official ranks to the painters employed there.

It was under the rule of Huizong that the Chinese grossly underestimated the power of the Jurchen armies, who conquered all of north China by 1127. Historians divide the Song dynasty into two periods. During the Northern Song (960–1126) when the capital was in north China in Kaifeng, the Song ruled all of China. In the Southern Song (1127–1276), the Song ruled only south China.

The cost to the Zhaos of this shift in power is told poignantly in Li's account. In 1127 the Zhaos were forced to move during the Jurchen invasion of north China. Li's description captures the difficulty first of reducing their enormous collection and then of moving south with the many remaining possessions: "We first gave up the bulky printed volumes, the albums of paintings, and the most cumbersome of the vessels. Thus we reduced the size of the collection several times, and still we had fifteen cartloads of books. When we reached Donghai, it took a string of

The Emperor as Artist

The emperor who saw north China fall to the Jurchen conquerors, Emperor Huizong was surely the finest painter among all of China's emperors and one of China's greatest calligraphers. Here he paints two delicate finchs resting on carefully rendered bamboo branches. His intensely realistic painting was as much the product of direct observation as was Zhang Zeduan's Qingming scroll.

boats to ferry them all across the Huai, and again across the Yangzi to Jiankang [Nanjing]."

Even though they had discarded much, the collection was still far too cumbersome for wartime. In 1128, the two were forced to separate when Zhao was given a new posting. The couple parted, with the wife in charge of the possessions, and Zhao took up his post, only to die of malaria in 1129. Li was left alone, still with far too many possessions to manage. At the time she heard her husband had died, "I still had twenty thousand *juan* [chapters] of books, two thousand copies of inscriptions on metal and stone with colophons, table services and mats enough to entertain a hundred guests, along with other possessions equaling those already mentioned."

Alone, she was unable to preserve the collection. She dispatched two servants to send her things to her brother-in-law, but the Jurchen sacked the city and her books "were scattered into clouds of smoke." Blocked from joining her brother-in-law, she changed course and went south to her brother. Left with a few baskets of goods, she stayed in a cottage, where much of what remained was stolen. At the end of her tale, almost all was lost.

The pull of these possessions is readily understood. They are all she has left of her marriage and of her husband. With a poet's prose, expressive yet concise, her account of her possessions vividly conveys the traumatic loss of the north to the Jurchens. Others with fewer goods than she and her husband were similarly forced to abandon their homes and flee to the south, unsure of what they would find.

Li's frank autobiography is an unusual piece of writing. The pretense that she is writing about her husband's collection frees her from the strictures against a woman's writing an autobiography, and she is able to give a verbal portrait of a marriage rivaling the visual tomb portrait of Master and Mrs. Zhao. Generations of Chinese have treasured her memoir for its warm depiction of her unusual relationship with her husband. Her later poems testify to her lasting grief over her husband's death. She entitled one poem "Written by Chance":

Fifteen years ago, beneath moonlight and flowers,
I walked with you
We composed flower-viewing poems together.
Tonight the moonlight and flowers are just the same
But how can I ever hold in my arms the same love.[11]

As open as it is, Li's autobiography leaves much unsaid. Nowhere does she discuss her own renown. A much better writer than her husband, Li was one of the great poets of her time. She intends to depict the idyll of her early marriage, but the reader can detect the seeds of resentment in her text. She loves her husband and their books, but he gradually takes control of their collection, keeping the key for himself, and when he dies, she has no means of support.

When Li Qingzhao wrote this memoir in the eighth month of 1132, she had already remarried. Her second husband was a poor choice. She sued him for embezzling funds and divorced him when he was found guilty and exiled. They had been married less than one hundred days.

Later Chinese scholars were troubled by the idea that so great a poet would divorce. Some even denied it, but they did not realize that divorce and widow remarriage occurred much more often in the twelfth century than in subsequent centuries. As the widowed daughter of a prominent family, Li Qingzhao was able to rely on her in-laws and her own siblings for help. Women, even childless women, in succeeding centuries would increasingly be viewed as members of their husband's families. As such, they found it impossible to return home, and they needed the permission of their in-laws to remarry. Both widow remarriage and divorce became

易安居士三十一歲之照

清麗其詞端莊其品歸去來兮
真堪偕隱
政和甲午新秋德父題於歸來堂

CHINA'S MOST FAMOUS WOMAN POET

This painting of Li Qingzhao is dated 1114, when Li was 31. Her husband wrote the dedication in the upper-right-hand corner of the portrait:

> Her poetry is pure and elegant,
> Her person modest and dignified,
> A real companion for me in my retirement.

(Hu Pin-ching, *Li Ch'ing-chao*, New York, 1966, p. 34)

His text conveys more affection than does this stylized portrait, showing an emaciated Li, with an elaborate hairdo, holding a sprig of chrysanthemums. Most likely a later forgery, the portrait depicts the ethereal appearance Li took on in people's minds, not her actual looks.

279

more and more disreputable. It was too easy to forget that China's most famous woman poet had both remarried and divorced.

Li makes it sound as if the fall of the north to the Jurchen in 1127 shattered the comfortable world of the bureaucratic families into which she was born. But the dissolution of that exclusive club predated 1127 by several decades and was the result of factional politics. She begins her memoir by saying, "In 1101, in the first year of the Jianzhong reign, I came as a bride to the Zhao household. At that time my father was a division head in the Ministry of Rites, and my father-in-law, later a Grand Councillor, was a vice-minister in the Ministry of Personnel." She does not reveal that her father and her father-in-law were members of opposing factions.

Her father, Li Gefei, was a prominent follower of Su Shi, who opposed Wang Anshi's attempt to impose educational uniformity because it stifled individual freedom of expression. Two years after her marriage, her father was expelled from the capital, along with sixteen other historicists. Although Li wrote poems of protest to her father-in-law, Zhao Tingzhi, the lieutenant of the man who had issued the order, the purge continued. In 1105, the names of 309 historicists were carved on a stone tablet, their writings banned, their kin barred from office. Because the ban on books was difficult to enforce, people continued to read the writings of these men, but not openly and certainly not in school. Far more damaging was the order preventing the relatives of the historicists from holding office. Although it was rescinded almost immediately and Li's father was able to return to Kaifeng, a lasting precedent had been set.

Li Qingzhao chose not to write about the unpleasant aspects of her world, whether factional infighting or her disastrous remarriage. And few marriages can have equaled Li Qingzhao's in emotional intensity. Her vivid descriptions of the passionate ties binding husband to wife, and of her grief at her husband's early death, are moving even today. In a society in which parents arranged their children's marriages, Li Qingzhao's experience was hardly typical. Her contemporaries, most of whom could only yearn for matches like hers, were drawn to the romantic ideal Li so beautifully evoked in her writings.

REMEMBERING THE NORTH

The loss of the north, so critical in Li Qingzhao's account, loomed large in the mental landscape of all those living in south China after 1127. There, they found themselves in a land of rivers and streams, so different from the loess plains of the north. Unlike the silt-filled Yellow River, the Yangzi was navigable, as were its many tributaries. The cost of transporting goods was much lower than it had been in the north, helping market networks to expand dramatically.

An enormous number of people fled to the south at the same time Li did in the early twelfth century. Hundreds of thousands of people, including twenty thousand high officials, tens of thousands of their office staff, and over four hundred thousand military and their families moved to the new capital of Hangzhou and its surrounding towns.[12] The sudden influx of people caused many difficulties. During the first chaotic years of the Southern Song dynasty, the Jurchen troops continued to attack along the Huai River valley and south of the river. As the following tale shows, the government was hard-pressed to keep social order.

In the early 1130s, a native of Kaifeng, the former capital, moved 800 kilometers (500 miles) to the newly designated capital of Hangzhou where he was to take up office. Determined to leave their assigned house in the red-light district, he told his wife to pack their belongings and await a sedan chair, which would take her to their new house in a residential district. When he came back to get her, the landlord said that she already left in a sedan chair. The man could do nothing to get her back. Five years later, at an official banquet in Quxian (Zhejiang), he began to sob at a dinner featuring freshwater turtle, the favorite dish of his missing wife. A servant was sent to console him, and it turned out to be his lost wife. She had been taken away by a broker in women and sold to the host for thirty strings. The man offered to compensate his host, but the man was so embarrassed to have taken someone else's wife as a concubine that he returned her without accepting any payment.[13]

In 1147, another refugee, a writer named Meng Yuanlao, recorded his own personal memories of what life in Kaifeng had been like. He called his book *A Record of the Dream of the Eastern Capital's Splendor*. The book was frankly nostalgic, seeking to depict life in the northern capital before the ravages of 1127. The city had had a population of over one million, not matched by London until the late seventeenth century. All these people were crowded into a space of just over 60 square kilometers (23 square miles). The density was over 2000 people per square kilometer (32,000 per square mile).[14] Meng does not talk about the crowding, the dirt, or the disease that must have been part of city life. His is an idealistic view, and the comparison with Hangzhou always implicit: "People of Kaifeng were kind and friendly.... A family newly arrived in Kaifeng would always find their neighbors most helpful: those kindly souls would bring tea and hot water, offer to lend them things or run errands for them, and give them practical tips."[15] This was a far cry from the experience of the woman kidnapped in Hangzhou!

Meng's real topic is the pleasures available to those who had money in their pockets. Kaifeng had seventy-two large and many more small restaurants, with fancy facades in front and small gardens in back. Unlike Changan, with its evening curfew, the pleasure quarters of Kaifeng were open around the clock, and customers flocked to these restaurants in all seasons. The most elaborate of the restaurants had five different buildings, each three floors high, linked by bridges and passageways. People dined out at restaurants, and they spent money on the various street entertainers. Meng's description of the lantern festival is typical:

> In the arcades along the broad avenue entertainers of every description plied their wares cheek by jowl, all displaying ingenious skills and wondrous talents. The singers, dancers, and acrobats caused a din that could be heard miles away. Some of them demonstrated their skill in archery or at kicking balls, others walked on tightropes strung between tall bamboo poles. Wildman Zhao would eat and drink while hung upside down: Zhang Jiuge would swallow an iron sword; Li Waining would pop up puppets with explosives. . . .

The list of performers and their acts goes on. This is a city filled with people deciding where to go, what to eat, or what to watch next. Meng makes little mention of officials or of examination candidates—his workmanlike prose suggests he may not have been a member of the literati. Meng does not belabor the point that all these pleasures are gone. His readers would have known that many of the entertainers had been taken captive by the Jurchen. The simplicity of his description is what makes it so poignant: everything he describes is part of a by-gone existence, and that is why he has recorded it.

City Life as Shown in the Qingming Scroll

The same impulse underlies one of the greatest examples of Chinese art, the hand-scroll of urban life by Zhang Zeduan, *Peace Reigns Over the River*, which is often referred to as the Qingming scroll. Although the scroll is sometimes on display in Beijing's Palace Museum laid out to its full length under a glass case, originally the viewer determined the pace of viewing by unrolling the 5.25-meter-long (5.74-yard-long) scroll section by section. The scroll was painted after the fall of the north, sometime before 1186, and its portrayal of urban life is as frankly idealistic as Meng's. Zhang's cityscape shows none of the discomforts of city life, possibly in order to convey a muted political message—that life under the reigning emperor was not as carefree as it appears on the scroll.

We know as little of Zhang's life as of Meng's. Our only source for his biography is the first colophon on the scroll, dated 1186. Chinese scholars felt free to write comments directly on paintings they owned or viewed; we call these reactions *colophons*, which often provide valuable information about a given painting.

The first colophon on the scroll prefaces Zhang's name with the title Hanlin, but no other documents record his membership in the Imperial Painting Academy. It continues, "When young, he studied and traveled to the capital for further study. Later he practiced painting things."

The Qingming scroll presents a free-flowing landscape, starting in the countryside and gradually moving into a city. Although the scroll is often called a depiction of Kaifeng, nothing in the scroll stands out as a landmark. The scroll begins at dawn, with a man leading donkeys down a path. As the viewer unrolls the scroll from right to left, he sees a small procession coming from the top of the scroll. Two men are carrying a sedan chair, around which they have wedged brooms. As the scroll progresses and time passes, the path meets a river where a small restaurant is opening for the day. Zhang provides extraordinary detail: each plank of each boat is delineated carefully. The first colophon says, "He showed talent for fine-lined architectural drawing, and especially liked boats and carts, markets and bridges, moats and paths."[16]

In this scene, the scroll shifts to the water, and we follow the river to the rainbow bridge. The detail of the painting is so mesmerizing that it is easy to forget that this is a careful composition. The scroll unfurls slowly, with the work of a narrator done by a path, then the river, and finally a road. The bridge, the dramatic peak, lies at the exact center of the scroll. This often-reproduced scene shows boatmen struggling to regain control of their boat, whose lead line has snapped. On the bridge above, someone tosses them a rope, which the artist shows unfurling in midair. Other sailors frantically take down the mast so they can go under the bridge. As the viewer unrolls the scroll, there is a close-up of a confrontation on the bridge itself. Servants in front of a sedan chair carrying a hidden figure gesticulate vigorously at the servant of two figures on horseback, yet neither gives way.

The people in the scroll have appetites to match those described by Meng Yuanlao. Along the sides of the bridge are various stands, some where customers can sit down and have a bowl of noodles, others where people can grab a snack standing up. As the scroll continues, the outskirts of the city come into view. An elaborate wooden edifice in front of a restaurant marks the festival day. The river winds out of sight, and a road leads the viewer to the city wall. As many restaurants and shops

CHINA'S COMMERCIAL REVOLUTION

Unlike earlier periods, when markets remained within government-designated commercial areas, in the Song dynasty merchants plied their wares on every street, and markets appeared in every village. The world's first paper money came into circulation at the beginning of the eleventh century. Many peasant households began to grow specialized crops and make handicrafts for the market. Historians still wonder why this commercial growth

did not lead to an industrial revolution.

This scene—taken from the 5.25-meter (5.74-yard) long Qingming scroll held in the Beijing Palace Museum—shows laborers carrying loads pausing in front of a cool drinks seller, a stand with tools laid out on the ground in front of it, and several restaurants on the left side of the bridge. On the right side of the bridge, bystanders gather to watch a grain boat below just avoiding a crash.

lie outside the wall as within it, suggesting that cities often overflowed their walls. The road goes by a garrison, with dozing soldiers in front of it, and the wall lies equally unguarded. This is an idyllic landscape, with no hint of the actual fortifications northern cities had to have to protect themselves against incursions, and it matches Meng Yuanlao's description: no beggars or poor people here.

The last stretch of road depicts many different establishments and the full range of Song society. A storyteller at the three-story restaurant, marked by a festive scaffolding, has attracted a crowd of listeners. Across the street sits a man selling religious statues, and next to him men draw water from a well. Three women sit in a doctor's office, behind which is a small garden.

Zhang's figures show how clothing corresponded to social status: the lower the social rank, the scantier the clothes. Peasants and oarsmen have on short tops and rolled up trousers. Townsmen wear kerchiefs, with longer shirts and trousers. Shop assistants are clad in long gowns and simple hats, while the Daoists and the lone Buddhist have robes made with long, draped sleeves. The low-level officials, clerks, students, and examination candidates all sport long gowns with kerchiefs tied over a stiff black form.

This is an artfully constructed scene, rich with human activity, but there are few women. One or two are gathered around the basket with the brooms in front of the restaurant. A woman peers out from a sedan chair, and a braid dangles down the back of a woman on horseback directly behind the Daoists. Three women sit in the doctor's shop. This same imbalance skews the entire scroll: out of the more than five hundred people shown, only about twenty are female. Those with bare heads are at home in their boats or their shops. Otherwise the women are in sedan chairs, on donkeyback or horseback, usually with their heads covered and always accompanied by men. The only women enjoying themselves outside are the women in front of the inn by the brooms.

Women Move Inside: The Spread of Footbinding

Zhang painted this scroll in the twelfth century, just as the practice of footbinding was catching on, and women were increasingly confined to the home. Because paintings of women in the Song do not show their feet, we must look to textual evidence to trace the spread of the practice.

One observer writing in the 1130s commented that Tang poets never wrote about footbinding: "From this one can know [that] flattened feet began only since the Five Dynasties. Before the Xining (1068–77) and

Yuanfeng (1077–86) reigns, the practice was rare. Recently people have copied each other and no longer feel shame."[17] Most observers thought the practice began with adult dancers binding their own feet in the tenth century, but then mothers began to bind the feet of their daughters, because the feet were more malleable before puberty.

To bind the feet a bandage, about 5 centimeters (2 inches) wide and 3 meters (10 feet) long, was wrapped with one end on the inside of the instep; from there it was carried over the small toes so as to force the toes in and toward the sole. The large toe was left unbound. The bandage was then wrapped around the heel so forcefully that the heel and toes were drawn closer together. This was done over and over again, until the bandage was used up. If it was done skillfully, after the foot healed in two years, the young woman could walk short distances with no pain. If

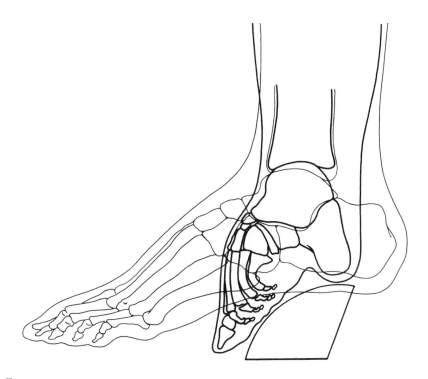

FOOTBINDING

Starting when their daughters were young girls, mothers bound their daughters' feet by wrapping a cloth around the toes and forcing them to grow under the foot. The practice began to spread during the Song dynasty, though some regions never adopted the custom. This diagram superimposes an unbound foot on top of a bound foot, which was about half the size of a normal foot.

done poorly, walking was always painful. Those few writers who commented on footbinding said little about why people found bound feet attractive. Wrapping the feet in long bindings meant that a woman's feet became a private part of her body, viewed only by herself, her mother when she was young, and her husband after marriage. Later sources describe husbands cleaning and sucking the feet of their wives, as though binding the feet had transformed them into sexual objects.

The practice of footbinding spread among women, even those of good families, after the fall of the north. When a wife of a local official, a vice-prefect, died during childbirth in 1274, she was buried with the fetus of her second son. Along with a money-filled purse and many silk clothes were buried six pairs of shoes 18 to 22 centimeters (7 to 8.5 inches) long and 5 to 6 centimeters (1.9 to 2.3 inches) wide. She needed wrappings to maintain such small feet, and they too have been found, 2 meters (6.5 feet) long and 10 centimeters (3.9 inches) wide. She was not a concubine but the wife and daughter of low-ranking officials.

It is always difficult to explain the spread of a fashion, especially one so painful. The practice of footbinding spread during the twelfth and thirteenth centuries as a market in women grew. In earlier periods men had taken concubines, usually when wives were unable to bear sons, but

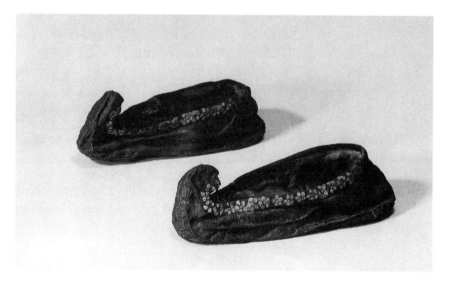

SHOES FOR BOUND FEET

This pair of shoes for bound feet was in the tomb of an official's wife who, in 1274, died in childbirth. The length of the shoes—from 18 to 22 centimeters (7 to 8.5 inches)—shows that during the Song, the practice of footbinding had not reached the extremes it would by the nineteenth century, when shoes 7 or 8 centimeters (about 3 inches) long were common.

the practice became more common in the twelfth and thirteenth centuries. Families began to sell their daughters and husbands their wives to make money. Song sources tell of brokers, like the one mentioned earlier who kidnapped the woman in Hangzhou, and of those who bought women legally.

The spread of commercial activity in the Song transformed women into commodities who were bought and sold on the basis of appearance—not married on the basis of family ties as they had been in earlier centuries. By the time of the Southern Song, the market in women had expanded so much that all women, even those from noncourtesan families, were affected. Women of good families still hoped to make good marriages, but they knew they would be rivals of concubines for their husband's attention, and they knew the concubines would have bound feet. Under the circumstances, mothers chose to bind their daughters' feet so as to maximize the girls' chances in the marriage market. They may not have been conscious of the damage they were doing to their daughters. The practice continued into modern times; footbinding died out in the 1930s. Like breast implants in twentieth-century America (which are less common than footbinding was), women bound their feet because other women bound theirs.

LIFE UNDER THE SOUTHERN SONG (1127–1276)

At first, the leaders and subjects of the Song emperor did not realize that they would never recapture the north from the Jurchens. Fighting with the Jin dynasty continued until 1141, when the Song emperor signed a humiliating treaty with his Jin counterpart (see chapter 8, p. 318). Eventually people realized that Hangzhou would have to be more than a temporary capital, and the emperor began to concentrate on the problems of governing an empire that was only half its original size. Although always threatened by the Jin in the north, the Southern Song enjoyed great economic prosperity as the first commercial revolution continued during the twelfth and thirteenth centuries.

Gods and Goods

Like women, popular gods were also affected by the expanding markets of the twelfth and thirteenth centuries. In addition to Buddhist and Daoist monasteries, each district in China had a group of temples housing local gods. Many of these had been human beings who came to be worshiped after their deaths as gods in their native places. Others were nature deities who included tree, mountain, and river gods. The Spirit of the Bamboo Grove, to whom the fictional Li Wa and her lover prayed for a child in Tang-dynasty Changan, typified such deities in the period before the Song dynasty. These gods performed miracles suited to the agricultural society from which they sprang. Local people prayed to them to bring rain, or end excessive rains, to keep drought and locusts away, and to protect them from plague, famine, and the dangers of childbirth.

Lay people could consult a host of religious specialists—some affiliated with Buddhism and Daoism and some not—or they could pray directly to deities for assistance. They were looking for someone or some god with the power to perform miracles, which they called *ling*, or efficacy. If someone, whether human or divine, could cure an ill person or make rain come, then people would seek that one's help, regardless of their religious affiliation.

With the move of the capital south and the continued increase in market activity, deities assumed new, more commercial powers. A collection of miscellaneous tales records the experience of a merchant who sold mats made of reeds. In 1158 he was traveling by boat with a shipment of mats when he agreed to give a Daoist practitioner a ride on his vessel. After they arrived, the Daoist bade him farewell saying, "I will enable you to get twenty thousand to reward you." At the time, the merchant did not understand.

When he went to market to sell his mats, he found that the demand for them was unusually high due to a shortage in Chengdu, almost 1,600 kilometers (1,000 miles) up the Yangzi River in Sichuan province. To ensure a sufficient supply for imperial sacrifices, the governor of Hangzhou raised the official purchasing price of each mat by two cash. Since the merchant had ten thousand mats, he made an extra profit of twenty thousand cash, just as the mysterious figure had promised him.

This was not a traditional miracle. The hitchhiker, who must have been a deity who assumed human form, did not bring rain or end illness. Instead he manipulated a shortage in Sichuan and twisted the government purchasing system to reward the favor. This miracle hinged on understanding the dynamics of a market stretching all the way from Hangzhou to Chengdu. The tale credits the god with having such an understanding, but the people telling the tale also had to grasp the complexities of the national market that had come into existence during the Song dynasty.

Problems with currency persisted even after the fall of the north when the Song continued to mint debased bronze coins and to print inflated paper money. Because each generation of money differed in value from its predecessors, no one could be certain of the exchange rates among the different generations of money. Contracts from the period give prices in paper money, but they specify the year of issue so as to avoid misunderstandings. In one dispute that reached court, one friend lent money to another, who paid him back with several paintings. After the man who received the paintings died, the man's children sued their father's friend, saying he had not paid back the full amount. The judge hearing the case agreed with them and ordered their father's friend to take back the paintings and to repay them in money—but in the currency of the original loan, which had occurred some forty years earlier. The lack of a stable currency may have made trading difficult, but people continued to produce for markets.

As merchants and traders went farther afield to buy and sell goods, they started to take their gods with them. One group of cultivators in Huzhou, the district next to Hangzhou, worshiped a Six Dynasties hero. They grew lotus pods and roots, which they sold at market, and they credited their god with sending rain that swept locusts away from their valuable lotuses. When they put up a stone commemorating their god's accomplishments, they had this to say about themselves:

> Many of this district's residents travel by boat to distant places to trade. On the day of departure, the people always pray to the deity and paint his image in their boats. They pray to him morning and night. When they travel on a river or a lake, even when they encounter winds or waves, he provides them with safe passage every time.[18]

So they took their god with them on their business trips, and they credited him with keeping them safe, even when they ventured far from home.

The realms of these deities stretched out as their followers traveled ever farther to trade goods and the market networks expanded. A national market came into being, in which goods were traded across all of south China, and even into the Jurchen-controlled north. Most of the goods traded nationally were rare luxuries or special treats, such as tangerines or lichees from Fujian. During famines, grain-poor provinces often purchased rice from distant, more productive areas. People were traveling farther and longer to trade, and the changes in the popular pantheon reflected their contact with other groups.

Shrines to Worthies

Temples to popular deities, with their ever-expanding catchment areas, were not the only religious institutions in the countryside. Alongside the temples to deities were shrines to worthy men, often located in schools or Confucian academies. Unlike the gods in temples, these were men who had performed good deeds. They were not thought to have any divine powers. Most of those commemorated were statesmen, officials, generals, famous loyalists, or writers who had done something worthwhile during their lives. They were local men, whose memory the community sought to keep alive by putting up a tablet in a shrine to them. Many had been virtuous local officials. The shrines were memorial halls that aimed to inspire the living to emulate the accomplishments of the dead; they were also sites of veneration. At periodic intervals in the schools, students and teachers were to prostrate themselves and offer incense and food offerings as an expression of respect for the honored dead.

The years following the fall of the north saw a change in the type of person worshiped in these shrines. The famous men who had held positions in the central government were joined by less famous men who had even occasionally been rejected by the state. These were intensely learned men, but men whose contemporaries misunderstood them. One such figure, Gao Deng, had joined the thousands of students who urged the emperor to declare war on the Jurchens who had just taken the north. A meeting with the prime minister who made peace with the Jurchens led to Gao's first demotion; his second demotion came after he wrote an examination question critical of that minister. He never served again in the government. Zhu Xi (1130–1200) one of the leading Confucian thinkers of his generation, wrote a text commemorating Gao's virtues, and he said: "The whole day long, like a torrent, he spoke of nothing but being a filial son and loyal minister and of sacrificing one's life in favor of righteousness. Those who heard him were in awe; their souls were moved and their spirits lifted."[19] Gao was able to live a life of virtue and learning, both Confucian values, because he had not served the corrupt government that had failed to win back the north.

Like the temples of popular deities, shrines to worthy men shed their local character in the twelfth and thirteenth centuries. They came to be built even in districts to which the deceased had no direct ties. The men commemorated had not been born in, had not served as officials in, and had never even visited the districts housing their shrines. Three men came to have shrines built to them all over south China; Zhou Dunyi (1017–1073), Cheng Yi (1033–1107), and Cheng Hao (1032–1085). In 1181, Zhu Xi wrote a text commemorating the three in his native Wuyuan county in Huizhou, and he did so after registering his initial protest: "It is my view that the Way of the three masters is grand and marvelous. However, this county, Wuyuan, is neither their native home, nor a place where they sojourned or served in office." He then explained why he overcame his objections: "In the past decade or so, school officials strove to establish sacrificial halls, their intentions being to honor and offer sacrifices to the three masters. This occurred even in places that were not the masters' native homes, that the masters did not serve or visit."[20]

Inscriptions to their shrines credited these three men, joined later by Zhu Xi in some shrines, with correctly understanding the Way of Confucius, and his disciple Mencius, the Way that had been lost by the intervening generations. These men "had retrieved and retransmitted the one, true Confucian Way in the Song." Even though these shrines ran counter to the local ideal, they became the most popular of the shrines, far outnumbering those to other worthy men in the twelfth and thirteenth centuries.

The Emphasis on Local Society

In the same centuries that temple, shrine, and market networks expanded, the world of the governing families contracted. In the years before the fall of the north, powerful bureaucratic families had assumed that their sons would pursue careers in officialdom. But the factional infighting between the classicists and the historicists forced them to rethink their strategies. When the classicists banned all the sons of leading historicist families from taking the examinations, they cut off what had been a certain career course—preparation for the examinations, sitting for the exams, and taking office. The powerful historicist families had to devise career paths outside the bureaucracy, and when the tables were turned and the historicists banned the sons of the classicists from taking the exams, they too had to shift gears.

These once prominent families turned away from government service. Instead they lived on their estates and devoted themselves to local society. They donated money to religious institutions, to Buddhist or Daoist monasteries, and popular temples. They sought to help their communities and incidentally to enhance their local reputations by building bridges and roads, distributing grain during famine, and making loans to the needy. They also organized the all-important local militia who tried to keep order.

This shift away from national politics affecting the standing of women in these families. As long as families concentrated on forming political alliances with other prominent families to maximize the benefits of the shadow privilege, daughters, like sons, had an important role to play. If married off successfully, they could bring benefits to their natal family. But as these families' confidence in their ability to place their sons in the

bureaucracy declined, they began to marry their daughters into other local families, and brides found themselves increasingly dependent on their
in-laws for their support. If widowed, brides had to secure the permission of their in-laws to remarry, and many continued to live with their
in-laws rather than risk the stigma of remarriage. Li Qingzhao's com-
ings and goings after her husband's death and her decision to remarry
were seen as practices of a bygone era.

One official, Yuan Cai (1140–90), wrote a manual of advice for his contemporaries. In it, he enumerated the possible careers that sons from good
families could pursue:

> If the sons of a gentleman have no hereditary stipend to maintain and no per-
> manent holdings to depend on, and they wish to be filial to their parents and
> to support children, then nothing is as good as being a scholar. For those
> whose talents are great, and who can obtain advanced degrees, the best course
> is to get an official post and become wealthy. Next best is to open his gate as a
> teacher in order to receive a tutor's pay. For those who cannot obtain advanced
> degrees, the best course is to study correspondence so that one can write letters
> for others. Next best is to study punctuating and reading so that one can be a
> tutor to children.
>
> For those who cannot be scholars, then medicine, Buddhism and Daoism,
> agriculture, trade, or crafts are all possible; all provide a living without bring-
> ing shame to one's ancestors.[21]

This is a revealing list. Yuan starts on the assumption that many such
sons will have a private income, either from the government in the form
of a stipend or from their own landholdings. If they do not, official service offers the greatest rewards. If one cannot pass the civil service examinations, then one can tutor older students or write letters. Yuan
suggests that the less able study punctuating and reading, because one
can teach those arts to children. Everyone had to learn how to punctu-
ate texts because no text written in classical Chinese was punctuated, and
deciding where sentences and clauses ended was the first step to grasp-
ing the contents of a text.

All these options would have been open to the sons of good families
before the fall of the north. The list with which Yuan closes his advice
is new: he advocates that those who cannot be students learn to be doctors, religious specialists, farmers, merchants, or craftsmen. His assertion
that none of these careers brings shame hints at the underlying truth: all
these professions would have brought shame in the previous century, but
the great families of China have had to adjust to a new social reality in
the twelfth. Because not all their sons could be officials or even school-
teachers, they had to pursue other careers.

Yuan's list of alternative occupations suggests that the business of educating examination candidates was a thriving one. More and more tutors were needed to prepare the candidates for the examinations. Even as the total population of China—in both the north and the south—remained around one hundred million, the number of men studying for the exams grew dramatically. In some districts after 1200 as many as three hundred men competed for one slot—a far higher ratio than had existed earlier.[22] Scholars agree that the increased interest in the examinations must have raised the literacy rate, with some estimating that one in ten men, but many fewer women, could read.

Although more men were taking examinations, more were also exercising the shadow privilege, with the result that the number of positions going to those who had passed the open examinations declined throughout the dynasty. In 1046, 57 percent of new officials had passed the regular, nonpreferential exams; in 1213 only 27 percent did so, with the bulk of the remaining positions going to those who had used the shadow privilege.[23]

More competition and fewer slots reduced the chances of any one person considerably, but contemporaries complained more often about other problems. Those taking the exams had to obtain a family guarantee in which the signatory vouched that the exam candidate had lived in the area for so long that his ancestors were not merchants, clerks, or priests. These guarantees meant that only the sons of established families could take the examinations.

Like people taking examinations everywhere, the candidates were most upset by the widespread cheating they felt was taking place. As woodblock printing became more sophisticated, students smuggled "small basted-together volumes with minute fly's head sized characters into the examinations."[24] The government ordered bookstores to stop printing and selling these aids, but the stores continued to do so as it was a profitable venture. Smuggling notes into the exams was popular, as was paying others to take the exams on someone's behalf, bribing the officials who graded the exams, and copying others' answers.

By the twelfth century, the idea of anonymity had triumphed. A piece of paper was pasted over the name of those taking the exams and examinations were recopied so that those grading them would not favor someone whose handwriting they recognized. Still, aggrieved candidates complained that members of a faction were able to make themselves known to their examiners by using unusual phrases and terms.

Some of those who had become disenchanted with the civil service examinations contributed money to build local academies where they sent their sons to be educated in the new approach to the Confucian classics. Starting in 1181, Zhu Xi (1130–1200) taught at the White Deer Academy, where he stressed that the goal of education was moral self-cultivation, not the pursuit of civil service examination degrees. The students studied the Confucian classics, especially *The Analects*, *Mencius*, and two chapters taken from the *Book of Rites*. These texts, *The Four Books*, were felt to offer the best models for those wanting to understand the Way of the ancient sages. Zhu stressed "apprehending the principle in things" (sometimes translated as "the investigation of things"), the cornerstone of his Neo-Confucian teachings. If someone very carefully examined the world around him and the teachings contained in the classics, he could perceive the pattern, or principle, underlying all human affairs.[25]

Zhu Xi and his followers also encouraged members of the community to help one another without causing the government to intervene, although their plans enjoyed little success. They founded community granaries, which, unlike Wang Anshi's ever-level granaries, were to be run privately by local people, not government officials. These granaries were to make interest-bearing loans to poor people. They, however, quickly encountered the same problem that Wang had experienced—widespread default; the most successful of them limited loans to famine years only. Some of the granaries ended up distributing grain as a charitable measure rather than insisting that the borrowers pay off the loans. Like Wang Anshi's Green Sprouts reforms, the private granaries also lost money, and all were defunct by 1308.

The significance of the private academies and community granaries was that they expressed the growing suspicion of government institutions among those who advocated the Confucian revival. Shut out of the examination system, these men chose to dedicate themselves to a new ideal. They wanted to attain sagehood, not by government service but by devotion to the community. From the very beginning, Confucius and his followers had been torn about whether to join government as ministers, and most had not. The students of Zhu Xi and the other Confucian revivalists looked to Confucius himself as a model. They claimed to have a direct line of transmission of the Way from him, and they thought they could best pass on his teachings outside of the government. No wonder they built so many shrines to Zhu Xi's teachers, Zhou Dunyi and the Cheng brothers.

The three centuries of Song rule—one hundred fifty years of a united China, and one hundred fifty years in only the south—were a time of continuous economic growth as the market expanded and professional specialization increased. The market economy affected people of all social strata. The poorest peasants fell deeper and deeper into debt in spite of Wang Anshi's best efforts to save them. The very wealthy, like the couple buried at Baisha, decorated their tombs with the latest in home decorating—including painted screens and chairs—and included detailed contracts specifying the high prices they had spent to purchase their burial plots. People living in Kaifeng spent money to eat in restaurants and to watch various urban entertainments, some of which are pictured in the scroll *Peace Reigns Over the River*. Li Qingzhao and her husband had sufficient disposable income to buy an enormous collection of bronzes and books, only to lose them as they fled south from the Jurchen invasion.

The loss of the north posed a psychic blow to the Song, but in the move south the Chinese were able to use the extensive waterways of the region to foster economic growth. People traveled increasingly large distances to sell goods, bringing their deities with them on their travels. As the economic world of producers and consumers expanded, so too did their religious world. People began to worship deities from other places in addition to their own local deities. Many people embraced the sages of the Neo-Confucian government who were worshiped across all of south China.

The prosperity that opened up the consumers' world had the opposite effect on the bureaucracy. That world contracted as fewer and fewer of the sons of former bureaucratic families were able to get positions in the bureaucracy, and as official life was fractured by factionalism. Disputes over managing the money economy created the conflict between the historicists and the classicists that drove the bureaucratic families out of the government and into the countryside. Even so, when compared with later periods, the Song stands out as a period of civility. Members of one faction might prevent their enemies from holding office, but they did not physically attack them, and no one lost his life for standing up to the emperor. There were no secret police, massive persecutions, or long jail sentences for those who crossed the people in power. Factional infighting, however, did leave the country's economic problems unsolved.

We should not be too harsh in judging the Song officials. They were the first bureaucrats in the world to use paper money, and naturally they succumbed to the temptation to print more money than they could back in an effort to lessen their budgetary woes. The same motive prompted them to make bronze coins with ever lessening quantities of copper. Their constant devaluations undermined the very currency they sought to support, yet the economy still managed to grow, fueled as it was by the expansion of markets. Without realizing the real causes for the chronic shortage of coinage, they blamed the crisis on the huge outlays they made to fight the northern peoples, the subject of the next chapter.

CHRONOLOGY

ca. 907–1125	LIAO DYNASTY
ca. 907–926	*Reign of Liao founder, Abaoji*
926–947	*Regency of Empress Chunqin*
1004	*Peace between Liao and Northern Song*
1055	*Timber Pagoda built*
1080	*Paintings in Kulun Banner tomb started*
1112–1170	*Lifetime of Wang Zhe, founder of the Complete Self-Realization School of Daoism*
1115–1123	*Reign of Jin founder, Aguda*
1115–1234	JIN DYNASTY
1125	*Jin troops defeat the Liao and take their territory*
1125–1220	WESTERN LIAO, SUCCESSOR STATE IN CENTRAL ASIA
1161–1180	*Reign of the Jin Emperor Shizong*
1189–1208	*Reign of the Jin Emperor Zhangzong*
1190–1208	*Master Dong writes* The Romance of the Western Chamber
1202	*The Jin claim to be the rightful successors to the Northern Song*
1215	*Mongols take the Jin capital at Beijing*
1234	*Mongols defeat the Jin and take north China*

THE NORTHERN DYNASTIES: NON-CHINESE RULE IN NORTH CHINA (907–1215)

In 907, after the last Tang emperor had been killed, China's history divided into two streams. The much better known stream was that of the Five Dynasties and the Song dynasty, discussed in the previous chapters. Equally important, though much less-studied, was the second stream—that of the non-Chinese dynasties who ruled increasing amounts of territory until 1127, when they took all of China north of the Huai River.

Despite the conquests of these nomadic or forest-dwelling peoples, the sedentary Chinese looked down on them. They developed writing systems only after they encountered the Chinese and produced fewer records than the bureaucratic Chinese did. Because their scripts are only now being deciphered, historians of the past have encountered them through prejudiced Chinese records. Traditional Chinese historians depict these peoples as illiterates who eagerly sought to learn Chinese ways and were finally subsumed by Chinese culture. They credit them with no lasting influence on China, and they describe the Chinese resident in these conquered areas as unwilling captives who never cooperated with their captors.

There is exciting new research, however, to show that these peoples selected and modified elements of Chinese civilization that appealed to them. They rejected other elements just as decisively. They rapidly adopted Chinese treaties, architecture, and religion, often with the enthusiastic cooperation of the Chinese under their rule.

We label each period of their rule with the name of the ruling tribe—Khitan, Jurchen, or Tangut; but these were not racially homogenous societies. For that matter, neither were the Chinese. All these groups included members of many different tribes and considerable numbers of Chinese in what are better thought of as federations. These federations proved fertile ground for new and innovative hybrid cultures that combined elements of non-Chinese cultures with Chinese contributions. Each of the different cultures these peoples developed had a decided and lasting—if still largely unrecognized—influence on later Chinese history.

The Khitans

The first peoples to conquer north China, the Khitans, practiced pastoral steppe nomadism. Although we do not know exactly how these people pronounced their own name, scholars have reconstructed the pronunciation as either Khitan or Kitan, which the Chinese pronounced Qidan. They initially had no permanent settlements, moving from site to site with their tents and herds of horses and camels. Although they controlled only a small section of what had been the Tang empire—sixteen prefectures in the area of modern Beijing—they ruled a wide band across the north of China, including modern Mongolia and Manchuria. From 916 to 1125, this swath of land served as a buffer between Europe and China. When, in subsequent centuries, Europeans like Marco Polo referred to China, they called it Cathay, which was a variation of the word Khitan (as is the modern Russian word for China, Kitaia).

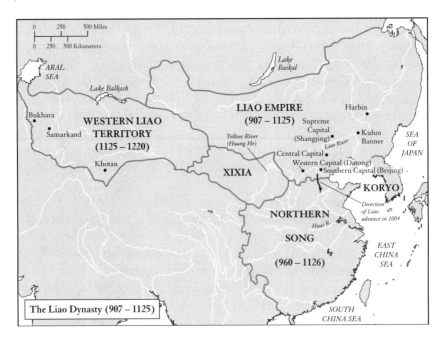

Little is known about the origins of the Khitans, but they claimed descent from the Tabgach, who had ruled China in the fourth and fifth
centuries as the Northern Wei (see chapter 4). Although the Khitans had
the same skin and hair coloring as the Chinese, the men's distinctive hairstyle set them apart. Like the Tabgach before them, the men shaved the
tops of their heads, leaving a fringe along the hairline from one ear to
the other. They allowed the hair in front of the ears to grow into long
braids, and they often wore a hat over their hair.

One dynamic leader, known to us only by his Chinese name Abaoji,
brought together a loose grouping of Khitan tribes in the years immediately after the collapse of the Tang. Abaoji (reigned 907–926) was fully

aware of the significance of the timing, and Khitan histories claim he first unified the Khitans in 907, the last year of the Tang dynasty. Historians agree that while he may indeed have been named leader in that year, he was only able to consolidate his power nine years later. The Khitans, like other nomadic peoples, called a *khuriltai*—or congress—that all tribal leaders attended so they could select a leader. This method of selection differed considerably from Chinese traditions.

Abaoji's Rise to Power

The Khitan conferred leadership on the most skilled among them. Unlike other tribal peoples who selected a new leader only on the death of the previous one, the Khitans followed a unique practice of meeting every three years to select a new leader or to reconfirm the existing one. Abaoji was sufficiently powerful that he bypassed the usual selection process in 910 and in 913, each time angering his brothers, who organized unsuccessful rebellions against him. Family ties kept Abaoji from killing his brothers, but he did manage to eliminate over three hundred of their supporters. In 916, rather than risk another rebellion, he organized a formal ceremony in which he assumed the throne and gave himself a reign title, in the Chinese tradition. Here he was making a clear claim to inherit the mantle of the Tang. He also forswore the Khitan tradition of the triannual congress to select a leader.

This coronation shows how Abaoji adapted Chinese ideas about rulers for new purposes, in this case consolidating his hold on power. Also in violation of Khitan traditions but in accordance with Chinese practice, he named his favorite son to succeed him. Abaoji did not adopt a name for his dynasty, but soon after his death the Khitan state took on the dynastic name Liao, for the Liao River where the Khitans originated. Because the early Khitan chronicles did not keep strict records of chronology, the date for the naming of the Liao dynasty is uncertain; it could be 926, 937, 938, or 947.

The Liao Innovation of Dual Administration

Abaoji's most successful melding of Chinese and Khitan traditions occurred in his restructuring of the Khitan government. He replaced traditional tribal rule with a dual administration: the north-facing section of the bureaucracy served the Khitans, while the south-facing half governed their Chinese subjects. Officials were appointed to the northern government on the basis of family ties; those in the southern government often had to pass civil service examinations. The questions retained a tribal flavor, as on one examination that required the candidates to write an essay on the topic of killing thirty-six bears in one day.

As time went on, the differences between the two governments became more pronounced. By the mid-tenth century, officials of the northern administration wore Khitan clothing and spoke only Khitan, while those in the southern part wore Chinese clothing and spoke both Chinese and Khitan. The northern administration officials used Khitan titles; the southern administration borrowed their titles from Chinese ministries. Although the two administrations appeared equal on paper, the northern officials had much greater access to the emperor, who was always on the move. Twice a year the emperor scheduled meetings with the officials of both the southern and northern administrations, but because the officials of the northern administration traveled with the emperor, they had year-round access to him. Also, all military authority rested decisively in northern hands, leaving the southern administration in a much weaker position.

Abaoji's desire to borrow and embellish Chinese ways extended beyond governmental structure. One of his first acts as emperor was to order a new city built (Huangdu, then Shangjing, now Boro Khoton, Inner Mongolia) as his capital. The Khitans first came into contact with the Chinese in the early tenth century when they began to build cities for the Chinese and the Central Asian Uighurs who flocked to their territory to flee the chaos of north China. These were Chinese-style cities, built on a grid, complete with walls, gates, and drum and bell towers, but they were inhabited in a nomadic way. The Khitans established five different capitals, in which they lived at different times of the year.

Liao Cities

To build the new capital, Abaoji used the traditional Chinese technique of required labor service, but he summoned the workers during the agricultural season rather than in the slack season because he was not yet fully conversant with the traditional Chinese system of taxation. Little is known about Khitan taxation, but it seems likely that the northern administration collected a share of each person's herds in peace and of their booty during war. The southern administration adapted the two-tax system of the late Tang.

In the new capital, government buildings were located in the north, while the Chinese residents lived in the southern section of the city. Laid out on a strict grid, the northern section of the city also housed Buddhist and Daoist monasteries, a Confucian temple, and a school. Although cities were new to the Khitan nomads, and they incorporated many Chinese elements, their cities were not completely Chinese. There was no fixed palace district, because the Khitan ruling family continued to live in tents, and to move from city to city. Oxen pulled wagons carrying the royal household's goods each time they moved. While the Khitans adopted some Buddhist practices, they continued to worship their tribal spirits and to conduct monthly ceremonies in honor of the sun on the temporary palace grounds.

Abaoji was also inspired by the Chinese language to order the introduction of a large script in 920 and a small script in 924. Each of these was derived from the Chinese. For years scholars have debated the relationship between the two scripts, and they have recently concluded that elements in the small script represented sounds and were combined to form units in the larger script, which represented words. Both scripts were required to write Khitan. One Chinese account tells of Khitan children reordering Chinese sentences so that the verb came last, after the subject and object. This is exactly how the Japanese today read Chinese and shows that Khitan, like Japanese, belonged to the Inner Altaic language family, while Chinese belongs to the Sino-Tibetan family. Today, no books in Khitan are extant. Some four hundred Khitan characters survive in bronze and stone inscriptions, and scholars have deciphered fewer than half of the surviving symbols.

Abaoji was the greatest leader of the Khitans, and his innovations in governance, urban planning, and writing all proved to have lasting significance. Yet, his adoption of Chinese dynastic succession, the one innovation about which he cared most, proved impossible to implement after his death in 926. Both the tribal leaders and his widow, the Empress Chunqin (active 920–947) opposed the son he had chosen to succeed him. He was not, they felt, a sufficiently powerful fighter, still the main requisite for a tribal leader. The empress succeeded in naming a different son to follow Abaoji, and she retained great influence over the new emperor, ruling de facto as regent.

The Position of Women in Liao Society

Empress Chunqin had already proved herself a force to contend with during Abaoji's lifetime. On one occasion she developed a plan for Abaoji to kill off several rival leaders, and at the time of his death she commanded two hundred thousand men in her own right. After Abaoji's death, hundreds of men from his retinue were killed so they could be

THE WRITING SYSTEM OF THE KHITAN

The Khitan writing system superficially resembles Chinese characters, but the Khitan language belonged to a different language family (Inner Altaic) from Chinese (Sino-Tibetan). Because the Chinese were the first Asian people to develop a script of their own, many of their neighbors, including the Japanese, Koreans, and Vietnamese, used Chinese characters to write their own languages. The Khitans went one step further and developed two scripts made out of sections of Chinese characters: the small script showed sounds while the large script showed words.

This rubbing taken from a brick shows a word in the large script of the Khitan language (right) and six words in the small script (in the left-hand column). The six characters give the date: "On the third day of the first month of the first year of the Dakang reign period [1075] of the Great Liao Empire."

buried in the imperial tomb. According to tribal custom, the empress should have joined them. A Chinese source informs us that the empress urged a high Chinese official to die with the emperor: "You were very close in serving the deceased emperor," she said. "Why don't you go?"

The minister replied: "As for intimacy, no one equaled Your Majesty. If Your Majesty goes, I will follow."

The empress dowager said, "I am not unwilling to follow the deceased emperor underground. But my sons are young and the country has no ruler. I cannot go."[1] She offered to cut off an arm to be buried with the emperor. When the court officials protested, she cut off her hand to be placed in Abaoji's coffin.

After Abaoji's death, this determined woman took over as ruler, making decisions on military and governmental affairs. Empress Chunqin was one of several Khitan empresses who exercised great influence. Many observers have noted the extraordinary power of women in Khitan society in particular and in nomadic societies in general. When the men went off to fight in battle, they entrusted their wives with the care of all their animals, and so the division of labor between men and women was much less pronounced than in sedentary Chinese society.

War with China

Empress Chunqin initiated a century of successful Khitan attacks on the Chinese, who were unable to mount an effective defense against the much superior armed Khitan horsemen. In 938 she led the Khitan armies and managed to take the sixteen prefectures in the immediate vicinity of modern Beijing that would remain in Khitan hands until the fall of the dynasty. The Khitan military machine continued to deal the different Chinese kingdoms defeat after defeat. Empress Chunqin lost power when her grandson took over in 947, and he in turn led a successful attack on Kaifeng. The Khitans proved unable to govern the area and withdrew after three months. In the years immediately following their withdrawal, the founders of the Song were successfully uniting the Chinese empire for the first time in fifty years, and flush with their victories, the Song attacked the Khitans in 979. A Khitan arrow struck the Song emperor, who had grossly underestimated the fighting power of the Khitans and who was forced to flee south in a donkey cart. This victory was the first of many the Khitans would achieve at the expense of the Song.

In 982, Dowager Empress Xiao took over the regency at the age of thirty (her son the emperor was only sixteen), and until 1009, she ruled with the assistance of three ministers, two of whom were Chinese. The Song and Khitan forces continued to skirmish regularly, and in 1004 the Khitan launched a successful invasion into north China, taking control of much of the Yellow River region.

Peace with the Chinese

Following their defeat in 1004, the Chinese sued for peace. They wrote to a former advisor of the Song emperor who had been taken prisoner and whom the Khitans subsequently appointed to be their finance commissioner. He worked out a face-saving settlement with the Chinese in which the Khitan retreated from the territory they had conquered in exchange for annual payments of two hundred thousand lengths of silk and one hundred thousand ounces of silver. These payments ensured that the Khitans were able to obtain most of the goods they needed. From the Chinese point of view, the payments were not unreasonably high, probably equal to the revenue from one or two prefectures. In absolute terms, these payments were less than 1 percent or 2 percent of the costs to the Chinese of waging war, making peace seem cheap at the price. The Chinese were loath to call the payments tribute, which would have implied Khitan superiority, and so they insisted on calling these indemnities "economic gifts."

The Chinese were not the only side concerned with diplomatic niceties. The treaty marked the first time the Khitans and the Chinese adopted Chinese kinship terms for each other, with the Khitan emperor and the Song emperor addressing each other as younger or elder brother, depending on who had been born first. This choice of terms suggests that the two sides were on equal footing, and indeed they referred to each other as the northern dynasty (the Khitans) and the southern dynasty (the Song). With this terminology, the Song recognized a multistate system, in which the Chinese state was simply one among several in the region.

This treaty, like all the others between the Chinese and the nomadic states, and those among the non-Chinese states, consisted of two oath letters, both in Chinese. Each side signed both copies, and each then retained one. This format was the distant descendant of the blood-oath treaties of the Spring and Autumn period. The Chinese may have been one among many states, but the Chinese language remained the language of diplomacy, and Chinese cultural patterns shaped the diplomatic interactions among these different states. In every instance, the oath letters were written in Chinese and not translated.

The Tanguts

The peace of 1004 held until the 1040s, when another state joined the Khitans and the Song in contesting territory. This was the Xia kingdom in the west that was populated by the Tanguts, a nomadic people who drove herds as their primary means of support. As in the case of Abaoji, one man was able to unite many tribesmen when in 1038 a successful leader declared himself emperor of the Xia kingdom and demanded recognition as an equal from the Song. When the Song refused to receive his presents, he wrote a letter to the Song emperor:

> The Fan [the Tanguts] and Han are each different countries, and their lands are vastly dissimilar. This is not a case of usurpation. Why is your resentment so deep? Moreover I was elevated by the throng and, in accordance with ancient Tuoba tradition, aspire to be emperor. What is wrong with that?[2]

This is a revealing letter. The Tangut ruler asserted status equal to that of the Song emperor. Like the Khitan emperor, he saw himself as the descendant of the Tuoba, or Tabgach, rulers.

The Tanguts were as intrigued as the Khitans by the possibilities of Chinese kinship terms. In 1043, the Tangut ruler made a new offer. Rather than be an equal to the Chinese emperor, he offered to call himself the son, and to call the Song emperor his father. The Chinese made a counteroffer: the Tangut ruler could be called a ruler, which was higher than a king but lower than an emperor. The Tanguts agreed, on the condition that the Chinese paid them an annual subsidy, but a year later the Khitans invaded the Xia and the entire arrangement collapsed.

We learn all this from Chinese records; otherwise the Tanguts remain shrouded in obscurity. The Mongols later commissioned an official history in Chinese for the Khitans, and for the Jurchen, but not for the Tanguts. In 1036, the Tanguts developed their own script. Their language included six thousand different ideograms, even though they used only twenty-five hundred of these to translate Chinese works. Over three thousand of the remaining ideograms were used exclusively in ritual songs, whose contents were meant to be understood only by those who had been initiated into the esoteric Buddhist traditions the Tanguts embraced. Modern scholars have understandably been challenged by a language that was deliberately esoteric. The secrets of the Tanguts remain hidden, though the kingdom held onto its territory in northwest China until the early thirteenth century when it fell to the Mongols.

Khitan Treatment of the Dead

During the time Emperor Xingzong (reigned 1031–1055) was campaigning against the Chinese and the Tanguts, his son, the future emperor Daozong (reigned 1055–1101), was growing up in a small town 85 kilometers (52 miles) south of Datong, Shanxi province, one of the Khitan capitals, where his mother's family lived. Khitan rulers were traditionally raised by the lineage of their mothers. Daozong was a devout Buddhist, and when his father died in 1055, he chose to commemorate him in an unusual way: he combined Buddhist and Chinese traditions to build the Timber Pagoda for him, which stands some 67 meters (220 feet) high.

The traditional Khitan treatment of the dead surprised and horrified the Chinese. When a parent died, the Khitans did not cry. Nor did they bury the dead. They placed the corpse in a tree for three years, and after the bones had been cleaned, they burned them. This means of disposal was well suited to a pastoral lifestyle, but the Khitans were quick to modify their practices once they saw what the Chinese did.

The Timber Pagoda

Daozong took an architectural form intended for the remains of the Buddha, the stupa, and he transformed it into the joint site of his father's remains and a giant image of the Buddha. The tall wooden, octagonal structure he built bore all the hallmarks of Khitan buildings. A two-hour drive south of Datong city, the Timber Pagoda is well worth a visit today. One glimpses the imposing structure from more than 16 kilometers (10 miles) away, but nothing prepares the visitor for its massive size. Its diameter of 30 meters (98 feet) makes it stand squatter than other Chinese pagodas. One cannot help being moved by the sight of a twelfth-century structure over 67 meters (220 feet) tall. Twelfth-century European cathedrals reach equivalent heights, but they, of course, were built of stone and not wood. The modern tourist can climb only to the third floor, but even so one can see the fascinating details of the structure from within the pagoda and outside on its surrounding porches.

Famed for its unique construction, the Timber Pagoda also houses breathtaking artworks from the Liao period. When one enters the main doorway, one sees the massive statue of the Buddha that dominates the first three stories. Each story holds several Buddhist images. Because of long-term damage, some have been replaced by garish modern statues bought from a factory, but the original wooden statues, with their faint

 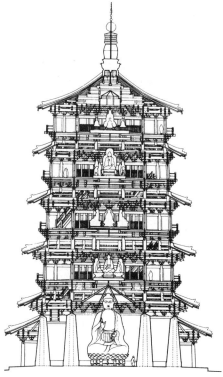

CHINA'S GREAT WOODEN BUILDINGS

The most impressive wooden pagodas in China—dating to the eleventh century—were built by the Khitans, a nomadic people with no previous experience building tall structures. In the eight hundred years since being built, these structures have withstood numerous earthquakes. The Khitan buildings also have the peculiarity of having more stories on the inside than appear when viewed from the outside. Although the Timber Pagoda shown here appears to be five stories high (left), it actually contains nine stories on the inside (right). It stands some 67 meters (220 feet) high, making it both the tallest wooden building in China and the oldest wooden building still standing.

traces of the original paint, are far more impressive. During the Cultural Revolution, activists attacked many of these images, which sustained further damage from ground squirrels. When scholars visited the temple in 1973 to assess the damage, they were amazed to find torn and damaged pages from Buddhist texts sticking out from an open crack in the back of a Buddha image on the fourth floor. When they investigated further, they realized the image contained a large cavity in which many texts and a few paintings had been hidden.

Combined analysis of stylistic attributes and carbon-14 sampling indicated the fourth-floor Buddha image was built during the eleventh century, contemporary with the Timber Pagoda, and sealed around 1125, when the Liao dynasty fell. The circumstances of the sealing recall those of the library cave at Dunhuang. Fearing that their libraries might be destroyed by conquering troops, the Buddhist monks at the Timber Pagoda hid beautifully hand-copied and elegantly printed Buddhist texts as well as scribbled notes, prayers for good fortune, and monks' licenses.

Innovations at the Timber Pagoda marked a renaissance in wooden building. The Khitan buildings, unlike the Chinese architecture of Changan, were built to last. Some fourteen wooden structures built by the Khitan survived until the beginning of the twentieth century. It may seem incongruous that a nomadic people would prove to be the greatest builders of wooden structures in premodern China, but that was indeed the case. The Khitan established their own architectural benchmark for all future builders to follow.

The emperor Daozong's solution to his father's burial was an unusual one, even among the Khitan. Much more common was the building of Chinese-style tombs, over a hundred of which have been excavated. Many of these tombs contain wall paintings, the main evidence of Khitan painting tradition, and some of the most beautiful paintings come from the tomb of an imperial princess buried in 1080, during Daozong's reign. They show a distinct Khitan style.

Portrait of a Wedding—Liao Style

By the year 1080, the Khitan tradition of killing the living to be buried with the dead was waning. Located in Jilin province in southeastern Manchuria, the Kulun Banner tomb contains only one skeleton of someone buried alive so that he or she would serve as a guardian spirit for the tomb. The presence of parts of ten charred bodies in the tomb indicates that the Buddhist practice of cremation was followed. The same mixture of tribal religion and Buddhism characterizes the objects found in the tomb. Sacrificial remains of sheep, deer, and fowl, and the presence of a silver-saddle decoration point to a traditional shamanistic funeral, although Buddhist guardian deities also appear on the doors of the tomb.

Two murals more than 30 meters (98 feet) long appear on both sides of the corridor leading down into the tomb. First sketched in red chalk, they were then filled in with colors, and the details were finally drawn with black ink. They show the wedding of an imperial princess with a high-ranking Khitan man. The figures, who bear gifts, talk to each other,

THE GROOM

The groom (second from left) stands with several other Khitan men, who have the same distinctive hairstyle. Shaving the crowns of their heads, they have kept a band of hair across their forehead that connects the pigtails on both sides of their face. In contrast, Chinese men did not shave their hair at all.

THE BRIDE

The bride (left), peering into a mirror held by a servant, stands next to a cart. Written sources from the time report that a crucial part of the bride's trousseau was the coffin she would be buried in, here shown pulled by a deer.

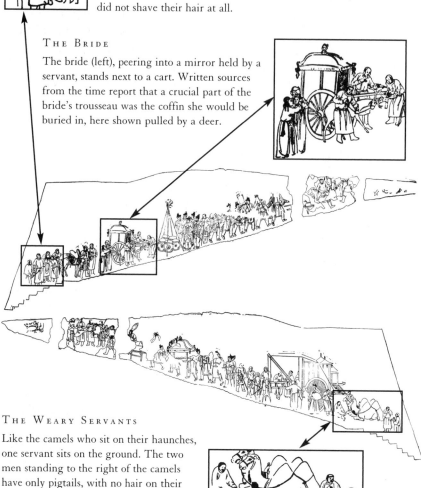

THE WEARY SERVANTS

Like the camels who sit on their haunches, one servant sits on the ground. The two men standing to the right of the camels have only pigtails, with no hair on their foreheads, suggesting that Khitan men of lower rank may have shaved off more of their hair than did high-ranking men.

A PANORAMA OF KHITAN SOCIETY

This drawing of a painting that appears on two facing walls flanking the corridor down to a tomb in today's Jilin province offers a rare glimpse of a wedding procession—high-ranking bride and groom accompanied by their extensive retinue. Even though the Khitans had their own distinctive writing system, no body of Khitan texts survives. In conjunction with occasional Chinese-language descriptions, historians must use the unique visual evidence provided by such paintings to piece together Khitan customs.

rest, and tend to the animals, look to be of the same social status. The bride and her attendant are standing in full view of their kinsmen, suggesting that the segregation of men and women was less pronounced than in China.

Unlike the Chinese tomb paintings at Baisha (discussed in chapter 7), these pictures do not center on the deceased couple. Archeologists are not even certain which figure is the husband, although they think it is probably the man gesturing to a servant who is about to give him a scepter. Another man stands behind the groom ready to give him his hat. The top of the groom's head is shaven, but the rest of his hair hangs loose; his companion's hair has been shaved off to leave only one lock hanging down over his ear, with a similar lock over the unseen ear. If archeologists are right about the groom's identity, high-ranking Liao men shaved off less of their hair than did their servants.

His bride is easily identifiable because she (in a small round hat) is looking into a mirror held by an older woman (wearing earmuffs). Written descriptions of weddings specify that the bride is to walk toward her husband while an older woman in front of her walks backward, although this practice is not explained. On the bride's right is a small cart. Next to it are three men, who tend an antlered deer. This cart, one of the bride's gifts, was actually a funeral bier, intended for use at her death, as was the deer, who would have been sacrificed then. To their right is a cluster of drums and a group of Chinese-looking officials, who may well have served in the south-facing administration. The opposite wall includes an object that is probably the groom's funeral bier. On the right end of the painting, exhausted servants and weary camels take their rest near a large cart.

The Kulun Banner tomb and fan painting show the marriage practices of the upper social stratum of Khitan princes and princesses. Marriage among lower social classes was much simpler, with elopement common. Khitan men would gather to race horses, gamble, and drink, and if a man happened to meet a woman he liked, he would go off with her. When their first child was born, the couple would present it to his family.

The Legacy of the Khitan

Even after two hundred years, although the Khitans had adapted Chinese architecture, burial practices, and diplomacy for their own purposes, they retained a distinct cultural identity. They had also designed a dual-facing administration, the political innovation that allowed their successors in the north, the Jurchen, and then the Mongols, to govern China. The Khitans, under Abaoji's leadership, had made the crucial administrative breakthrough, but they themselves never governed much settled territory. They retained control of the huge band of grassland to the north of China, and to the continued discomfort of the Song, they managed to hold onto their sixteen prefectures around Beijing without ever extending their control beyond that small area. They were fully capable of conquering the area north of the Yellow River, as they showed in 947 and again in 1004, but they could not run the civil administration in such a large area. Instead, they set huge indemnities as the price of their withdrawal, which the Song agreed to pay.

The successors to the Khitans, the Jurchen, succeeded where the Khitan failed. They not only conquered north China but also ruled it for over a century as the Jin dynasty. The early Jin emperors encouraged the adoption of Chinese cultural ways and a Chinese-style state as a means of enhancing their own authority, and when their successors ordered their subjects to return to the Jurchen language and customs, they were hard-pressed to do so. The price of adopting a Chinese-style administration required an obliteration of much of their tribal past. At the end of the Liao dynasty, the Khitan had avoided much contact with the Chinese, and they traveled as a distinct group to settle in Central Asia. In contrast,

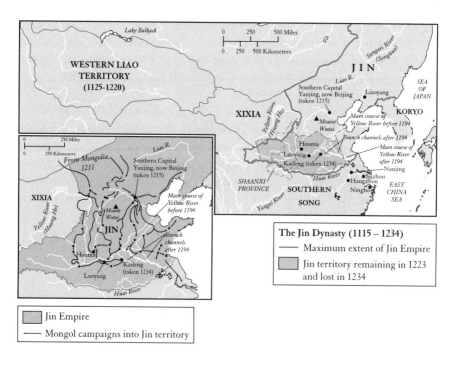

the Jurchen blended almost indistinguishably into Chinese society, and only the Jurchens who lived in the Manchurian heartland retained their traditional ways.

THE RISE OF THE JURCHEN

The uneasy balance of power between the Song and the Khitans held through the eleventh century, but everything changed at the beginning of the twelfth century when a new leader suddenly appeared. Like Abaoji in his time, Aguda (reigned 1113–1123), the leader of the Jurchen, used his extraordinary abilities to unite a large group of tribes who had previously lived on the eastern fringe of the Khitan polity in what is now the Liaoning peninsula. They proved to be a powerful fighting force, intent on obtaining loot from conquered peoples.

Like the Khitans, the Jurchen spoke an Inner Altaic language. They did not have their own alphabet but used the small Khitan script for most of the twelfth century. Yet the Jurchen differed from the Khitans in important ways. They were not a nomadic people of the steppe but a forest-dwelling people whose traditional home was Manchuria. They made their living hunting and fishing, and they lived in villages of wooden houses, not tents. Some of the Jurchen were farmers who grew rice and wheat. They also wove their own hemp and raised silkworms, and they wore simple clothes of white linen. They worshiped deities and nature, and they believed shamans had special powers, one of which was to punish murderers.

The Khitans classed the Jurchen into two groups: the "cooked" Jurchen, who had had more contact with Chinese ways, and the "uncooked," who lived to the north. Whether exposed to Chinese ways or not, all Jurchen men participated in group hunts, and all served as soldiers when their tribe fought. The largest groups in Jurchen society were the clans, which consisted of several lineages. Each lineage was headed by one man, who ruled all the other men in his lineage. During the course of the eleventh century, the Wanyan clan, one of the uncooked clans, was expanding its power in the region around the modern city of Harbin.

The first hint of a new order occurred at the First Fish Feast in 1112 when the Wanyan leader Aguda appeared before the drunken Khitan ruler, who commanded him to dance. Aguda refused. The Khitan ruler asked again, and again Aguda refused, causing great embarrassment to the Khitan ruler. The following year, the Jurchen launched the first of what was to be many successful campaigns against the Khitan. In 1115, after the Jurchen conquest of Manchuria, Aguda himself became the ruler of a Chinese-style dynasty that he called Jin, or gold, after the Ashi River, a tributary of the Sungari, where gold had been found and where his clan had originated.

Like other nomadic leaders, Aguda proved to be an avid student of the fine points of diplomatic convention. He rejected letters from the Liao court because they failed to address him as emperor. The Song were quick to recognize Aguda, because they thought—in what was to prove a wild miscalculation—they could use Aguda as a counterweight to the Khitans. At this point, the Jurchen was still an egalitarian, tribal state, as we can see from the following description of Jurchen decision making:

> From the commanding general down to the soldiers, everybody . . . had millet gruel and roast meat for food, and there was no difference in quality between high and low. When their country is involved in great affairs [war], they all go out into the wilderness and sit down in a circle, drawing in the ashes. Then they deliberate, starting from the lowest one present. When the council has come to an end, they wash away the charcoal and not a human voice is heard—such is their secrecy. . . .
>
> When the army returns after a victory, another great reunion takes place, and it is asked who has won merits. According to the degree of merit, gold is handed out; it is raised and shown to the multitude. If they think the reward too small, it will be increased.[3]

Little distinguished the most powerful members of the Jurchen from the soldiers. Eating the same food, they participated equally in decision-making councils. Aguda made this tribal council of the Jurchen the main body of his new central government.

In 1116 Aguda took the Khitan heartland of the Liao River. With each victory he recruited the defeated Khitan forces into his army, which was divided into units meant to include three hundred men, but in fact often numbering fewer. These units were formed on the basis of preexisting clans. Ten of those "three-hundred" units formed a larger unit of three thousand, led by a hereditary leader, or battalion commander. The leaders of the "three thousand" units served as de facto administrators of the territory they had conquered. In 1120 the Chinese and the Jurchen agreed to attack the Khitans simultaneously, and when the Jurchens took both the Upper and Central Capitals, the Khitan emperor fled westward. After the Southern Capital (Yanjing, now Beijing) and the surrounding sixteen prefectures fell in 1123, Aguda adopted the dual administration of the Khitans, and significantly, he retained those Chinese officials employed by the Khitans. Aguda died in the same year, and his younger brother succeeded him. In 1124 the Jurchen captured the Khitan emperor; Khitan rule ended in 1125.

After their defeat, the Khitans did not become Chinese. Most fled to the hostile but tribal territory of the Jurchen, while a small group of nobles moved to the western steppes to modern Xinjiang and Uzbekistan. This last group, the Western Liao or Black Khitans, were particularly significant because the Mongols encountered them before they reached either the Jurchen or the Song, and they recruited some of their most influential advisors from among them. These advisors introduced the Mongols to the important concept of the dual-facing administration.

The Jurchen Conquest of North China

In 1123, the Song agreed to pay the Jurchen two hundred thousand ounces of silver and three hundred thousand bolts of silk annually. The Jurchen knew enough about textiles to demand silks embroidered with dragons and phoenixes, the motifs traditionally reserved for the Chinese emperor. Like the treaty between the Song and the Khitans, this one took the form of identical oath letters, but these letters called the Song and the Jurchen leader by the same title, "august emperor," and no terminological differences indicated that the two were not full equals. In fact, the Jurchen was the more powerful state, as it decisively demonstrated in 1125, when war broke out again, but this time directly between the Song and the Jurchen. In a desperate attempt to fend off the Jin, Emperor Huizong abdicated in favor of his young son, Qinzong (reigned 1125–1127), but to no avail. In 1127 the Jurchen crossed the Yellow River and took the Northern Song capital of Kaifeng. After sweeping through north China, the Jurchen forces took both men prisoner.

The second series of oath letters that followed were even more burdensome to the Song. They agreed to pay 300,000 ounces of silver, 1,000,000 strings of coins, and 300,000 bolts of silk annually to the Jurchen—in addition to a devastating one-time payment totaling 180 annual payments. The oath letters referred to the Jurchen ruler as the elder uncle and the Song only as his nephew. No longer a multistate world, this was a world in which the Jurchen were superior to the Song.

As the Jurchen were quick to learn the prerogatives of imperial power, they delighted in tormenting the captured Northern Song emperors. In a humiliating spectacle, the Jurchen forced Huizong and Qinzong to march north. In 1127 the former rulers were degraded to commoners, and in 1128 they were made to bow before Aguda's tablet in his mausoleum. Worst of all, the Jurchen gave the two rulers new and ignominious Chinese titles. The former emperor Huizong was dubbed the Marquis of Muddled Virtue, and his son, Doubly Muddled.

Jurchen forces continued to pursue the Song armies south of the

Yangzi River for the following fifteen years, taking the major cities of the lower Yangzi—Nanjing, Suzhou, Hangzhou, and Ningbo—in succession. Finally they forced the new Song emperor to escape on ship, which was the first time in history that an emperor had resorted to the sea to flee an enemy attack. In their conquered territories to the north, they began to establish a government. They allowed their generals to establish de facto rule, and in 1137, they created an important new institution, the Mobile Presidential Council, which was in charge of all civil and military affairs, including the recruiting of government officials. This council presided over a new unit of regional government, the circuit, which consisted of twenty or so prefectures and was the forerunner of the modern province. These early years of Jin rule also witnessed the conscious acceptance of many Chinese cultural elements such as the adoption of the calendar in 1137, of titles in 1138, of court rituals in 1139, and of court music in 1140.

The Humiliating Peace with the Jin, or Diplomacy by Corpse

In 1141, a peace treaty was signed with the Song that set annual payments at two hundred fifty thousand ounces of silver and two hundred fifty thousand bolts of silk. The drafters of the treaty cast aside all the euphemisms protecting Chinese pride. The payments were from an "insignificant state" to a "superior state," and they were called tribute. The treaty made official the outcome of fifteen years of war: the Song had become the subject state of a non-Chinese dynasty, the Jin.

With the peace, the Jin promised to return the bodies of the deceased Northern Song emperor Huizong (Marquis of Muddled Virtue), who had died in 1135, with that of his wife and his mother. They did not, however, send back the still-living Qinzong, who would have been not just an embarrassment but also a rival to his younger brother, the first emperor of the Southern Song. The return of his father's dead body and his still-living mother made it possible for the Southern Song emperor to fulfill his filial duties. This odd diplomacy by corpse is recorded in a painting commissioned by Cao Xun (1098–1174), one of the architects of the 1141 peace.

The painting shows a large enclosed sedan chair, which is carried on poles, with numerous bearers. Many people are watching the progress of the sedan chair, which carries the mother of the Southern Song emperor. Behind her are the encoffined remains of the deceased Song emperor Huizong, his wife, and his mother.

THE DEAD EMPEROR COMES HOME

When the Jin dynasty took north China, they also captured the emperor Huizong and his son Qinzong. By the time Huizong died in captivity in 1137, a debate raged in the Southern Song court at Hangzhou, in modern Zhejiang.

The official Cao Xun, who commissioned this painting, tries to put a positive spin on the humiliating peace of 1142, in which the Song promised to pay the Jin dynasty a huge annual indemnity. The group of officials who advocated peace with the Jin celebrated the return of the dead emperor along with the corpses of his wife and his mother, shown in this painting, "Welcoming the Imperial Carriage." At the same time, an opposing group of officials remained steadfastly opposed to the loss of the north and advocated attacking the Jin-dynasty armies.

Why would someone commemorate such a gruesome event? Cao Xun wrote on the painting, "I made this picture to hand down to my family,"[4] even though he did not paint it himself. Cao commissioned this private painting because he wanted his descendants to honor him for his role in recovering the corpses. By emphasizing the only positive feature of the 1141 treaty, the return of the corpses, the painting conveys the patron's support for the peace. It does not show the enormous payments the Song had to make to the Jin, nor does it show the loss of territory.

Like Cao, many Chinese living in the south welcomed the peace with relief. Other Chinese argued that the Southern Song should have attempted to reconquer the north. This split shaped twelfth-century poli-

Once peace was restored, the Jin dynasty did not disrupt the daily life of their Chinese subjects. In this scene from a drawing of a wall painting in the Yanshan Monastery in today's Shanxi province, we see women sitting in a pavilion. The viewer can even make out the writing on a flag: "Wild flowers from throughout the land bloom here; full jars of fragrant local wine," which advertises female companionship. On the street below them are a seller of drinks, a man washing clothes, a beggar with a staff, and several monks.

tics, and the 1141 decision to sue for peace still arouses great anger among the Chinese today. In retrospect, though, it is difficult to see what other choices the Song had. With the Jin armies manifestly more powerful, continuing to fight hardly seemed an option.

JIN RULE AFTER THE 1141 PEACE WITH THE SOUTH

Once peace had been arranged with the Southern Song, the Jin emperors faced the challenge of governing a society of some fifty million in which they remained a minority of four million. The emperors of the twelfth century saw two distinct strategies: either they could adopt Chinese-style governance completely or they could do their best to retain traditional Jurchen ways. Whatever choice they made, though, they had to face the reality that most Jurchen quickly adopted Chinese ways, and the emperor could do little to stem the trend.

One Jurchen ruler adopted so many Chinese practices (such as tea drinking) that his contemporaries nicknamed him "aping the Chinese" even before he seized power in 1150. His violent accession was the beginning of a long series of murders of his opponents, almost all members of the Jurchen ruling clan. Most historians now understand his embrace of Chinese culture as an attempt to lessen the power of his opponents. His tendency to add the wives and consorts of his victims to his own household only contributed to his unpopularity with subsequent historians, who never called him emperor, but simply the prince of Hailing (reigned 1150–1161).

The prince of Hailing replaced the regional Mobile Presidential Councils with a more traditional bureaucracy modeled on the Chinese state, complete with the Six Boards (Revenue, Civil Appointments, Rites, Works, Punishments, and War) and the Secretariat (see chapter 5, p. 203). The most powerful body was the Presidential Council, which included the prime minister and many members of the imperial clan. Not all the terminology matched exactly, but the Jin government covered the same areas as did the Chinese, even with bureaus for astronomy and historiography. The Jin governmental structure was much more like a Chinese state than was the Liao, with its separate bureaucracies for its Chinese and Khitan subjects. Still, the Jin did recruit Chinese and Jurchen officials on different tracks. The Chinese sat for civil service examinations while the Jurchen were appointed to office, often on the basis of their father's position. The Jin also followed the Liao practice of having five capitals, which the emperor visited at different times during the year.

After doing his best to establish a Chinese-style autocracy, the prince of Hailing began preparations for an attack on the Southern Song in 1159. Realizing that the assault on the south would require a large navy, he mobilized some thirty thousand Chinese for that purpose. The one hundred twenty thousand Jurchen troops formed most of his cavalry, with one hundred fifty thousand Chinese who constituted the bulk of the infantry. The Chinese soldiers outnumbered the Jurchen troops three to two. These troops succeeded in taking the Huai River, but the Southern Song forces managed to defeat them at the Yangzi in 1161. While the prince of Hailing was at the front, a cousin of his who led a coup in

Liaoyang was proclaimed emperor in October of that year. The prince of Hailing was killed several weeks later, and the cousin, who became Emperor Shizong (reigned 1161–1189), then proceeded to negotiate a new peace with the Southern Song. Although the amount of the payments did not change, the Song changed the terminology of the treaty. No longer were they the humiliating "vassals" of the Jin. Instead, they adopted the fictive kinship terms of uncle and nephew.

Emperor Shizong reacted to the rule of his predecessor by passing a series of measures designed to strengthen Jurchen identity. He saw signs of the weakening of Jurchen identity all around him. In Aguda's time, Jurchen tribesmen seem to have had equal shares of wealth. With the conquest of north China and the ensuing creation of military colonies for those in the "three thousand" and "three hundred" systems, the distribution of wealth became increasingly uneven. In 1183 the emperor ordered the first in a series of censuses that provide an extraordinarily detailed view of Chinese society under Jin rule. Unlike most population surveys of China, the Jin enumerators tallied both the number of households and the size of the population, as shown in the following table.

CENSUS TAKEN UNDER JIN RULE

YEAR	HOUSEHOLDS	INDIVIDUALS	PERSONS PER HOUSEHOLD
1187	6,789,499	44,705,086	6.59
1190	6,939,000	45,447,900	6.55
1195	7,223,400	48,490,400	6.71
1207	8,413,164	53,532,151	6.33

Although most Chinese households were estimated to have five members, the slightly higher figures here are due to the greater number of slaves in Jin households. When they conquered north China, the Jurchen forces took a number of captives, whom they then enslaved. The 1183 census shows that the imperial clan, the Wanyan family, consisted of 982 clan members in 170 households, with an average of 5.7 people per household. These 982 imperial clan members held over 27,000 slaves, or an average of 163 slaves per household. The census did not distinguish ethnicity. One scholar estimates that of a total population of over forty-four million, in Jin territory, less than 10 percent were Jurchen or Khitan.[5]

Jin documents show a wide range of wealth, with some families owning large estates and others being forced to work the land, as was true in south China at the time. When the census takers documented that some Jurchen had managed to amass huge amounts of land at the expense of their brethren, the emperor ordered the distribution of free foodstuffs to poor Jurchen. Emperor Shizong saw the disparity in wealth as yet another sign of the decay of the Jurchen society all around him.

Reviving Jurchen Ways

As part of his effort to revive Jurchen identity, Emperor Shizong forbade the Jurchen from taking Chinese names or wearing Chinese-style clothing, and he urged the Jin to return to their traditional ways. All those resident at court were ordered to speak only Jurchen. Despite these measures, he may not have really wanted to revive traditional Jurchen ways. The emperor grew up in an outer branch of the imperial clan, and his mother belonged to the minority Bohai people who had completely adopted Chinese culture by the twelfth century. The emperor himself had received a Chinese education in the classics, and although he encouraged the Jurchen to use their native tongue at court, it was already a dying language, which even the emperor's own son refused to study. The emperor professed great pleasure when a grandson spoke to him in Jurchen, but evidently the boy, who would succeed his grandfather as Emperor Zhangzong (reigned 1189–1208), could say only the word for thank-you.

The Jurchen people in general, and certainly those Jurchens employed at court, may simply have found Chinese more useful than their own language. Jurchen had no script of its own, although many Jurchen used the smaller Khitan script to write. Emperor Shizong ordered the creation of a separate Jurchen script, but it was never successful. Jurchen did not become a language with its own literature. All books in Jurchen were translations, with most of them court-sponsored versions of the Chinese classics.

Emperor Shizong's attempt to revive Jurchen extended to the civil service examinations. In 1164 the government selected three thousand students to study Jurchen, and nine years later, it established a Jurchen language school to prepare Jurchen students to sit for the civil service examinations. The Jurchen language exams never became an important means of recruiting officials, and the vast majority of Jurchen officials continued to be appointed, not selected by the examinations.

Emperor Shizong's support for the Chinese language civil service examinations prompted their dramatic expansion. Whereas under the prince of Hailing some 60 or 70 candidates passed the exams every 3 years, the number leaped to 500 men who passed in the 1180s and then 600 in the 1200s. This level of recruitment matched that of the Southern Song, although many more men sat for the exams in the south than in the Jurchen-occupied north, where the pass rate fluctuated between 25 percent and 33 percent.[6]

The increase in the level of recruitment through the civil service examinations led to a revival of Chinese learning in the second half of the twelfth century, a trend far more pronounced than the emperor's well-publicized efforts to support the Jurchen language. The teachings of the Northern Song thinker Su Shi enjoyed a great following as the rulers of the Jin embraced Su's emphasis on learning and culture. The Confucian teachings of Zhu Xi, so popular in south China at this time, were little studied in the north, although they first became available during the 1190s.

The Popularity of the Ethic of Filial Piety

The Confucian emphasis on children's obligations to their parents struck a chord with the Chinese population living under Jin rule. As part of his translation project, Emperor Shizong commissioned a Jurchen edition of the Han-dynasty Confucian text, *The Classic of Filial Piety*. Members of other religious traditions also evinced an interest in filial piety. One Buddhist monastery, Yanshan, on Mount Wutai (where Ennin visited in the ninth century) contains beautifully detailed wall paintings with filial themes. The artist of the Yanshan paintings, like the artist of the Qingming scroll, depicted vivid scenes of everyday life using an overhead perspective, so that the viewer can look into houses and boats. Although the Yanshan monastery paintings date to 1167, most scholars see them as continuing the Northern Song tradition of painting and think that their artist may have been a Northern Song court painter who remained in Jin territory after 1127.

Reflecting the widespread interest in tales of filial piety, the Yanshan wall paintings show Buddha's disciple Sariputra cutting off his flesh to feed his parents. Also linked to the interest in filial piety is the rise of a new Daoist sect, the Complete Self-Realization (Quanzhen) school, whose founder, Wang Zhe (1112–1170), consciously adopted aspects of Buddhism, Daoism, and Confucianism to form a new philosophy.

Complete Self-Realization Daoism

Wang Zhe, born to a Chinese family in Shaanxi, witnessed the Jurchen conquest of north China. After receiving a traditional Chinese education, he failed the civil service examinations, abandoned his studies, and seems

A New Sect of Daoism

A new branch of Daoism, called the Complete Self-Realization school, that mixed elements of Buddhism, Daoism, and Confucianism, emerged in north China under Jurchen rule. This pottery pillow dated 1178 in the Philadelphia Museum is a rare artwork in which a Confucian, Buddhist, and Daoist are shown together playing chess. The Complete Self-Realization school is still active today and supports temples in the New Territories of Hong Kong.

to have lived off his family's wealth until he had a religious vision of Daoist immortals at the age of forty-eight. Wang then moved to Shandong where he began to teach his new philosophy to groups of literati who formed societies. He saw the three teachings of Confucianism, Buddhism, and Daoism as three legs of a tripod, with the tripod representing the Dao, or the Way. Wang selected three texts, one from each religion, for his followers to study: *The Classic of Filial Piety* from Confucianism, *The Way and Integrity Classic* from Daoism, and the concise *Heart Sutra* from Buddhism. He borrowed freely from the different traditions, encouraging his followers to be celibate, to fast regularly, to follow a vegetarian diet, and to avoid drinking alcohol.

Wang modified traditional Daoist promises of immortality to offer his followers a kind of inner peace—or self-realization, in his terms—to be achieved through meditation. If his followers were able to practice meditation correctly, then they could achieve a kind of detachment from this world even while their bodies remained in this world. A ban on the teachings in 1190, twenty years after Wang Zhe's death, seems only to have made them more popular.

Scholarly Culture under the Jin

Emperor Shizong's efforts to expand the civil service examinations contributed to the flourishing of Chinese scholarly culture in the years leading up to and following 1200. Chinese scholars living in Jin territory saw no contradiction between serving an alien dynasty—which grew less and less alien over time—and the lifestyle of a scholar, which is richly described in plays called "all-keys-and-modes" (*zhugongdiao*), a new literary form. These plays alternated passages of prose with stanzas of poetry sung to preexisting tunes. The playwrights frequently changed tunes, hence the name of the genre. Later generations who looked down on these plays did not preserve them, and only three all-keys-and-modes plays survive today. One of them is a rewrite of Yuan Zhen's story of his abortive love affair with Oriole (see chapter 6, p. 233). Because only the playwright's last name is known, he is usually referred to as Master Dong, and he wrote *The Romance of the Western Chamber* sometime between 1190 and 1208. One scholar calls this wonderful, lively play "the chief gem in the crown of Jin literature,"[7] even though it was written in Chinese, as was all Jin-dynasty literature.

Oriole and Zhang under Jurchen Rule

Although the characters bear the same names as those in the Tang-dynasty story, they have greatly changed. The focus of attention is no longer Oriole but the young man who courts her, Zhang. He embodies the scholarly ideal of the Jin dynasty:

> In beauty and grace young Zhang of Xile [Luoyang]
> Vies with the paragons of old.
> Passionately fond of poetry and calligraphy,
> An expert painter and musician,
> He's an impeccable prose-writer (and a scrupulous man) as well.

Zhang, then, is a classical scholar, a painter, a musician who can play the Chinese lute, and an essay writer. In comparison to his Tang predecessor, Zhang has become much more effeminate. Once he falls in love with

Oriole, he becomes so ill that he nearly dies, prompting her decision to go to bed with him. Oriole has changed, too. The all-keys-and-modes Oriole has had her feet bound so that when she first appears, Zhang sees "Her feet, dainty but firm, are like lotus buds." It makes sense that a character who was born to a respectable family would have had her feet bound; remember the official's wife in Jiangxi who was buried with her foot-wrappings.

Oriole's maid Crimson assumes a much more important role than she did in the Tang story. She arranges all the meetings between the two lovers, and she is responsible for their successful union. Her witty tongue and ingenuity, like Figaro's in Beaumarchais's *The Marriage of Figaro*, show that the servant classes can be just as smart, if not actually smarter, than those they serve, a theme directly counter to the age-old tradition of privileging the educated among the Chinese. The monk, Dharma Wit, who lends the hapless Zhang money (so that he can marry Oriole), serves as the maid's male counterpart. Master Dong has altered the plot, too, so that the two lovers are joined at the end of the play, after Oriole manages to extricate herself from her engagement to her cousin on the legal technicality that she had never received any engagement presents from him. Gone, too, is the subtle tension between the narrator's stated support for Zhang and the reader's sympathy with Oriole.

The transition from the marvelous tale of the Tang to the all-keys-and-modes play of the Jin resulted in a much longer literary work. Yuan Zhen's tale is a classic of terseness and subtlety, with major plot shifts occurring in just a few well-chosen phrases in classical Chinese. But where the Tang original is tight, the Jin version is prolix. Written in the vernacular Chinese of the time, the play's actions take much longer to occur. It is as if Master Dong has to explain at great length the matters that Yuan Zhen could leave to the imagination of the reader.

With its vivid love story and repeated scenes of fighting on stage, the Jin version of the play enjoyed great popularity in its day, even among a less-educated audience. Recently one scholar has offered a new interpretation that suggests another reason for the play's enduring appeal. Its language works on two levels: in one it simply conveys a love story, but indirectly it contains an involved series of sexual references. In some places, Master Dong talks directly about sex, as when Zhang "fondles her [Oriole's] fragrant body ecstatically;/Stroking,/Licking, sucking."[8] But most of the play works less directly, though the playwright gives broad hints about the symbolic language he employs. For instance, in the Tang story, it is Oriole who plays the zither, but in the Jin play, Zhang plays the zither in his attempts to woo Oriole. Since one term for the lips of the vagina was the same as the word for strings of a zither, Master Dong could also be alluding to the caressing that takes place before a woman reaches orgasm. Zhang's speech to her extends the double meaning:

> My longing for you grows only more intense,
> So I idly entrust it to my zither playing.
> Such a joy, and in spring, moreover—
> The flower-heart is bound to be moved.[9]

The flower-heart was another term for clitoris.

The play does not celebrate premarital sex. Its complex imagery suggests that sex has to take place within marriage, where it can be regulated. Indeed Zhang and Oriole's union succeeds only at the end of the play after they have eloped. Although the play celebrates a traditional Chinese view of marriage, it does so in an explicitly sexual way, very different from the more restrained efforts of later generations. The play offers eloquent testimony to the tolerant cultural environment that flourished under the Jurchen.

The Romance of the Western Chamber prompted further rewrites in later centuries, and later sources record that Jin authors produced close to seven hundred plays in the all-keys-and-modes genre. The presence of miniature stages in Jin-dynasty tombs, including that of a Complete Self-Realization Master, also testifies to the immediate success of the new drama.

Confucian Learning under the Jin Emperors

The popularity of the Complete Self-Realization school indicates that scholars in the north were feeling much the same disillusionment with the civil service examination system as their counterparts in the south. Even though the pass rate was much higher in the north than in the south, one's chances of getting a post remained very slim, especially in the highest reaches of the Jurchen-dominated bureaucracy. Confucian intellectuals began to express their doubts about the nature of true learning in an environment that stressed only success in the examinations. One Chinese scholar described the development of studies in the last years of the Jin dynasty, saying:

> I recall the old gentlemen saying that in the Taihe era (1202–1209) the examiners determined who would pass and fail as soon as they had looked at the rhapsody (*fu*) and poem. When they read the essay and discourse they only used their brushes to check off taboo characters and imperial names and to count the number of characters and revisions. With such examiners it was hard to expect candidates to be concerned with excellence.[10]

This commentator worried that those who had simply mastered the art of test taking did better on the examinations than did those who had genuine learning and literary talent, and his views were echoed by the Jin scholars who tried to reform the examinations in the years after 1206.

In looking at the Jin debate over the meaning of the examinations, one cannot help noticing how everyone involved in the debate—scholars, both in support of and opposed to the examinations, bureaucrats, both Jurchen and Chinese, and the emperor himself—had embraced the traditional Chinese emphasis on classical learning. Whatever their position, no one saw any discordance between serving a Jurchen emperor and striving for a full knowledge of the Chinese classics.

Confucian Measures under Emperor Zhangzong

When Emperor Shizong died in 1189, he was succeeded by his grandson, who reigned until 1208. The new emperor Zhangzong continued his grandfather's support for the civil service examinations, both in Chinese and Jurchen, and he carried out a series of measures designed to show just how Chinese the Jin dynasty had become.

The first such measure he took was the promulgation of a new law code, the Taihe Code. This code was the culmination of a century of legal change. The founder of the Jin, Aguda, had presided over a tribal society with a law system whose underlying principle was an eye for an eye. If they had sufficient funds, criminals could pay penalties and forgo punishment, although their ears or nose would be cut off to show that they had broken the law. Although the prince of Hailing and Emperor Shizong codified all the precedents based on the Tang Code, neither issued a new code. The Taihe Code drew heavily on the Tang Code while making some concessions to Jurchen custom. It revised earlier statutes to give masters more power over their slaves and to allow Jurchen sons to divide their households while their parents were still alive, a practice contrary to the Chinese ideal.

Even more significant than the promulgation of a Chinese law code was Emperor Zhangzong's resolution to select one of the five elements as the emblem of his dynasty. Emperor Zhangzong and his advisors faced a difficult decision that took them eight years to make. Depending on which element they chose, they could position themselves as the legitimate successors of the Tang, the Liao, or the Northern Song. In 1202 the emperor and his advisors decided that earth was the symbol of the Jin. In doing so, they were making the claim that the Jin rulers—not the Southern Song emperors—were the rightful successors to the Northern

Song. One leading Confucian scholar of the time saw this decision as one of the emperor's greatest accomplishments. In an essay praising the emperor, he wrote "The virtue of the earth was amplified so that the Central Plain was unified."[11]

Of course, as long as the Southern Song ruled south China and the Jin the north, China was anything but unified. This was an extraordinary claim for an alien dynasty to make, but, by the year 1202, the Jin dynasty did not seem alien at all to Confucian bureaucrats like him. This scholar was familiar with the teachings of the Neo-Confucians in the south, who valued understanding of the Dao, or Way, above political service, but he thought government service, even in the Jurchen government, an equally valid way to achieve the Dao. Whatever its cosmological significance, the choice of a ruling element could not solve the recurrent problems the Jin faced at the turn of the century.

The Last Years of the Jin

Since the 1120s, the Yellow River had been flooding over its dikes. In 1194 it shifted its course dramatically from north of the Shandong peninsula to south of it. The catastrophic flooding continued for thirty years after the river had changed course, wiping out crops over a large area. The resulting shortfall in Jin government revenues from the agricultural tax coincided with problems in currency. Like the Southern Song, the Jin faced a shortage of bronze coins, and they lacked the copper mines the Song had. Finance officials experimented with different currencies—iron, silver, paper money backed by silver—but, like the Song, they continued to issue notes with lower and lower face value, which created a complicated and unstable financial situation.

Just as the Jin government was struggling with these problems, the Southern Song decided to stage an attack. The chief councilor of the Southern Song, Han Tuozhou (1151–1207) led a force of some one hundred sixty thousand against the Jin forces of one hundred thirty thousand. He hoped that the Chinese living in Jin territory would shift allegiance, but they did not. In fact, the opposite occurred when a general in Sichuan and many of his seventy thousand troops defected to the Jin. Several clear Jin victories signaled to both sides that the Song could not reconquer the north. Han Tuozhou was dismissed from office and then killed. The Jin demanded Han Tuozhou's head, which the Song had no choice but to lacquer and send north in a box, in the most humiliating of gestures.

The Jin were eager to sue for peace and to resume payments from the

Song, which they raised to fifty thousand ounces of silver and fifty thousand bolts of silk. The Jin desperately needed the revenues from the settlement to mount a force against a new enemy to their north, the Mongols. In 1214 the Jin twice requested the annual payment from the Song to make up for alleged shortfalls, but the Song refused to pay anything at all. Continued flooding in the Yellow River coincided with a drought across most of north China, and the Jin emperor decided to retreat to the southernmost of his five capitals, Kaifeng. The Mongols interpreted the retreat as further preparation for war, and they drove the much-weakened Jin south to just a sliver of land between the Yellow and Huai River valleys. In 1215 the Mongols took the Jin capital of Beijing. The Jin managed to hang on until 1234, when their new capital at Kaifeng fell, but the once-powerful dynasty was reduced to a minor regional power for the last twenty years of its existence.

THE DIVISION OF NORTH AND SOUTH

Although the Jin ruled north China and the Song south China for only a century, the two societies diverged in important ways—much as the paths of East and West Germany, or China and Taiwan, took sharply different courses in similarly short periods. While trade between the north and the south was banned and while the only goods officially exchanged were indemnity payments, trade still occurred on a regular basis. Some scholars estimate that the Song was able to earn back everything it paid in war indemnities through trade. Books were traded as well as goods, and scholars in the north had access to the writings of southern thinkers like Zhu Xi. Both governments faced the same problems of devalued paper money and inconsistent money supply. Emperor Shizong tried to correct the sharp division of wealth among the Jurchen, a division mirrored in the south by the uneven growth of the commercial revolution.

Still, the differences between the cultures of the north and south are more striking than the similarities. Scholars in the north may have read the teachings of the Neo-Confucians, but they were more heavily influenced by the teachings of Northern Song thinkers like Su Shi, whose writings were reinterpreted by the Confucians of the Jin. They thought studying for the civil service examinations and the pursuit of a bureaucratic position, even in a Jurchen government, was an honorable career for a scholar, a view fewer and fewer Confucians in the south shared. In the north, scholars and commoners alike flocked to the new dramas like *The Romance of the Western Chamber*, but their southern counterparts did not. And when the northerners read the teachings of the Self-Realization school, southerners remained curiously untouched by the new amalgam of the three religions.

Ironically the Jin dynasty made its claim to greater legitimacy than the Southern Song just before its dramatic decline and ultimate surrender to the Mongols. The Liao had ruled only a small section of China proper, and they had never integrated Chinese bureaucrats into their government. The Jurchen took the Liao innovation of dual government an important step further. They adopted the structure of Chinese bureaucracy and the means of recruiting by examinations while reserving the highest positions for native Jurchen, whom they selected on the basis of recommendation.

The various measures the Jin emperors took to support Jurchen ways had little effect. Emperor Shizong banned Chinese names and clothing, but he also encouraged the translation of Chinese classics into Jurchen, which exposed even more Jurchen to Chinese thinking. The Jurchen language civil service examinations probably had the same effect. After all, no original books in Jurchen existed for the tribesmen to read. Not all of Emperor Shizong's measures aimed to strengthen Jurchen culture. He encouraged the collection of precedents for a new law code based on Chinese law, not on tribal precedent. Although he instituted Jurchen language civil service examinations, they never attracted a large clientele. The expansion of recruitment via Chinese language exams, and the ensuing growth of the Chinese scholarly class, was more noticeable.

Short-lived as their dynasty was, the Jurchen made a crucial breakthrough in Chinese history. Under their rule, the best-educated Chinese scholars could serve a non-Chinese ruler and still feel that they were advancing the cause of Chinese civilization. Chinese soldiers outnumbered Jurchen in the Jin army, and the Southern Song generals were sorely disappointed in 1206 when the north Chinese failed to rise up against the Jin. Chinese scholar-bureaucrats cooperated with the Jurchen by teaching them how to govern Chinese style and by helping them to design a bureaucracy on the Chinese model.

These Chinese scholars explained the theory of the five elements and participated in the debates in Zhangzong's court over which element best suited the Jin view of their place in Chinese dynastic history. The Jin made their claim to succeed the Northern Song just as the Mongols appeared, but they were right to see themselves as pathbreakers. The Southern Song made no innovations in governance that shaped the rest of Chinese history, but the Jurchen, in concert with their Chinese advisors, devised the formula that allowed much more powerful non-Chinese dynasties than themselves—the Mongols and then the Manchus—to rule China. Later Chinese historians did their best to argue that Chinese civilization under non-Chinese rule was a departure from the norm, but for the last one thousand years of Chinese history, it was more often the norm than an aberration.

CHRONOLOGY

ca. 1200	*Different peoples of the steppe unite to form Mongol confederation*
1206–1227	*Reign of Chinggis Khan (Genghis Khan)*
1219–1241	*Mongols conquer much of Asia and eastern Europe*
1234–1276	*Mongols rule north China*
1253–1255	*Journey of William of Rubruck to Mongolia*
1254–1322	*Lifetime of Zhao Mengfu, painter of* Sheep and Goat *scroll*
1260–1294	*Reign of Emperor Khubilai Khan*
1262–1319	*Lifetime of Guan Daosheng, female painter*
1271	*Mongols adopt the dynastic name "Yuan"*
1271–1295	*Marco Polo travels away from Venice, possibly in China*
1276	*Mongols take south China*
1276–1368	YUAN DYNASTY, WHEN MONGOLS RULE NORTH AND SOUTH CHINA
1300–1400	*Circulation of encyclopedias and dramas in vernacular Chinese*
1301–1374	*Lifetime of Ni Zan, painter of trees*
1313–1320	*Reign of Emperor Ayurbarwada*
1315	*Civil service examinations held for the first time since Mongols unified China*
1330s–1350s	*Plague causes extensive loss of life*
1368	*Mongols overthrown by peasant rebels*

C H A P T E R   9

THE MONGOLS
(ca. 1200–1368)

In the early 1200s, the Mongols exploded out of their steppe homeland to stun, attack, and conquer Eurasia. The Jurchens were among their first victims, but ultimately much of Eastern Europe and Asia—including all of China—would come under the rule of the stampeding armies, so infamous for their use of terror. Much of the territory they conquered soon reverted to non-Mongol rule, but in China they established a dynasty that ruled in the north for a century and a half, and in the south for a century. This was the first time in Chinese history that a foreign people had conquered all of China, not just the north.

The Mongols built on the Liao model of dual government and Jurchen experience of rule in north China to construct a new dynasty, which they named the Yuan dynasty, that systematically excluded the Chinese from government service. They suspended the civil service examinations until 1315, forcing educated Chinese to adopt new strategies of advancement. Some became doctors, and others clerks to the Mongol officials. In spite of the obstacles, a few even adopted Mongol names and joined the government. But the vast majority of the Chinese elite had to carve new lives for themselves outside of government service, and they often did so on their rural estates.

It took over fifty years for the Mongols to conquer all of China, and the destruction and casualties, especially in the north, took a great toll. Yet the Yuan dynasty proved to be one of great cultural vitality. Drama, born under the Jurchens, continued to develop under Mongol rule. Court-room dramas, often punctuated by lively slapstick scenes, attracted large audiences, even among those who did not understand Chinese. Many of the playwrights had used vernacular Chinese while drafting government

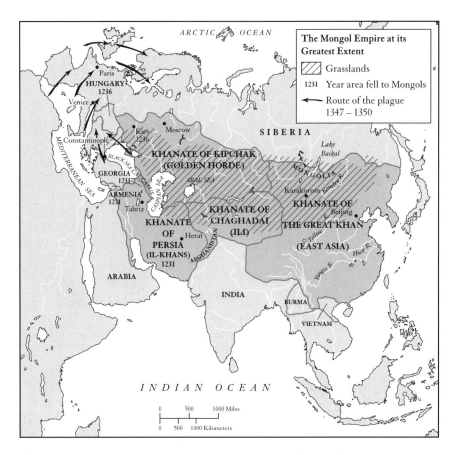

The Mongol Empire at its
Greatest Extent

///// Grasslands

1231 Year area fell to Mongols

←— Route of the plague
1347 – 1350

documents and went on to exploit its potential as a literary medium. Painting was also popular, and the first Chinese woman to achieve recognition as a great artist did so under Mongol rule.

Although some scholars speak of a Pax Mongolica, or a Mongolian peace parallel to the peace of the Roman Empire, the period of Mongol rule over Asia and Eastern Europe was short-lived. Although travel remained difficult, some Europeans, including possibly Marco Polo (1254–1324), managed to visit Mongolia or perhaps China itself when under Mongol rule. One inadvertent by-product of Mongol rule was increased transmission of disease-carrying bacteria across Eurasia. The Black Death, or bubonic plague, caused widespread suffering in China decades before it ravaged Europe in 1348, and it was one of the causes of the religious rebellions that brought down the Mongol dynasty in 1368.

THE ORIGINS OF THE MONGOL CONFEDERATION

Historians are hard-pressed to explain why the Mongols moved out of their homelands when they did. For centuries, different tribes had lived in the steppe areas of what is now the independent state of Mongolia and the Chinese autonomous region of Inner Mongolia, but they coalesced into a fighting confederation only once in history, sometime around 1200. In the years prior to 1200 they were one of many peoples who traveled on a yearly basis from grassland to grassland so they could feed their flocks of sheep, cows, and horses. Theirs was a largely self-sufficient economy. Sheep provided skins for clothing, milk and cheese for food, dung for fuel, and wool for the Mongols' distinctive felt yurt-tents. Horses provided crucial transport, especially during hunting expeditions and military campaigns.

One possible reason for the Mongols' expansion outside their traditional homeland was climatic. There seems to have been a steep and regular decline in the mean annual temperature in Mongolia between 1175 and 1260. A temperature drop would have resulted in less grass for the Mongol herds and would have prompted the Mongols to seek new grasslands, which meant conquering new territory.

The Social Organization of the Mongols

The tribal structure of the Mongols was well suited to the demands of war. All tribesmen were obliged to join group hunts and battles. The men left their women in charge of their flocks, affording women correspondingly more power than their Chinese counterparts. The Mongol women who had to be able to ride and move quickly did not adopt the Chinese custom of footbinding. Their nomadic lifestyle meant the Mongols were far better suited for the constant movement of war than were their sedentary Chinese neighbors, who had much more to lose.

The Mongols chose their leaders as other tribal peoples did, on the basis of who in the ruling tribe was best fitted to succeed the previous leader, or khan. In some cases the tribal leaders would choose a brother of the dead leader; in others, the most powerful son. As in other polities governed according to this principle of tanistry, a *khuriltai* council of all the men ratified the choice of a new leader only after he had defeated all his rivals. One of the most powerful men in a Mongol tribe was its shaman, who was thought to have the power to communicate with divine forces and whose support the khan needed.

Other ties linked individual tribesmen. Mongol men who vowed to support each other became sworn brothers, who could call on each other in time of need. They could also swear loyalty to a leader from another tribe and become his personal supporter. Tribesmen did not have to follow a leader from their own tribe, and the Mongol federation included speakers of different Mongolian and Turkic dialects. When a tribesman became the personal supporter of a leader, he swore his absolute obedience to him only during wartime. After a successful battle, the khan had first pick of captured women and horses, and his supporters then divided the remaining booty. In peacetime, a personal supporter promised simply not to act counter to his leader's interests. As a result, the khan had every reason to be at war, when he could command the obedience of his troops by distributing booty to them, and no incentive to be at peace, when his troops would not obey him. Only continuous conquest, coupled with a steady supply of booty, could hold such an army together. For a leader to stop moving was tantamount to disbanding his troops.

Chinggis Khan's Rise to Power

Most of us know Chinggis by his Persian name, Genghis Khan, since so many of the sources about the Mongols are in Persian. The Mongols themselves had no written language. Only one source from the Mongol point of view survives, *The Secret History of the Mongols*, and it uses Chinese characters to record the sounds of the Mongolian original. Like many oral epics, *The Secret History* includes much that is legendary, starting with the descent of the Mongols from a blue doe. Still, *The Secret History* makes it possible to sketch the rough outlines of Chinggis's rise to power.

Chinggis Khan (ca. 1167–1227) was born to a chieftain's family living in the forests east of Lake Baikal in what is now the People's Republic of Mongolia. His father's personal supporters abandoned the nine-year-old Chinggis, his mother, and his siblings on his father's death, and they were forced to live in the forest. Although it was initially a disadvantage to be fatherless, Chinggis began launching his own campaign to win followers. As he grew up he was able to resume contact with his father's supporters, and his father's sworn brother gave him his daughter in marriage in exchange for a coat of black sable. When he did so, he made the promise to Chinggis, in the words of *The Secret History*:

> In return for the coat of black sables
> I shall collect for thee
> Thy people which have separated themselves.
> In return for the coat of black sables
> I shall gather for thee
> Thy people which have dispersed themselves.[1]

Like Abaoji of the Khitans and Aguda of the Jurchen (see chapter 8) before him, Chinggis gathered supporters, defeated opponents, and gradually rose to head a loose confederation of tribesmen. Skill in battle must have helped him, but luck too played its part. After all, he was never wounded in battle, which was little short of miraculous given the ferocity of arrow warfare and the light armor of the Mongols.

Chinggis initially did nothing to mark himself off from other tribal leaders, but in 1203 he made a deliberate attempt to break the loyalties of his followers to their own chieftains. He reordered his army into decimal units of tens, hundreds, and thousands, each with its own commander. This reorganization was only partially successful, for the troops retained their traditional tribal designations in addition to the decimal ones. Three years later, a shaman gave him the title Chinggis Khan, which literally means ruler of the ocean, and by extension, world ruler. In 1206, when Chinggis had defeated his rivals, he assumed leadership of all nomadic peoples dwelling in felt tents. The structure of the Mongol army, with its unending hunger for the spoils of war, pushed Chinggis to conquer new lands.

A Woman Rises to Provincial Governor

By 1215, the Mongols took all of north China for the Jin dynasty, leaving the Jurchens only a narrow band of land around the Huai River valley (discussed in chapter 8). Because the three-way contest among the Mongols, the Jin, and the Southern Song left the Shandong peninsula with no clear leaders, rebels and bandit leaders formed small armies and temporary alliances with each other. In the town of Yidu (near modern Jinan, Shandong), after 1215 a young woman named Yang Miaozhen, who "was crafty and assertive as well as skillful in horsemanship and archery," inherited leadership of an army of over ten thousand men. Following her brother's death, she subsequently married the leader of another private army, and the two successfully negotiated a series of alliances first with Song officials and then with the Mongols.

On one occasion, when her forces were outnumbered, she even seduced a former brigand who had been named a general by the desperate Song state. Her husband's biography in the official history of the Song gives a sense of her ironic wit: "With my husband reported dead, how can I, a woman, fare for myself? May I, then, serve you, my lord, as your wife?" In fact, her husband was alive but just too far away to rescue her. The official history continues that the brigand-general "retired with Yang to her chamber and felt as if he had returned home." But the next day she refused him entrance, he was forced to surrender to the Jurchen, and she eventually rejoined her husband. After his death, the Mongols named her to the position of provincial governor—probably the highest post to be held by a civilian woman in imperial China.[2]

The Mongol Conquest of Eurasia

After taking north China, the Mongols turned away from the rice paddies of south China to conquer the Eurasian steppe, the terrain with which they were most familiar. It took them only thirty years to cut a swath through the grasslands of Europe and Asia. No army succeeded in defeating them. By 1219 they had taken Russia and by 1222, all of north India. Chinggis's death gave Europe a two-year respite, but he had secured the consent of his four sons concerning the succession. The conquests resumed when a khuriltai council acknowledged his son Ögödei (reigned 1229–1241) as the new khan in 1229. Georgia, Persia, and Armenia fell in 1231, and Kiev and Hungary followed in 1236. Finally the conquests ended in 1241 with Ögödei's death. This plunged the Mongols into a succession dispute that was resolved only in 1264 with the division of the empire into quadrants, one each for the descendants of Chinggis's four sons.

The Reasons for the Mongols' Success

The Mongols took territory with breathtaking speed. Although the army numbered only one hundred thirty thousand, its impact was that of a much larger force. Each soldier, equipped with several horses, could ride for three or four days without tiring his mounts. Atop the riderless mounts sat dummy soldiers, who appeared to swell the ranks of the attackers.

The Mongols had mastered the art of using horses to the best advantage. A wall of heavily armed horsemen bearing lances led the advance. Behind them were light cavalry and bowmen whose strong weapons were made of layers of horn and sinew on a wooden frame. These mounted bowmen were deadly shots. If the first row of heavily armed men could not move fast enough, they would leave gaps so that the faster moving, lightly armed men behind could press to the front and attack. Their varied formations gave the Mongols a flexibility no other army could match.

The Mongols recruited new soldiers from among the conquered. They put captive men in the infantry, often in the front ranks to force the captives' compatriots to shoot at their countrymen. The conquerors also sought the counsel of non-Mongol artillery experts in the use of new weapons. The iron stirrups they adapted from the Jurchen enabled their mounted archers to shoot at the enemy on the gallop. Following the Chinese example, they tipped their arrows with iron that would penetrate more deeply. They developed giant slingshots whose accuracy was enhanced by counterweights, and they used Chinese gunpowder to make firebombs. They even developed an ancestor of the gun: a flamethrower made out of bamboo tubing in which a mixture of charcoal, iron, and porcelain chips was expelled by gunpowder.

Although the Mongols employed excellent formations and were quick to adopt new technologies, they are best known for the violence of their attacks, which their victims depicted as wanton. Matthew Paris (1200–1259), an Englishman, gives the following contemporary account:

> Swarming like locusts over the face of the earth, they have brought terrible devastation to the eastern parts (of Europe), laying them waste with fire and carnage. . . . they have razed cities, cut down forests, overthrown fortresses, pulled up vines, destroyed gardens, killed townspeople and peasants.

The Mongols' use of captured troops on the front lines particularly horrified Paris, who offers the following explanation for their ruthlessness:

> For they are inhuman and beastly, rather monsters than men, thirsting for and drinking blood, tearing and devouring the flesh of dogs and men, dressed in ox-hides, armed with plates of iron, short and stout, thickset, strong, invincible, indefatigable, their backs unprotected, . . . They are without human laws, know no comforts, are more ferocious than lions or bears. . . . And so they come with the swiftness of lightning to the confines of Christendom, ravaging and slaughtering, striking everyone with terror and incomparable horror.[3]

In Paris's view, the Mongols were not like other people. They were not Christian, they behaved like animals, and their violence was feral.

The Systematic Use of Terror

Many observers, terrorized as they were, overlooked an important component of the Mongol strategy. Every action the Mongols took had the same objective: to force the residents of each walled city to surrender and give up their plunder. It took time to lay siege to a city, to cut off its food and water supply, and to wait for its residents to surrender, but the Mongol armies worked best when they were moving. If they could establish a sufficiently terrifying reputation before they attacked, the residents of any given city would surrender without fighting. In these instances, the Mongols did not kill the inhabitants. Once they had taken their share of plunder, they kept on going, leaving the inhabitants to govern themselves and to follow the same religious practices as they had before.

It was in hopes of encouraging rapid surrender that the Mongols behaved so viciously. In 1221, after a son-in-law of Chinggis had died in the fighting outside the city of Herat in Afghanistan, the Mongols gave the order, as recounted by the Persian historian Juvaini (1226–1283), "that the town should be laid waste in such a manner that the site could be ploughed upon; and that in the exaction of vengeance not even cats and dogs should be left alive." Only the four hundred craftsmen who were sent to the capital in Mongolia survived. Everyone else was killed, and the Mongols severed the victims' heads from their bodies, forming separate piles for men, women, and children. They took every action possible to cultivate a reputation for senseless violence. In other instances, once they had taken a city, they killed only those inhabitants over a certain height. Or they cut off the ears of all the residents and piled them up as a warning to those who came after them. A brilliant strategic device, terror as used by the Mongols created a climate of fear that enabled the Mongol armies to conquer new territory without having to fight for it.

Terrified as the Europeans were of the Mongols, they were also curious about them, and several European travelers made the long trip to see the Mongols in their homeland. Since 1100, the Europeans had been fighting for outposts in Syria and Palestine, and in 1205—three years before Chinggis unified the Mongols—the Fourth Crusade took the city of Constantinople (now Istanbul). Hoping to make an alliance with the Mongols against the Muslim Turks, Pope Innocent IV sent John of Plano Carpini (fl. 1240s) to the Mongol court in 1245, and in 1253 Louis IX of France sent William of Rubruck (ca. 1220–ca. 1257). The Polo brothers had a different goal. Merchants in search of profit, they first set off in 1261, and they went again in 1271. The accounts these men wrote provide a level of detail far superior to the impressionistic comments of those who remained in Europe.

WESTERN VISITORS TO THE KHAN'S COURT

In 1253 the French king sent a personal envoy to visit the capital of the Mongols at Karakorum.[4] William of Rubruck's letter home gives a clear picture of the difficulties of travel and the arduous living conditions the Mongols, even the Mongol khan, endured. The envoys lived in a hut so small they could not stand up. With only skins for warmth, they were always cold, and their diet was a monotony of gruel and gristle. Once they were given "the meat of one small, scrawny ram as food to last for six days, and each day a bowl full of millet and a quart of ale made from millet." The Mongols, even the khan, ate the same simple food.

William and his companion first met Möngke Khan (reigned 1251–1259) on Christmas day, 1253. After being searched for weapons, they were allowed to speak with the khan, whom William described as "snub-nosed, a man of medium build, and aged about forty-five." The missionaries refused the khan's offer of wine, but "unfortunately for us [William and his companions], our interpreter was standing next to the stewards, who gave him a good deal to drink, and in no time he grew tipsy."

William began to communicate better once he met some of the Europeans resident at the Mongol court. One of these was a French woman who had been taken prisoner in Hungary in the 1230s. After the difficult journey to Mongolia, she had married a Russian builder of houses and settled in Karakorum. The Mongols' capital did not impress William, who thought the city smaller than the village of Saint Denis outside Paris. The city had few comforts, but William describes a lavish silver fountain in the shape of a tree with four lions at its base, which a French goldsmith had just completed. The goldsmith's son, a fluent speaker of French and Mongolian, became William's interpreter.

Although William could not speak Mongolian, he was able to find out more about the Mongols than had any previous visitor. He provides the sole account of how Möngke's men discovered a plot against him just as the assembly was convening to acclaim him the new khan.

On the Armenians' Easter, when William and some Nestorian Christians visited Möngke, William saw a servant carrying charred shoulder-blade bones of sheep out of the khan's tent. He later discovered that the Khan "does nothing in the world unless he has first consulted these bones, with the result that he does not allow a man to enter his residence without previous reference to the bone." The khan followed the traditional religious practices of the Mongols, including daily divination by fire, which resembled those of the ancient Shang kings:

> When [the bones] have been charred black, then, they are brought to him again, and he looks to see whether the heat of the fire has split them cleanly lengthwise. In that case the way is clear for him to act; if, on the other hand, the bones are cracked horizontally or round fragments have splintered off, then he refrains.

Although the Khan was friendly to the Christians, William soon realized that he was equally hospitable to all the religious teachers in his court and that he had no intention of converting to Christianity.

Reporting directly to the French king, William provided detailed accounts of the other Christians he met at Möngke's court, most of whom were Syrian and Armenian Nestorian Christians who observed different festivals from those celebrated by the Europeans. Very much a man of his time, he classed all he met as Christians or pagans, and he criticized all those whose practices differed from his own.

William's account carefully distinguishes between what he himself saw, what others told him, and what was hearsay. The reader of his account feels the sting of the biting Christmas wind that swept across the steppe and tastes the frustration of trying to convert the Mongols to Roman Catholicism. No one can doubt that William went where he said he did and saw what he records.

The World of Fantasy: Marco Polo

The same cannot be said of the much more famous account by Marco Polo. Anyone reading Polo's account has to question the reliability of what he says about China. Sources external to his memoir do not record his presence in China, much less his service in the positions he professes to have held. He claims to have built the Mongols the catapults that made it possible for them to take Xiangyang in 1268—two years before his arrival in China. Further casting doubt on his account, Chinese sources record the fall of the city in 1273 with the help of Arab—not European—engineers. Polo says he served as governor of Yangzhou, but the lists of governors are complete and do not give his name.

Still, we do know that the Polos traveled outside of Italy. By 1264, Italian merchants had established an outpost in the city of Tabriz in Iran, and it is likely that Polo traveled at least that far. Unlike the sections concerning China under the rule of Khubilai Khan (reigned 1260–1294), those parts of Polo's account about Iran contain geographically accurate information. Marco's father and uncle left Constantinople in 1261 and returned to Venice in 1271. They traveled again in 1271, this time with Marco, and returned to Venice only in 1295, on a ship with a Chinese princess who was to be married to a Middle Eastern king. Polo's description of their journey tallies with Chinese accounts, which do not, however, explicitly mention the Polos by name.

As is well known, Marco Polo wrote his account in prison during 1298 and 1299, assisted by Rusticello de Pisa, who specialized in romances, and who, like many modern ghostwriters, felt no compunction about embellishing the truth to enhance the readability of his account. One scholar has shown that Khubilai's welcome to Marco was simply lifted from Rusticello's rewrite of the passage from the Arthurian legend when Tristan first goes to court. However unlikely this partnership was, the two men succeeded in producing a best-seller for all times, a book so well known that Christopher Columbus carried it with him on his voyages to the New World. In contrast, William of Rubruck's scrupulously accurate and much more informative account languishes largely unread.

Polo gives none of the detail Rubruck does. As his account meanders from place to place, he sometimes records the number of days necessary for the journey, sometimes not. At times large chunks of the itinerary are left out, and he writes as if he flew to the Mongol capital. The reader never learns the gritty details of the trip. With whom does Polo travel? What does he eat? Where does he stay? What language did he speak? Who were his interpreters? Further undercutting his credibility, his account suffers from a mind-numbing repetitiveness. In almost every city in China he records, "The inhabitants are idolators and burn their dead. They are subject to the Great Khan and use paper money," or some variation of this formula. The typical passage about a given place will mention its major products, such as silk, jujubes, foodstuffs, or armaments, comment on the numbers of ships there, and then lurch to the next site.

Despite its formulaic narrative and outright inventions, one cannot reject Polo's account totally because it occasionally includes kernels of important information. One has to wonder when Polo reports that women test brides for their virginity by scratching their hymens with a clean cloth, "so that the linen may be slightly stained with the virginal blood," which cannot be washed out. But when Polo records "to ensure this strict preservation of virginity, the maidens always walk so daintily that they never advance one foot more than a finger's breadth beyond the other," it seems as if he is actually describing the effects of footbinding. Marco seems to know about practices with which people in Europe could not have been familiar: he meets a spirit medium who specializes in finding lost or stolen goods, and he describes the Chinese custom of equipping the dead with "horses and slaves, male and female, and camels and cloth of gold in great abundance—all made of paper!"[5]

Distorted and secondhand as it is, Polo's *Travels* testifies to the cultural brilliance of China under the Mongols, especially in comparison to the Europe of his time. William of Rubruck found Karakorum sorely lacking, but Polo's informant finds the Southern Song capital of Hangzhou (which he calls Kinsai) "without doubt the finest and most splendid city in the world." It was a city of many bridges and waterways, with markets everywhere. The variety of goods stuns the visitor, who reports "There is always abundance of victuals, both wild game, such as roebuck, stags, harts, hares, and rabbits, and of fowls, such as partridges, pheasants, francolins, quails, hens, capons, and as many ducks and geese as can be told." Once again, Polo gets carried away. "Among the articles regularly on sale in these squares are all sorts of vegetables and fruits, above all huge pears, weighing ten pounds apiece." Still, whatever the exaggerations, Polo's description captures life in the Chinese capital, graced as it was by numerous urban amenities like hospitals, fire brigades, pleasure boats, paved roads, public baths, and stone houses.

What we have in Polo's *Travels*, then, is the strung-together accumulated hearsay of travelers who went to China. Some Europeans did make the trip, as the tombstone of the daughter of an Italian merchant shows.

An Early European Tombstone in China

One of the earliest pieces of evidence showing European presence in China is the tombstone of Katerina Ilioni, who died in the city of Yangzhou, Jiangsu, in 1342, fifty years after Marco Polo allegedly visited China. She is the only Western woman before the nineteenth century whose activities in China appear in the historical record.

The daughter of a Venetian merchant, she was buried with a tombstone showing a haloed figure—possibly her namesake St. Catherine of Alexandria—being beheaded and then lifted from her tomb by two angels. At the top of the headstone sit the Madonna and Jesus, with two angels to the left. The Latin text records her name and the year of her death. We should not be surprised if the figures look slightly Chinese; the Chinese artist who composed the scene drew the four characters of his seal just to the left of the second and third lines of the Latin text.

Some of the expressions Polo uses are Persian, suggesting his informants could have been from Iran. Failure to visit China would not have prevented Polo from writing. His contemporary Pegolotti wrote a dry book that gave price data from China, yet its author had never journeyed there. In an age when so few Europeans had been to China, one could easily write about it on the basis of others' reports.

In fact, the success of Marco Polo's account may have encouraged other authors to write their own "Marco Polo" texts in which they recorded hearsay about places beyond Europe. The survival of over one hundred forty manuscripts in a host of different languages—Court French, Latin, German, Spanish, Portuguese, Irish, English, the Spanish dialects of Aragonese and Catalan, the Italian dialects of Venetian and Tuscan, and a mixture of French and Italian—suggests that a new type of travel account gained popularity in the centuries after Polo. Different kings commissioned their own "Marco Polos," and different authors borrowed liberally from other manuscript versions. The translations we use today give the misleading impression that there was one definitive manuscript, rather than many variants.

Although Polo alleges he helped the Mongols in their conquest of China, or Cathay, his account gives little sense of how hard the Mongols had to struggle to take south China.

THE MONGOL CONQUEST OF SOUTH CHINA

The watery terrain of south China proved a formidable obstacle to the Mongols' fast-moving forces, accustomed as they were to the steppe. After the final defeat of the Jurchen armies and the fall of their capital in 1234, the Mongol armies began a sustained attack against south China. It would take forty years for the Mongols to defeat the last of the Southern Song armies. The ferocious armies and swift cavalry of the Mongols faced the much larger army and navy of the Chinese. Cut off from supplies of fresh horses, the Chinese never managed to adapt to the horse warfare of the Mongols, while the Mongols, incongruous as it seems for a nomadic people, managed to organize a navy capable of defeating the Chinese in less than decade.

The Chinese never succeeded in fielding a powerful cavalry. The nomadic peoples of the north—whether Khitan, Jurchen, or Mongol—had the edge over the sedentary Chinese, who did not grow up on horseback. When fighting the Khitan and the Jurchen forces, the Chinese could buy strong horses from other tribes, but as more and more of the north fell and trade routes were blocked, they could no longer obtain good horses. The horses bred in south China never grew as tall as their strong par-

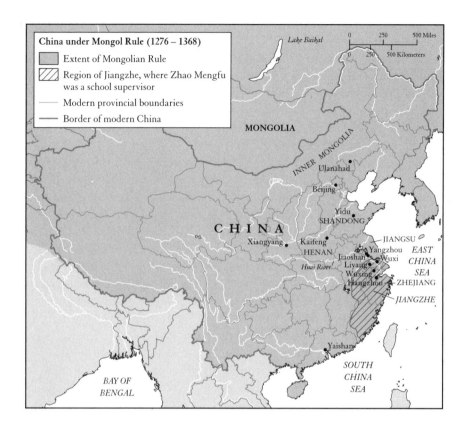

China under Mongol Rule (1276 – 1368)

- Extent of Mongolian Rule
- Region of Jiangzhe, where Zhao Mengfu was a school supervisor
- Modern provincial boundaries
- Border of modern China

ents, possibly because the south did not offer the necessary grasslands. Horses fed on grass carried to their stables could never outrun horses who foraged for their own food.

By the thirteenth century the Mongols controlled most of the supply routes, limiting the Song to purchases of only ten thousand horses a year. The horses they managed to buy were short, sickly, sometimes as small as large dogs, and woefully unfit for fighting the Mongol horses. As a result, the Chinese cavalry suffered a chronic shortage of horses. Usually supplied with one horse per rider, Chinese soldiers fought an army that gave its soldiers three horses per soldier as a matter of course. When the supply of horses dwindled, as it did frequently, Chinese soldiers sometimes had to share one horse between two men. Among the Mongols, one man could have as many as five mounts for himself.

If battle on horseback was unfamiliar to the Chinese, naval warfare was even more unfamiliar to the Mongols. Originally the Mongols had used inflated animal skins, not ships, to cross rivers. But, just as they had quickly adapted to warfare using iron stirrups, iron arrow tips, gunpowder, and catapults, after 1270 they built themselves a navy to rival that of the Chinese. They staffed their fleet with non-Mongols and appointed a Tangut and a northern Chinese to lead it.

The Chinese themselves had little experience of ships, and the Chinese navy regularly committed strategic errors in battles with the Mongols. Naval commanders deployed heavy oceangoing vessels on the inland waterways even though these ships could not move rapidly. As the Mongols took more territory, Chinese commanders tried to stem defections of their sailors to the enemy by staffing their ships with infantry incapable of sailing the ships. In a battle at Jiaoshan in 1273, Jiangsu, on the Yangzi River, the Mongols used their cavalry in support of the navy. Mounted horsemen rode down the coast and barraged the Chinese ships with arrows at the same time the Mongol ships attacked. Because the Chinese commanders, still fearful that their troops would flee, had moored all their fighting ships with anchors and chains, their ships could not dodge the onslaught. When one of the ships caught fire, the wind spread the fire from one ship to the next, and thousands of Chinese died, trapped as they were on the immovable boats.

In the final battle of the war between the Chinese and the Mongols, the remnants of the Chinese navy, some thousand ships, formed a single line of boats stretching out into the harbor at Yaishan, just south of Guangzhou. The last Song emperor, a boy of nine, and his mother boarded one of the ships. With their ships outnumbering those of the Mongols three to one, the Chinese anticipated victory and mistakenly believed the Mongols would attack quickly. Instead the Mongol navy adopted the siege warfare strategy that had served it so well on land. After cutting off the navy's supply routes and waiting two weeks so that the Chinese fell short of both food and water, the Mongols attacked on a rainy, foggy morning. Sources report that one hundred thousand Chinese died in the battle, many after committing suicide. Only one hundred Chinese surrendered at the end of the battle; the rest were dead. The Song emperor and his mother perished in the carnage, but a rumor persisted that somehow the two had managed to escape.

Although vastly outnumbered by the Chinese, the Mongols had proven themselves more skillful horsemen and better innovators. They had won the prize of south China, but they did not reckon with the difficulties of ruling a sedentary civilization, far different from their own tribal society.

Governing China

An apocryphal tale holds that after conquering north China the Mongols decided to kill all its inhabitants so they could use the land as pasture for their horses. They changed their minds when the Khitan statesman Yelü Chucai (1189–1243) argued that the Mongols would do better to let the

Chinese live and tax them annually. This story, though fictitious, illuminates the predicament of the Mongols. The tribesmen knew how to sack cities, collect plunder, and move on, yet they had no experience governing conquered territory. With China in their thrall, they had to develop a new strategy. Distrustful of the Chinese, the Mongols preferred to deal with the Turkic peoples of Central Asia—the Khitans, the Tanguts, and the Uighurs among others—who could speak both Mongolian and Chinese. They called these people the people of various categories, or *semu* people. The statesman Yelü, himself a Khitan, was descended from the founder of the Liao dynasty, Abaoji. Yelü also served as the intermediary between Chinggis and the leader of the Complete Self-Realization school of Daoism (see previous chapter) to whom Chinggis granted special tax-exempt privileges.

Chinggis's son, Ögödei, placed Yelü in charge of taxation in 1229, and Yelü drew on his experiences as a Jin-dynasty official to structure the Mongols' financial policies in north China. He drew up regional administrations based on the Jurchen circuits, and he established bureaus in each circuit to collect taxes. Instead of the irregular levies the Mongols collected, he established fixed rates for a land tax and for a poll tax, with people in cities and the countryside paying different rates. Yelü also tried to implement other traditional measures, like a census and the civil service examinations, but the Mongol administration lacked the manpower to enforce these measures. After 1235, when Yelü lost power at court, these attempts to govern in the Chinese style stopped.

There are different founding dates for the beginning of the Mongol dynasty. The earliest is 1260, when all the succession disputes had ended and Khubilai Khan took control of Mongolia and north China. Ten years later, in 1271, he founded a dynasty with the Chinese name Yuan, which means "origin." The last Song emperor died in 1279. The best date for the start of Yuan-dynasty rule is 1276, when the Mongol conquest of the south was completed.

Only after the conquest of the south did the Mongols once again tackle the problem of governing China. Yelü had already identified the major differences between the Chinese and Mongolian administrations: taxation and government recruitment. Because the Mongols usually collected booty once a city had fallen, the Chinese practice of annual, low-level taxes was new to them. So too was the Chinese practice of recruitment through the civil service examinations. The Mongols tended to recruit on the basis of heredity, with a son taking over his father's position; as an illiterate people, they had never used examinations.

At the time of the conquest, Mongolian had no script, and the language could not be written down. Chinggis Khan, his son Ögödei, and

'Phags-pa	Uighur	Mongolian

MONGOLIAN WRITING

When the Mongols conquered Eurasia they were illiterate, but, under Chinggis Khan, they soon developed their own script, which they borrowed from the Uighurs. In 1269 the Tibetan monk 'Phags-pa, who advised the Mongol emperor Khubilai Khan, designed a script whose use was made compulsory in all government documents. In the long run the 'Phags-pa script proved too cumbersome, and the Uighur script is still used today in Inner Mongolia. (Cyrillic displaced the Uighur script in Outer Mongolia.) Unlike the Mongols, whose different scripts were all phonetic, the Chinese subjects of the Mongols continued to use characters

his grandson Möngke could neither read nor write. Chinggis ordered the Mongols to adopt a new alphabet from the Uighur script (which, like our alphabet, was derived from the Aramaic). Even though the Uighur script did not represent all the sounds of Mongolian, and it omitted vowels, it gained popularity because it was so easy to write. Unlike Chinese, written Mongolian had the same word order and grammar as the spoken language.

Social Change

Khubilai and his advisors followed the Liao precedent of dual government in that they envisioned separate societies—non-Chinese and Chinese—under Mongol rule. The Mongols divided the population of China into four groups: themselves, the people of various categories, the northern Chinese, and the southern Chinese. They attempted to freeze local society by classing the population into the four racial groups and then assigning individual households to different job categories. Most people were classed as agricultural workers, but some were assigned more specific tasks preparing goods for the emperor. Suspicious of the Chinese, they forbade intermarriage between Mongols and Chinese, although much mixing actually occurred. Numbering only two million during the course of the Yuan dynasty, the Mongols lacked enough men to serve as officials, so they appointed men of the various categories to office. They installed a non-Chinese and a Chinese in all high offices, with the two men to govern in tandem.

The Mongols left many sections of the Chinese bureaucracy in place, while also establishing new branches to deal with specifically Mongolian problems, such as the Section for Retrieving Lost Animals. The Mongols quickly succeeded in establishing themselves as legitimate rulers, but they had difficulty bringing order to China. Bandit gangs eluded the authorities for much of the dynasty and eventually swelled to such large numbers that they were able to overthrow the Mongols.

The Mongols' decision to suspend the civil service examinations had the greatest effect on educated Chinese families, who had devoted themselves to placing at least one son in the bureaucracy. In one stroke, the Mongols cut off the primary route to office. Chinese families adjusted quickly. Some accepted classification into the category of Confucian households whose job it was to teach in local schools, although teaching did not offer the same rewards it had in former periods when so many boys studied for the civil service examinations. Others obtained positions as clerks in the government offices where they could serve two thirty-month terms as county clerks, and then three successive terms as a clerk to a subprefect. Under the Mongol regulations, the same man could serve twelve and a half years and continue to be a clerk. The long service required and the low salary one could earn, however, discouraged many from this route.

One career that gained new prestige under the Mongols was medicine. Remember that during the Southern Song, Yuan Cai (see chapter 7, p. 294) had advised families that, if their sons could not become scholars, they could become doctors, religious specialists, farmers, merchants, or craftsmen. Under the Mongols, the sons of many officials turned to the study of medicine instead. Medicine made it possible to earn money, and, because one could choose one's patients, one could avoid treating the socially undesirable. If very successful, one could even be appointed a court physician. The highly textual study of medicine resembled the study of Chinese classics in that both fields remained removed from practice. Once one had passed the civil service examinations, the classics offered little specific guidance in governing, and most officials learned on the basis of doing. So too with medicine. Doctors studied highly theoretical medical treatises, but they learned how to treat patients only once they began to practice.

Because the sons of many prominent families joined the medical profession, the social standing of doctors rose under the Mongols. A temple inscription records:

> The shallow knowledge that is the fashion classifies medicine as a mere technical skill. This shows unawareness that the power of a doctor in aiding the world may be a match for that of Heaven and Earth. Why? Heaven and Earth give life to men but cannot make men free of sickness. When men are sick they beseech Heaven; Heaven is unmoved. They call upon Earth; Earth is silent. If their sickness does not abate, they must turn back and seek healing from a doctor. With a doctor—if one finds the right man for it—agonizing pain will cease, the emaciated will grow stout and strong, and those on the verge of death will not die. Is it wrong to say that the physician's power is a match for that of Heaven and Earth?[6]

Even this author, with his favorable view of doctors, conceded that one had to find the right physician before one could be cured.

Others took a more critical stance of medical practitioners. One Yuan-dynasty play pokes fun at two doctors who pretend to have mastered the Confucian classics. As the two doctors engage in a mock battle over who should enter the sickroom first, Doctor Muddly Head says to Doctor Finishemoff:

> Surely you must have heard that our Holy Sage, Confucius, says: "He who walks slowly behind his seniors is said to have due younger-brotherly reverence, while he who rushes on ahead of his seniors is said to be irreverent. . . . Now you, elder brother, are my senior, and I'm your younger brother. . . . Verily the ancient Kings of Virtue were perfectly correct in their rules of etiquette! And should I go in before you, I would be an ass, a swine, a thorough hypocrite![7]

To someone who did not know the classics, this absurd citation might sound as if it were indeed from *The Analects*. The disjuncture between the pseudopoliteness and the obscenities of the last line would surely make the unschooled laugh. But an educated person, who would recognize the quotation as spurious, would have found this passage even funnier. This play mocks the pretenses of doctors who put on all the airs of scholars but had none of their erudition.

Linguistic Change under the Mongols

Like English in the years after the Norman invasion, the Chinese language absorbed many loanwords during the century of Mongol rule. The needs of government prompted many linguistic changes. Since the Mongols found the written colloquial much easier to understand than literary Chinese, they insisted on its use in government documents. So all decisions of state were recorded in vernacular Chinese. Of course, the written vernacular predated Mongol rule. Popular narratives from Dunhuang, such as Turnip's trip to visit his mother in hell, and the new plays of the Jin dynasty, such as the updated story of Oriole and Zhang, used the vernacular, but they were exceptions, written in times when almost all literary writing was still done in the classical language.

The great playwrights of the Yuan, who drafted documents in the vernacular while at work, used the same language to write their plays. The influx of new words and new grammar gave written Chinese a vigor that the traditional language lacked, filled as it was with allusions and classical references. The Mongols were not alone in finding the vernacular easier to learn. Even Chinese found it easier. If one wanted to write a letter, one could do so in the vernacular. One did not have to have a classical education to write a letter or read one of the new plays. The publishing industry continued to grow in the Yuan, producing large numbers of encyclopedias aimed at a popular audience. These books reprinted forms so that the readers could fill in the blanks to produce contracts for the sale of land, a boat, a horse, a cow, and for the hiring of a servant. They also include model forms to be used when suing someone for breach of payment. On the occasion of a child's engagement, they give hundreds of sample letters, from which the reader could select according to the occupations of the engaged couple's parents.

These cheaply printed encyclopedias, with crudely drawn characters on rough paper, achieved a wide circulation, as the high number of reprints testifies. They also influenced the visual vocabulary of those living under the Mongols. A much simpler portrait than that of the deceased couple from Baisha (chapter 7), the portrait of the deceased from a Yuan-dynasty tomb at Yuanbao Shan (in Ulanahad, Inner Mongolia) shows a Mongolian man and his wife. The man wears the characteristic blue robe and boots of the Mongols, while his wife has a Chinese hairstyle and facial features. If this portrait is accurate, she must have been

Chinese, but it is also possible that she was a Mongolian woman whose descendants wanted her to be painted as if she were Chinese.

At the same time that more and more people were reading the encyclopedias, the continued suspension of the civil service examinations discouraged the populace from studying the classical language. If a classical education did not bring a boy closer to office, many people reasoned, why study the classics at all? One drama, *Grandee's Son Takes the Wrong Career*, illustrates the appeal of the vernacular, even to those with a classical education. The play, set in Kaifeng under Jin-dynasty rule, treats a traditional theme: the scholar who falls in love with an uneducated girl. The son of a Jurchen official, he studies only halfheartedly, and his girlfriend, Golden Notice, chides him, surprisingly, for studying too hard! When she says, "You've been swotting/those what-do-you-call-them classics in your study all these days," he replies, "Let's not talk about such things, they just don't matter,/just hand me over the latest popular plays."[8]

PORTRAIT OF A MONGOL COUPLE

After conquering China, some Mongols adopted Chinese ways and were buried in Chinese-style tombs. The gentleman shown here wears a typical Mongolian outfit of a blue robe and boots, while his wife wears Chinese clothes and hairstyle, making it difficult to determine whether she was Chinese, Mongolian, or of mixed heritage.

The two then turn to their favorite task, learning speeches from the plays. Golden Notice can read the vernacular well enough to understand the promptbooks of twenty-nine plays she proceeds to list.

This play twists an old theme in several new directions. Most surprisingly, the play ends with the scholar abandoning his studies and joining his in-laws as itinerant performers. His father-in-law reacts to his proposal grudgingly, saying, "The only man I want for my son-in-law is a writer of play books." Unlike any earlier fathers in Chinese literature, he has no use for a scholarly son-in-law. Only after the boy has demonstrated his knowledge of the plays, his ability to draft new speeches, and his willingness to carry a drum and their costumes does Golden Notice's father consent to the union.

One man is universally acknowledged as the greatest Yuan playwright of them all, Guan Hanqing (ca. 1220–ca. 1307), whose masterpiece, *Dou E's Revenge*, tells the story of a young girl whose mother is dead and whose father is a scholar. When her father leaves to sit for the civil service examinations, a woman adopts the girl on the condition that she will marry her son when she grows up. Dou E matures into an extremely moral and blameless woman, but, after being framed for poisoning her father-in-law, she is wrongfully executed. Her father later returns to his hometown as an official whose job it is to review all capital cases. As he is conducting his inquiry, his daughter's spirit appears in court before all those who are present and, to their surprise, identifies the real murderer.

Plays about justice delayed proved enormously popular in the Yuan dynasty and spawned many imitators. One judge in particular, Judge Bao, who appears in seven extant plays, was based on an actual historical personage, who wrote about the iron industry (see chapter 7, p. 265). As the prefect of Kaifeng, he won a reputation for fairness and incorruptibility that persists even today. In each play the judge visits the scene of a crime, often committed years earlier, and uses an ingenious stratagem to smoke out the real culprit. In *The Contract*, a scheming aunt plots to deprive her nephew of his rightful inheritance so that her own daughter and her husband can get the money. After she rips up the contract that proves her nephew's claim, she denies the boy is her relative. Judge Bao then spreads a false rumor that the boy has died. If a relative is responsible, he announces, the penalty will be a fine, yet if the murderer is a stranger, he will be executed. Frightened, the evil woman admits she is the boy's aunt, and she exhibits her copy of the destroyed contract to substantiate her statement. The judge triumphantly produces the boy, forcing the woman to hand over his contested inheritance, to the delight of the audience.

Reinstating the Civil Service Examinations

A long period of instability followed Khubilai's death in 1294, even in the absence of war or rebellion. The legacy of tanistry meant the Mongol royal clan had no orderly means of determining the succession. From 1294 to 1333, nine emperors ruled, but only one, Emperor Ayurbarwada (reigned 1313–1320), succeeded in naming his successor. Ayurbarwada's reign offered a brief respite from the infighting, which resumed after his son's death in 1323. The other eight emperors were overthrown, with two killed. All nine emperors encountered severe financial problems. Their tribal traditions meant they were all obliged to distribute gifts among the royal entourage at regular intervals, but the long peace also meant they had no booty to give to their kinsmen. Instead, they printed more paper money, oblivious to the long-term consequences. The developed market economy of the Song continued to expand under Mongol rule. Yet, by the end of the dynasty, the constant printing of inflated money had undercut the populace's faith in paper money, and people reverted to the use of copper and silver for their transactions.

As a child, the emperor Ayurbarwada had studied with Confucian tutors, who instilled in him the love of traditional Chinese learning. One of his first acts on taking office was to reinstate the civil service examinations. The emperor and his advisors debated the curriculum. If they followed the precedent of the Jin dynasty, the examinations would test the candidates' knowledge of the classics as well as their literary talents. But an influential group of scholars argued that the examinations should emphasize only knowledge of the classics, especially the four Confucian texts on which Zhu Xi had written commentaries (see chapter 7, p. 296). They advocated the elimination of the literary essays. These Neo-Confucian scholars prevailed.

In 1315 when the examinations were held, the Mongols and Central Asians sat for a different examination than did the Chinese. The peoples of various categories were required to answer detailed questions on Zhu Xi's editions of *The Four Books: The Great Learning* and *The Mean* (two individual chapters Zhu Xi had taken from *The Book of Rites*) as well as *The Analects* and *Mencius*. They also had to write a five-hundred-character essay on a contemporary issue. Theirs was a much more truncated syllabus than scholars in previous dynasties had been required to master, and it was also a much less demanding examination than that for the Chinese. The Chinese had to write detailed short essays three-hundred-characters long about Zhu's commentaries to *The Four Books*. In addition, they had to select one of the longer classics from among *The Book of Songs,*

The Book of Documents, The Book of Rites, and *The Spring and Autumn Annals,* on which they wrote a five-hundred-character essay. Finally they had to draft a one-thousand-character essay on a modern problem of governance.

Both sets of requirements were much simpler than those Zhu Xi had advocated for the students at his academy in the twelfth century. The narrow curriculum the Mongols had selected in conjunction with their Chinese advisors suited the limited linguistic abilities of the Mongols and the Central Asians, but it restricted the native speakers of Chinese, who spent all their time memorizing a small amount of material. This abbreviated curriculum proved to have an influence no one could have predicted when the first examinations were held, because subsequent dynasties retained it.

Even after the reestablishment of the examinations, most offices continued to be filled by appointments or on the basis of heredity. The Chinese taking the exams faced much more difficult odds than the Mongols and the Central Asians who did so. The regulations specified that half the successful candidates (fifty men) would be Mongols or Central Asian; the remaining fifty would be Chinese. But fifty successful candidates were drawn from a Chinese population of 85 million, and fifty from the Mongol and Central Asian population of some two million. Although the quota specified that one hundred men could succeed in a given year, in practice, fewer men passed, and 1333 marked the first time in which the full one hundred men passed. The list of the one hundred successful candidates from that year survives and includes the requisite fifty Chinese and fifty Mongols and Central Asians. Ninety-two percent of the Chinese, whose average age was thirty-one, had married, versus 74 percent for the others, whose average age was twenty-eight. Fully 58 percent of the non-Chinese had Chinese mothers, and almost 70 percent were married to Chinese women, a statistic that shows how unsuccessful had been the Mongols' attempt to ban intermarriage with the Chinese.[9] Even though much racial mixing occurred under the Mongols, they still retained their strict system of racial preferences, which privileged the Mongols and other minorities over the Chinese.

By 1333 only 2 percent of the officials serving the Mongols, some 550 men, had received their positions after passing the civil service examinations, and by the end of the dynasty only 1,139 degrees had been awarded (of a possible 1,600).[10] A much smaller proportion of officials than during either the Jin or the Song dynasty, this figure shows that most Chinese scholars could not hope to pass the examinations in the Yuan dynasty. Although very few Chinese passed the examinations, many Chinese served in the Mongol administration, often in a lower capacity as a clerk, but sometimes in higher appointed positions.

In 1287, a descendant of the Song ruling family, Zhao Mengfu (1254–1322), accepted a position in the Mongol government, much to the consternation of the Chinese literati around him. Considered the greatest calligrapher of the Yuan dynasty, Zhao painted several pictures depicting the choices of Chinese scholars whether or not to serve the Mongols. He, in concert with other artists, developed a new symbolic vocabulary of painting in order to do so. Their use of visual allusions known to only a few highly educated viewers altered the course of Chinese painting.

ZHAO MENGFU AND THE ART OF HEIGHTENED EXPRESSIVENESS

In 1295, after Khubilai's death, Zhao returned home to Wuxing (Huzhou, Zhejiang), the neighboring county to Hangzhou, where he spent several frustrating years of idleness. In 1300 he accepted office again, this time to serve as the director of Confucian schools in the region of Jiangzhe (modern Jiangsu and Zhejiang provinces), a position he enjoyed. It was at this time that he painted his *Sheep and Goat* scroll, a picture that makes sense only if one understands the allusions it contains.

This handscroll shows two animals, the goat on the right and a sheep on the left, whose contrasting coats illustrate Zhao's deft brushwork. The goat's long hair prompted the artist to use a dry brush that could suggest individual hairs, while he captured the black and white, wooly rounded body of the sheep with a wet brush. Commentators have speculated about the relationship between the two animals, with some even suggesting the two are about to fight, but Zhao wrote these lines to the left of the animals:

> I have painted horses but have not tried sheep or goats. Since Zhongxin asked me for a painting, I have playfully painted these from life. Although the painting cannot approach those of the ancient masters, it seems to have somewhat captured their spirit consonance.[11]

Zhao's approach is lighthearted and animated by real pleasure in his ability to capture the essential quality of the animals. The meaning of the term *spirit consonance* is difficult to convey in English, but it refers to the overall feeling of the great works of the past. As he penned these words, Zhao knew that he had painted a masterpiece.

Zhao expected his viewers to be sufficiently knowledgeable to recognize the allusions in his painting. As he said around the time he painted the *Sheep and Goat* scroll, "My own paintings seem to be quite simply and carelessly done, but connoisseurs will realize that they are close to the past and so may be considered superior. This is said for the cognoscenti, not for ignoramuses."[12] The colophons written by later owners and viewers explain that the goat and the sheep symbolized two Han-dynasty generals, Su Wu and Li Ling (see chapter 3, p. 128). One refused to serve the Xiongnu and spent his days as a shepherd; the other, represented by the goat, chose to work with the non-Chinese conquerors. The traditional Chinese view, of course, was that the shepherd was more noble than the collaborator, but Zhao's painting does not support such a reading. If anything, the self-satisfied sheep looks less imposing than the more lively goat. Instead, let us interpret both animals as representing the two sides of Zhao's own self: the sheep when he was idle and the goat when he was more happily employed, even if it happened to be by the Mongols.

China's First Recognized Woman Artist

Zhao's wife, Guan Daosheng (1262–1319), is the one female name regularly appearing on lists of great Chinese painters. The first woman to have left behind a significant body of work, Guan painted Buddhist figures, flowers, landscapes, and, most characteristically, bamboos. She was born into a prominent local family with no sons, which may explain her unusual upbringing. In 1289, Zhao Mengfu married Guan. After her death, Zhao wrote an epitaph for her that explains the circumstances of their marriage:

> Her father was Guan Shen. . . . Mr. Guan was known for his exceptional talent and unconventionality, and his chivalrous conduct was the talk of the neighborhood. My wife since birth had intelligence that surpassed others. Her father cherished her, definitely wanting to get a fine son-in-law. Her father and I were from the same district, and because he also had a high regard for me, I knew someday that she would become my wife.[13]

At the time of their marriage, he was thirty-five and she twenty-seven, old by the standards of the day, though Zhao does not explain why she married so late. Zhao had one son and four daughters from his first marriage, and although Guan gave birth to two sons and two daughters, she found time to paint, quite possibly with her husband as her instructor.

Also in the epitaph Zhao records that he entrusted all household affairs to Guan. In an unusually detailed letter she wrote to her servants, we can see her commanding role in household management. She instructs her brother to collect a loan of one hundred ingots from a monastery and

A CHINESE PAINTING BEFORE AND AFTER

Much Chinese art looks cluttered with seals because Chinese owners and connoisseurs felt that a crucial aspect of appreciating a painting was writing one's response to the image in a colophon or impressing one's seal on the painting.
Here we see Zhao Mengfu's painting of a sheep and a goat as he painted it (top).

Here we see Zhao Mengfu's painting as it looks today (bottom)—littered with no less than thirteen seals of the Qianlong emperor (reigned 1736–1796). He even felt sufficient authority to put his seals in the eloquent white space between the goat and the sheep that Zhao had left empty.

then use the money to buy land. She then specifies how much cash, oil, and rice should be given to the monastery to commemorate the death of the abbot. She closes with detailed instructions about the upkeep of the family's fields:

As for the dike along the field at Su bay, have Xu Shouer repair it well. Do not neglect the mulberry trees, and be sure to water them well. You should also look after those on the mountain. Have Elder Brother Zipei [another servant] direct other men to graft more chestnut trees and plant more pepper plants.[14]

Like other women from well-off families, she played an important role in conducting family affairs.

Guan and Zhao's marriage was a happy one, although at one point Zhao wanted to take a concubine. Guan voiced her protest in a moving poem entitled "Married Love":

> You and I
> Have so much love,
> That it
> Burns like a fire,
> In which we bake a lump of clay
> Molded into a figure of you
> And a figure of me.
> Then we take both of them,
> And break them into pieces,
> And mix the pieces with water,
> And mold again a figure of you,
> And a figure of me.
> I am in your clay.

BAMBOOS BY THE WOMAN PAINTER GUAN DAOSHENG
The wife of Zhao Mengfu, Guan Daosheng was China's most famous woman painter, who specialized in painting bamboo. Like many well-bred women of her day, she also managed the family estate, right down to instructing servants which crops to plant and which dikes to repair. Madame Guan also raised nine children, four of them her own.

You are in my clay.
In life we share a single quilt.
In death we will share one coffin.[15]

Zhao did not take the concubine.

Guan's surviving paintings all date to the years of her marriage. The family moved back and forth between the Hangzhou area and the capital, Beijing, where she was able to see paintings from the Tang and Song dynasties. There, the emperor Ayurbarwada thought her calligraphy so fine that he commissioned her to write *The Thousand Character Classic*, a book in which no character is repeated. After mounting her rendition, he sent it to the imperial library so that future generations would "know that our dynasty had a woman who excelled in calligraphy," as her husband recorded in his epitaph for her. In 1319 Guan fell ill and asked permission to return to the south. She died before she was able to reach home.

For all her success, the prejudices of her day constrained Guan. In one colophon she admitted to painting with some trepidation: "To play with brush and ink is a masculine sort of thing to do, yet I made this painting. Wouldn't someone say that I have transgressed propriety? How despicable, how despicable."[16] Her comments must have been in tongue-in-cheek for she went on to paint frequently. Given her husband's leading role in the movement toward expressiveness, we can assume she too hoped to capture the bamboo's essence, and so to express her own personality. Her bamboos are never monotonous, for each branch has its own distinct identity, rendered with her mastery of the brush. Guan also broke with tradition to paint bamboos in red, although none of these paintings survive.

We have seen that the highest praise given to Li Qingzhao was to say that her poems were not like a woman's. So too with the paintings of Guan Daosheng. Her success as an artist, like Li Qingzhao's as a writer, reflects her prominent social standing and the unusual encouragement of her male kin.

Ni Zan's Non-Representative Art

Ni Zan (1301–1374), the son of a wealthy land-owning family, was an artist whose work continued the tradition of Zhao Mengfu and Guan Daosheng. After Ni Zan inherited the family fortune, he lavished great sums on books, paintings, and calligraphy. An anonymous portrait done at the time reveals much about Ni Zan's unusual personality. His obsession with cleanliness spawned many later stories, perhaps the most amus-

NI ZAN: AN EXPONENT OF EXPRESSIVE ART

One of the great turning points in the history of Chinese art took place under Mongol rule, when artists began to paint subjects that stood for more than simply the object depicted. Ni Zan, shown here sitting on a platform in front of a painting in his signature style, repeatedly used the same three elements—trees, rocks, and a blank expanse of water—to paint landscapes that expressed human relationships. In many of his pictures bamboo trees possessed the qualities of human individuals.

Famous for his obsession with cleanliness, Ni Zan is depicted with a female servant holding a water bottle and a cloth, while the male servant holds a duster. The poem on the painting, written by a friend, explicitly refers to Ni Zan's obsession:

> Waving a jade-handled duster, he is immaculately neat and supremely elegant.
> If an uncouth person washes without using a towel, he is not allowed to speak of cleanliness.

(Wen C. Fong et al., *Images of the Mind: Selections from the Edward L. Elliott Family and John B. Elliott Collections of Chinese Calligraphy and Painting at the Art Museum, Princeton University,* Princeton, 1984, figure 106.)

ing about a night he spent with a famous courtesan. Wary that she was not clean, Ni Zan asked her to wash herself over and over, and when the dawn came, he sent her home without having ever gone to bed.

Throughout his life, Ni painted endless variations on the same theme of a landscape with trees, rocks, and a blank expanse that represented water, the topic of the painting shown in his portrait. He continued the move toward expressiveness that marked all Chinese painting under the Mongols. Zhao Mengfu painted himself as a sheep and a goat, and his wife Guan Daosheng depicted herself as bamboo, while Ni Zan portrayed himself and others as trees. In 1353, he painted bamboos to commemorate leaving the house of a friend with whom he had spent four months. *Twin Trees by the South Bank* shows two very different trees. The taller one bears many twigs, while the shorter one, at a different angle, sprouts new buds. The trees are so expressive that they do not really resemble trees, an effect Ni Zan seems to have sought deliberately. He wrote on one painting of bamboo:

> Now, my bamboo painting is nothing more than the writing down of the untrammeled feelings in my breast. Why should I trouble myself over whether it resembles something or doesn't, whether the leaves are thick or sparse, the branches slanting or straight?[17]

This willingness to depart from natural models in order to convey one's feelings marked the culmination of the trend that began at the time of the Mongol conquest. Several centuries later a writer recorded this story about Ni Zan:

> One night by candlelight he drew a bamboo-and-tree picture and was very proud of himself. When he got up the next morning and looked at it, it had no resemblance to bamboo at all. He laughed and said: "Ah, but a *total* lack of resemblance is not an easy thing to achieve."

Whether true or not, this story contains a valuable insight. Ni Zan commands an important position in Chinese painting history because of his willingness to embrace nonrepresentative art, centuries ahead of his time.

THE FALL OF THE MONGOLS

The problems causing the fall of the dynasty surfaced most clearly in the years after 1332, when powerful figures at court succeeded in naming the thirteen-year-old boy, Toghōn Temür (reigned 1332–1368), to be emperor. The Mongol chancellor then set about restoring Mongol policies from the early years of their conquest. One such effort was to reduce imperial expenditures to the level occurring during Khubilai's reign, a worthy goal during a period of raging inflation and rampant printing of money. But this sound economic initiative was paired with an invidious ethnic policy. The chancellor wanted to keep the Chinese and Mongol peoples completely separate, as if he did not realize just how much cultural mixing and intermarriage had taken place since the years of Khubilai's reign.

As different factions at court debated the pros and cons of cultural mixing, a series of disasters led to the fall of the dynasty. In 1331 an epidemic in the province of Hubei wiped out nine-tenths of the population.

Two years later, in both the Yangzi and Huai River valleys, some 400,000 people perished. The death toll in China under the Mongol dynasty was enormous. Scholars estimate the combined population of north and south China to have been between 110 million and 120 million at the time of the Mongol invasion. In 1290 the Mongol census takers counted fewer than 59 million people. Most scholars view this census with skepticism, thinking many people went uncounted, but a census done in 1393 registered 10.7 million households, or some 60 million people. A recent estimate suggests 85 million would be more accurate.[18] Scholars have traditionally thought the Mongol invasions caused the drop.

More recently, William H. McNeill has offered another explanation for the massive losses.[19] The shift of trade routes away from the desert silk routes to the grasslands facilitated the spread of the plague bacillus. As the Mongols traveled overland, infected fleas rode in the Mongols' grain bags attached to their saddles. The plague, which originated in the lowlands near the Himalayas, arrived in China in 1331 and simmered there until the 1350s when more epidemics ravaged the nation. In some areas, two-thirds of the people were reported to have died. Archeologists who have done autopsies on human skeletons concluded that the plague reached Central Asia sometime in 1338 or 1339, with the plague bacillus traveling along the trade routes until the plague-infested rats arrived in the Crimea in 1346. The Mongols introduced China to an unfamiliar disease pool, with much the same deadly effects as occurred with the arrival of the Europeans in the New World.

The massive deaths resulting from the plague led to drastic revenue shortfalls for the central government. A coup in 1340 brought a new chancellor. In 1344 the Yellow River flooded, yet the chancellor waited seven years before summoning one hundred seventy thousand men to rechannel the river. The displaced and hungry men who worked on this project provided the perfect breeding ground for rebellion, and the chancellor's decision to pay them with worthless paper money only heightened their anger.

The first uprising, which occurred in 1351, claimed that the age of the Mongols had ended and that the Buddha of the future, the Maitreya Buddha, had come to rule on the earth. Many of the rebels subscribed to a story predicting that a one-eyed man would lead them, and the leaders buried a stone figurine of a one-eyed man at the scene of the river works. Although government forces arrested their leader, the rebels succeeded in taking the entire Huai River valley.

The Mongols managed to contain this particular rebellion by 1354, but rebels continued to fight for territory all over China. Great disorder marked the last years of the Mongol reign. No place was safe from the rebels. The disorder prompted Ni Zan to live on board his houseboat in the hope of avoiding the rebels. Zhu Yuanzhang (1328–1398) was a peasant who joined the rebels in the 1350s. With each victory against government troops, he rose up in the ranks of the rebels' army and emerged the triumphant founder of a new dynasty in 1368. The era of Mongol rule had come to a close.

The Legacy of the Mongols

Traditional stereotypes about Chinese cultural superiority have combined with modern Chinese nationalism to obscure the contributions the Mongols made to Chinese history. Some of their contributions resulted from deliberate policy decisions. The Mongols redrew the map of China along the same lines as the Jin dynasty had, and the provinces they established underlie the provincial borders of modern China. The examination curriculum, which Emperor Ayurbarwada selected in 1315, remained the basis of the civil service examinations throughout the Yuan dynasty and the succeeding Ming and Qing dynasties. A simplified curriculum originally designed for nonnative speakers shaped the education of the literati for six centuries. Until 1905 all candidates for the civil service examinations memorized Zhu Xi's commentaries on *The Four Books*.

Some of the most important changes occurring under Mongol rule occurred as the by-products of other decisions. When the Mongols suspended the civil service examinations, they had no idea that they were creating the beginnings of gentry society. The suspension of the examinations before 1315 and the minimal recruiting done afterward prompted many scholarly families to devote themselves to their country estates.

Some of the Mongols' policies had long-term deleterious effects. The Mongols' tradition of generosity to fellow tribesmen created a chronic deficit at the center, and they issued far much more paper money with insufficient backing than had their predecessors. Because paper money, one of China's great inventions, fell out of use in the years following the end of the Yuan dynasty, China headed into a period of great economic change with a crippled monetary system.

CHRONOLOGY

1368–1644	MING DYNASTY
1368–1398	*Reign of Ming founder, Ming Taizu*
1370	*First ban on private sea voyages*
1387	*Registration of land throughout the empire*
1400–1700	*Second commercial revolution*
after 1400	*Korean-Chinese textbook,* Old China Hand, *circulates*
1403–1424	*Reign of Yongle Emperor*
1405–1433	*Zheng He voyages*
1420	*Capital moved from Nanjing to Beijing*
1449	*Mongols take Ming emperor prisoner at Tumu*
1450	*Paper money falls into disuse*
1472–1529	*Lifetime of Wang Yangming, advocate of the unity of thought and action*
1560s–1570s	*Portuguese gain a foothold at Macao*
1567	*Lifting of ban on trade with foreign countries—except with Japan*
1571	*Peace reached with the Mongols*
1583–1610	*Matteo Ricci, Jesuit missionary, in China*
1500–1600	*Single Whip reform of taxes*
1619	*First military victory of Manchus against Ming dynasty*
1644	*Manchu conquest of China*

CONTINUING THE WAR AGAINST THE MONGOLS: THE MING DYNASTY

(1368–1644)

When Zhu Yuanzhang (1328–1398) founded the Ming dynasty in 1368, a native Chinese dynasty unified the empire for the first time in two hundred fifty years. Although his troops had forced the Mongols back to Mongolia, the Chinese never succeeded in vanquishing them. After 1368, the Mongols divided into several confederations, one of which ruled in the name of the Yuan dynasty. The Chinese lived in constant fear that the Mongols would regroup under the leadership of a second Chinggis Khan and reconquer China. Although they never managed to do so, different confederations posed a real, if intermittent, threat to the Chinese throughout the course of the Ming. One such confederation, the Oirats, kidnapped the emperor in 1449, and a century later, the troops of the Altan Khan (1543–1583), himself a descendant of Chinggis Khan, reached the walls of Beijing.

Fixated on the Mongols, the Ming court built a series of fortifications that taken together constitute the Great Wall as we know it today. They periodically forbade trade with other countries (although not successfully). These defensive measures did not tame the Mongols, and the pursuit of such a close-minded, narrow foreign policy—so different from the approach of earlier dynasties—blinded the court to another threat. Obsessed with the Mongols, the Ming ignored the Manchus in the northeast until 1619, when the Manchus had their first major victory. They went on to invade China in 1644 and establish the Qing dynasty (1644–1911).

The Ming founder did not allow for even the kinds of changes in population, economy, or agriculture that had occurred in previous dynasties. Accepting his vision of an unchanging economy, his successors froze land

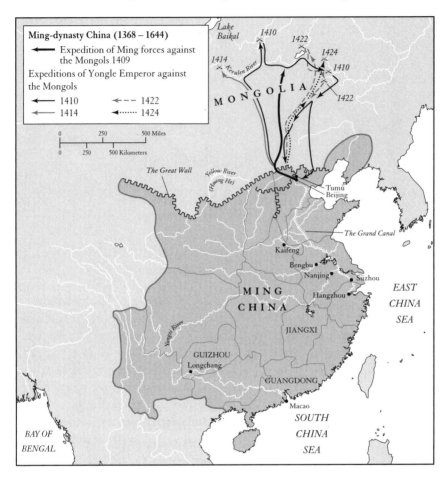

taxes at their late-fourteenth-century levels, even though the revenue needs of the state continued to increase.

These conservative measures made it difficult for the Chinese government to respond to the global events of 1492 and their momentous consequences. To be sure, contact between Europe and the New World did not affect China immediately. It took half a century for New World silver to reach China, but when it did, it poured into the veins of the Chinese market system, which had already absorbed much Japanese silver. By 1600 many cultivators were paying their land taxes in silver. New crops came too, with dramatic effects on Chinese cuisine and far-reaching consequences for the Chinese population, which grew exponentially on a diet supplemented by corn and potatoes.

The first European missionaries to reach China, the Jesuits, had the extraordinary experience of going where few Europeans had been be-fore. In their previous contacts with nomadic peoples, the Chinese had always enjoyed a superior position, priding themselves on their literate civilization. Their only rival had been the Indians, who saw themselves at the center of the Buddhist civilization. The Europeans posed a differ-ent type of threat, the enormity of which dawned on the Chinese slowly.

THE MING FOUNDER AND THE SYSTEM HE DESIGNED

Zhu Yuanzhang was the only founder of a Chinese dynasty born to a genuinely poor peasant family. The sole child of six siblings who was not given up for adoption or married off at a young age, he witnessed his parents' death during an epidemic when he was only sixteen. His trau-matic childhood convinced him of the importance of agriculture and shaped his fundamentally conservative vision of government. The main obligation of the state was to protect farmers, he felt, who would in turn provide all its revenues. The Ming founder designed a fiscal system for a frozen, unchanging agrarian economy—an economy far different from the commercialized market system existing at the time. Each man was to register his occupation with the authorities, who fully expected his de-scendants to perform the identical task in perpetuity. In line with his agrarian policies, the Ming founder in 1370 and again in 1398 forbade the Chinese to embark on private voyages overseas. The Ming initially enjoyed great success in registering both population and land, and the central government was able to collect sufficient land taxes for its needs.

The dependence of the Ming on agrarian revenue marked an impor-tant reversal. Since the years after 755, inadequate land revenue had forced the central government to develop commercial taxes and monop-olies. The success of the Ming in registering people and land allowed them to ignore all nonagrarian sources of revenue. Paper money, which the Chinese had been the first in the world to invent, and which the Mon-gols had printed in such large quantities that it lost its value, completely fell from use by 1450, leaving copper coins the main medium of exchange for small transactions and precious metals for large ones. Once Zhu Yuanzhang's forces drove the Mongols back to the steppe, Zhu had to decide which earlier dynasty his would emulate.

Fiercely proud that he was Chinese and intensely aware that the de-feated dynasty was foreign, Zhu looked to the great native dynasties of the past as models. Those with short reigns, like the Qin and the Sui, he dismissed quickly, because he hoped—correctly as it turned out—that his descendants would rule for centuries. The Han, rulers for four centuries, had become the dynastic symbol of the Chinese. Like Zhu, the Han founder Liu Bang was born into a low-ranking family, but he had attained a low official position under the Qin, a distinction which the founder of the Ming had not. The Tang dynasty posed the next obvious candidate for emulation, for it had presided over an age of great expansion and lasting artistic accomplishments. The Song had also ruled for centuries, but their defeat first at the hands of the Jurchen and then the Mongols tainted them, and the Ming founder saw nothing to emulate in their weak military. Opting for the example of the Tang, Zhu Yuanzhang modeled his court robes and ritual on its precedent. In 1368 and again in 1390, he ordered his subjects to follow the hairstyles and clothing of the Tang and to abandon foreign styles.

The Unacknowledged Legacy of the Mongols

The source of most Ming governance, however, lay in its predecessor, the Mongol dynasty. Even the name of the new dynasty, *ming*, meaning "light" or "bright," resembled the name of the Mongol dynasty (*yuan* means "original," and by extension "primary") more than it did the regional names of earlier dynasties. The word *ming* had two sets of associations. For the peasants who had followed the millenarian rebel leaders, it suggested the triumph of light over darkness, but to Confucians it also meant bright and discerning. Although the emperor had received only a rudimentary education himself, he used classical Chinese in his own writings, and government clerks used classical Chinese once again to draft documents. When the emperor reinstituted the civil service examinations in 1384, he adopted the heavily Neo-Confucian curriculum of the Mongols.

The Ming followed Mongol precedent in other important areas. Under the Mongols, the chancellor had ruled as a kind of prime minister, with authority over the Six Boards—Revenue, Civil Appointments, Rites, War, Punishments, and Works. The chancellor was, in theory, second only to the emperor, although, in fact, the chancellors at the end of the Mongol dynasty overshadowed the emperor. The Ming emperor initially structured his central government in the same way, with a chancellor ranking above the Six Boards, but he felt threatened by having such a high official in his government and in 1380 abolished the position. The Ming also took over some five hundred thousand soldiers directly from the Yuan army, and it retained much of the Mongolian-influenced nomenclature for official titles. On the regional level, the Ming followed Mongol practice and left their regions—the provinces—in place. Underneath the provinces were prefectures and counties, the basic building blocks of government since the Han.

Counting the Population

Once he had taken power, the Ming founder, Emperor Taizu, initiated a series of far-reaching reforms that gave the central government detailed information about individuals and their landholdings for the first time since the demise of the equal-field system in the eighth century. Like the Tang, the Ming used household registers to gather this information. The Ming continued the Mongol practice of recording the occupations of individual families in the registers and of requiring them to perform their labor obligations depending on their assigned category. In 1381 the emperor called for officials to record the same information about all residents of the empire: the name, age, and birthplace of the head of the household, his occupational category, his land and animal holdings, and the size of his residence. Four copies were made so that each district, prefecture, and region had one, with the central government keeping its copy in yellow-colored covers—hence the name Yellow Registers.

Most families belonged to farming households, but many were classed as military households, some of whom were expected to fight, and more of whom lived in military colonies where they grew crops for the use of the soldiers. The emperor used this expedient to reduce the burden of supporting the army, but the military colonies were never able to provide all the grain the soldiers required.

Because the Ming founder did not envision any social change, the registers permanently assigned families to particular tasks, like providing wine, sweeping tombs, or growing lotus roots for the imperial household. It would have been more efficient to collect taxes from all households and pay individuals to do these tasks as needed, but the emperor assumed all taxpayers would continue to perform the same services, without ever changing occupations. The emperor's own family had been classed as gold panners under the Mongols, even though no gold mines existed in their home district in Bengbu, Anhui, so he should have been aware of the inaccuracies of such classifications. But he replicated the Mongols' labor system and required that the labor obligation of each individual be shown on all government documents along with his name. Because of this requirement to register, we know that successful examination candidates during the Ming came not only from official households, as the government expected they would, but also from agricultural, military, artisan, and salt-producing households. Evidently, the assignment of occupational categories did not prevent people from changing their occupations. In fact, many families paid other families to perform their labor service obligations for them.

The Ming founder also hoped to sustain an unprecedented level of surveillance through the Yellow Registers. Families retained one copy of their household registration, which could be checked against the government copy, and they were responsible for making sure that they filled in the registers correctly. Every one hundred ten families formed a new unit. The ten richest families assumed the post of headmen, with each headman ensuring that the ten poorer families under him performed their labor obligations and paid their taxes. The authorities initially experimented with holding the richer families responsible for tax collection in their districts and forcing them to make good when the poorer families could not pay, but the rich families soon succeeded in protecting themselves from such demands, and government income fell as a result.

Registering Land

In 1387 the loss of revenue prompted yet another reform, the detailed registration of landholdings all over the empire. These land charts were called fish-scale registers, because the sketches of plots resembled the overlapping scales of a fish. Government officials hoped to register all land, dividing it into nine grades of productivity that determined the owner's tax obligation, but they soon adopted the expedient of a fiscal sixth-acre. (The sixth-acre, or *mu*, was the most common unit of land). Someone who owned a fiscal sixth-acre owed the taxes due on a productive sixth-acre, regardless of the amount or quality of land cultivated. By 1393 the authorities had collected sufficient data—either through land surveys or by using registers from earlier dynasties—to draw up quotas by province and by district.

Ming officials even collected the same two taxes, one in the summer and one in the autumn, that the Tang had instituted after the An Lushan rebellion and that the Song had continued. The Ming founder planned to update the Yellow and the fish-scale registers, but as in the case of the equal-field registers, the government lacked the manpower to do so. Like the provincial quotas set in the years after the An Lushan rebellion, the amounts that individual districts paid in the 1390s became the basis of all subsequent exactions, regardless of changes in land ownership or productivity. The Ming succeeded in collecting twice what the Mongols had in land tax, which proved to be more than enough for the needs of the central government in the 1380s and 1390s. Yet, once inflation began, as it did in the fifteenth century, these land-tax revenues no longer sufficed.

The Ming founder attempted to reform the currency by issuing paper money that could not be exchanged for silver. The law forbade the private use of either silver bullion or copper coins, though the Chinese were encouraged to pay their taxes in silver and copper in order to remove these metals from circulation. At the same time, the government maintained its monopoly on copper and silver mines; private mining was forbidden. So too was any sea trade by private merchants. Issued regularly in the late fourteenth century, these bans stayed in effect throughout the fifteenth, although private trade certainly continued.

The Failure to Impose a Confucian Morality

The Ming founder began his rule by implementing various Confucian measures designed to ensure that his subjects adhered to traditional norms of behavior. He periodically drafted texts exhorting them to follow a moral course, and he even required that all villagers attend readings of community compacts to remind them of their obligations. He ordered village officials to draw up lists of residents who had behaved immorally, the so-called dishonor rolls, but he abandoned these once he found "the authorities have been listing the miscellaneous small crimes of the commoners in such a way that good people guilty only of some momentary error have become indelibly marked for life with no way to reform and renovate themselves at all."[1]

Yet the failure of his subjects and his officials to live up to ethical standards frustrated him enormously, and he found himself abandoning Confucian exhortations for Legalist measures designed to force people to behave. The Ming founder occasionally took the law into his own hands. He described his treatment of a man who had sold poison to a palace guard, saying:

> I ordered the drug seller Wang Yunjian to swallow one of his own poison pills. Wang held the pill in his hand and his face changed color. He was upset and hesitated to swallow it. After I made him swallow it, I asked him: "What are these pills made of?" He answered, "Arsenic, Sichuan peas, kneaded into a pill, with cinnabar coating." I asked: "How long after swallowing the pill does a man die?" He said: "Half a day." After he said this, the tears poured down.

Since the law did not allow execution by poison, the emperor then forced the unfortunate Wang to swallow an antidote. When he had recovered, the emperor ordered him decapitated as the law specified. Eventually the emperor found that the most extreme measures did not cause people to reform. After several granary officials were caught stealing grain, they were sentenced to having their faces and bodies branded, and their kneecaps removed. Even so, when they returned to their previous jobs, they resumed their corrupt practices, much to the emperor's surprise and dismay.

Famous for his erratic treatment of officials, the Ming emperor oscillated between periods of relative lenience and excessive violence. Although the official histories give few details, one purge is documented, occurring in 1376 because the Ming founder objected to a traditional practice among bureaucrats. Provincial officials who submitted tax reports to the Board of Revenue routinely left their forms blank so that the tax amounts paid could be entered later and more accurately checked against the records held in the center. The emperor felt that such a practice facilitated corruption. After he had launched a massive purge of the bureaucracy, dismissing some ten thousand officials, he solicited criticism. When one official dared to explain that honest local officials had no way of knowing how much tax grain would actually arrive in the capital, and averred that many innocent officials had been unfairly dismissed, the emperor sentenced him to forced labor. The Ming emperor's brutal measures fully deserve the label "purge." In 1380, when the emperor fired his chancellor and dismantled the Grand Secretariat, thirty thousand people disappeared. In 1385, some ten thousand were sentenced to death in another corruption scandal over grain, and in 1393, fifteen thousand died when the emperor suppressed a challenge to his authority.

The Ming founder could not prevent a prolonged succession dispute in the years following his death. After the death of the heir apparent in 1392, the Ming founder had named a grandson to succeed him, but when the founder died in 1398, civil war broke out. The new emperor's uncles did not accept his claim to rule, and in 1402, his senior uncle led an army who stormed the capital at Nanjing. The troops set the palace on fire, and the unfortunate grandson, then only twenty-one, probably burned to death. Rumors of his survival circulated in the years after his uncle succeeded to the throne, and the new emperor ordered periodic searches for his missing nephew. The new emperor chose Yongle as his reign title, meaning "Eternal Happiness."

THE VOYAGES OF THE YONGLE EMPEROR

Intensely conscious of his father's great accomplishments, yet at the same time uncomfortably aware that he had seized power from his father's designated heir, the Yongle emperor launched a series of ambitious policies designed to demonstrate his own greatness. The most ambitious and the most famous were his spectacular ocean voyages. Equally dramatic was the new emperor's decision to shift the capital north to Beijing, where it remained for the following five hundred years, and where it is today.

The Yongle emperor, who commanded a personal force of over one hundred thousand soldiers, was more at home in the north than in Nanjing, where many sympathized with the cause of his deposed nephew. As soon as he took power he named Beijing the capital, but he was able to move his government there only in 1420 after the Grand Canal had been rechanneled. Before the repairs to the canal, the Ming had shipped tax grain by sea, but the dangers of ocean travel, combined with the threat of Japanese piracy, persuaded officials to shift to inland waterways. They launched a massive rebuilding of the Grand Canal, and by 1415 a series of forty-seven locks had been constructed, linking Hangzhou with Beijing. Then some 335 battalions, comprising 235,000 men and their families, moved to the capital, swelling the population of Beijing to over 2 million, all supported by grain shipped along the refurbished canal. Where Nanjing had been oriented to the south and to the ocean, Beijing faced toward the steppe and the Mongols who lived there.

The Yongle emperor took further measures to preserve his memory. He himself wrote a text expressing his understanding of the teachings of Zhu Xi, and in 1414 he ordered the scholars in government employ to prepare a definitive edition of *The Four Books*, to be used in studying for the civil service examinations. He named his most ambitious project for himself. *The Yongle Encyclopedia* copied passages from almost all extant works. Containing over twenty-two thousand chapters, the completed text was far too large to be published so only a few manuscript copies were made by hand. Although most of the encyclopedia burned in various library fires occurring during the nineteenth century, the few thousand pages that survive today testify to the ambition and the scope of the project. (Some observers believe that the complete original version lies buried in the tomb of the Yongle emperor.) We can read the texts of several late Southern Song and Yuan dramas only because they were included in the encyclopedia. Separated from the rest of the work by chance, and so saved from destruction, the surviving pages resurfaced among the secondhand booksellers of Beijing, where book collectors found them at the beginning of the twentieth century.

The Yongle emperor hoped to expand the borders of the empire even beyond where his father had gone. He ordered troops dispatched north to Mongolia, where the Mongols had broken up into separate feuding confederations. Between 1410 and 1424, the Ming committed five separate expeditions to the defeat of the Mongols, but they never succeeded in that effort. The Yongle emperor also sent troops south to Vietnam (then called Annam), but the Chinese troops withdrew after twenty years with no new conquests. He had more success with his ocean voyages, begun in 1405 and continuing after his death, which reached Indonesia, Vietnam, India, Somalia, and farther down the east coast of Africa. These voyages did not seek to conquer new territory nor to conduct private trade, which was still banned during the years of the voyages. The emperor claimed that the voyages were designed to locate the escaped prince he had overthrown, but it is more likely that the emperor sought to enhance his reputation by achieving something his father had not.

Under the leadership of a Muslim eunuch named Zheng He (1371–1433), an imperial fleet of over three hundred ships traveled to Southeast Asia, India, and Africa one hundred years before Columbus's and da Gama's more famous voyages. Some of these treasure ships were 120 meters (400 feet) long and 48 meters (160 feet) wide, making them the largest wooden boats in the world. The ships carried over twenty-eight thousand men, who traveled in relative luxury, dining on fresh fish kept in separate compartments filled with water. Dwarfing those of the European explorers in size, these Chinese ships made a statement to the world about the power of the Ming dynasty. But it was a temporary, even vainglorious, statement, for the Chinese conquered no territory and retained no seaports. The voyages ended as quickly as they had begun, can-

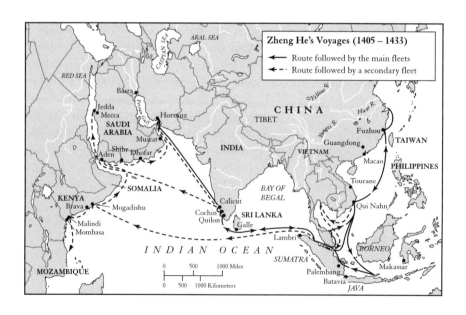

celed on grounds of unnecessary expense soon after the death of the eunuch admiral in 1433.

The eunuchs were a power center that the Ming founder and his successors struggled to contain. By the time of the Ming, the central government rarely recruited eunuchs from among war captives. Most eunuchs were selected by their parents, who hoped to improve their sons' lives by castrating them and rendering them eligible for palace service. Yet, because the eunuchs had supported the Yongle emperor's coup, he appointed them to new positions, most notably deputing Zheng He, who had been castrated as a boy of ten or eleven while a prisoner of war, to lead his navy. In addition, the new emperor dispatched some eunuchs as envoys to other countries. He also hired them to obtain goods for the palace and to spy on both civilians and soldiers. The eunuchs ran a separate jail, the "Eastern Depot" established in Beijing in 1420, where they imposed their own sentences and where they tortured their victims, sometimes to death. A strong personality, the Yongle emperor managed to maintain control of the eunuchs, but succeeding emperors, who chafed at the onerous demands of ruling, ceded much power to them.

The Nature of the Trade

The Ming fleet engaged in tribute trade, following the traditional pattern of giving gifts to foreign rulers and receiving gifts in return. The Chinese gave items of great prestige value, like suits of clothing, umbrellas, calendars, and books, but with little intrinsic value. They also gave out grants of paper money and copper coins to local peoples, who tended to buy back Chinese goods with the money and to trade valuable horses, copper, wood, animal hides, gold, and silver. Ming accounting practices make it impossible to estimate the balance of trade the Chinese had with these outlying peoples—or even the cost of the expeditions—but the terms seem to have favored the Chinese. A ship was worth 1,000 piculs (approximately 100,000 liters or 2,800 bushels) of rice, but the city of Suzhou paid three thousand times as much rice every year to the central government in taxes.[2] Suzhou (the former base of a rival to the Ming founder) was admittedly the most heavily taxed area in China, but even so the cost of the ships took only a small part of the government's annual revenues.

One ancient measure of an emperor's rule was his ability to attract auspicious beasts, and this conveyed great prestige on the exotic animals like rhinoceroses, ostriches, lions, and leopards brought back by the admiral's fleet. In 1414 Zheng He's men encountered an African giraffe in Bengal, where it had been sent as a gift from Kenya. The Bengali king agreed to

The Emperor's Zoo in 1414

Unlike the Spanish and Portuguese explorers who reached the New World within one century of Zheng He's voyages, the Chinese did not colonize the ports they visited, and they found no precious metals. But they did bring back rare animals—including this giraffe—which the emperor treasured as a sign of his auspicious rule and occasionally brought out to display to honored dinner guests.

This painting depicts the arrival of the giraffe in Beijing in 1414. Entitled, "In Praise of the Qilin, the Auspicious Sign," the text says:

> When a sage possesses the virtue of the utmost benevolence so that he illuminates the darkest places, a unicorn [qilin] appears. This shows that Your Majesty's virtue equals that of Heaven: its merciful blessings have spread far and wide so that the harmonious vapors have emanated a unicorn as an endless bliss to the state for a myriad myriad years.

(Philip Snow, *The Star Raft: China's Encounter with Africa*, New York, 1988, p. 24)

The inscription is far more enthusiastic than the portrait is accurate. Curiously, the artist drew the overall shape of the giraffe correctly, but its markings look like the scales of a fish, suggesting that the artist may have never seen the giraffe.

send the animal on to Beijing, where the Yongle emperor first refused to greet it, but in 1415, when a second giraffe arrived, the emperor agreed to participate in a lavish welcoming ceremony. The giraffe reminded the Chinese of a mythical, auspicious unicorn-like animal, the *qilin* (in Japanese, *kirin*, today the logo for the Japanese beer of the same name). The *qilin*, last sighted in ancient times, was thought to have the body of a deer and the tail of an ox. The Somali word for "giraffe" was *gerrin*, which sounded remarkably like the Chinese word. The giraffe joined the imperial entourage and made occasional appearances at subsequent feasts, which must have made a striking impression on those in attendance.

The Chinese Vessels Compared to European Ships

The product of a long tradition of shipbuilding, the Ming fleet displayed all the technological innovations Chinese boatbuilders had made in previous centuries. The ships navigated by means of star maps and compasses. Chinese ships carried compasses starting in the ninth or tenth century, a century or two before the Europeans and Arabs. Dating back to the second century, Chinese stern-post rudders were also more advanced, because a smaller or larger rudder could be used on the same pin, depending on the depth of the water. The grain ships in the Qingming scroll are equipped with such rudders, which the Europeans adopted at the beginning of the thirteenth century, probably from the Arabs.

Chinese shipbuilders outpaced their European counterparts in yet another respect. They built separate watertight compartments, like the different sections of a bamboo, so that if a ship sprang a leak, only one part of it took in water. This technique allowed the craftsmen to repair the leaks while the ship was still sailing. These compartments also housed the fish and fresh water to supplement the rations of the Chinese sailors.

Whereas Columbus's crew eked out the days on their diet of hardtack supplemented by bread baked with ocean water, Zheng He's men traveled in style. Columbus traveled with 4 boats, Zheng He with 317. The Santa Maria was 24 meters (80 feet) long, with a capacity of 250 metric tons (280 English tons). The treasure ships were at least 120 meters (400 feet) long and carried 2,200 metric tons (2,500 English tons). Eunuch officers commanded a navy of 28,000 men, most of whom were banished criminals. Specialists in protocol, astrologers, judges, and even Arabic translators were also on board. The doctors and herb specialists on the Chinese ships numbered 180, which was the size of da Gama's entire crew.[3] All comparisons between the Chinese and the European ships make the same point: the Chinese ships exceeded the European ships, often by a factor of ten or more, in size, staff, and equipment.

CHINA'S EARLY MASTERY OF THE SEA

In 1435, fifty-seven years before Columbus, the Chinese admiral Zheng He led a fleet of enormous ships from China to the Indian Ocean and beyond. His largest vessels exceeded 121 meters (400 feet) in length—five times larger than the 24-meter- (80-foot-) long Santa Maria. No contemporary drawings of either Zheng He's treasure ships or the Santa Maria survive, but this illustration shows reconstructions of both ships. Although the Chinese ships were much larger and more impressive, smaller ships were more practical for exploration, and Columbus actually complained that his ships were too big to maneuver in alien waters.

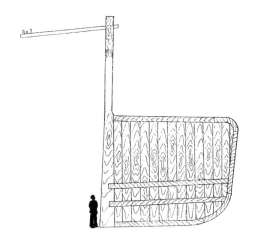

THE SIZE OF ZHENG HE'S VESSELS

In this sketch a man stands beside the 10.8 meter- (36.2 foot-) long rudder used by Zheng He's vessels to show its relative size. This sketch is based on a post excavated in Nanjing, which confirms that the boats were as large as Chinese historical records maintain.

The Chinese and the European expeditions differed in another important way: the Europeans were exploring territory previously unknown to them. Not so the Chinese. Zheng He's men carried a 6.3 meter- (21-foot-) long map of the oceans. Not drawn to scale, it showed the coasts of Africa and India, with sailing directions, giving the degrees and the number of watches to be followed between pairs of destinations. The African section includes some vague terms, like "Black Kids" (Hei-er), but some surprisingly accurate place names—*Malindi* for Malindi, and *Menbachi* for Mombasa (both in Kenya). Once the ships reached land, they had to use local pilots to navigate the coastal waters, which are not shown in detail. This map reveals that the Chinese were following courses discovered by earlier explorers.

The End of the Voyages

The Chinese ships had every advantage over the Europeans but one: the Chinese lacked continuing government support. After the death of the Yongle emperor in 1424, the voyages were suspended, with the central government reluctantly allowing a seventh, and final, voyage in 1433. Zheng He died in the same year. The ostensible reason for the suspension was the excessive cost of the voyages, yet clearly civil officials seized this pretext to rein in the eunuchs who controlled the navy. At first the treasure ships were placed in dry storage, but as time went on, the ships rotted. The mariners were reassigned to tax boats on the Grand Canal, and in 1477 the records of the voyages were destroyed.

A novel written at the end of the sixteenth century gives further insight into why the Chinese did not use the voyages to build up a colonial empire. Writing in the age of long, vernacular novels, during the sixteenth and seventeenth centuries, the author Luo Maodeng added deities and supernatural guardians to spin a four-volume picaresque novel out of Zheng He's voyages, *Voyage of the Three-Treasures Eunuch*. In one incident the Chinese ships arrive on the African coast to find that the local ruler did not welcome them. The officers wanted to attack, but their admiral advised a different course, arguing that they could not conquer simply by using superior force. Instead he ordered a demonstration of Chinese weaponry, which persuaded the African king to submit. Taking a Confucian view, the novelist suggests that a righteous ruler does not use force to win over his subjects. Near the end of the novel, when one of the characters stumbles into the underworld (where he sees his late wife), victim after victim comes forth to charge the Chinese with war crimes. The section concludes with the king of the underworld sending a message to Zheng He that he and his sailors should return to China.

To argue that the Chinese lacked the stomach for empire would be too simple. Zheng He's men did commit atrocities, and they did not hesitate to forage for and even steal food when the local people were not forthcoming. In one instance, the Chinese ships killed five thousand pirates in Sumatra on the Malacca Strait, and in another, they became enmeshed in a dispute between two rulers in Siam and Java. But these military campaigns were exceptions. *The Voyage of the Three-Treasures Eunuch* suggests that the Chinese had reservations about conquering less civilized peoples so far removed from their own cultural sphere. The objects of Ming attempts at conquest, the Mongols to the north and the Vietnamese to the south, both lay directly on China's borders, and their residents had long exposure to Chinese ways.

By the time of the seventh expedition, the Chinese fleet had established a regular series of ports they visited in Vietnam, Java, Sumatra, Sri Lanka, and the west coast of India. If the voyages had continued, these cities might have become treaty ports, similar to the fueling stations the Europeans were to establish within the century. In fact, when da Gama's men reached the east coast of Africa, the inhabitants told them they had already seen white people, by which they meant the Chinese of Zheng He's fleet. Local rulers permitted da Gama to build a trading post at the same fortress where the Chinese had earlier stored their goods. But the Chinese did not continue their voyages. During the seventy-year hiatus between the final departure of the Chinese and the first arrival of the Portuguese, events inland caused the Chinese government to turn away from the sea.

Border Conflicts with the Mongols

The Ming shifted their sights from the sea to the steppe, where their rivals, the Mongols, had begun to reorganize. The Mongols had posed a problem for the Ming founder and for the Yongle emperor, but they remained largely unorganized during the reigns of the first two emperors. Then, in the years after the death of the Yongle emperor, a new leader named Esen (d. 1455) unified a branch of Mongols called the Oirats, who began to make incursions into Chinese territory. In 1449 the Oirat confederation went into battle with the Ming imperial troops at a site called Tumu. Now a truck stop two hours from Beijing, Tumu, then a desolate posting station, was a six-day march from the capital.

The emperor, who came to the throne in 1435 at the age of eight, was controlled by a faction of palace eunuchs who advised him to lead his troops into battle. Against the strenuous objections of his civil officials, the emperor did so. The Ming forces went north to attack the Oirat Mongols, but a disastrous defeat caused them to reverse course. As the Chinese were making their way back to Beijing, a hard rain began to fall. The imperial entourage stopped in Tumu to make camp, and tried to dig wells, but the terrain was too dry. By the time they realized a river lay close to their camp, the Oirats had secured the river bank, cutting off the water supply. The weary troops suffered the double misfortune of being soaking wet at the same time they had no drinking water. The emperor ordered his chief eunuch to sue for peace, but the eunuch disobeyed, giving unauthorized orders for a new attempt to reach the river. A day-by-day account reports:

> In considerable confusion the army, surrounding the imperial palanquin, struggles forward a mile or so. On observing this action, the enemy now attacks in full force from all sides. The Chinese army breaks, gives ground in great disorder, becomes a mob. The Mongols shout, "Throw down your arms and armor and be spared." Ignoring their officers, the Chinese soldiers go wild, strip off their garments, and run toward the Mongol cavalry, only to be cut to pieces. The air rains arrows, and the Mongols close in. The emperor's personal cavalry guards surround him and try to break through but make no headway. The emperor dismounts and sits on the ground amidst a hail of arrows that kills most of his attendants. He remains unharmed and waits calmly.[4]

The Oirats then captured the Ming emperor and took him to Mongolia.

The Chinese suffered one of their most ignominious defeats at the battle of Tumu, yet the victorious Mongols exacted almost no concessions from them. In Beijing, the anti-eunuch forces rallied behind a new emperor, who gave the kidnapped emperor the title of "The Grand Senior Emperor." The Oirats subsequently attacked Beijing but withdrew after an unsuccessful five-day siege. The following year they returned the emperor, who was able to regain the throne after another succession dispute broke out.

Although the Mongols did not realize any lasting gains from their victory, the focus of Ming foreign policy permanently shifted after 1449. All subsequent Ming rulers saw the Mongolian border as the real threat to the well-being of the empire and thought the dangers across the seas could be disposed of simply by forbidding Chinese contact with foreign nations. The Mongols forwarded periodic requests to resume trade, but court officials, who viewed all trading missions as harboring potential spies, generally rejected such requests.

In their continuing battles with the Mongols, the Chinese had the great disadvantage of trying to defend a border over a thousand miles long, while the Mongols enjoyed the tactical advantage of mobility. Their cavalry could strike the border at any point. Lacking the funds to send further expeditions into Mongol territory, Chinese officials opted to build individual sections of wall, starting in the far west of China and moving east. These walls constitute today's Great Wall, but no one in the Ming conceived of them as a single entity. As long and formidable as these walls were, they did not achieve their purpose of protecting the Chinese. In 1550 the Mongols, under the leadership of the Altan Khan, simply went around a wall, and seven hundred of his men reached a gate in the Beijing city walls. Luckily for the Chinese, they turned around once they had presented their demand for access to Chinese markets.

The Mongol attacks prompted the court to take the most conservative of approaches to foreign powers. It regularly passed decrees banning contact and trade with overseas nations while officials bemoaned the depredations of pirates, whom they incorrectly assumed were Japanese, on the southeast coast. Most of these pirates were Chinese who dared to violate the court's ban on foreign trade.

The mid-sixteenth century saw an important change in the court's hostility toward foreign trade. The Portuguese first arrived on China's southeast coast in Guangzhou in 1517, but early relations were marred by Portuguese attempts to conquer Chinese territory by force, and it was only in the 1560s and 1570s that the Portuguese obtained a foothold in Macao. There trade boomed. In 1573 a wall and a gate to separate the Portuguese from the Chinese were erected, and, until 1999, Macao was governed directly from Portugal.[5] Under the grand secretaryship of a powerful minister named Zhang Juzheng (1525–1582), the Ming reached peace with the Mongols at the end of the sixteenth century. In 1571, the Ming state conferred the rank of prince on the Mongol leader, the same Altan Khan who had attacked the walls of Beijing some twenty years earlier, and gave his subordinates titles as well. In turn, they promised to recognize the Ming emperor; trading—and peace—resumed. All these developments pointed to a softening in the Ming suspicion of foreign trade. As relations with the Mongols eased, the court rescinded the ban on trade with foreign countries—with the exception of Japan—in 1567. The lifting of the ban, though, did not grant Europeans freedom of movement within China. They remained subject to strict surveillance and could be expelled at any time.

SOCIAL CHANGE UNDER THE MING

After 1433, no emperor succeeded in implementing domestic policies with the far-reaching effects of those of the Ming founder or his son, the Yongle emperor. As recruitment by civil service examination became the norm, the teachings of the Neo-Confucians gained in influence. Chinese thinkers opted for a conservative vision of society that offered women little freedom. Yet the years between 1450 and 1600 witnessed genuine social change. Over and over, learned men advised young girls to stay inside, but more and more young girls learned to read classical Chinese so they could study the rigidly conservative manuals of their time. Although the examinations tested students' knowledge of Zhu Xi's commentaries on *The Four Books*, the unchanging curriculum did not prevent new thinkers from making their mark. Nor did rigid government policies prevent economic change. Even though paper money disappeared, China's market economy continued to expand and sucked in large quantities of New World silver. Many peasants had come to pay their taxes in silver by the year 1600.

Changing Moral Standards for Women

Literature gives a few hints of changes in women's lives during these centuries. The romance of Oriole and student Zhang, as portrayed in Wang Shifu's (ca. 1250–1300) *The Story of the Western Wing*, continued to win large audiences. Early in the fifteenth century one observer wrote "Of all new comedies/And old musical plays,'/ *The Story of the Western Wing*

388 Continuing the War against the Mongols

takes first place all over the world."[6] Yet it became increasingly difficult to reconcile Oriole's conduct with her pedigree as the daughter of a prominent family. When Yuan Zhen wrote his autobiographical story in the eighth century (chapter 6, p. 233), and when Master Dong wrote his play in the late twelfth or early thirteenth century (chapter 8, p. 326), girls from powerful families might engage in premarital sex, but by the 1500s, a more restrictive morality had gripped Chinese society. Oriole began to be played by a "flowery female lead," a role type reserved for prostitutes and other female protagonists with lax morals.

The new Oriole appears in a farcical skit entitled "A Noontime Dream in the Garden Grove," by Li Kaixian (1502–1568).[7] A fisherman dozes off in the afternoon and dreams of a meeting between Oriole and Li Wa, the female protagonist of Bai Xingjian's story (see chapter 5, p. 211). In her Tang incarnation, Li Wa began life as a prostitute but was able to marry a student. With her encouragement, he does well in the civil service examinations, and they go on to have a family together. The Ming playwright uses the conceit of having the two fictional characters meet. Li Wa and Oriole begin their conversation on an acrimonious note, which continues throughout the skit:

> [Oriole speaks:] What makes you so much better than me?
> [Li Wa]: What makes me less than you?
> [Oriole speaks:] You flirted with passing strangers at the Serpentine Pond.
> [Li Wa]: At Universal Salvation Monastery you set your eyes on roving monks.

The two women proceed to trade accusations and eventually arrive at the topic of sex. Oriole makes the first charge—that Li Wa entrapped innocent girls in prostitution: "You purchased good girls and made them base; by precedent you should have been divorced!" Even though Li Wa was a prostitute, she is able to attack Oriole on moral grounds, which she proceeds to do with no holds barred: "You had sex first and married later; according to what's right, you two should have been whipped apart." The conflict goes on, with their servants joining the fray, but the playwright has made his main point. Being a prostitute is reprehensible, and premarital sex is equally reprehensible.

This skit testifies to the stricter morality that evolved throughout the Ming. The Ming founder contributed to this new moral sense by discouraging widow remarriage. He established government subsidies for the support of widows: should a woman be widowed before the age of thirty and remain unmarried until she was fifty, she was eligible to have a commemorative arch built in front of her house, and her in-laws' labor obligations were waived. This measure enshrined a new, more restrictive morality for women. Widow remarriage carried no stigma in earlier ages, when even a well-born woman like the Song poet Li Qingzhao could remarry (chapter 7); but widow remarriage, like premarital sex, became increasingly unthinkable for women of good families in the years after 1400.

Large families continued to invest in corporate property, often in south China, where lineages assumed the shape they were to retain for the next five hundred years. Lineage rules survive specifying that women are to be kept inside and that widows are not to remarry. Several women who refused to remarry following the death of their husbands committed suicide, and the first recorded shrine to a faithful widow dates to 1498. These were the first women to be worshiped alongside the male local worthies in Confucian shrines and schools.[8]

Footbinding continued to spread during this period, and it was thought undesirable for women to venture outside the home. Of course, rich families with servants would have been able to enforce the new restrictions with far greater ease than poor families. Those who depended on the labor of their women could not restrict them to the home, for they needed them to work in the fields.

Books Aimed at a Female Audience

At the beginning of the dynasty, the Ming founder sought to inculcate the palace women with female virtues by ordering them to study the three obediences and four virtues described in the Han-dynasty writer Ban Zhao's *Lessons for Women* (chapter 3, p. 139). At the same time that he drafted various books of exhortations, he commissioned a new, updated *Lessons for Women*. Part of a boom in woodblock publishing during the Ming, over fifty different books appeared on female morality. These included versions of Ban Zhao's precepts as well as group biographies of virtuous women. These books all trumpeted the virtues of women who submitted to the authorities in their lives, whether their parents when they were young, their in-laws when married, or their husbands and sons as they aged. Stressing the imperative for women to remain chaste and to uphold the traditional family virtues, they called for women to remain inside their homes.

Many observers commented on how common it was for young girls, whether in villages or cities, to study these books. The author of one Ming manual of advice tells girls to start the study of *Lessons for Women* at the age of six, which was exactly what Ban Zhao had hoped for when she called for girls to begin their education at the same time boys did. This manual goes on to urge that girls be restricted to the women's quarters at the same time.[9] As they learned to read and so gained access to the broader world of learning, large numbers of women began to form literary societies, to publish their own poetry, and to edit anthologies. Many developed literacy in classical Chinese.

Relations between Fathers and Daughters

Strictly construed, the teachings contained in the women's instruction books meant that a girl belonged to her natal family only until the time of marriage, when she joined her husband's family. Even if widowed and childless, she was to continue living with them. Such a belief should have discouraged parents from becoming too close to their daughters, but several epitaphs for the dead show how attached to their daughters some fathers became. One father, who lost two daughters to smallpox, wrote the following moving account of his older daughter's childhood:

> When you were born I was not pleased. A man over thirty wanted a son, not a daughter. But you won me over before you had completed your first year. Even then you would respond with giggles each time I made a face at you. . . .
>
> You often knocked on the door and then quickly went inside and asked: "Who is there?" . . .
>
> Sometimes you would play a guessing game with me and the winner would chase the loser around the house. When you finally caught me you laughed jubilantly and clapped your hands. Who would have believed that not quite half a month later you would breathe your last?[10]

This was a lively daughter, whose father doted on her and who disagreed with her mother about how best to raise her. He explains:

> Your mother was too strict. From time to time she would discipline you for fear that your habits would be carried into adulthood. Although I agreed with her, I said to her when you were not around: "A little child cannot be expected to know right and wrong. Let her be until she is a little older."

It is impossible to imagine this lively youngster growing up to become the docile woman depicted in women's instruction books, whatever subsequent measures her mother might have taken to discipline her. Her father concludes his requiem by describing her trip to the underworld:

> It is the way of the world that one does not weep over the death of a daughter. . . . Ten days before you were stricken your sister Axun, younger than you by two years, came down with the same illness. Three days after she died, you too were gone.

Now that you no longer have playmates, you should at least have the company of your sister, whom you knew well. You can walk now but she is still unsteady on her feet. Hold her by the hand wherever you go. . . .

I have been thinking of you all the time. If you know how much I miss you you will come back, again and again, in my dreams. If fate permits, be reborn as my next child. For such hopes I am sending you a copy of the Diamond Sutra as well as other books of spells and incantations. . . . When you see the King of the Underworld, kneel down with raised hands and plead for mercy. . . .

Just say the words to him and don't cry or be noisy. You must not forget that the underworld is different from home.

This memoir prompts one to question how deeply the new morality managed to penetrate. The mourning father admits that he disagreed with his wife's attempts to discipline their young daughter, and others may have questioned the new morality as well.

Certain fifteenth-century thinkers encouraged parents to treat their children gently. The most famous Confucian of the period, Wang Yangming (1472–1529), shared Mencius's faith in human nature. Wang taught that as they grew up, people strayed from the innate knowledge they had once possessed at birth. "Everybody, from the infant in swaddling clothes to the old, is in full possession of this innate knowledge," taught Wang. He encouraged a much freer education for children than was practiced at the time: "When we teach children we must kindle their enthusiasm and make everything a joy. Then they will advance of their own accord without ceasing."

Wang Yangming and the Unity of Knowledge and Action

Wang's views may have stemmed from his unusual childhood. His biography, which was written by his disciples and verges on hagiography, reports that he spoke for the first time at the late age of six. Although he then went on to do brilliantly in school, he was unable to equal his father's first-place finish on the civil service examinations and passed only on his third try. Soon after joining the civil service, Wang wrote a memorial to the emperor defending two imprisoned officials who had urged the emperor to dismiss his favorite eunuch; in response, Wang was given forty strokes and exiled to Longchang, Guizhou, in the remote deeply forested regions of southwest China. This was an area inhabited by several non–Chinese speaking tribal peoples.

While in southwest China, Wang Yangming reached his most important insight. Whereas the great Song Neo-Confucian scholar Zhu Xi (see p. 296) had called for the investigation of things external to the individual, Wang Yangming advocated turning one's gaze inward on oneself. Each person was capable of becoming a sage, whether he held office or gained fame in any area. Wang also taught that it was wrong to divorce study from action, as was the educational norm during his lifetime. He advocated the "unity of thought and action," and himself enjoyed great fame during his lifetime as a successful military general who once captured a rebel leader. For Wang, the way to learn anything was to try carrying it out; only then could one adjust what one had learned to the realities of action.[11]

Wang Yangming's teachings implied that infants, who were born with their innate moral knowledge intact, offered their parents insights into human nature. Some of his followers opened a school that extended Wang's teachings more broadly. His most eccentric follower, Li Zhi (1527–1602), claimed, "The heart of the child is absolutely not false but pure and true. . . . If one loses the heart of the child then he loses his true heart."[12]

Li Zhi was especially interested in a new literary genre—the vernacular novel—that took shape in the fifteenth century. He edited and wrote commentaries to two of China's earliest and subsequently most-beloved novels: *The Romance of the Three Kingdoms* and *The Water Margin*. Attributed to a fourteenth-century author, *The Romance of the Three Kingdoms* was first published in 1522 and went through twenty more editions before the end of the Ming dynasty. Its protagonists are all based on historical figures who vied for power at the end of the Han dynasty. *The Water Margin* recounts the nefarious activities of a group of bandits whose hideaway lies in the marshes of Shandong, for whom this classic novel is named.

Li Zhi's free interpretation of Wang Yangming's teachings coupled with his enthusiastic embrace of Buddhist teachings culminated in his arrest for heresy in 1602 and his subsequent suicide while in jail awaiting trial. One of the witnesses to the controversy was a Jesuit father who had arrived in Beijing in 1601. Li Zhi described Matteo Ricci (1552–1610) to a friend, saying:

> Now he can speak our language fluently, write our script, and act according to our rules of conduct. He is an extremely impressive man—a person of inner refinement, outwardly most straightforward.[13]

Ricci commanded unusual talents. He had devoted long years to learning to speak and write Chinese. His Chinese was sufficient to debate with Chinese scholars, an accomplishment all the more impressive in an age before dictionaries and refined teaching methods.

Matteo Ricci in China

Ricci had developed his own system of memorizing large quantities of material, in which he imagined a house with different rooms all containing packets of information. He used this system to memorize *The Four Books*, an accomplishment few Chinese could match. With the help of Chinese friends, he was even able to write philosophical treatises.

The objects Ricci brought along to China also aided his cause. Some of these items, like books, struck Chinese viewers with their beauty while others, like clocks and telescopes, could be put to practical use. The Jesuits could predict the movement of the stars, and even more important, the time of eclipses, with greater precision than could Chinese astronomers. Like the Chinese, the early Jesuits posited that the sun and the planets revolved around the earth. After 1516, when the Catholic church forbade Galileo's (1564–1642) teachings, the Jesuits adopted Tycho Brahe's (1546–1601) model of the universe, which held that the planets revolved around the sun. According to Brahe, the sun in turn revolved around the earth. The theory may have been wrong, but the rigor of Brahe's naked-eye observations allowed him to predict the movement of planets with unprecedented exactitude. Brahe's model of the universe prevailed in China until the nineteenth century, when Protestant missionaries first introduced the teachings of Copernicus (1473–1543) and Kepler (1571–1630). Chinese scholars also acknowledged the greater precision of Western clocks. At the time, the Chinese had water clepsydras and incense clocks, but the Jesuits had more precise hourglasses. The early European chiming clocks were notoriously inaccurate, and they began to keep good time only after the introduction of a new type of pendulum at the end of the seventeenth century.

The beauty of the lavish illuminated manuscripts Ricci brought from Europe contrasted with the austere woodblock illustrations of Chinese books. European books achieved wide circulation among educated circles in Beijing, prompting Chinese artists to adopt certain techniques from the Western etchings. The use of chiaroscuro to show shadows dazzled the Chinese. And Chinese artists enthusiastically adopted the new technique of vanishing-point perspective, which offered a whole new way of depicting space.

The books the Jesuits carried looked different from traditional Chinese books. Ricci brought a copy of the Plantin Bible with him that was eight volumes long, each of fine paper with excellent bindings. The text was printed in Greek, Latin, Hebrew, and Chaldean. When, on one occasion, the book fell overboard, it floated to the surface of the water, where a boatman retrieved it. Since the incomprehensible book bore no

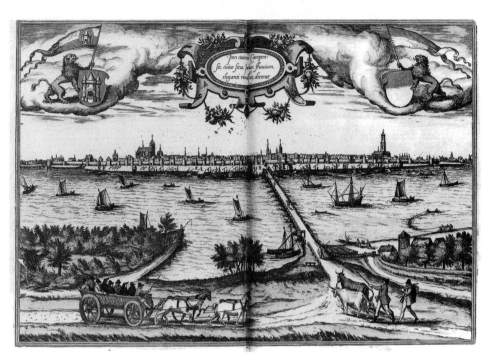

THE ADOPTION OF VANISHING-POINT PERSPECTIVE

Although traditional Chinese artists had used perspective, they did not adopt a vanishing point until the late sixteenth and seventeenth centuries, when Jesuit teachers introduced European engravings like this cityscape to the Chinese (top). This landscape by Zhang Hong (1577–after 1652) (bottom) uses a bridge to connect a foreground with a city across a lake.

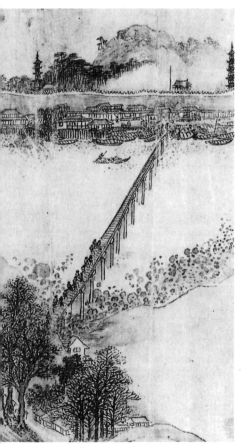

obvious value to the boatman, the Jesuits were able to buy it back for a small amount, three-tenths of a ducat, which they noted was the exact cost of a boy child during a famine. The Jesuits remained proud of their books, but scholars criticized their new religion for having so few texts available in Chinese. Like the early Buddhists, the Jesuits faced the enormous task of translating their texts into Chinese, and a full edition of the Bible became available only in the 1820s.

Obstacles to Conversion

The Jesuits' problems began as soon as they started to translate the major concepts and doctrines of Catholicism. They faced the choice of using preexisting Chinese words, with all their non-Christian associations, or of creating new words. Early Buddhists responded to the same dilemma by adopting Daoist vocabulary to express their religious ideas. Only after several centuries, when the concepts of Buddhism had become more familiar, did later Buddhist translators use loanwords from Sanskrit, confident that their readers could understand them. At first the Jesuits tried the term *Tianzhu* ("lord of heaven") for God, but Ricci realized that an unfamiliar term for the supreme Christian deity would confuse potential converts. He eventually opted for *Shangdi* (literally "sovereign on high"), a term that incorporated the name of the god Di, who had appeared in the oracle bone texts dating to 1200 B.C. The term was not apt: the sovereign on high of ancient Chinese texts was one god among many, while the Jesuits' god demanded recognition as the sole deity.

Because the strict monotheism of the Christians ran counter to every religious tradition existing in China, the Chinese brought their own interpretations to Christian teachings. Most Chinese assumed the Christian God, like Chinese deities, to have been a person who had lived and who had become a deity after his death. Even leading converts, like Michael Yang Tingyun (1557–1627), explained that, in former lives, the Christian deity had "become incarnate in China several times in the persons of Yao, Shun [the legendary sage kings], Confucius, several kings and even a number of ordinary individuals."[14]

Even the most basic of teachings, such as the Ten Commandments, proved difficult for the Chinese to accept because so many fundamentally alien assumptions underlay the Christian teachings.

"I am the Lord your God. . . . You shall have no other gods before me"
The Jesuits' demand that the Chinese give up their own gods before they could accept their Christian god proved a major stumbling block. In con-

trast, Buddhist missionaries had required only that the Chinese accept the Buddha as the supreme deity, and they had incorporated many local deities into their faith, often as guardian deities.

Although the Jesuits condemned the Chinese propensity to worship people after their deaths as gods, many Chinese worshiped the foreigners as gods. The clockmakers of Shanghai made Matteo Ricci their patron deity. The Jesuits unwittingly claimed the same proofs of divinity as had indigenous holy men. They were delighted to report that, when the bodies of Jesuit holy men were exhumed, they were found intact, with no signs of decay.

"You shall not make for yourself a graven image"   The Jesuits were quick to condemn indigenous religious practices, even though they resembled their own to a surprising degree. Like traditional Chinese practitioners, the Jesuits used rosaries, holy water, and religious images, yet they tore down statues of Chinese deities, often only to replace them with Christian images. As early as 1583, Ricci noticed the Chinese tendency to worship images of the Madonna as if she were a local deity, and some early Jesuits replaced the Madonna with a picture of Jesus for fear the Chinese would think their primary deity was female.

Images of Jesus presented their own problems. In his memoirs, Ricci described how a eunuch traveling with him misunderstood the meaning of Ricci's own crucifix. Seeing that it was "carved in wood, painted with blood, and seemingly alive," the eunuch seized the crucifix, assuming it to be an instrument of black magic. Given their view that one traveled to the underworld in one's own body, the Chinese thought crucifixion, with its permanent damage to the feet and hands, a particularly shameful way to die because one dishonored one's parents when the body was disfigured. And throughout his preaching, Ricci avoided explaining that Jesus had been condemned to death for breaking the law.

"Honor your mother and father"   The correct interpretation of this commandment also troubled the Jesuits. Strictly construed, of course, it referred to one's everyday relations with one's living parents, but many Chinese saw it as a justification for ancestor worship. The Jesuits, in turn, viewed ancestor worship as a violation of monotheism. Many potential Chinese converts could not conceive of abandoning their household shrines to their ancestors. With Ricci's acquiescence, the Jesuits adopted a middle course. They hoped that all converts would give up ancestor worship, and indeed, the most knowledgeable ones did. But, as their critics noted, the Jesuits allowed some converts to continue to worship the images of their kin in their household shrines.

"You shall not commit adultery" The Christian ban on adultery, and by extension concubinage, posed the greatest difficulty for Chinese converts, especially those of the upper classes who were accustomed to taking more than one wife. Even the emperor had many consorts. In Chinese eyes, one's obligation to produce an heir justified any number of concubines, regardless of what the Westerners preached about monogamy. As the Buddhists before them had discovered, the ideal of chastity for the clergy collided head-on with each individual's desire to have a family.

At the time of Ricci's death in 1610, the Jesuits had established a small number of missions in Beijing, Nanjing, Hangzhou, and a few other southern cities. Only twelve Jesuit missionaries from Europe or Macao were in China, and one estimate puts the total number of converts at five thousand.[15] Clearly very few Chinese came into contact with the Jesuits; most who did belonged to the lower levels of the literati. As interesting as we find Ricci, we must remember that Wang Yangming's views about the unity of thought and action influenced many more people in China than did Ricci's Christianity.

Although the fifteenth and sixteenth centuries witnessed a high degree of intellectual ferment, with thinkers like Li Zhi and Matteo Ricci crossing paths and debating each other, fortune-telling and predicting the future still remained popular. Building a house was a particularly dangerous activity in which much could go wrong, and many people consulted *The Classic of Lu Ban*, a carpenter's manual dating before 1550, to ensure that everything went smoothly.

Building a House in the Sixteenth Century

The patron deity of all those in the building trade, Lu Ban is the putative author of a manual about house-building. Those building a new house sought the advice of professional specialists called *fengshui* masters in finding an auspicious site for their house.[16] The siting of a house was thought—as it is today by modern *fengshui* masters—to be of paramount importance in determining the fortunes of the family who lived in it. Next to agriculture and textile manufacture, building was the most important industry in premodern China. As in our own day, constructing a house brought the uninitiated house-owner into contact with those who were knowledgeable about building and hence in a position to take advantage of the customer. Carpenters belonged to guilds whose strict labor rules kept costs artificially high.

We have seen that the Qin-dynasty bamboo slips at Shuihudi contained long lists of auspicious and inauspicious days for different activities (chapter 3). So too does *The Classic of Lu Ban*, but the list is expanded to include hundreds of tasks. We have also seen how Wang Chong scorned the people of the Han dynasty for their fear of digging into the earth as a dangerous act and the measures they therefore took to placate the spirits before they built a house (p. 136). Written over one thousand years later, *The Classic of Lu Ban* contains much that would have drawn Wang Chong's ire. The anonymous author warns that digging into the ground still poses risks including water poisoning, dropsy, and burglary by thieves, against which he recommends specific precautions. For the people of the Ming—whether literati or peasants—the moment of greatest danger was the placing of the ridgepole, the main piece of wood holding the house together. The manual describes an elaborate ceremony to be held before hoisting the ridgepole.

The increase in woodblock printing in the Ming meant that all kinds of new books, whether building manuals like *The Classic of Lu Ban* or women's manuals, became available. Chinese printing experienced no sudden breakthroughs in technology like the invention of movable type in Europe (ca. 1450) by Gutenberg (ca. 1395–1468). Instead, Ming printers used the same technique of carving individual pages into wooden blocks that had been developed in the ninth and tenth centuries. But the Ming publishers produced many more books and used more extensive distribution systems than had the printers of previous periods. The size of private libraries grew dramatically: in 1400 a book lover might dream of a large personal library of ten thousand chapters, perhaps more than a thousand books, yet by 1600 some scholars owned as many as ten thousand titles.[17] Certain texts, such as the Chinese classics, the official histories, or the official law code, were required reading for all scholars and officials. Others, like the new novels, appealed to readers for their sheer entertainment value.

The printing boom of the Ming has given historians another precious gift: a Chinese-language textbook that offers a detailed glimpse of how China's market economy functioned in the fifteenth and sixteenth centuries.

A Travel Survival Kit for Businessmen Going to China

Old China Hand details the travels of a group of Koreans who go to Beijing to sell horses. Written sometime after 1400 as a language textbook for non-Chinese, it survives today in a bilingual Korean-Chinese edition.[18] This anonymous book provides a hands-on introduction to the conversational Chinese necessary for travel and for conducting business. One of the Korean protagonists explains that he averages one trip a year between Beijing and Korea so that he can sell Korean horses, ginseng, and ramie cloth in China and purchase Chinese textiles and other light manufactured goods for sale in Korea. Merchants like him created a continuing demand for a phrasebook like *Old China Hand*, which was frequently reprinted and subsequently translated into Mongolian, Manchu, and Japanese.

The similarities between this textbook and those in use today are striking because the colloquial language of *Old China Hand* evokes today's spoken Mandarin. A stock character in all Chinese textbooks, a wonderfully knowledgeable and helpful native speaker, here a Mr. Wang, travels with the Koreans. Mr. Wang explains the intricacies of Chinese commercial law, including the procedures for canceling a sale after a contract has been signed. He also helps the Koreans with their financial transactions.

The Chinese in the book show the same unquenchable curiosity about the experiences of foreigners who study Chinese as they do today. After generously praising the Koreans' Chinese, Mr. Wang asks one of the Koreans how long he has studied and whether his teacher was Chinese. The Korean provides a description of the pedagogical methods current at the time:

> In the evenings we drew lots to recite by heart in front of the teacher. To those who could recite by heart, the teacher gave a "free token." If someone could not recite by heart, the student on duty started to recite and the student who could not recite was hit three times as punishment.

He explains that the tokens could be used to avoid beatings on days when the students had not prepared their lesson. The Koreans speak the perfect level of Chinese for such a textbook. They have a good command of basic Chinese, but they must ask Mr. Wang for help when anything untoward happens.

The Koreans' response to China also seems uncannily modern. At every inn, at every meal, they constantly ask if they are being charged the "actual price," because clearly they do not think they are. As it details the Koreans' trip, *Old China Hand* provides the reader, or language student, with all the phrases necessary to conduct a successful business trip. One learns how to order a meal, get a bed in a hotel, bargain, and draw up a contract.

The manual depicts a sale of ten inferior and five good horses, for which the Koreans ask one hundred forty ounces of silver. The buyer responds indignantly, "How can you ask such a price? Just tell me the selling price, there is no need to bargain in such an unreasonable way." The buyer, the broker, and the Korean haggle for a while until the broker proposes a price of one hundred ounces. Now it is the Korean's turn to be outraged: "As to the price you have fixed, even in Korea you couldn't buy horses for that price. You don't really want to buy horses, you're just have a nonsensical discussion." Finally the broker orders the two men to stop shouting and sets a price at one hundred five ounces—just a little over what the broker originally proposed and thirty-five ounces under the Korean's asking price. The Korean immediately acquiesces, indicating his asking price was as unrealistic as the buyer had maintained.

The Use of Silver as Money

The Korean then makes this request: "There is just one thing. Don't give me silver that is low in purity. Give me some good silver." The buyer offers to let him have a look at the silver, but the Korean admits he cannot distinguish pure from impure silver. Silver has replaced paper money, the source of inflation in the Yuan and early Ming. In earlier centuries, merchants had to overcome an unreliable currency, with paper money varying in value depending on the year of issue. The use of specie eliminated that problem. Silver was not made into coins by the government but instead circulated in large pieces, such as ingots, or in small slivers. Consumers collected the slivers, putting them in a wax ball and melting them down when they reached sufficient quantity to make an ingot.

The problem was that one could adulterate the silver, and only a metalsmith could detect the difference between pure and impure silver. Ming-dynasty markets always had a silversmith who weighed slivers and tested the purity of the metal. Yet individuals could not consult a silversmith for every transaction they made.

We see this problem several times in *Old China Hand*. At one stop Mr. Wang pays for wine at an inn, but the waiter refuses to accept his currency, saying, "Elder Brother, give me some good silver. This is only 80 percent silver. How can one use it?" Mr. Wang defends the silver. The waiter finally accepts the silver reluctantly: "Leave it here and I'll have to make the best of it. Even if I can't use it, I'll just have to suffer with it." Wang's savvy response reveals that he sees through the waiter's scam: "What on earth are you talking about? If you couldn't use it would you be willing to accept it?" The problem of impure silver was an irritant to all commercial transactions, a pretext for the Chinese to cheat the unwary. The Koreans ultimately work out a successful strategy of negotiating the purity of the silver as well as the price of their goods.

Old China Hand leaves the impression of a smoothly functioning money economy, even in the absence of paper money. The Koreans work on a cash-and-carry basis, with all their transactions in silver. Even though they are carrying trade goods, no one ever suggests bartering them for services. Barter probably occurred within villages, but *Old China Hand* makes no mention of the practice.

Consumer Goods in Ming-dynasty China

Having sold their goods, the Koreans discuss what to buy and take back home. Their shopping list presents the author with another marvelous opportunity to introduce new vocabulary, and it conveys a rich sense of the variety of goods available at a single store in Beijing. The shopping list includes seven types of beads, tweezers, hats, buttons, makeup, needles, combs, knives, chess sets, scissors, and officially approved weights. The Koreans plan to buy one hundred bolts each of coarse cotton, woven satin, plain satin, and patterned satin, and for children, bells, tassels, and iron rings. Beijing is admittedly the capital at the time and an important market center, but the availability of such an array of goods indicates that the inconvenience of using slivers of silver as the main currency did not impede the distribution of goods.

The list of books the Korean merchants want to buy provides a glimpse of the Chinese publishing industry. Among them are *The Book of Songs*, the writings of the Tang Confucian thinker Han Yu and the Song poet Su Shi. Some of the books, like Zhu Xi's commentary on *The Four Books* and *A New Book for Preparing for State Examinations*, are aimed at examination candidates; others, like *The Political Deeds of Emperor Tang Taizong* (who visited hell after killing his brothers), are for entertainment.

The Victims of the Market Economy

Among the Chinese the Koreans meet in *Old China Hand*, most prosper, but the foreign merchants also encounter some needy peasants along the way. One peasant explains that in a famine year, he does not have enough extra rice to sell, but then he generously shares his scarce cooked rice. Lacking meat or cooked vegetables, his family eats their rice only with salted cucumber. At their next stop, when the travelers ask to buy food for their horses, their host informs them that people are going hungry but eventually allows them to graze their horses in a nearby field. Although the market system of China continued to expand during the fifteenth and sixteenth centuries, downturns occurred with sufficient regularity for *Old China Hand* to mention them.

The most vivid record of suffering during this period is visual. In 1516, the artist Zhou Chen (active ca. 1472–1535) painted an unusual set of paintings, *Beggars and Street Characters*, which recorded the condition of street people in Suzhou, then China's most magnificent city. Like the Qingming scroll, his work was a political painting. The painter of the earlier scroll made his point by depicting an ideal city and leaving his viewers to ask why their city differed. Zhou took a much more direct approach. He showed the suffering occupants of the city in all their misery, claiming that he painted people just as he saw them in the autumn of 1516:

> I was idling under the window, and suddenly there came to my mind all the appearances and manners of the beggars and other street characters whom I often saw in the streets and markets. With brush and ink ready at hand, I put them into pictures in an impromptu way. It may not be worthy of serious enjoyment, but it certainly can be considered as a warning and admonition to the world.

Zhou does not specify to whom the warning is addressed, but another colophon is more forthcoming:

> This album presents us with the many aspects of misery—hunger and cold, homeless destitution, infirmity and emaciations, deformity and sickness. Anyone who can look at this and not be wounded to the heart by comparison is not a humane person. . . . I imagine also that the officials and nobles were seldom able to nurture and succor the common people. . . . Thus this work . . . was meant as an aid to government and is not a shallow thing—one can't dismiss it as a "play with ink."[19]

Zhou Chen felt that the officials in charge had failed to carry out their obligations to the people and that they were obliged to do something about the suffering in the streets he could see from his window. Because his was a protest painting aimed at Suzhou's government, he may well have magnified the misery of those he saw.

Even allowing for exaggeration, the viewer cannot help being shocked by the plight of the people the artist painted. Suzhou, the most prosperous city of the Ming, attracted the poor much as modern cities draw in the homeless. The pictures show skeletal figures in rags. Some, like the man crouching on the ground, are outright beggars, but others have occupations. One blindman is a drummer and there is a monkey trainer with a hoop. Zhou Chen painted these album leafs during a period when eunuchs controlled the central government. When the head eunuch (the same man who ordered Wang Yangming beaten and exiled) was overthrown in 1510, he had stored up a personal fortune greater than the annual budget of the government.

EARLY SOCIAL COMMENTARY

These three portraits are among fourteen surviving paintings done in 1516 by the artist Zhou Chen who painted the people he saw on the streets of Suzhou as, he said, a "warning and admonition to the world." These realistic portraits are among the very few surviving paintings of destitute people in China.

The Shortage of Silver

The poverty Zhou Chen witnessed may well have reflected the pervasive shortage of silver in China. The collapse of paper money at the beginning of the Ming had forced the Chinese to return to a metal currency.

With copper reserves sparse, the government came to depend on un-minted silver as the main medium of exchange. Gold was always viewed as an inferior metal to silver. The Chinese price for silver was almost always higher than the world price and the Chinese price for gold almost always lower. Accordingly, silver tended to flow into China while gold flowed out.

Under the Yongle emperor, the government began to mine silver intensively. Since the demand for silver was so great, government employees and thieves siphoned off much of the mined silver. Government figures thus reflect a fraction of actual production, which experts estimate to have been three times higher than stated. Government records from the reign of the Yongle emperor show production peaking at over 10 metric tons (11 English tons) a year; and after 1440, it declined to less than 3 metric tons (3.3 English tons) a year and to less than 1.5 metric tons (1.65 English tons) a year after 1500.[20]

The world's largest economy at the time desperately needed silver so it could expand. By the 1530s, the situation had become so severe and the potential profits from the silver trade so great that merchants dared to ignore the government's ban on trade with foreign nations. Silver first came in from Japan, whose mines were producing large quantities. Like pilferage, smuggling generates no records unless detected, but in 1542 the Chinese government seized three ships from Japan carrying 1 metric ton (1.1 English tons) of silver each, more than China's annual production since 1450. If ten or twenty ships carried that much silver annually, China was importing 20 metric tons (22 English tons) of silver each year, and many analysts estimate the figure to have been even higher.

The amount of silver flowing into China reached new heights after the first silver from the New World reached Asia. The Spanish discovered huge reserves of silver in Peru in the 1540s, but only thirty years later did they perfect the use of mercury to refine it. Spanish galleons carried the silver from the New World to Spain's colony in the Philippines, at Manila, where Chinese merchants from Fujian and Guangdong traded Chinese goods, most often tea, porcelain, and high-quality silks. The Chinese merchants insisted on payment in silver, for European-manufactured goods held little appeal for them, and they retained their prejudice against gold. The lack of records coupled with the extensive smuggling of silver makes it impossible to estimate how much silver flowed annually from the New World to China, but one expert suggests the silver carried in a single Spanish galleon surpassed China's annual production. Another estimates that, between 1570 and 1600, 7.5 percent of the total output of silver from Peruvian mines ended up in China, where it constituted an infusion equal to eight times China's own silver stocks.[21] The size of the Chinese community in Manila provides an indirect measure of the growth in trade between Spain and China. In 1570, forty Chinese lived in Manila. By 1600, the Chinese community had exploded to fifteen thousand people.

The Impact of New World Silver on Ming Taxation

New World silver transformed the Chinese economy down to its roots, although the central government never formally acknowledged it. The tax system established by the Ming founder presumed a barter economy in which individual cultivators paid their taxes in grain and labor once every ten years. As the sixteenth century progressed, though, and as more New World silver entered the economy, certain areas began to pay their taxes with money. The first stage toward commutation was to use cloth; as the century progressed, this changed to silver. The formal reassessment of taxes in grain and labor into silver was called the Single Whip reform, because each cultivator paid all his taxes in a single currency. Because the character for "whip" has the same pronunciation as that for "register," the name of the tax actually meant a single-register tax, in which all taxes were amalgamated into one.

The Single Whip reforms were carried out in different ways in different regions, and wide disparities in how taxes were collected and assessed persisted even after 1600. Most taxpayers ended up paying taxes every year. Their tax was assessed partially on the basis of how many able-bodied men were in the household and partially on the basis of landholdings. With the exception of households that performed certain labor services, such as delivering grain, most households paid a tax in silver in place of their original labor assignment. A county official—rather than the head of a 110-family unit as designated by the Ming founder—collected the tax.

THE SECOND COMMERCIAL REVOLUTION OF THE MING DYNASTY

All the silver pouring into China clearly had an effect, but in the absence of reliable data, assessing the extent of commercialization during the Ming dynasty is difficult. It is also difficult to compare Ming commercialization with that during the first commercial revolution of the Tang and Song dynasties. We have seen in chapter 7 that many households began to produce either part time or full time for the expanding markets of the Song dynasty and to purchase foodstuffs at markets rather than growing it themselves. Song-dynasty commercialization occurred largely in the major cities of the lower Yangzi valley. In succeeding centuries, market networks extended to include smaller cities and ultimately countryside producers. Others, in less developed regions, continued to farm at a subsistence level, growing their own foodstuffs and buying few goods, perhaps only salt, at market. Throughout the Ming, subsistence farming persisted, especially in border areas and remote mountain regions, and it continues today in the poorest regions of modern China like Guizhou province in the southwest.

During the second commercial revolution of the Ming period, the market economy became more extensive. The size of landholdings declined sharply in the areas with the greatest concentration of markets: the lower Yangzi valley, Fujian, and the area around Beijing. In the prosperous lower Yangzi region around Suzhou, during the twelfth and thirteenth centuries, many families owned farms of 4 hectares (10 acres), which they cultivated themselves with the help of draft animals. In the Ming, farms of .67 hectares (1.67 acres), with an ox or a buffalo, were common, while those with no animals might consist of less than a third of a hectare (.83 acres).[22] This decline in the size of farms coupled with an increase in population is evidence that more people were making their living in nonagricultural pursuits.

The economic growth of the Ming period was varied. More towns—especially in the lower Yangzi region and in Fujian—began producing specialty handicrafts such as distinctive types of pottery and porcelain, certain weaves of silk, and varying weights of paper. The variety of edible goods increased—specialized fruits like lichees and tangerines or processed foods like sugar and candy. The size and scale of enterprises also grew, especially those linked with mining. Many new towns came into being, often along waterways or the coast. These frequently had the word for market in their name. Cotton production increased dramatically in the course of the dynasty. In 1400, individual households cultivated cotton, processed it, and manufactured cotton goods, by themselves; by 1600, weaving households in the lower Yangzi imported ginned cotton (with seeds removed) from northern provinces such as Shandong and Henan and the southern ones of Fujian and Guangzhou. Trade, especially in grain, occurred more frequently between the lower Yangzi region and neighboring provinces than it had during the first commercial revolution of the Song dynasty.

A growing economy, expanding market networks, freely flowing money, a large merchant class—all these factors point to a prosperous economy with a larger commercial, nonagricultural sector than had existed in earlier periods. Zhou Chen's street people suggest that a widening disparity in incomes accompanied this economic expansion. Changes in population provide a final, imperfect indicator of steady growth in Ming China. Because the central government gathered population data only as part of its effort to collect revenues, and because it often recorded the number of households (and rarely the total number of people), all population data must be used with caution; scholars have yet to reach a consensus about population growth after 1400. Broadly speaking, we can distinguish two versions of population history during the Ming. The most frequently cited view accepts the official 1393 census of 60 million and proposes 150 million for the dynasty's close, while a newer, more persuasive, calculation revises the census of 1393 upward to 85 million and proposes 310 million for 1650.[23] As much as the two hotly debated views diverge, they agree in one important way: China's population increased more than twofold over a period of two hundred fifty years. Both estimates point to steady, unprecedented growth during the dynasty—convincing evidence that the effects of China's second commercial revolution were widespread and long lasting.

The population data for the first commercial revolution of the Tang, Song, and Jin dynasties are less controversial. The population of 53 million in 755 reached 120 million in 1200, which means that China's population doubled over four hundred years.[24] The demographic evidence strengthens our impression that the second commercial revolution affected more people and was more intense than the first commercial revolution, whose effects were limited largely to the single region of the lower Yangzi valley.

China enjoyed prosperity and growth during the Ming dynasty. In comparison to earlier periods, the empire's economic expansion was unprecedented. But by 1600, China was no longer the world's leader; Europe, so long in China's shadow, had begun to outpace her.

EPILOGUE

Until 1600, China's economy was more developed than Europe's. Any European visiting China during the long time span covered by this book would have been impressed by China's large cities, high-quality textiles, extensive libraries, and sophisticated technology. In his *Travels*, Marco Polo (or his unnamed informants) describes China's capital at Hangzhou (which he calls Kinsai) as "without doubt the finest and most splendid city in the world."[1] In the sixteenth century, Francis Bacon (1561–1626) credited three inventions with transforming the world: printing, gunpowder, and the compass. All had come to Europe from China.

Starting in 1600, European perceptions of Chinese superiority began to erode. Matteo Ricci and his Jesuit companions recognized Chinese technological skill in some areas—fine silk textiles and porcelain—but they knew that European clocks, cannons, and astronomical instruments were better than their Chinese counterparts. In the centuries after 1600 the gap between Europe and China widened, always at China's expense. By the nineteenth century the European nations commanded military forces far more powerful than Chinese armies, and only China's size and a series of historical contingencies prevented her from being conquered and colonized. Instead, the European powers—and Japan—carved China up into spheres of influence governed indirectly by foreign powers.

What accounts for the reversal? The simplest answer is that Europe achieved first a scientific revolution and then an industrial revolution that powered its development to unprecedented levels. So, while China experienced both intensification of agriculture and expansion of commercial networks, its growth paled in comparison to Europe's.

New World food crops, which Chinese cultivators adopted with great enthusiasm, were the greatest source of innovation after 1600.

New World Food Crops

New World food crops transformed Chinese cuisine. Red chili peppers, sweet peppers, and peanuts joined some of China's traditional ingredients in its most beloved and familiar dishes. Other New World crops had little nutritional value but altered lifestyles in lasting ways. Tobacco cultivation and use spread quickly. In the seventeenth century one observer described how tobacco had entered China:

> Smoke leaves. These . . . originally came from Fujian. When I was young I heard my elders say that in Fujian there were some who smoked them by inhaling, and that doing this made people drunk. They were called "dry wine." But there were none in this locality. At the end of the Chongzhen reign (1628–1644) a man surnamed Peng in the county capital got some seeds from I know not where, and grew them here. He picked the leaves and dried them in the dark. Then those who worked at this business cut them into fine shreds, and they were sold to merchants from places far away.[2]

Tobacco became a popular stimulant, especially among laborers, who were tired and chronically undernourished. It still enjoys an enormous following, although recent regulations ban smoking in public places.

As dramatic as the introduction of tobacco was, the staples from the New World—corn, potatoes, and sweet potatoes—had the greatest long-term effects. Since the beginnings of agriculture, the Chinese had settled in river valleys and lowlands where they grew millet, wheat, and rice. The introduction of new rice strains from Vietnam had improved productivity, but even those strains could grow only in terraced, irrigated fields. A New World food crop such as corn could grow in areas too dry for rice yet too wet for wheat, and it grew faster than either crop. Potatoes could grow in the same climate as wheat, but they produced several times as much food. A hardy crop, potatoes required little care and could grow at high altitudes. Peanuts, another high-calorie crop, grew along rivers and coastlines where other crops could not be cultivated.

Although the new crops required a shorter growing season and less careful tending than indigenous Chinese crops, they never displaced rice and wheat from their primary positions as the staple foods of the Chinese. No crop new to China ever rivaled the success of the potato in Ireland. In plentiful years Chinese farmers continued to plant wheat and rice, and no one voluntarily ate the New World food crops, except for the occasional snack of a roasted sweet potato or corn fritter. It was during famine years that the New World food crops mattered. Cultivators could harvest a crop of potatoes or corn in years in which both the rice and wheat crops failed, averting starvation.

New World food crops were only one factor contributing to China's population explosion after 1600. After 1368, the empire was unified and no long wars interrupted the continuous growth of population. The size of the population under the Shang and Zhou dynasties is impossible to assess, but most analysts agree that the population during the Han and Tang dynasties remained near sixty million. It continued to grow, reaching one hundred twenty million in 1200, during the period of division between the Southern Song and the Jin dynasty in the north. Under the Mongols, the population declined, possibly because of deaths resulting from the Mongol conquest, possibly because of Black Death, and reached a startlingly low 85 million in 1380. The following table offers a reconstruction of China's demographic history.[3]

SUMMARY OF CHINA'S DEMOGRAPHIC HISTORY

YEAR	POPULATION	CENSUS
2		59,594,978
200	60,000,000	
755		52,919,309
1000	100,000,000	
1200	120,000,000	
1380	85,000,000	
1393		60,545,812
1500	165,000,000	
1600	260,000,000	
1650	310,000,000	
1812		360,282,000
1900	500,000,000	
1950	600,000,000	
2000	1,300,000,000	

The Effects of China's Population Increase

However one interprets these figures, one trend is crystal clear. China's population began to increase steadily after 1380 when the burden of feeding the population began to weigh more heavily than it ever had in the centuries before the Ming dynasty.

The contrast with Europe here is stark. In 1500, right after Columbus's voyage, Europe's population totaled some one hundred million people. Many of these left Europe to settle the conquered territories of the New World in the sixteenth and seventeenth centuries, reducing European population density even further.[4] Small family size and the movement of so many Europeans overseas provided a steady demand for labor-saving devices, a precondition for technological innovation.

In China, large family size and continued population growth after 1380 produced an excess of labor. Accordingly, demand for labor-saving devices remained weak. A 1313 manual, Wang Zhen's *Treatise on Agriculture*, depicts a spinning machine not too different from the spinning jenny and the spinning frame that were so important to Europe's Industrial Revolution. This machine, powered by human or animal labor, had thirty-two spindles that could spin 58.5 kilograms (130 pounds) of thread in a day. Wang Zhen's written description gives the dimensions of this machine as 6 meters (20 feet) long and 1.5 meters (5 feet) wide. This spinning machine never enjoyed widespread use, and by 1600, people seem to have forgotten its existence; no Chinese subsequently used anything like it.

In an era of population increase, there was simply no demand for a machine that could save labor. As Mark Elvin has stated, "What China thus needed was something not within the bounds of technological possibility—namely, a machine that would produce cotton cloth with half the previous input of raw cotton rather than half the previous input of human labor."[5] China had labor—lots of it. What China lacked was a surplus of raw materials that could be processed into manufactured goods. Given the increasing pressure of population, less and less land could be devoted to nonagricultural crops like cotton, and any surplus that might have financed technological innovation was consumed by the growing population. Conditions simply were not ripe for the introduction of labor-saving machinery.

Historians have come to realize that the Ming-dynasty system of handicraft production differed in important ways from the European putting-out system that preceded the industrial revolution. In industrializing Europe, merchant-entrepreneurs supplied weavers with machinery and thread that they wove into cloth in their own homes; the merchants returned to collect the woven goods and deliver more supplies. The merchant-entrepreneurs controlled the production process throughout, and they could introduce technological innovations at any time. In China, however, middlemen came between the entrepreneurs and the peasant producers. The middlemen sold the weavers thread and then bought the output of the household. Each household determined the production process. Many layers of middlemen stood between the producers of handicrafts and the entrepreneurs who sold the goods at market. The middlemen made it difficult to transmit innovations between the entrepreneurs and the peasant producers.

One final contrast with Europe is worth consideration. The Europe that underwent both the scientific and industrial revolutions comprised a number of competing states, which some analysts see as crucial to both revolutions. Military competition among the European states was one spur to innovation. And inventors or scholars who encountered repression in one country could seek refuge in another.

China, on the other hand, was reunified in 1368 and remained so until 1911. In 1644 the Ming dynasty fell to the invading Manchus, a non-Chinese people who dwelled in the forests of Manchuria. Like the Jurchen, whom the Manchus claimed as their ancestors, the Manchus formed a confederation powerful enough to conquer China within the space of a generation. In 1621 the Manchus controlled only two cities in the northwest (Shenyang and Liaoyang). By 1642 they controlled all of Manchuria. Although the Ming rulers were surely aware of the threat to the northeast, they were preoccupied with an empire-wide peasant rebellion. In April of 1644 the rebels took Beijing, and only one month later a Ming general surrendered to the Manchus. Pouring through the Great Wall, the Manchus conquered China and established the Qing dynasty, China's last.

But one should not exaggerate the degree of centralized control under Manchu rule. The Qing state was not uniformly powerful enough to stifle invention. Many Chinese proved themselves more than capable of mastering and adopting Western science and technology in the nineteenth century.

Still, the point suggests a fruitful assessment of China's own past. Certain eras in Chinese history stand out for the liveliness of their thinkers, their artistic creativity, and sudden bursts of economic growth. The first such era occurred during the sixth to the third centuries B.C., when Confucius taught his students, and when rival schools propounded ideas about nature, man, and the role of government. This was the age when warring states forged alliances, disbanded, and formed new alliances. The constant fighting prompted the first coinage, labor specialization, and the formation of cities.

The era of the Silk Road trade, from the fall of the Han dynasty in A.D. 220 to the end of the first millennium, was also a remarkable time in Chinese history. China's population was exposed to foreign traders, commodities, and teachings, and foreign motifs transformed Chinese silver, textiles, and figurines. People were drawn to the new religions of Daoism and Buddhism. Aided by generous state support, Buddhist teachers developed new teachings that allowed laypeople to remain filial to their parents even as they converted to Buddhism.

The final period of significant change has to be China's first commercial revolution, occurring in the centuries after 800 under the Song. Many people took up side pursuits in addition to agriculture to expand their incomes. The development of woodblock printing facilitated the exchange of ideas, and, as the new Confucian synthesis of Zhu Xi circulated among scholars in South China, the ideas of Su Shi about culture spread among scholars in north China under Jurchen rule. A considerable border trade between north and south ensured that ideas and inventions traveled all over the empire.

During these periods of dramatic growth China was not unified. During the Warring States period, several large kingdoms contested each other for control of the empire. During the first centuries of contact with Buddhist missionaries, the empire was divided into north and south, and it was the non-Chinese rulers of the north who gave Buddhist missionaries their start. And during the crucial centuries of commercial growth, China was divided into two: first a tiny northern section controlled by the Khitans and the huge southern empire of the Song, and then the much larger northern kingdom of the Jurchens and the smaller kingdom of the Southern Song. The enormous tribute payments the Song agreed to pay first the Khitans and then the Jurchen provided a spur to the developing economy and contributed to the dramatic economic growth of the period.

All the observers who lived during these ages of innovation bemoaned the lack of unity and wished for a ruler strong enough to unite the empire. They do not seem to have realized how much vitality resulted from the disunity, from the fighting, and from the ensuing chaos.

NOTES

INTRODUCTION

1. Many of the translations have been taken from Victor Mair's *The Columbia Anthology of Traditional Chinese Literature* (New York, 1994). I cite translations, whenever available, for the convenience of English-speaking readers. I have checked the original texts of all Chinese passages, and in rare instances I have modified the translation to increase accuracy. I have also changed the romanization so that all Chinese terms are in pinyin romanization, and I have dropped brackets and other sinological conventions to enhance readability. To reduce the number of footnotes, only direct quotations and statistics are cited. If a series of quotations comes from one source, only one note will be given after the first citation, with page numbers for subsequent citations in that same note.

2. Samuel Beal, *Buddhist Records of the Western World translated from the Chinese of Hiuen Tsiang (A.D. 629)* (Delhi, 1982 [1884]), xxiii–lxxxiii, xlv (travelers from afar), lxxi (rebirth in India).

CHAPTER 1   THE BEGINNING OF THE WRITTEN RECORD
(ca. 1200 B.C.–771 B.C.)

1. David N. Keightley, *Sources of Shang History* (Berkeley, 1978), 78–79.
2. David N. Keightley, "Sources of Shang History: Two Major Oracle-Bone Collections," *Journal of the American Oriental Society* 110.1 (1990): 49.
3. David N. Keightley, "A Late Shang Divination Record," Selection 1, in Victor Mair, *Columbia Anthology of Traditional Chinese Literature*, 3–4. The version I give here has been modified by Keightley; compare Keightley, *Sources*, 41.
4. K. C. Chang, *Art, Myth, and Ritual: The Path to Political Authority in Ancient China* (Cambridge, 1983), 103.
5. David Hawkes, *The Songs of the South* (New York, 1985), 227–228.
6. K. C. Chang, *Shang Civilization* (New Haven, 1980), 158–194.
7. *Kaogu xuebao* (Reports in archeology) (1979) 1: 27–120 (English abstract, 119–120).
8. To use David N. Keightley's term from "Early Civilization in China: Reflections on How It Became Chinese," in Paul Ropp (ed.) *Heritage of China: Contemporary Perspectives on Chinese Civilization* (Berkeley, 1990), 30.
9. K. C. Chang, *Shang Civilization*, 228.

415

10. Edward L. Shaughnessy, "Historical Geography and the Extent of the Earliest Chinese Kingdoms," *Asia Major* 3rd series 2.2 (1989): 1–22.

11. K. C. Chang, *Shang Civilization*, 194.

12. Edward L. Shaughnessy, "Historical Perspectives on the Introduction of the Chariot," *Harvard Journal of Asiatic Studies* 48.1 (1988): 189–237, citation on 214.

13. They also claimed that the Shang had taken the Mandate of Heaven from their predecessors, the Xia dynasty. Historians and archeologists vigorously debate whether a Xia dynasty preceded the Shang, with some arguing that the pre-Shang Erlitou culture is the same as the Xia culture mentioned by Sima Qian in his chronicle of ancient Chinese history. Others, more skeptical, point out that the Erlitou sites provide no written evidence linking their culture to the Xia and think the Xia may simply have been the creation of Zhou-dynasty propagandists. *The Cambridge History of Ancient China: From the Origins of Civilization to 221 B.C.*, ed. Michael Loewe and Edward L. Shaughnessy (New York, 1999), presents the pro-Xia view (K. C. Chang) and the opposing view (Robert Bagley).

14. William H. Nienhauser, Jr. (ed.), *The Grand Scribe's Records,* Volume 1: *The Basic Annals of Pre-Han Ching by Ssu-ma Ch'ien* (Bloomington, 1994), 49–52; K. C. Chang, *Shang Civilization*, 13–15.

15. Edward L. Shaughnessy, "Historical Perspectives on the Introduction of the Chariot," 231.

16. Edward L. Shaughnessy, *I Ching: The Classic of Changes* (New York, 1996), 159.

17. We are fortunate, too, that some of the greatest translators and linguists of the twentieth century translated the poems into English. The classic translations are by Bernard Karlgren, *The Book of Odes* (Stockholm, 1950), and Arther Waley, *The Book of Songs* (New York, 1937), while *Columbia Anthology of Traditional Chinese Literature* contains more recent selections by Jeffrey Riegel, and *An Anthology of Chinese Literature* (New York, 1996) contains those by Stephen Owen. Interested readers will want to compare all versions. Because the original Chinese (included by Karlgren) drops many pronouns, each translator must decide who is speaking in any given passage and choose the appropriate pronouns accordingly. This text uses Waley's translations of the work song detailing the seasons (164–167, Mao number 154), "Big rat" (309, Mao number 113), and the "dead doe" (60, Mao number 62); Riegel's for "very stupid dolt" (155–156, Mao number 58).

18. Lothar von Falkenhausen, "Issues in Western Zhou Studies," *Early China* 18 (1993): 151; "The Etiquette of Communication," unpublished paper, April 1989.

19. Edward L. Shaughnessy, "Two Bronze Inscriptions of the Western Chou," Selection 2, in Mair, *Columbia Anthology of Traditional Chinese Literature*, 4–5; Shaughnessy, "The Date of the 'Duo You Ding' and Its Significance," *Early China* 9–10 (1983–1985): 55–69.

20. Lothar von Falkenhausen, "Issues in Western Zhou Studies," *Early China* 18 (1993): 149–150, modifying Karlgren's translation of ode number 209.

CHAPTER 2   THE AGE OF THE WARRIOR AND THE THINKER:
             DOUBLE EARS AND CONFUCIUS

1. *The Spring and Autumn Annals* is the first surviving source to provide a year-by-year account of events from 722 to 481 B.C. (In poetic phrasing, "spring and autumn" means "year.") Written down sometime in the fourth century B.C., *The Annals* must have drawn on earlier written sources, or perhaps oral traditions. Early scholars credited Confucius with the book's authorship, though few now do. Several authors later formulated commentaries in which they expanded on the entries in *The Spring and Autumn Annals*. The most important source for the history of the Spring and Autumn period, *The Commentary of Mr. Zuo*, purports to be a commentary to *The Spring and Autumn Annals*, but most modern scholars think it was originally a separate narrative, also organized year by year, that was written down (on silk?

on bamboo?) a little before 300 B.C. After being cut up into different sections, it was later appended to *The Spring and Autumn Annals*. Because the narrative is not always continuous, but sometimes backtracks or jumps ahead, it seems quite likely that *The Commentary of Mr. Zuo* combined several different sources by different authors. See the entry in Michael Loewe (ed.), *Early Chinese Texts: A Bibliographical Guide* (Berkeley, 1993).

2. There is some disagreement about when to start the Warring States period. The end date of the earlier Spring and Autumn period, 481 B.C., is a logical break, but others prefer 453 B.C., when the Jin kingdom was partitioned into the Wei, Han, and Zhao kingdoms, or 403 B.C., the date of formal recognition by the Zhou king of the division of the Jin kingdom.

3. Melvin Thatcher, "Marriages of the Ruling Elite," in Rubie S. Watson and Patricia Buckley Ebrey (eds.), *Marriage and Inequality in Chinese Society* (Berkeley, 1991), 49.

4. Burton Watson, *The Tso Chuan: Selections from China's Oldest Narrative History* (New York, 1989), 42–43 (promise to withdraw for three days' march), 60–63 (battle of Chengpu).

5. Nicola Di Cosmo, essay in Michael Loewe and Edward Shaughnessy (eds.), *The Cambridge History of Ancient China* (New York, 1999).

6. Mark Edward Lewis, *Sanctioned Violence in Early China* (Albany, 1990), 116. Compare Roger T. Ames, *Sun-tzu: The Art of Warfare* (New York, 1993), 111.

7. J. I. Crump, *Chan-kuo Ts'e* (Ann Arbor, 1996), 289 (Zhao king), 195–198 (Longsword).

8. Interested readers will want to consult the arguments for dating individual chapters and the new translation by E. Bruce Brooks and A. Taeko Brooks in *The Original Analects: Sayings of Confucius and His Successors* (New York, 1998), which was not available to me at the time of writing.

9. All passages are followed by the chapter and verse number from Simon Leys, *The Analects of Confucius* (New York, 1997).

10. Margery Wolf, "Beyond the Patrilineal Self: Constructing Gender in China," in Roger T. Ames et al. (eds.), *Self as Person in Asian Theory and Practice* (Albany, 1994), 251–267.

11. Robert Eno, *The Confucian Creation of Heaven: Philosophy and the Defense of Ritual Mastery* (Albany, 1990), 33.

12. Susan R. Weld, "The Covenant Texts from Houma and Wenxian," in Edward L. Shaughnessy (ed.), *New Sources of Early Chinese History* (Berkeley, 1997), 140–142.

13. Robert Eno, *The Confucian Creation of Heaven*, 239.

14. A. C. Graham assigns the authorship of the different chapters to three sects he classes as "purist," "compromising," and "reactionary," in *Disputers of the Tao, Philosophical Argument in Ancient China* (La Salle, Illinois, 1989), 36.

15. Burton Watson, *Basic Writings of Mo Tzu, Hsün Tzu, and Han Fei Tzu* (New York, 1963–1964), 59 (physician), 127 (Confucian pleasure in funerals), 75–77 (three non-Chinese peoples).

16. Benjamin Schwartz, *The Word of Thought in Ancient China* (Cambridge, 1985), 148 (thieves), 140 (guests).

17. Robert Eno, *The Confucian Creation of Heaven*, 50–51.

18. Victor Mair (trans.) *Tao Te Ching: The Classic Book of Integrity and the Way* (New York, 1990), 59. This book has two halves, *The Integrity Classic* and *The Way Classic*. This verse is the first verse in *The Way Classic*, which traditionally preceded *The Integrity Classic*, but an archeologically discovered text at Mawangdui reverses the two halves, as does Mair in this translation. See also excerpt 10 in Mair's *The Columbia Anthology of Traditional Chinese Literature*.

19. Victor Mair, *Tao Te Ching*, 138 (definition of wuwei), 54 (verse 43 [original number 78], immutability), 31 (verse 24 [original number 61], female stillness), 30 (verse 23 [original number 60], cooking fish), 39 (verse 30 [original number 80], small state), (verse 63 [original number 19], Confucianism).

20. Burton Watson, *Chuang Tzu Basic Writings* (New York, 1964), 87 (Yan Hui), 45 (butterfly), 42–43 (Lady Li), 115 (skull), 60 (tree).

21. Donald Harper, "Resurrection in Warring States Popular Religion," *Taoist Resources* 5.2 (1994): 13–28.

22. W.A.C.H. Dobson (trans.), *Mencius*, Selection 8. In Victor Mair, *Columbia Anthology*, 43.

23. Burton Watson, *Basic Writings*, 62, 70–71 (section 15, "Debating Military Affairs" about Qin rule), 42, 43 (section 9, "The Regulations of a King" about meritocracy and trade).

Chapter 3   The Creation of Empire (221 b.c.–a.d. 200)

1. J. J. L. Duyvendak, *The Book of Lord Shang: A Classic of the Chinese School of Law* (Chicago, 1928), 172–173.

2. Mark Lewis, *Sanctioned Violence in Early China* (Albany, 1990), 61–62.

3. Karen Turner Gottschang, "Chinese Despotism Reconsidered: Monarchy and its Critics in the Ch'in and Early Han Empires," University of Michigan Ph.D. dissertation, 1983, 31–32.

4. Denis Twitchett and Michael Loewe (eds.), *The Cambridge History of China*, Volume 1: *The Ch'in and Han Empires 221 B.C.–A.D. 220* (New York, 1986), 61.

5. Maxwell K. Hearn, "The Terracotta Army of the First Emperor of Qin," in Wen Fong (ed.), *The Great Bronze Age of China: An Exhibition from the People's Republic of China* (New York, 1980), 357.

6. Jack L. Dull, "Anti-Qin Rebels: No Peasant Leaders There," *Modern China* 9.3 (1983): 285–318. The cited passage appears on p. 303.

7. *The Cambridge History of China,* Volume 1, 85.

8. Jens Petersen, "Which Books Did the First Emperor of China Burn?" *Monumenta Serica* 43 (1995): 1–52. The list of books to be burned appears on p. 7.

9. A. F. P. Hulsewé, *Remnants of Ch'in Law: An Annotated Translation of the Ch'in Legal and Administrative Rules of the 3rd Century B.C. Discovered in Yün-meng Prefecture, Hu-pei Province, in 1975* (Leiden, 1985), 7–15.

10. Michael Loewe, "Wood and Administrative Documents of the Han Period," in Edward L. Shaughnessy (ed.), *New Sources of Early Chinese History* (Berkeley, 1997), 162.

11. Hugh T. Scogin, "Between Heaven and Man: Contract and the State in Han Dynasty China," *Southern California Law Review* 63.5 (1990): 1386.

12. Turner Gottschang, "Chinese Despotism Reconsidered," 190 (harsh corners), 65 (soup).

13. Yü Ying-shih, "The Hsiung-nu," in Denis Sinor (ed.), *The Cambridge History of Early Inner Asia* (New York, 1990), 123.

14. Fu You and Chen Songchang, *The Cultural Relics Unearthed from the Han Tombs at Mawangdui* (Changsha, 1992), "A Comprehensive Introduction," 13.

15. Yü Ying-shih, "Han China," in K. C. Chang (ed.), *Food in Chinese Culture: Anthropological and Historical Perspectives* (New Haven, 1977), 74.

16. Michael Loewe, "Wood and Administrative Documents of the Han Period," in Edward L. Shaughnessy, *New Sources of Early Chinese History*, 162.

17. Karen Turner, "The Theory of Law in the Ching-fa," *Early China* 14 (1989): 55–76, citation on 60.

18. Jerry Norman and Tsu-lin Mei, "The Austroasiatics in Ancient South China: Some Lexical Evidence," *Monumenta Serica* 32 (1976): 274–301.

19. Cyril Birch, *Anthology of Chinese Literature* (New York, 1965), 97–101.

20. Esson M. Gale (trans.), *Discourses on Salt and Iron: A Debate on State Control of Commerce and Industry in Ancient China* (Leiden, 1931), 15–16.

21. Michèle Pirazzoli-t'Serstevens, *The Han Civilization of China* (Oxford, 1982), 139, 144.

22. Victor Mair, "The Contract for a Youth," (selection 189), *The Columbia Anthology of Traditional Chinese Literature*, 510–513.

23. Hans Bielenstein, "Lo-yang in Later Han Times," *Bulletin of the Museum of Far Eastern History* 48 (1976): 1–142, especially 11, 88.

24. Valerie Hansen, *Negotiating Daily Life* (New Haven, 1995), 152.

25. Victor Mair, *Columbia Anthology*, selection 11, 62–77, citation on 66.

26. Victor Mair, *Columbia Anthology*, selection 194, 534–541, citation on 536; Nancy Lee Swann, *Pan Chao: Foremost Woman Scholar of China* (New York, 1932), 82–91.

27. Anne Behnke Kinney, "Infant Abandonment in Early China," *Early China* 18 (1993): 124.

28. Victor Mair, *Columbia Anthology*, selection 219, 629–630, gives Lin Yutang's translation of *Shuofu* 110: 5066 "Han za shi mi xin," from *The Importance of Understanding* (Cleveland, 1960) 225–228.

29. Rafe de Crespigny, "Politics and Philosophy under the Government of Emperor Huan, 159–168 A.D.," *T'oung Pao* 66.1–3 (1980): 41–83, citation on 54.

30. Wu Hung, *The Wu Liang Shrine: The Ideology of Early Chinese Pictorial Art* (Stanford, 1989), 25, 97.

31. *Weishu* (The History of the Wei) 8: 263–265.

CHAPTER 4   CHINA'S RELIGIOUS LANDSCAPE (200–600)

1. Erik Zürcher, *The Buddhist Conquest of China: The Spread and Adaptation of Buddhism in Early Medieval China* (Leiden, 1972), 27.

2. W. B. Henning, "The Date of the Sogdian Ancient Letters," *Bulletin of the School of Oriental and African Letters*," 12.3–4 (1948): 601–615, citation on 605.

3. Arthur Wright, "Fo-t'u-teng: A Biography," in Arthur F. Wright and Robert M. Somers (eds.), *Studies in Chinese Buddhism* (New Haven, 1990), 47 (blue lotus), 59 (Buddha as foreign deity).

4. Kathryn Ann Tsai (trans.), *Lives of the Nuns: Biographies of Chinese Buddhist Nuns from the Fourth to Sixth Centuries: A translation of the Pi-ch'iu-ni chuan, compiled by Shih Pao-ch'ang* (Honolulu, 1994), 20.

5. Arthur F. Wright, *Buddhism in Chinese History* (New York, 1959), 37.

6. Zenryū Tsukamoto, *A History of Early Chinese Buddhism: From Its Introduction to the Death of Hui-yüan*, trans. Leon Hurvitz (New York, 1985), 175.

7. Larissa Schwartz and I learned this in May 1996 from our two guides, Wen Aiqiong and Ms. Tang, and the director of the Kizil Research Institute, Chen Shiliang.

8. *Zhongguo shiku Kezier shiku* I (Beijing, 1989), 210. This book contains beautiful plates of many of the caves.

9. Samuel Beal, *Buddhist Records of the Western World Tsiang (A.D. 629)*, xxiii–lxxxiii, lxxiii (fan), lxxxi (Faxian).

10. Joseph Fletcher, "The Mongols: Ecological and Social Perspectives," *Harvard Journal of Asiatic Studies* 46.1 (1986): 11–50, citation on 17.

11. Han Guopan, *Weijin Nanbeichao shigang* (Beijing, 1983), 446–447.

12. W. F. J. Jenner, *Memories of Loyang: Yang Hsüan-chih and the Lost Capital (493–534)* (Oxford, 1981), 147–148.

13. Jacques Gernet, *Buddhism in Chinese Society: An Economic History from the Fifth to the Tenth Centuries*, trans. Franciscus Verellen (New York, 1995), 3–4 (types of monasteries), 11–12 (the size of the monastic population), 256 (presence of Buddhist sanctuaries).

14. Albert Dien, "A New Look at the Xianbei and Their Impact on Chinese Culture," in George Kuwayama (ed.), *Ancient Mortuary Traditions of China: Papers on Chinese Ceramic Funerary Sculptures* (Los Angeles, 1991), 54.

15. Pei-yi Wu, translation of the "zhijia" section of Yan Zhitui's memoir, personal communication to the author, September 9, 1996.

16. Yen Chih-t'ui, *Family Instructions for the Yen Clan: An Annotated Translation with Introduction (Yen-shih Chia-hsün)* (Leiden, 1968), 20.

17. Jacques Gernet, *Buddhism in Chinese Society*, 6.

18. Erik Zürcher, "Perspectives in the Study of Chinese Buddhism," *Journal of the Royal Asiatic Society of Great Britain and Ireland* 2 (1982): 161–176.

CHAPTER 5   CHINA'S GOLDEN AGE (589–755)

1. Arthur Waley, *Ballads and Stories from Tun-huang: An Anthology* (New York, 1960), 172.

2. Wallace Johnson, *The T'ang Code,* Volume I: *General Principles* (Princeton, 1979); *The T'ang Code,* Volume II: *Specific Articles* (Princeton, 1997).

3. Antonino Forte, *Political Propaganda and Ideology in China at the End of the Seventh Century* (Naples, 1976), 187–200, citations on 187, 195.

4. Arthur Wright, "Symbolism and Function: Reflections on Changan and Other Great Cities," *Journal of Asian Studies* 24.4 (1964): 667–679, citation on 671.

5. Chi-chen Wang (trans.), *Traditional Chinese Tales* (New York, 1944), 62 (curfew), 67 (constable of the quarter), 73 (qualities of a courtesan).

6. Ikeda On, "T'ang Household Registers and Related Documents," in Arthur F. Wright and Denis Twitchett (eds.), *Perspectives on the T'ang* (New Haven, 1973), 121–150, citation on 124–125.

7. Valerie Hansen, "Why Bury Contracts in Tombs?" *Cahiers d'Extrême-Asie* 8 (1995): 59–66.

CHAPTER 6   THE AN LUSHAN REBELLION AND ITS AFTERMATH
(755–960)

1. Witter Bynner (trans.), in Cyril Birch (comp. and ed.), *Anthology of Chinese Literature from Early Times to the Fourteenth Century* (New York, 1965), 266–269.

2. Denis Twitchett, "The Salt Commissioners after An Lu-shan's Rebellion," *Asia Major* n.s. 4.1 (1954): 60–89.

3. Arthur Waley, *The Life and Times of Po Chü-i* (New York, 1949), 18.

4. Denis Twitchett, "Merchant, Trade and Government in Late T'ang," *Asia Major* n.s. 14 (1968): 3–95, citation on 90–91.

5. Arthur Waley (trans.), *A Hundred and Seventy Chinese Poems* (New York, 1949), 199–200.

6. Chi-chen Wang, *Traditional Chinese Tales*, 75–86, citations on 83–84, 86; the story is also Selection 252, Mair, *Columbia Anthology*, 851–861.

7. James R. Hightower, "Yüan Chen and 'The Story of Ying-ying,'" *Harvard Journal of Asiatic Studies* 33 (1973): 90–121, citation on 112–117.

8. Arthur Waley, *The Life and Times of Po Chü-i*, 78.

9. Jacques Gernet, *Buddhism in Chinese Society*, 237.

10. Denis Twitchett, *Financial Administration*, 165–166.

11. Edwin O. Reischauer (trans.), *Ennin's Diary: The Record of a Pilgrimage to China in Search of the Law* (New York, 1955), 239 (flowers), 257–258 (maigre feasts).

12. Edward H. Schafer, "The Last Years of Ch'ang-an," *Oriens Extremus* 10 (1963): 133–180, n. 243.

13. Aurel Stein, *Serindia*, Volume II (Oxford, 1921), 808.

14. Lionel Giles, "Six Centuries at Tunhuang: A Short Account of the Stein Collection of Chinese Mss. in the British Museum" (London, 1944), 5.

15. Jeannette Mirsky, *Sir Aurel Stein, Archeological Explorer* (Chicago, 1977), 278–280.

16. Paul Pelliot, "Une bibliothèque médiévale retrouvée au Kan-sou," *Bulletin de l'Ecole Française d'Extrême Orient* 8 (1908): 528–529.

17. Rong Xinjiang, "Dunhuang cangjingdong de xingzhi ji qi fengbi yuanyin" (The nature of the document-cave at Dunhuang and the reasons for its being sealed), *Dunhuang Tulufan yanjiu* 2 (1996): 23–48.

18. Lionel Giles, "Six Centuries," 18.

19. Victor H. Mair, *Tun-huang Popular Narratives* (Cambridge, 1983), 87–121, 92 (meeting with father), 106 (underworld terrors), 110 (ungrateful mother).

20. Liu Xinru, "Buddhist Lay Associations in Tunhuang," unpublished paper, translation of Pelliot, 3037.

21. Lionel Giles, "Six Centuries at Tunhuang," 38; compare Gernet, *Buddhism in Chinese Society*, 272.

22. Valerie Hansen, *Negotiating Daily Life*, 68–73.

CHAPTER 7 COMING TO TERMS WITH MONEY: THE SONG DYNASTY (960–1276)

1. Robert M. Hartwell, "Regional Economic Development and the Transformation of Chinese Society, 750–1250 A.D.," unpublished paper presented at SORCE Conference on Regionalism and Economic Development in China, Philadelphia, 1978.

2. Robert M. Hartwell, "Markets, Technology, and the Structure of Enterprise in the Development of the Eleventh-Century Chinese Iron and Steel Industry," *The Journal of Economic History* 26 (1966): 29–58, citation on 45.

3. Christoph Schifferli, "Le système monétaire au Sichuan vers la fin du Xe siècle," *T'oung Pao* 72 (1986): 269–290.

4. Robert M. Hartwell, "The Evolution of the Early Northern Sung Monetary System," *Journal of the American Oriental Society* 87.3 (1967): 280–289.

5. Yuan Yitang, "BeiSong qianhuang: song bizhi dao liutong tizhi de kaocha," *Lishi yanjiu* 1991.4: 129–140, statistics on 131.

6. Paul J. Smith, "Shen-tsung's Reign (1068–1085)," draft chapter for *The Cambridge History of China*, Volume 5: *The Sung* (dated August 1993).

7. Yang Lien-sheng, *Money and Credit in China: A Short History* (Cambridge, 1952), 53.

8. The great Chinese archeologist Su Bai wrote the site report, which has been published in a lavish volume, complete with a long English abstract and English key to the plates, to facilitate consultation. *Baisha Songmu* (The Song tomb at Baisha) (Beijing, 1957).

9. For a full translation of this text and an explanation of the different clauses, see chapter 6 of Valerie Hansen, *Negotiating Daily Life*, citation on 166.

10. Translated in full by Stephen Owen, *An Anthology of Chinese Literature* (New York, 1996), 591–596.

11. Ling Chung and Kenneth Rexroth, *Li Ch'ing-chao: Complete Poems* (New York, 1979), 52.

12. Yoshinobu Shiba, "Urbanization and Development of Markets in the Lower Yangtze Valley," in John Winthrop Haeger (ed.), *Crisis and Prosperity in Sung China* (Tucson, 1975), 19.

13. Hong Mai, *Yijianzhi* (The record of the listener) (Beijing, 1981) 4.11: 631–632.

14. E. A. Kracke, "Sung K'ai-feng: Pragmatic Metropolis and Formalistic Capital," in John Winthrop Haeger (ed.), *Crisis and Prosperity in Sung China*, 65–67.

15. Pei-yi Wu, "Memories of Kaifeng," *New Literary History* (1994) 25: 47–60, 51 (about friendliness of Hangzhou natives), 53 (about performers).

16. Valerie Hansen, *The Beijing Qingming Scroll and Its Significance for the Study of Chinese History* (Albany, 1996), 3.

17. His comment is contained in a Yuan collection of miscellaneous notes, Tao Zongyi's *Nancun chuogenglu* (Beijing, 1980), 126–127.

18. Valerie Hansen, *Changing Gods in Medieval China, 1127–1276* (Princeton, 1990), 77 (miracle of mats), 117 (lotus pod merchants).

19. Ellen Neskar, "Shrines to Local Former Worthies," in Donald S. Lopez, Jr., *Religions of China in Practice* (Princeton, 1996), 293–305, citation on 301.

20. Ellen Neskar, "The Cult of Worthies: A Study of Shrines Honoring Local Confucian Worthies in the Sung Dynasty (960–1279)," Columbia University Ph.D. dissertation, 1993, 59 (three masters), 238 (failure to visit), 267 (true Confucian way).

21. Valerie Hansen, *Changing Gods*, 8.

22. John W. Chaffee, *The Thorny Gates of Learning in Sung China: A Social History of Examinations* (New York, 1985), 35.

23. Peter K. Bol, review article, "The Sung Examination System and the Shih," *Asia Major* 3rd series 3.2 (1990): 149–171; figures on 152.

24. John W. Chaffee, *Thorny Gates*, 114.

25. Daniel K. Gardner, *Chu Hsi Learning to Be a Sage: Selections from the Conversations of Master Chu, Arranged Topically* (Berkeley, 1990), 53.

CHAPTER 8   THE NORTHERN DYNASTIES: NON-CHINESE RULE IN NORTH CHINA (907–1215)

1. Karl A. Wittfogel and Feng Chia-sheng, *History of Chinese Society Liao 907–1125*. Transactions of the American Philosophical Society n.s. 36 (Philadelphia, 1946), 254, n. 27.

2. Ruth Dunnell, "The Hsi Hsia," in Herbert Franke and Denis Twitchett (eds.), *The Cambridge History of China*, Volume 6: *Alien Regimes and Border States, 907–1368* (New York, 1994), 1987.

3. Herbert Franke, "The Chin Dynasty," in *The Cambridge History of China*, Volume 6, 265–266.

4. Julia Murray, "Ts'ao Hsün and Two Southern Sung History Scrolls," *Ars Orientalis* 15 (1985): 1–29, citation on 10.

5. Herbert Franke, "The Chin Dynasty," in the *Cambridge History of China*, Volume 6, 239–240 ("aping the Chinese"); 278, Table 7 (population figures); 282 (slaves per household); 279 (estimate of Jurchen and Khitan population).

6. Peter Bol, "Seeking Common Ground: Han Literati under Jurchen Rule," *Harvard Journal of Asiatic Studies* 47 (1987): 461–538, figures on 475–476.

7. Stephen West, *Vaudeville and Narrative: Aspects of Chin Theater (1115–1234)* (Wiesbaden, 1977), 125.

8. Li-li Ch'en (trans.), *Master Tung's Western Chamber Romance (Tung Hsi-hsiang chu-kung-tiao)* (New York, 1994), 6–7 (about Zhang's education), 15 (bound feet), 147–148 (fondling).

9. Wilt Idema, "Satire and Allegory in All Keys and Modes," in Hoyt Cleveland Tillman and Stephen West (eds.), *China under Jurchen Rule* (Albany, 1995), 238–280, citation on 255.

10. Peter Bol, "Seeking Common Ground," 497.

11. Tao Jing-shen, *The Jurchen in Twelfth Century China* (Seattle, 1976), 88.

CHAPTER 9   THE MONGOLS (CA. 1200–1368)

1. Francis Cleaves, *The Secret History of the Mongols* (Cambridge, 1982), 33. Compare Paul Kahn, *The Secret History of the Mongols* (San Francisco, 1984).

2. Pei-yi Wu, "Yang Miao-chen, a Woman Warrior in Thirteenth-Century China," unpublished paper given at the University Seminar on Traditional China, Columbia University, April 9, 1996.

3. John Andrew Boyle, "The Last Barbarian Invaders: The Impact of the Mongol Conquests upon East and West," *Memoirs and Proceedings of the Manchester Literary and Philosophical Society* 112 (Manchester, 1970). Reprinted in *The Mongol World Empire 1206–1370* (London: Variorum Reprints, 1977), 1–15, 6–7 (Paris); 5 (Juvaini).

4. Peter Jackson (trans.), *The Mission of Friar William of Rubruck: His Journey to the Court of the Great Khan Möngke 1253–1255* (London, 1990), 188 (rations), 178 (the khan's nose), 179 (drunk interpreter), 193 (divination with bones).

5. Ronald Latham (trans.), *The Travels of Marco Polo* (New York, 1958), 197 (virgins), 224 (paper funeral goods), 213 (splendid city), 214–215 (market).

6. Robert Hymes, "Not Quite Gentlemen? Doctors in Sung and Yuan," *Chinese Science* 8 (1987): 9–76, citation on 53.

7. William Dolby, *Eight Chinese Plays from the Thirteenth Century to the Present* (New York, 1978), 24–25.

8. William Dolby, *Eight Chinese Plays*, 37 (swotting), 48 (son-in-law).

9. John Dardess, "Shun-ti and the End of Yüan Rule in China," *Cambridge History of China*, Volume 6, 565.

10. Frederick W. Mote, "Chinese Society under Mongol Rule, 1215–1368," *Cambridge History of China*, Volume 6, 638.

11. Li Chu-Tsing, "The Freer Sheep and Goat and Chao Meng-fu's Horse Paintings," *Artibus Asiae* 30.4 (1968): 279–326, citation on 281.

12. Li Chu-Tsing, "Grooms and Horses by Three Members of the Chao Family," in Freda Murck and Wen Fong (eds.), *Words and Images: Chinese Poetry, Calligraphy, and Painting* (New York, 1991), 199–220, citation on 208.

13. Marsha Weidner, *Views from Jade Terrace: Chinese Women Artists, 1300–1912* (Indianapolis, 1988), 66.

14. Elizabeth Toll, "Kuan Tao-sheng: A Study and Translation of the Primary Sources," Harvard University unpublished A.B. thesis, 1978: Appendix VII.

15. Kenneth Rexroth and Ling Chung, *Orchid Boat: Women Poets of China* (New York, 1972), 53.

16. Marsha Weidner, *Views from Jade Terrace*, 67.

17. James Cahill, *Hills beyond a River: Chinese Painting of the Yuan Dynasty, 1279–1368* (New York, 1976), 175 (untrammeled feelings), 175 (total lack of resemblance).

18. Martinus Johanne Heijdra, "The Socio-Economic Development of Ming Rural China (1368–1644): An Interpretation," Princeton University Ph.D. dissertation, 1994: 52; see also his "The Socio-Economic Development of Rural China," in Denis Twitchett and Frederick Mote (eds.), *The Cambridge History of China*, Volume 8: *The Ming Dynasty*, Part 2 (New York, 1998), 417–578.

19. William H. McNeill, *Plagues and Peoples* (New York, 1976).

CHAPTER 10   CONTINUING THE WAR AGAINST THE MONGOLS:
THE MING DYNASTY (1368–1644)

1. John W. Dardess, *Confucianism and Autocracy* (Berkeley, 1983), 241 (crimes), 239 (poison).

2. Jung-pang Lo, "The Decline of the Early Ming Navy," *Oriens Extremus* 5:2 (1958): 149–168, figure on 153.

3. Robert Finlay, "Portuguese and Chinese Maritime Imperialism: Camões's *Lusiads* and Luo Maodeng's *Voyage of the San Bao Eunuch*," *Comparative Studies in Society and History* 34 (1992): 225–241.

4. Frederick W. Mote, "The T'u-mu Incident of 1449," in Frank A. Kierman Jr. and John K. Fairbank (eds.), *Chinese Ways in Warfare* (Cambridge, 1974), 262.

5. John E. Wills, Jr. "Relations with Maritime Europeans, 1514–1662," in Denis Twitchett and Frederick W. Mote (eds.), *The Cambridge History of China*, Volume 8: *The Ming Dynasty, Part 2* (New York, 1998), 333–375.

6. Stephen West and Wilt L. Idema, *The Story of the Western Wing* (Berkeley, 1995), 5.

7. Stephen West and Wilt L. Idema, *The Story of the Western Wing*, 299–304.

8. Katherine Carlitz, "Shrines, Governing-Class Identity, and the Cult of Widow Fidelity in Mid-Ming Jiangnan," *Journal of Asian Studies* 56 (1997): 612–640.

9. *Pangshi jiaxun* (Counsels of Woman Pang) (*Lingnan yishu* edition), 5a.

10. Pei-yi Wu, "Childhood Remembered: Parents and Children in China, 800 to 1700," in Anne Behnke Kinney (ed.), *Chinese Views of Childhood* (Honolulu, 1995), 149–152 (Shen Cheng), 146 (Wang Yangming).

11. Tu Wei-ming, *Neo-Confucian Thought in Action: Wang Yang-ming's Youth (1472–1509)* (Berkeley, 1976); Wing-tsit Chan (trans.), *Instructions for Practical Living and Other Neo-Confucian Writings by Wang Yang-ming* (New York, 1963).

12. Pei-yi Wu, "Childhood Remembered," 147.

13. Jonathan Spence, *The Memory Palace of Matteo Ricci* (New York, 1984), 255.

14. Jacques Gernet, *China and the Christian Impact* (New York, 1985), 231 (Michael Yang), 122 (crucifix).

15. Erik Zürcher, "The Jesuit Mission in Fujian in Late Ming Times: Levels of Response," in E. B. Vermeer (eds.), *Development and Decline of Fukien Province in the 17th and 18th Centuries* (Leiden, 1990), 418.

16. The manual has been beautifully translated into English by Klaas Ruitenbeek, *Carpentry and Building in Late Imperial China: A Study of the Fifteenth-century Carpenter's Manual Lu Ban Jing* (New York: 1993).

17. Timothy Brook, *The Confusions of Pleasure: Commerce and Culture in Ming China* (Berkeley, 1998), 169.

18. Svetlana Rimsky-Korsakoff Dyer, *Grammatical Analysis of the Lao Ch'i-ta with an English translation of the Chinese Text* (Canberra, 1983). This wonderful translation reproduces the Chinese text on facing pages to the English translation; 307–309 ("free tokens"), 411–417 (horses), 389–391 (waiter). See also Valerie Hansen, *Negotiating Daily Life*, 140–145.

19. James Cahill, *Parting at the Shore: Chinese Painting of the Early and Middle Ming Dynasty, 1368–1580* (New York, 1978), 191–192.

20. William S. Atwell, "International Bullion Flows and the Chinese Economy *circa* 1530–1650," *Past and Present* 95 (1982): 68–90, 76 (annual silver production); 76 (Japanese ships); 77 (estimate of annual production).

21. Richard von Glahn, *Fountain of Fortune: Money and Monetary Policy in China, 1000–1700* (Berkeley, 1996), 135, 141.

22. Martin Heijdra, "The Socio-economic Development of Rural China during the Ming," in Denis Twitchett and Frederick Mote (eds.), *The Cambridge History of China,* Volume 8, 417–578, estimates on 522.

23. Ping-ti Ho, *Studies on the Population of China, 1368–1953* (Cambridge, 1959), represents the traditional view, challenged vigorously by Martin Heijdra, "The Socio-economic Development of Rural China during the Ming," population data on 440.

24. Ping-ti Ho, "An Estimate of the Total Population of Sung-Chin China," in Françoise Aubin (ed.), *Sung Studies in Memoriam Étienne Balazs* (Paris, 1970), 3–53; Denis Twitchett, "Population and Pestilence in T'ang China," in Wolfgang Bauer (ed.), *Studia Sino-Mongolica Festschrift für Herbert Franke* (Wiesbaden, 1979), 35–68.

Epilogue

1. Ronald Latham, *The Travels of Marco Polo*, 213.

2. Mark Elvin, "Skills and Resources in Late Traditional China," reprinted in Mark Elvin, *Another History: Essays on China from a European Perspective* (Sydney, 1996), 74; originally in Dwight H. Perkins (ed.), *China's Modern Economy in Historical Perspective* (Stanford, 1975).

3. William Lavely, James Lee, and Wang Feng, "Chinese Demography: The State of the Field," *Journal of Asian Studies* 49 (1990): 807–834, statistics on 816–817; Martin Heijdra, "Ming Rural China," 52. The estimates for 1500, 1600, and 1650 average Heijdra's high-growth and middle-growth hypotheses. Heijdra provides a detailed explanation for why population growth occurred in the Ming dynasty and not later.

4. E. L. Jones, *The European Miracle: Environments, Economies, and Geopolitics in the History of Europe and Asia* (New York, 1981), 83.

5. Mark Elvin, "The High-level Equilibrium Trap," reprinted in Mark Elvin, *Another History*, 38; originally in W. E. Willmott ed., *Economic Organization in Chinese Society* (Stanford, 1972).

SUGGESTIONS FOR
FURTHER READING

These readings are listed for the convenience of readers who may wish to consult them in addition to the sources listed in the endnotes to each chapter, which are not repeated here.

CHAPTER 1   THE BEGINNINGS OF THE WRITTEN RECORD (CA. 1200 B.C.–771 B.C.)

As is obvious from the endnotes, two American scholars, David N. Keightley and K. C. Chang, have introduced the history of the Shang and Zhou dynasties to Western readers. Other important works by Keightley include "The Religious Commitment: Shang Theology and the Genesis of Chinese Political Culture," *History of Religions* 17.3–4 (1978): 211–225, and "The Late Shang State: When, Where, and What?" in David N. Keightley (ed.), *The Origins of Chinese Civilization* (Berkeley, 1983).

For the linguistic evidence concerning non-Chinese peoples, see E. G. Pulleyblank, "The Chinese and Their Neighbors in Prehistoric and Early Historic Times," in David N. Keightley, *The Origins of Chinese Civilization*, 411–465. Robert W. Bagley provides a good introduction to the Sanxingdui site in "A Shang City in Sichuan Province," *Orientations* 21.11 (November 1990): 52–67, and "Sacrificial Pits of the Shang Period at Sanxingdui in Guanghan County, Sichuan Province" *Arts Asiatiques* 43 (1988): 78–86. Volume 23, numbers 3 and 4 of *The Journal of Indo-European Studies* is devoted to the topic of the Xinjiang corpses; see, in particular, the essays by Victor Mair, Edwin G. Pulleyblank, and Donald Ringe.

The volume by W. Thomas Chase, with Jung May Lee, *Ancient Chinese Bronze Art: Casting the Precious Sacral Vessel* (New York, 1991), explains the technology of bronze casting with very clear illustrations. The topic of food in ancient China is covered by E. N. Anderson, *The Food of China* (New Haven, 1988).

Edward L. Shaughnessy's *Sources of Western Zhou History: Inscribed Bronze Vessels* (Berkeley, 1991) provides an excellent introduction to the sources, as does the volume he edited entitled *New Sources of Early Chinese History: An Introduction to the Reading of Inscriptions and Manuscripts* (Berkeley, 1997).

CHAPTER 2   THE AGE OF THE WARRIOR AND THE
THINKER: DOUBLE EARS AND CONFUCIUS
(770–221 B.C.)

Hsu Cho-yun's *Ancient China in Transition: An Analysis of Social Mobility 722–222 B.C.* (Stanford, 1965) still contains much useful information. James Legge's *The Ch'un Ts'ew with the Tso Chuen*, Volume V: *The Chinese Classics* (Hong Kong, 1960) offers a full if archaic translation along with the complete Chinese text. For the introduction of cavalry, see the classic article by H. G. Creel, "The Role of the Horse in Chinese History," *American Historical Review* 70.3 (1965): 647–672.

Much has been written about the great thinkers of the Warring States. Herbert Fingarette's *Confucius: The Sacred as Secular* (New York, 1972) still remains influential. Many translations of the classics are available in English. In addition to the originals and the translations cited in the endnotes, I have used D. C. Lau's *Mencius* (New York, 1970). While the only full translation of Mozi (Yi-pao Mei, *The Ethical and Political Works of Motse*, London, 1929) is dated, John Knoblock's recent three-volume translation, *Xunzi: A Translation and Study of the Complete Works* (Stanford, 1988–1994) sets a high standard for all future translators of Chinese classics to follow.

Mary H. Fong's "The Origin of Chinese Pictorial Representation of the Human Figure," *Artibus Asiae* 49.1-2 (1988–89): 5–38, discusses the bronzes that show the celebratory rituals accompanying victory in battle.

Mark Elvin's "Three Thousand Years of Unsustainable Growth: China's Environment from Archaic Times to the Present," *East Asian History* 6 (1993): 7–46, is one of the few articles in English to address the issue of environmental change in ancient China, and Francesca Bray, *Agriculture* (Volume 6, Part II of *Science and Civilization in China*, New York, 1984), provides a very useful overview of agriculture. Li Xueqin's *Eastern Zhou and Qin Civilizations* (translated by K. C. Chang, New Haven, 1985) surveys the archeological discoveries of the period, kingdom by kingdom and commodity by commodity. *The Cambridge History of Ancient China: From the Origins of Civilization to 221 B.C.* edited by Michael Loewe and Edward L. Shaughnessy (New York, 1999), will no doubt become the standard reference for this period; the essays by Nicola di Cosmo, Lothar von Falkenhausen, Donald Harper, Cho-yun Hsu, Mark Lewis, and David Nivison proved very helpful.

CHAPTER 3   THE CREATION OF EMPIRE
(221 B.C.–A.D. 200)

In addition to the first volume of *The Cambridge History of China*, see Li Yu-ning, *The Politics of Historiography: The First Emperor of China* (White Plains, 1975). Sarah Queen, *From Chronicle to Canon: The Hermeneutics of the Spring and Autumn, according to Tung Chung-shu* (New York, 1996), reexamines Dong Zhongshu's role in Emperor Wu's reign.

While the two-volume archeological report for tomb number 1 at Mawangdui has been published (*Changsha Mawangdui yihao Hanmu*, Beijing, 1973), those for tomb number 2 and tomb number 3 have not. Among the most important secondary works about the find are Wu Hung, "Art in a Ritual Context: Rethinking Mawang-dui," *Early China* 17 (1992): 111–144; Michèle Pirazzoli-t'Serstevens, *The Han Civilization of China* (Oxford, 1982); Michael Loewe, *Chinese Ideas of Life and Death: Faith, Myth, and Reason in the Han Period (202 B.C.–A.D. 220)* (London, 1982), and Michael Loewe, *Ways to Paradise* (London, 1979). The texts in the Mawangdui tomb have also been the subject of several first-rate studies: R. P. Peerenboom's *Law and Morality in Ancient China: The Silk Manuscripts of Huang-Lao* (Albany, 1993), and Li Ling and Keith McMahon, "The Contents and Terminology of the Mawangdui Texts on the Arts of the Bedchamber," *Early China* 17 (1992): 145–185.

For more about Ban Zhao, see Nancy Lee Swann, *Pan Chao: Foremost Woman Scholar of China* (New York, 1932), and Yu-shih Chen, "The Historical Template of Pan Chao's *Nü Chieh*," *T'oung Pao* 82 (1996): 229–257.

Wang Yü-ch'üan describes the changes in the structure of the Han government in "An Outline of the Central Government of the Former Han Dynasty," *Harvard Journal of Asiatic Studies* 12 (1949): 134–187. Rafe de Crespigny has done a series of very useful translations from Sima Guang's history, *Zizhi tongjian* (The comprehensive mirror for aid in government); they are published by the Faculty of Asian Studies at the Australian National University and distributed by the University of Hawaii Press. See also his "Political Protest in Imperial China: The Great Proscription of Later Han, 167–184," *Papers on Far Eastern History* 11 (March 1975): 1–36. Howard Levy, "Yellow Turban Religion and Rebellion at the End of the Han," *Journal of the American Oriental Society* 76: 214–227, provides a good introduction to the Daoist rebellion that so weakened the Han dynasty. Anna K. Seidel describes the different Daoist groups coexisting in China in the first and second centuries in her *La Divinisation de Lao Tseu dans le Taoisme des Han* (Paris, 1969, 1992) and "The Image of the Perfect Ruler in Early Taoist Messianism: Lao-tzu and Li Hung," *History of Religions* 9.2–3 (1969–70): 216–247. R. A. Stein raises the possibility of aborigine influence on the Daoists in his "Remarques sur les Mouvements du Taoïsme Politico-Religieux au IIe Siècle ap. J.-C.," *T'oung Pao* 50 (1963): 1–78, while Anna Seidel traces the continuities before and after Zhang Daoling's religious vision in her "Traces of Han Religion in Funeral Texts Found in Tombs," in Akitsuki Kan'ei (ed.), *Dōkyō to shūkyō bunka* (Tokyo, 1987), 21–57.

CHAPTER 4   CHINA'S RELIGIOUS LANDSCAPE (200–600)

For a general introduction to the history of the Six Dynasties, see the conference volume edited by Albert Dien (especially his introduction and the essay by Denis Grafflin, "Reinventing China: Pseudobureaucracy in the Early Southern Dynasties"), *State and Society in Early Medieval China* (Stanford, 1990).

Arthur Wright, in his now-classic study *Buddhism in Chinese History* (Stanford, 1959), provides a good introductory study of Buddhism in China, as does Zenryū Tsukamoto, *A History of Early Chinese Buddhism: From Its Introduction to the Death of Hui-yüan*, trans. Leon Hurvitz (New York, 1985). In addition to his monumental *The Buddhist Conquest of China* (Leiden, 1972), Erik Zürcher has several important articles: (1) "Late Han Vernacular Elements in the Earliest Buddhist Translations," *Journal of the Chinese Language Teachers* 12 (1977): 177–203; (2) " 'Prince Moonlight' Messianism and Eschatology in Early Medieval Chinese Buddhism," *T'oung Pao* 68.1–3 (1982): 1–75; and (3) "Han Buddhism and the Western Region," in *Thought and Law in Qin and Han China: Studies Dedicated to Anthony Hulsewé on the Occasion of His Eightieth Birthday* (New York, 1990).

The study of Daoism is still in its early stages, but several articles provide good introductions to the new Daoist schools taking shape at this time: Anna Seidel, "Chronicle of Taoist Studies," *Cahiers d'Extrême-Asie* 5 (1989–90): 223–348; Michel Strickmann, "The Mao Shan Revelations: Taoism and the Aristocracy," *T'oung Pao* 63.1 (1977): 1–64; Richard B. Mather, "Kou Ch'ien-chih and the Taoist Theocracy," in *Facets of Taoism* (New Haven, 1979), 103–122; and Anna Seidel, "Imperial Treasures and Taoist Sacraments—Taoist Roots in the Apocrypha," in Michael Strickmann (ed.), *Mélanges Chinois et Bouddhiques volume XXI, Tantric and Taoist Studies in Honour of R. A. Stein,* Volume II (Brussels, 1983), 291–371.

For modern studies of the Silk Road, see the extensive work done on this topic by Liu Xinru who has published two pathbreaking volumes: *Ancient India and China, Trade and Religious Exchanges* A.D. *1–600* (Delhi, 1988), and *Silk and Religion: An Exploration of Material Life and the Thought of People* A.D. *600–1200* (Delhi, 1996). See also Victor H. Mair, "Mummies of the Tarim Basin," *Archaeology* 48.2 (1995): 28–35.

CHAPTER 5 China's Golden Age (589–755)

The Cambridge History, Volume 3: *Sui and T'ang China, 589–906,* Part 1, ed. Denis Twitchett (New York, 1979), provides a thorough overview of the political history of this period. Several articles by Denis Twitchett and David MacMullen published in the third series of *Asia Major* have expanded our knowledge of Tang political history; most helpful to me was Twitchett's "The T'ang Imperial Family," *Asia Major* 7.2 (1994): 1–62. Twitchett's earlier study, *Financial Administration under the T'ang Dynasty* (Cambridge, 1970), surveys government policy and translates many relevant documents. C. P. Fitzgerald, *The Empress Wu* (London, 1968), provides a general if old-fashioned introduction, while John E. Wills Jr.'s *Mountain of Fame* (Princeton, 1994) provides an up-to-date biography. For more about the lives of prostitutes in the capital, see chapter 8, "Honor among the Roues," in Paul Rouzer's forthcoming book, *Articulated Ladies: Gender and the Male Community in Early Chinese Literature.* See also Glen Dudbridge, *The Tale of Li Wa: Study and Critical Edition of a Chinese Story from the Ninth Century* (London, 1983). Turfan is the subject of the April 1999 issue of *Orientations* and of the 1998 issue of *Asia Major,* 3d ser., 11(2).

For the paintings of Yang Guifei, see Elizabeth Lyons, "Ming Huang's Journey to Shu: The History of a Painting," *Expedition* 28.3 (1986): 22–28. Arthur Waley's,

The Life and Times of Po Chü-i 772–846 A.D. (New York, 1949) is a lively study of the poet who wrote about Yang Guifei's death.

CHAPTER 6   THE AN LUSHAN REBELLION AND ITS AFTERMATH (755–960)

The Cambridge History, Volume 3, Part 1 provides a political and institutional history of the dynasty after the tumultuous events of 755, while Arthur Waley, *The Life and Times of Po Chü-i 772–846 A.D.,* gives a vivid sense of what it was like to live during this age of waning central government power. Denis Twitchett documents Yuan Zhen's unsavory activities in "The Seamy Side of Late T'ang Political Life: Yü Ti and His Family," *Asia Major* 3rd series 1.2 (1988): 29–63. For a thorough explanation of the examination system, see Denis Twitchett, *The Birth of the Chinese Meritocracy: Bureaucrats and Examinations in T'ang China* (London, 1976).

A few primary sources from this period are available. Bernard S. Solomon has translated a rare, surviving section of *The Veritable Record of the T'ang Emperor Shun-tsung (February 28, 805–August 31, 805): Han Yü's Shun-tsung shih-lu* (Cambridge, 1955); Charles Hartman, *Han Yü and the T'ang Search for Unity* (Princeton, 1986), has introduced and translated many of Han Yu's writings.

The discovery of the library cave at Dunhuang has spawned a new field of Dunhuangology. Victor H. Mair is the scholar who has worked most extensively on the vernacular literary texts from Dunhuang. *Tun-huang Popular Narratives* (Cambridge, 1983) gives a full translation of the text about Turnip and three other texts. *Tang Transformation Texts: A Study of the Buddhist Contribution to the Rise of Vernacular Fiction and Drama in China* (Harvard, 1989) describes the history of these texts more fully, and *Painting and Performance: Chinese Picture Recitation and Its Indian Genesis* (Honolulu, 1988) traces the practice of telling stories, accompanied by illustrations, all over the world. Denis Twitchett, "The Composition of the T'ang Ruling Class" in *Perspectives on the T'ang* (New Haven, 1973), uses Dunhuang documents to reconstruct the social classes at Dunhuang.

The cave paintings at Dunhuang have been reproduced many times. The most convenient set of photographs is a five-volume set published as *Dunhuang Mogaoku* (Beijing, 1982). For a recent study of the paintings of Mt. Wutai, see Dorothy C. Wong's "A Reassessment of the Representation of Mt. Wutai from Dunhuang Cave 61," *Archives of Asian Art* 46 (1993): 27–52.

CHAPTER 7   COMING TO TERMS WITH MONEY: THE SONG DYNASTY (960–1276)

The Song dynasty has been the subject of extended study by American scholars going back into the 1950s. *The Cambridge History*, Volume 5, is not yet available, though I have been much influenced by Paul J. Smith's draft of his chapter about the New Policies, "Shen-tsung's Reign (1068–1085)." This careful study represents a breakthrough in our understanding of the New Policies. See also the essays (particularly

Paul J. Smith's) in Robert P. Hymes and Conrad Schirokauer (eds.), *Ordering the World: Approaches to State and Society in Sung-Dynasty China* (Berkeley, 1993).

Robert M. Hartwell has delineated the extensive economic changes of this period in several important articles. In addition to those cited in the notes, see his "Demographic, Political, and Social Transformations of China, 750–1550," *Harvard Journal of Asiatic Studies* 42.2 (1982): 365–442.

Valerie Hansen, *The Beijing Qingming Scroll and Its Significance for the Study of Chinese History* (Albany, 1996), reproduces the scroll in black and white with an introduction. Roderick Whitfield, "Chang Tse-tuan's Ch'ing-ming shang-ho t'u," Princeton University Ph.D. dissertation (1965), gives full translations of all the comments written on the scroll by later owners and scholars. Richard Barnhart, "The Five Dynasties and the Song Period," in Yang Xin et al. (eds.), *Three Thousand Years of Chinese Painting* (New Haven, 1997), gives a stimulating survey of new scholarship.

Western historians have long been interested in the specific question of social mobility: Who could take the civil service examinations? Did passing the examinations guarantee one's family a place in the social elite for generations? Robert Hymes's careful study of social change in one locality, *Statesmen and Gentlemen: The Elite of Fu-Chou, Chiang-Hsi, in Northern and Southern Sung* (New York, 1986), shows convincingly that membership in the local elite hinged on far more than simply passing the civil service examinations.

Patricia Ebrey's *The Inner Quarters: Marriage and the Lives of Chinese Women in the Sung Period* (Berkeley, 1993) is the definitive work on women—and footbinding—in the Song; Stephen Owen's *Remembrances: The Experience of the Past in Classical Chinese Literature* (Cambridge, 1986) sensitively translates and brilliantly analyzes Li Qingzhao's postface.

Peter Bol's magisterial *This Culture of Ours: Intellectual Transitions in T'ang and Sung China* links the intellectual changes of the period with the social changes of the Song. Robert M. Hartwell's important early article, "Historical Analogism, Public Policy, and Social Science in Eleventh- and Twelfth-Century China," *American Historical Review* 76.5 (June 1971): 690–727, argues that Wang Anshi and Sima Guang differed most strongly in their understanding of the role of historical precedent.

CHAPTER 8   THE NORTHERN DYNASTIES: NON-CHINESE RULE IN NORTH CHINA (907–1215)

Although the study of the Northern dynasties has generally lagged behind that of Tang and Song China, several new publications have greatly advanced the field. *The Cambridge History of China,* Volume 6: *Alien Regimes and Border States 907–1368*, ed. Herbert Franke and Denis Twitchett (New York, 1994), brings together the work of Western scholars in one volume, with the essays by Herbert Franke on the Jin and by Denis Twitchett and Klaus-Peter Tietze on the Liao especially helpful. See also Franke's essay, "The Forest Peoples of Manchuria: Kitans and Jurchens," in Denis Sinor (ed.), *The Cambridge History of Early Inner Asia* (New York, 1990). Everyone must begin the study of the Liao with the pathbreaking volume by Karl A. Wittfogel and Feng Chia-sheng, *History of Chinese Society Liao 907–1125*, Transactions of the American Philosophical Society n.s. 36 (Philadelphia, 1946), which provides extensive, heavily annotated translations of passages from primary sources. See also Jennifer Holmgren, "Marriage, Kinship, and Succession under the Ch'i-tan rulers of the Liao dynasty (907–1125)" *T'oung Pao* 72 (1986): 44–91; and Jing-shen Tao, *Two Sons of Heaven: Studies in Sung-Liao Relations* (Tucson, 1988).

Nancy Shatzman Steinhardt's "Liao: An Architectural Tradition in the Making," *Artibus Asiae* 54.1–2 (1994): 5–39, provides a fascinating introduction to the buildings of the Khitan; her *Liao Architecture* (Honolulu, 1997) is even more thorough. The contents of the image found in the Timber Pagoda have been published in a lavish volume by Shanxisheng wenwuju and Zhongguo lishi bowuguan, *Yingxian muta Liaodai mizang* (Beijing, 1991). Linda Cooke Johnson's "The Wedding Ceremony for an Imperial Liao Princess: Wall Paintings from a Liao-Dynasty Tomb in Jilin," *Artibus Asiae* 44.2–3 (1983): 107–136, supplied much information about Liao tomb art, as did Robert Albright Rorex, "Some Liao Tomb Murals and Images of Nomads in Chinese Paintings of the Wen-chi Story," *Artibus Asiae* 45 (1984): 174–198.

The Xi Xia are the subject of a new book by Ruth Dunnell: *The Great State of White and High: Buddhism and State Formation in Eleventh-Century Xia* (Honolulu, 1996). See also Ksenia Borisovna Kepping (translated by George van Driem), "The Name of the Tangut Empire," *T'oung Pao* 80. 4–5 (1994): 357–376.

China under Jurchen Rule, ed. Hoyt Cleveland Tillman and Stephen West (Albany, 1995), contains many provocative studies of Jurchen culture, and I have drawn most heavily on those by Jin Qicong and Wilt Idema. Chan Hok-lam, *Legitimation in Imperial China: Discussions under the Jurchen-Chin Dynasty (1115–1234)* (Seattle, 1984), surveys the main events of Jurchen rule while Daniel Kane, *The Sino-Jurchen Vocabulary of the Bureau of Interpreters* (Bloomington, 1989), provides a valuable introduction to the language.

Ellen Johnston Laing surveys the art of the period in her "Chin 'Tartar' Dynasty (1115–1234) Material Culture," *Artibus Asiae* 49 (1988–89): 73–126. For more about the Yanshan Monastery, see Robert Maeda, "Chieh-hua: Ruled Line Painting," *Ars Orientalis* 10 (1975): 123–141, and *Yanshan Temple in Fanshi, Shanxi Province* (*Fanshi Yanshisi*, Beijing, 1980). For Wang Zhe, see Florian C. Reiter, "Ch'ung-yang Sets Forth His Teachings in Fifteen Discourses," *Monumenta Serica* 36 (1984–85): 33–54.

CHAPTER 9   THE MONGOLS (CA. 1200–1368)

For a general introduction to the history of the Mongol dynasty, see *The Cambridge History of China*, Volume 6, and Morris Rossabi's *Khubilai Khan: His Life and Times* (Berkeley, 1988). David Morgan's *The Mongols* (New York, 1986) provides a succinct survey, with greater attention to the Persian chronicles. The great Central

Asian historian Joseph Fletcher summarized several important themes of Mongol history and defines tanistry in "The Mongols: Ecological and Social Perspectives," *Harvard Journal of Asiatic Studies* 46.1 (1986): 11–50; see also Gareth Jones's provocative essay, "A Note on Climatic Cycles and the Rise of Chinggis Khan," *Central Asiatic Journal* 18.4 (1974): 217–226.

Frances Wood's *Did Marco Polo Go to China?* (London, 1995) argues that Polo did not visit China and cites the important early article by the expert historian Herbert Franke, "Sino-Western Contacts under the Mongol Empire," *Journal of the Hong Kong Branch of the Royal Asiatic Society* 6 (1966): 49–72. Ronald Latham's translation, *The Travels of Marco Polo* (New York, 1958), remains the standard translation into English, and the introduction points out a number of problems with Polo's account. I. de Rachewiltz, *Papal Envoys to the Great Khans* (London, 1971), provides wonderfully detailed biographies of the different European travelers to China.

Richard Davis, *Wind against the Mountain: The Crisis of Politics and Culture in Thirteenth-Century China* (Cambridge, 1996), analyzes the fall of the Song while providing gripping descriptions of battle. Two important articles treat the relationship between the Chinese and the Mongolians in the Yuan dynasty: (1) Igor de Rachewiltz, "Some Remarks on the Language Problem in Yüan China," *Journal of the Oriental Society of Australia* 5.1–2 (1967): 65–80; and (2) H. Franke, "Could the Mongol Emperors Read and Write Chinese?" *Asia Major* n.s. 3 (1952): 28–41. William Dolby offers brief selections from several Yuan-dynasty plays in his *Eight Chinese Plays from the Thirteenth Century to the Present* (New York, 1978), while Wilt Idema and Stephen H. West, *Chinese Theater 1100–1450* (Wiesbaden, 1982), offer more thorough coverage. William H. McNeill makes the case that the Black Death spread from China to Europe in *Plagues and Peoples* (New York, 1976).

For Guan Daosheng, see three important studies: (1) Marsha Weidner, "Women in the History of Chinese Painting," and the relevant entries for Guan's paintings in *Views from Jade Terrace: Chinese Women Artists 1300–1912* (New York, 1988); (2) Morris Rossabi, "Kuan Tao-Sheng: Woman Artist in Yuan China," *Bulletin of Sung Yuan Studies* 21 (1989): 67–84; and (3) Elizabeth Toll, "Kuan Tao-sheng: A Study and Translation of the Primary Sources," Harvard University, unpublished A.B. thesis, 1978, which presents all the relevant primary sources. Two recent studies shed significant light on the position of women in Yuan society: Bettine Birge, "Levirate Marriage and the Revival of Widow Chastity in Yüan China," *Asia Major* 8.2 (1995): 107–146; Paul J. Smith "Fear of Gynarchy in an Age of Chaos: Kong Qi's Reflections on Life in South China under Mongol Rule," *Journal of the Economic and Social History of the Orient* 41.1 (1998): 1–95.

James Cahill discusses Ni Zan in his *Hills beyond a River: Chinese Painting of the Yuan Dynasty 1279–1368* (New York, 1976), as do Wen C. Fong et al. in their *Images of the Mind: Selections from the Edward L. Elliott Family and John B. Elliott Collections of Chinese Calligraphy and Painting at the Art Museum, Princeton University* (Princeton, 1984). James Cahill, "The Yuan Dynasty," in *Three Thousand Years of Chinese Painting*, provides an excellent up-to-date survey.

CHAPTER 10   CONTINUING THE WAR AGAINST
THE MONGOLS: THE MING DYNASTY (1368–1644)

Given the abundant sources for the study of Ming history, surprisingly little work
has been done on the dynasty as a whole. *The Cambridge History of China,* Volume
7: *The Ming Dynasty (1368–1644),* ed. Frederick Mote and Denis Twitchett (New
York, 1988), and Volume 8: The Ming Dynasty, Part 2, ed. Denis Twitchett and
Frederick Mote, (New York, 1998) are the obvious places to begin. Biographies of
uniformly high quality are given in *Dictionary of Ming Biography 1368–1644,* ed. L.
Carrington Goodrich and Chaoying Fang (New York, 1976). Several studies cover
the early years of the dynasty: Edward L. Dreyer, *Early Ming China: A Political History* (Stanford, 1982); John W. Dardess, *Confucianism and Autocracy* (Berkeley, 1973);
Wang Yuquan, "Some Salient Features of the Ming Labor Service System," *Ming
Studies* 21 (1986): 1–44; Charles O. Hucker, *The Ming Dynasty: Its Origins and Evolving Institutions* (Ann Arbor, 1978); and Charles O. Hucker, *The Traditional Chinese
State in Ming Times (1368–1644)* (Tucson, 1961). Ray Huang's *Taxation and Governmental Finance in Sixteenth-Century Ming China* (New York, 1974) remains the
definitive work and a model of clarity on the complicated topic of Ming finance.
An important recent study by Martinus Johanne Heijdra, "The Socio-Economic Development of Ming Rural China (1368–1644)," Princeton University, Ph.D. dissertation, 1994 (in volume 8 of *The Cambridge History of China*), provides a cogent
rethinking of the literature in Chinese and Japanese in addition to that in Western
languages.

Shih-shan Henry Tsai's *The Eunuchs of the Ming Dynasty* (Albany, 1996) places
the eunuch admiral Zheng He in context. The first chapter of Philip Snow's careful study, *The Star Raft: China's Encounter with Africa* (New York, 1988) provides a
good introduction to the Zheng He voyages. Louise Levathes's, *When China Ruled
the Seas: The Treasure Fleet of the Dragon Throne, 1405–33* (New York, 1994) is a
popular treatment enlivened by excellent graphics and marred by many errors. Frederick Mote, "China in the Age of Columbus," in *Circa 1492: Art in the Age of Exploration,* ed. Jay A. Levenson (New Haven, 1991), and Joseph Needham, *Science
and Civilisation in China,* Volume 4, Part 3, Sections 28–29 (New York, 1971), provide information about ship construction. Arthur Waldron's *The Great Wall from
History to Myth* (New York, 1990) provides a good overview of Chinese relations
with the Mongols, while Frederick W. Mote focuses on one particularly dramatic
incident, "The T'u-mu Incident of 1449," in *Chinese Ways in Warfare,* ed. Frank A.
Kierman Jr., and John K. Fairbank (Cambridge, 1974), 243–272.

A complete translation of *The Romance of the Three Kingdoms* has been published
by Moss Roberts as *Three Kingdoms: A Historical Novel* (Berkeley, 1991). Patrick
Hanan's "The Development of Fiction and Drama," in Raymond Dawson (ed.), *The
Legacy of China* (New York, 1964), offers a good introduction to the novels of the
sixteenth century.

Alfred W. Crosby Jr.'s *The Columbian Exchange: Biological and Cultural Consequences of 1492* (Westport, 1972) remains the pathbreaking study of this topic. For

a detailed discussion of the Jesuits' astronomical teachings, see Nathan Sivin "Copernicus in China," in *Studia Copernica* 6 (Warsaw: Institute for the History of Science, 1973), which has been reprinted in Sivin's *Science in Ancient China* (Brookfield, 1995). James Cahill's *The Compelling Image: Nature and Style in Seventeenth-Century Chinese Painting* (Cambridge, 1979) documents Western influence on Chinese painting.

William T. Rowe's essay, "Approaches to Modern Chinese Social History," in Olivier Zunz, *Reliving the Past: The Worlds of Social History* (Chapel Hill, 1985), elegantly presents different views on whether the Chinese economy in the seventeenth and eighteenth centuries was capitalist.

E P I L O G U E

Two eminent Sinologists have written about China's failure to industrialize: (1) A. C. Graham, "China, Europe, and the Origins of Modern Science," in Shigeru Nakayama and Nathan Sivin (eds.), *Chinese Science: Explorations of an Ancient Tradition* (Cambridge, Mass., 1973) and (2) Nathan Sivin, "Why the Scientific Revolution Did Not Take Place in China—or Didn't It?" originally in *Chinese Science* 5 (1982), reprinted in his *Science in Ancient China* (Brookfield, 1995). Mark Elvin has also shaped the debate: see his *The Pattern of the Chinese Past* (Stanford, 1973) and his collected essays reprinted in *Another History: Essays on China from a European Perspective* (Sydney, 1996). E. L. Jones, *The European Miracle: Environments, Economies, and Geopolitics in the History of Europe and Asia* (New York, 1981) is the rare book that explicitly and provocatively compares European and Chinese economic history.

CREDITS

ILLUSTRATIONS

Chapter 1: **p. 16**, *Qiang Prisoners of War*, Courtesy of the Institute of History and Philology, Academia Sinica; **p. 25**, Sumitomo Collection; **p. 26**, Courtesy of the Institute of History and Philology, Academia Sinica; **p. 28**, Courtesy of the Institute of History and Philology, Academia Sinica; **p. 29**, Cultural Relics Publishing House (Wenwu), Beijing, China; **p. 30 (all)**, The Shanghai Museum; **p. 34**, Courtesy of the Institute of History and Philology, Academia Sinica; **p. 37**, Cultural Relics Publishing House (Wenwu), Beijing, China; **p. 38 (both)**, Cultural Relics Publishing House (Wenwu), Beijing, China; **p. 39**, After Li Chi, Anyang (Seattle, 1977), p. 115.

Chapter 2: **p. 54**, *Hometown of Confucius* (detail), Cultural Relics Publishing House (Wenwu), Beijing, China; **p. 58**, The Metropolitan Museum of Art, Gift of The Dillon Fund, 1973. (1973.120.2); **p. 59**, Shanghai Museum; **p. 69**, Cultural Relics Publishing House (Wenwu), Beijing, China; **p. 76**, Cultural Relics Publishing House (Wenwu), Beijing, China; **p. 77**, The Palace Museum, Beijing, China; **p. 92**, After Kaogu Yanjiusuo (ed.) Kaoguxue Jichu (Beijing, 1958) figure 24.

Chapter 3: **p. 96**, Kneeling Archer (front), Cultural Relics Publishing House (Wenwu), Beijing, China; **p. 106**, Cultural Relics Publishing House (Wenwu), Beijing, China; **p. 107 (all)**, Cultural Relics Publishing House (Wenwu), Beijing, China; **p. 118**, Cultural Relics Publishing House (Wenwu), Beijing, China; **p. 120**, Cultural Relics Publishing House (Wenwu), Beijing, China; **p. 122**, Cultural Relics Publishing House (Wenwu), Beijing, China; **p. 133**, Courtesy of the Chinese Culture Center of San Francisco; **p. 143**, After Edouard Chavannes, *Mission Archiologique dans La Chine Septentrionale* (Paris, 1909) plate 59.

Chapter 4: **p. 152**, *Life on the Silk Road* figurine, from Robert L. Thorp and Virginia Bower, *Spirit and Ritual: The Morse Collection of Ancient Chinese Art* (New York: The Metropolitan Museum of Art, 1982), p. 72 (figure 45); **p. 165**, Provided by Xinjiang Kucha Caves Research Institute; **p. 166**, Provided by Xinjiang Kucha

Caves Research Institute; **p. 167**, Provided by Xinjiang Kucha Caves Research Institute; **p. 168**, Provided by Xinjiang Kucha Caves Research Institute; **p. 172**, After Robert L. Thorp and Virginia Bower, *Spirit and Ritual: The Morse Collection of Ancient Chinese Art* (New York: The Metropolitan Museum of Art, 1982), p. 72 (figure 45); **p. 173**, © Copyright The British Museum; **p. 177**, The Schloss Collection.

Chapter 5: p. 190, *Lady Kuo-kuo and Her Sisters Setting Forth on an Outing* (detail), National Palace Museum, Taipei, Taiwan, Republic of China; **p. 194**, *Shina Bunka Shiseki*, vol. 12 (Kyoto, 1976), courtesy of Hozokan Publishers; **p. 201**, Cultural Relics Publishing House (Wenwu), Beijing, China; **p. 207 (both)**, The Schloss Collection; **pp. 208–9**, National Palace Museum, Taipei, Taiwan, Republic of China.

Chapter 6: p. 220, *Donor Image*, Cultural Relics Publishing House (Wenwu), Beijing, China; **p. 225**, National Palace Museum, Taipei, Taiwan, Republic of China; **p. 226**, All rights reserved, The Metropolitan Museum of Art, Rogers Fund, 1941. (41.138); **p. 238 (both)**, Cultural Relics Publishing House (Wenwu), Beijing, China; **p. 241**, Cultural Relics Publishing House (Wenwu), Beijing, China; **p. 243 (both)**, Cultural Relics Publishing House (Wenwu), Beijing, China; **p. 246**, Aurel Stein, *Serindia*, vol. II, 1921, by permission of Oxford University Press; **p. 248**, After M. Aurel Stein, *Ruins of Desert Cathay: Personal Narratives of Explorations in Central Asia and Westernmost China* (London, 1912); **p. 250 (both)**, Cultural Relics Publishing House (Wenwu), Beijing, China; **p. 255**, © Copyright The British Museum.

Chapter 7: p. 258, Qingming Scroll (detail), The Palace Museum, Beijing, China; **p. 273 (both)**, Cultural Relics Publishing House (Wenwu), Beijing, China; **p. 277**, The Metropolitan Museum of Art, John M. Crawford, Jr., Collection, Purchase, Dillon Gift, 1981. (1981.278); **p. 279**, After Li Qingzhao Ji (Beijing 1962), frontispiece; **pp. 284–85**, The Palace Museum, Beijing, China; **p. 287**, Fairbank, John, Edwin Reischaeur, and Albert Craig, *East Asia: Tradition and Transformation*, 1st ed. Copyright © 1973 by Houghton Mifflin Company. Used with permission; **p. 288**, Cultural Relics Publishing House (Wenwu), Beijing, China.

Chapter 8: p. 298, *A Tartar Prince Escorting Two Chinese Ladies* (detail), Museum of Far Eastern Antiquities, Stockholm, Sweden; **p. 301**, Museum of Far Eastern Antiquities, Stockholm, Sweden; **p. 305**, After Feng and Wittfogel, *History of Chinese Society Liao 907–1125*, Transactions of the American Philosophical Society, n.s. 36 (Philadelphia: The American Philosophical Society, 1946), p. 248; **p. 310 (left)**, Nancy Steinhardt; **p. 310 (right)**, Liang Ssu-Ch'Eng, *A History of Chinese Architecture* (MIT Press, 1984), Fig 31d; **p. 312**, Cultural Relics Publishing House (Wenwu), Beijing, China; **p. 319**, Shanghai Museum; **p. 320**, Cultural Relics Publishing House (Wenwu), Beijing, China; **p. 325**, Philadelphia Museum of Art: Gift of Mrs. Carroll S. Tyson.

Chapter 9: p. 334, *Portrait of a Mongol Couple* (detail), Cultural Relics Publishing House (Wenwu), Beijing, China; **p. 346**, Harvard-Yenching Library; **p. 351**, Fairbank, John, Edwin Reischaeur and Albert Craig, *East Asia: Tradition and Transformation*, 1st ed. Copyright © 1973 by Houghton Mifflin Company. Used with permission.; **p. 355**, Cultural Relics Publishing House (Wenwu), Beijing, China; **p. 361 (both)**, Courtesy of the Freer Gallery of Art, Smithsonian Institution, Washington, D.C.; **p. 362**, Kuan Shih Tai-Sheng, *A Bamboo Grove in Mist*, detail, Yale University Art Gallery, Gift of Mrs. William H. Moore for the Hobart and Edward Small Morse Memorial Collection; **p. 364**, National Palace Museum, Taipei, Taiwan, Republic of China.

Chapter 10: p. 368, *Tribute Giraffe with Attendant* (detail), Philadelphia Museum of Art: Gift of John T. Dorrance; **p. 380,** Philadelphia Museum of Art: Gift of John T. Dorrance; **p. 382,** From *The Ship, an Illustrated History* by Bjorn Landstrom. Copyright © 1961 by Bokforlaget Forum AB. Used by permission of Doubleday, a division of Random House, Inc.; **p. 383,** Cultural Relics Publishing House (Wenwu), Beijing, China; **p. 394 (top),** Georg Braun, *Civitates Orbis Terrarum* (Cologne, 1572–1616), courtesy of the Beinecke Library, Yale University; **p. 394 (bottom),** Zhang Hong, *Ten Scenes from Ydeh*, dated 1629, Moriya Tadashi Collection, Kyoto, after James Cahill, *The Compelling Image* (Cambridge, 1982), plate 1.18; **p. 403,** Zhou Chen, Chinese, c. 1940–after 1536, Ming dynasty. *Beggars and Street Characters* (detail), 1516. Handscroll, ink and color on paper, overall 31.9 3 244.5 cm. © The Cleveland Museum of Art, 1999, John L. Severance Fund, 1964.94.

TEXT

pp. 43–49, 84, 132–33, 137–39, Republished with permission of Columbia University Press, 562 W. 113th St., New York, NY 10025. *Anthology of Traditional Chinese Literature* (excerpt), Victor Mair ed., 1994. Reproduced by permission of the publisher via Copyright Clearance Center, Inc.

p. 32, From *The Songs of the South: An Ancient Anthology of Poems by Quan Yuan and Other Poets*, ed. David Hawkes. Reprinted by permission of the editor.

p. 43, From *I Ching: The Classic of Changes* by Edward L. Shaughnessy, trans. Copyright © 1996 by Edward L. Shaughnessy. Reprinted by permission of Ballantine Books, a Division of Random House, Inc.

pp. 43–48, From *Book of Songs*, edited and translated by Arthur Waley. Copyright © 1937 by Arthur Waley. Used by permission of Grove/Atlantic, Inc.

pp. 43–48, 277–78, From *An Anthology of Chinese Literature: Beginnings to 1911* by Stephen Owen, editor and translator. Copyright © 1996 by Stephen Owen and The Council for Cultural Planning and Development of the Executive Yuan of the Republic of China. Reprinted by permission of W. W. Norton & Company, Inc.

pp. 48–51, Lothar von Falkenhausen, "Issues in Western Zhou Studies: A Review Article," *Early China* 18 (1993): 149–50. Reprinted by permission.

p. 49, Edward L. Shaughnessy, "The Date of the 'Duo You Ding' and its Significance," *Early China* 9–10 (1983–1985): 57–58. Reprinted by permission.

pp. 68, 70, 72–74, From *The Analects of Confucius*, translated by Simon Leys. Translation copyright © 1997 by Pierre Ryckmans. Reprinted by permission of W.W. Norton & Company, Inc.

pp. 84–85, From *Tao Te Ching* by Lao-tsu, translated by Victor H. Mair. Translation copyright © 1990 by Victor H. Mair. Used by permission of Bantam Books, a division of Random House, Inc.

pp. 224, 226–27, From *The Jade Mountain: A Chinese Anthology* by Witter Bynner. Copyright © 1929 and renewed 1957 by Alfred A. Knopf, Inc. Reprinted by permission of the publisher.

INDEX